THE REALITIES AND FUTURES OF WORK

THE REALITIES AND FUTURES OF WORK

DAVID PEETZ

PRESS

To Ron Kelly
and Georgina Murray

Published by ANU Press
The Australian National University
Acton ACT 2601, Australia
Email: anupress@anu.edu.au

Available to download for free at press.anu.edu.au

ISBN (print): 9781760463106
ISBN (online): 9781760463113

WorldCat (print): 1117766917
WorldCat (online): 1117767111

DOI: 10.22459/RFW.2019

Cover design and layout by ANU Press
Cover artwork by Georgina Murray

Contents

Preface and acknowledgements

My wonderful wife, Georgina Murray, apart from being an excellent sociologist, is a great Leonard Cohen fan. So I get to hear his music a lot. Leonard Cohen wrote a song 'Everybody Knows', and so it seems that everybody knows about the future, or at least they pretend they know. But, in reality, nobody knows. In Dante's *Divine Comedy*, written over eight centuries ago, the eighth ring of hell had a special place for 'diviners, astrologists and musicians' or, as a later illustration put it, 'futurologists'. He was probably right.

So if you are reading this book hoping to be able to join the crowded ranks of those who boast 'I know about the future', you may be disappointed. But if you bought it (or at least downloaded it) to find out what others, who say they do know, don't know, you may be more pleased. What I can claim I know a lot about is the realities of work at present, and how we have to understand those realities to enable informed views on the future to be made. And how we do have to think about the future, and that the choices we make now will shape the way the future turns out. Because if we get those choices wrong, the future could be looking pretty grim—like in that longer song title of Neil Young's: 'Everybody Knows This is Nowhere'.

Dante isn't the only literary figure to get a mention in this book, though he's the most ancient. Littered throughout, but especially in Chapter 3, are references to books, movies (or, in this preface, songs) from popular or classical culture. That's partly because one of the most interesting ways people have had of talking about the future is through literature rather than through scholarly work (or speculative writing dressed up as scholarly work). And it's also because I happen to like some of those literary works and talking about them.

This book could not have been produced without the contributions of a number of other people.

The genesis for this book was over 20 years ago, when I began teaching a course at Griffith University on 'Workplace Industrial Relations'. Over time I produced notes for the students that morphed into weekly readings. At one stage, in the early 2000s, the course was taught externally and Cameron Allan and Keith Townsend helped turn the notes and readings into something more pedagogically oriented for students. They also shaped my thinking in several areas, with Keith, for example, providing a lot of material on consent and control by management that is reflected here, and later on about emotional labour when he updated the course. Cameron contributed useful material on culture, gender and disadvantage. Later on, Janis Bailey updated the course again, including on postmodernism and power. Keith is now a professor at Griffith but Cameron, after a late career in the public service, and Janis have both retired. I want to acknowledge all their contributions.

That course has now disappeared but quite a bit of the 'realities' part of this book originated with those earlier notes. Then Tony Dundon (without realising it at the time, and possibly without realising it until he reads this) sparked the specific idea for this book. After I'd started preparing a manuscript, Werner Nienhüser suggested the plural of the title (it was originally 'reality and future') and that made so much sense. He also developed my literary education by giving me a copy of Dave Eggers's *The Circle*. My ideas on the 'futures' side of this book were further developed through some talks I gave that were hosted by the T.J. Ryan Foundation and in various academic and practitioner conferences and sessions.

The Graduate Center at the City University of New York (special thanks to Ruth Milkman, Kay Powell and Don Robotham) gave me a fellowship that enabled me to finish work on the book, including writing most of Chapter 11 (as well as starting work on another book), and Griffith University allowed me to come here (special thanks to Ruth McPhail). Gregor Murray's Centre de recherche interuniversitaire sur la mondialisation et le travail, based in Québec, Canada, exposed me to many international ideas and helped me develop several of my own at its various events and conferences.

The quarterly *Griffith Review* kindly allowed me to use some material that I had published originally there—in *Griffith Review* 45 ('The Choices We Make: A *Sliding Doors* Moment') and *Griffith Review* 61 ('Debt in Paradise: On the Ground with Wage Theft')—as the basis for much of Chapter 1 and a smaller part of Chapter 10. Some more of the ideas in Chapter 10 arose from a report I did for the Queensland Parliament on the operation of the workers' compensation system in that state (thanks, Grace Grace), while others arose from work I did with Paul Harpur some time after he had completed his PhD on international labour standards, and his work has also contributed to the ideas and text in parts of this book (thanks, Paul). A number of the ideas in several other chapters derived from work with Georgina Murray, but she can't be blamed for what I got wrong because she doesn't always agree with me anyway. Indeed, I wish I could blame others for any mistakes in the book but, sadly, I cannot (well, not so far).

Georgina Murray and Ron Kelly read through the complete manuscript and gave worthy feedback, as did two thorough anonymous referees for ANU Press. Frank Bongiorno, also from that university, gave useful advice, and John Mahony undertook some excellent copyediting. I'm also pleased that ANU Press (thanks, Emily Hazlewood and Elouise Ball) is willing to offer refereed academic books in an open-access format that is affordable and consistent with the spirit of open inquiry that is so important in this era of commodification.

And finally, a reverse acknowledgement to the multinational corporation that now owns the copyright on lyrics for certain songs. It demanded a four-figure payment if I were to use a couple of lines from a deceased poet's song in the final chapter in this open-access book, and thereby demonstrated one of my points about the power of large corporations—in this case, the owner of rights to a tower of songs. Everybody knows I was waiting for a miracle, but it being a book about the future and democracy, in my secret life I thought I might be the man in Manhattan to cry out 'Hallelujah!'. But when it came to closing time on the editing of the book, I just had to think, hey, that's no way to say you can't use it.

David Peetz
New York
May 2019

Abbreviations

AAP	Australian Associated Press
ABS	Australian Bureau of Statistics
ACTU	Australian Council of Trade Unions
AGPS	Australian Government Publishing Service
AI	artificial intelligence
AIRAANZ	Association of Industrial Relations Academics of Australia and New Zealand
AMT	Amazon Mechanical Turk (crowdwork platform)
AODP	Asset Owners Disclosure Project
CEO	chief executive officer
CHI	computer–human interaction
CIPD	UK Chartered Institute of Personnel and Development
CPS	US Current Population Survey
CSIRO	Commonwealth Scientific and Industrial Research Organisation
CSR	corporate social responsibility
ERC	Expenditure Review Committee
ESG	environmental, social and governance
FWC	Fair Work Commission
GDP	gross domestic product
HR	human resources
HRM	human resource management
IEEE	Institute of Electrical and Electronics Engineers
IMF	International Monetary Fund

ILM	internal labour market
ILO	International Labour Organization
ISO	International Organization for Standardization
JIT	just-in-time
NESB	non–English speaking background
NSW	New South Wales, Australia
OECD	Organisation for Economic Co-operation and Development
OHS	occupational health and safety
OPEC	Organization of the Petroleum Exporting Countries
PBS	Public Broadcasting Service
POW	prisoner of war
Qld	Queensland, Australia
RMIT	Royal Melbourne Institute of Technology University
STEM	science, technology, engineering and mathematics
TNC	transnational corporation
UBI	universal basic income
UK	United Kingdom
USA	United States of America

List of tables

1

The big trends, the big choices

15 June 2049: Pat shuffles into the homeless shelter. They're hard to find and they've always been spartan places, but more so now than they ever were when she was a student and did some volunteer work here in 2019.

Not that she has time to dwell on those memories much. She knew she never wanted to come here, but she's finally given in. It's just too dangerous outside. The bashings are getting harder to avoid, sometimes shootings by the gangs or the cops. And if they get you, there's no point in going to a hospital. If you don't have private insurance ('whatever that is', she mumbles, though she knows what it is) you pay an up-front fee that she has no chance of handing over. Or they don't let you in.

Continued overleaf

15 June 2049: Pat has coffee with an old friend from her university days. She hasn't seen her for a quarter of a century. They've both aged since then, but both like to think the other hasn't.

They sit inside the cafe, next to the main window. Across the road is a sparkling new medical clinic. Her friend looks closely at it, then recognition dawns.

'Isn't that where we both did volunteer work for our degrees, back in 2019?'

'Yes, though of course the homeless shelter moved out long ago. They've much nicer premises now, but I hear it's rarely full.'

'You see quite a few homeless people sleeping out in the park. I guess there's nothing much to bother them.' She pauses. 'Ever used that clinic?'

Continued overleaf

Same with GPs, though at least the charge isn't so high there. It used to be called a 'copayment' when it was lower, but eventually, she remembers, the government just stopped paying anything to doctors. 'Rightsizing government', they said, or some other buzzword.

She wonders if she recognises the face on the other side of the soup ladle from her student days, but she says nothing.

'Where you from?' he asks, trying to make conversation as he half-fills a bowl.

'Round here. I went away. Came back a few years ago.'

'What brought you back?'

'I had some work—well, from time to time anyway.'

'Doing what?'

'Oh, through the app I got work as a sessional tutor at the uni. Had my last contract there about eighteen months ago, a few years after I got my PhD.'

'Couple of years ago, I had a cough, real bad. My chest hurt so much I thought I was having a heart attack. They hooked me up and ran all the expensive tests, figured it was just a cracked rib. Well, they weren't expensive tests for me—didn't cost me anything, of course. But it was really good.'

'And how's the job going, Pat?'

'Quite well. You know, it's pretty secure. I've got my hat in the ring for a promotion.'

'To senior lecturer?'

'Yes. It's a few years since I got my PhD, I've done my share of teaching and publishing. I think I'm about due. Is that app your baby crying?'

'I'll bring her in. I thought she might sleep better in the sunshine. Never mind.'

It's the same Pat in each vignette. The focus of our attention, though, is not the choices Pat made. She had limited choice. It's the choices *we* make. We, as a society, face choices that affect what we do, the way we work, the nature of work, who benefits, and who suffers from it. But it's the choices that we make that make the difference to her—and to millions of others. The movie *Sliding Doors*, released in 1998, presented two very different, alternative scenarios, distinguished by whether the main character caught or missed an underground train. In that movie, the defining event was essentially random (whether or not she got through the train's sliding doors), but in this book it is not random events, it is conscious choices that make the difference to our futures.

This book will outline the potential futures we face and the choices we make that will affect those futures. But it does so very much in the context of the reality of work *now*. Many books about the future of work start by talking about the latest technology, and focus on how *that* is going to change the way we work. And there is no doubt that technology will have huge impacts. However, to really understand the direction in which work is going, and the impact that technology and other forces will have, we need to first understand where we are.[1]

I wrote much of this book while based in Australia, and so some of the examples are Australian. But there are also examples from the USA, where I finished writing this book, and even from Scandinavia, where I spent a few months living quite some time ago. Those two areas—the USA and Scandinavia—represent the extremes of the industrialised world, from what would be called the archetypal liberal market economy, in which the state plays ostensibly a minimalist role and the market mostly rules, to the group of archetypal coordinated market economies in which the market is frequently subordinated to the demands of the state and civil society.[2] That range tells us something about the diversity of possibilities open to us all, and underlines one of the ideas in this book that there are, indeed, choices that can and will be made.

So where Australian examples have been used, they have been chosen with more than one eye on, and countless lessons from and for, the world at large. Australia also has many lessons for the rest of the industrialised world because, although Australian people have liked to think of themselves as egalitarian,[3] it is a liberal market economy that has undergone some of the more substantial neo-liberal transformations over the past three decades, and is in some ways an indicator, short of the extremes of the USA, of

1 Much of this chapter first appeared in *Griffith Review* in David Peetz, 'The Choices We Make—a "Sliding Doors" Moment'. *Griffith Review* 45 (July 2014): 44–75.

2 The terms 'liberal market' and 'coordinated market' economies come from the 'varieties of capitalism' literature, centred around Peter A. Hall and David W. Soskice, *Varieties of Capitalism: The Institutional Foundations of Comparative Advantage* (Oxford: Oxford University Press, 2001).

3 Donald Horne, *The Lucky Country: Australia in the Sixties* (Ringwood, Vic.: Penguin, 1964).

where other industrialised countries have been heading. So, before going further into the future, what's the back-story? How did we get to where we are? And where, exactly, are we?

Through parts of the eighteenth and nineteenth centuries, improved living standards were manifested first as increased health, and later as improved wages.[4] Inequality rose in the later part of the nineteenth century and peaked in the 'gilded age' before World War I, but thereafter reduced. Through several decades after World War II, living standards improved, unemployment was low and workers' slice of the cake gradually got more icing on it. Wages and benefits rose, annual leave got longer, working hours got shorter. Responding to pressures from numerous parts of civil society, fearful of the alternative (communism) and legitimated by the economic role the state had played in World War II, governments widened and deepened the range of services they provided.

This changed through the 1980s, in many countries. Major shifts in economy and society were brought about by financialisation, described by Thomas I. Palley as 'a process whereby financial markets, financial institutions, and financial elites gain greater influence over economic policy and economic outcomes'.[5] Increasingly, financialisation prioritised the monetary over the real, the volatile over the stable, the immediate over the sustainable, and the rich over the poor.

For many, financialisation in Australia was most symbolised in the decision by then treasurer Paul Keating and prime minister Bob Hawke to deregulate foreign exchange markets and substantially loosen regulation of financial markets in December 1983. For me, though, it was most symbolised by a meeting of the budgetary committee of the Labor Cabinet on 28 July 1986 when, fearing a run on the dollar in financial markets and possible intervention by the International Monetary Fund,[6] ministers hastily reversed an earlier decision affecting taxation of capital flows and loosened foreign investment policy.

4 Daniel Gallardo Albarrán, *A Composite Perspective on British Living Standards during the Industrial Revolution* (Groningen, NL: Groningen Growth and Development Centre, University of Groningen, 25 April 2016).

5 Thomas I. Palley, 'Financialization: What It Is and Why It Matters'. Working Paper No. 525 (Annandale-on-Hudson, NY: Levy Economics Institute, 2007), papers.ssrn.com/sol3/papers.cfm?abstract_id=1077923.

6 Paul Kelly, *The End of Certainty: The Story of the 1980s* (Sydney: Allen & Unwin, 1992), 207.

Since then, finance capital has grown in strength. Governments around the world have been attracted to 'market liberal' policies (sometimes described as neo-liberalism).[7] Unions have declined in coverage and influence in the face of increasingly hostile employers under pressure from financiers, indifferent or hostile governments, and their own 'institutional sclerosis', as Barbara Pocock described it:[8] unions' failure to make sufficient internal changes to accommodate the demands of the market liberal era. Globalisation has thus developed in an environment that has been most conducive to the interests of capital, and most antagonistic to the interests of labour.

The 'sliding doors' portraits of Pat illustrated two alternative visions of the future for workers. Which of these turns out to be true depends on the choices we make over coming years.

Management

In 1987, Wolfgang Streeck wrote of how the great 'uncertainty of management' was dealing with the 'management of uncertainty'.[9] Managers have responded—to the volatility of the product markets in which they sell and the financial markets in which their equity and debt are nested—by a range of strategies, some consistent, many contradictory.

Chief among the consistent strategies is the search for greater flexibility. We hear a lot about employers offering greater flexibility *for* employees—more choice in their start or finish times, perhaps in their total hours. This can be in response to demands from employees themselves—more on that later. It might, however, be a different story when people actually try to use such flexibility, for which they may be penalised.[10]

The *principal* form of flexibility is the flexibility *by* employees that employers seek, to help employers manage—and shift—their own risk. Sometimes they seek 'functional' flexibility: getting employees to take on multiple and quite different tasks and hence skills. Sometimes they

7 Erik Olin Wright, *Understanding Class* (London: Verso, 2015).

8 Barbara Pocock, 'Institutional Sclerosis: Prospects for Trade Union Transformation'. *Labour & Industry* 9, no. 1 (1998): 17–33.

9 Wolfgang Streeck, 'The Uncertainties of Management and the Management of Uncertainty'. *Work, Employment and Society* 1, no. 2 (1987): 281–308.

10 David Burkus, 'Everyone Likes Flex Time, but We Punish Women Who Use It'. *Harvard Business Review*, 20 February 2017.

seek 'numerical' flexibility, meaning that the number of workers, or the number of hours they work, or maybe even their pay rates, move up and down according to the needs of the enterprise.[11]

For a long time, greater numerical flexibility was seen as an unequivocal plus, creating greater stability, or at least resilience, in labour markets. Governments were encouraged, including by bodies like the Organisation for Economic Co-operation and Development (OECD), to make wages more variable, remove restrictions on hours and on hiring and firing, and attempt to emulate the most flexible of them all—the US labour market, where employers hire and fire 'at will'.[12] Then the global financial crisis came along, and, although Europe experienced a greater fall in economic activity than the USA, it was America that suffered the greater drop in employment. In its biggest test, the theory failed spectacularly.[13] The OECD had been having misgivings even before then. After the crisis it recommended governments improve income support and unemployment insurance benefit systems,[14] which it had previously said would decrease flexibility.

Alongside greater flexibility came the urge for control. But how? On the one hand, employees were demanding more voice at work and more control over their working lives. The decline of unions meant that, for many workers, an obvious mechanism for voice was no longer there. Some technologies inherently gave greater discretion to employees using those technologies. A case study by James R. Barker showed that employees were often more effective at exerting control over the behaviour of fellow employees, and extracting maximum effort, than were their supervisors.[15] So, many employers gave employees greater control over their work.

But it is hard for managers to 'let go'. The urge for control is human. How could they justify the 'big bucks' if the workers themselves were in charge? Other technologies gave the opportunity to micromanage employees—

11 John Atkinson, *Flexibility, Uncertainty and Manpower Management*. IMS Report No. 89 (Brighton, UK: Institute for Manpower Studies, 1985).

12 Organisation for Economic Co-operation and Development, *The OECD Jobs Study: Facts, Analysis, Strategy* (Paris: OECD, 1994).

13 David Peetz, Stephane Le Queux, and Ann Frost, 'The Global Financial Crisis and Employment Relations'. In *The Future of Employment Relations: New Paradigms, New Approaches*, ed. Adrian Wilkinson and Keith Townsend (Basingstoke: Palgrave Macmillan, 2011), 193–214.

14 Organisation for Economic Co-operation and Development, *Employment Outlook* (Paris: OECD, 2009).

15 James R. Barker, 'Tightening the Iron Cage: Concertive Control in Self-Managing Teams'. *Administrative Science Quarterly* 38, no. 3 (1993): 408–37.

in particular, to dictate their time. Swipe cards could tell warehouse bosses just how long their workers were taking to move a pallet of cans from shelf to truck.[16] Monitors could tell call centre bosses how many seconds 'customer service representatives' were pausing between calls, or taking to go to the toilet.[17] Barcode scanners could tell supermarket managers how long shop assistants took to process a trolley of groceries.[18] All could be used to tell staff, 'Work more! Work faster!' So, many employers gave employees *less* control over their work.

Regardless of whether they gave employees greater or less *individual* control over their work, employers typically sought to reduce the *collective* discretion employees exercised. The sort of control employers were happy to let employees have was only contingent control—management could always take it back. For some, keeping out, or throwing out, unions became important. While decades of research had shown that employees could be, and commonly were, simultaneously committed to both union and employer,[19] many employers could not stomach the idea of an alternative source of power. Sometimes through sophisticated human resource management policies that signalled 'We're all in this together', sometimes through aggressive policies of exclusion, those employers often succeeded in obtaining unilateral control of the workforce, precluding collective bargaining in favour of individual contracting.[20]

These employers would often cloak individualistic rhetoric with a collective demand on their employees (though the term 'employees' was often replaced with 'partners', 'members' or, more commonly, 'associates'). Corporate 'culturism', as it was described by Hugh Willmott,[21] sought simultaneously to make employees feel as if they were treated as individuals but needed to subvert their individuality in pursuit of the collective, corporate goals. Those who failed to toe the corporate rhetoric

16 Christopher Wright and John Lund, 'Best Practice Taylorism: "Yankee Speed-up" in Australian Grocery Distribution'. *Journal of Industrial Relations* 38, no. 2 (1996): 196–212.

17 George Callaghan and Paul Thompson, 'Edwards Revisited: Technical Control and Call Centres'. *Economic and Industrial Democracy* 22 (2001): 13–37.

18 Robin Price, 'Controlling Routine Front Line Service Workers: An Australian Retail Supermarket Case'. *Work, Employment and Society* 30, no. 6 (2016): 915–31.

19 For example, D.G. Gallagher, 'The Relationship between Organizational and Union Commitment among Federal Government Employees'. *Academy of Management Proceedings* (1984): 319–23. More extensive references are in footnote 80 in Chapter 5.

20 David Peetz, 'Decollectivist Strategies in Oceania'. *Relations Industrielles* 57, no. 2 (2002): 252–81.

21 Hugh Willmott, 'Strength Is Ignorance; Slavery Is Freedom: Managing Culture in Modern Organizations'. *The Journal of Management Studies* 30, no. 4 (1993): 515–52.

line, as Diane Van den Broek found in her study of a telecommunications company, would be performance-managed out.[22] It was reminiscent of the scene in Monty Python's *Life of Brian*, in which Brian, facing an adoring but uncomprehending crowd, calls out 'You're all individuals!' They respond, 'Yes, we're all individuals!' He pleads, 'You're all different!' 'Yes, we are all different!' Then a little voice at the back pipes up: 'I'm not!'

Willmott took a more sinister view of it all, likening 'culturist' strategies to Big Brother's attempts at totalising control in George Orwell's *Nineteen Eighty-Four*.[23] Yet often these attempts failed because, unlike in *Nineteen Eighty-Four*'s Oceania, workers were exposed to all sorts of ideas outside the workplace. The HR Department could never be as softly persuasive as Orwell's Ministry of Truth, or as violently persuasive as his Ministry of Love.[24]

Services

One of the biggest shifts in the location of work has been from the public to the private sector. In the public sector, 'new public management' became the rage from the 1980s.[25] Some activities were totally privatised. Services were outsourced to the private sector, policy separated from delivery. But not all changes in work can be traced to market liberal policies or financialisation. Some simply emerged as part of the normal process of development in a trading world.

In all industrialised countries, manufacturing has, in relative terms, declined. Manufacturing instead provides the engine for rapidly growing Third World or transition economies, for dragging people out of poverty.[26] Still, government policies in industrialised countries influence how much manufacturing declines, and what it would look like. Most employment

22 Diane Van den Broek, 'Human Resource Management, Workforce Control and Union Avoidance: An Australian Case Study'. *Journal of Industrial Relations* 39, no. 3 (1997): 332–48.

23 George Orwell, *Nineteen Eighty-Four: A Novel* (Harmondsworth: Penguin, 1949, repr. 1976).

24 Willmott, 'Strength Is Ignorance'.

25 Christopher Hood, 'A Public Management for All Seasons'. *Public Administration Review* 69, no. 1 (1991): 3–19.

26 United Nations Conference on Trade and Development, *Trade and Development Report: Capital Accumulation, Growth and Structural Change*. UNCTAD/TDR/2003 (New York and Geneva: United Nations, 2003).

growth now and in the future in developed countries is in 'services', a term so broad it can mean 'anything that isn't primary production or manufacturing'.

Much of the structural growth in new service sector jobs is in occupations that involve personal interactions. These jobs put demands on employees that were relatively unknown in manufacturing or mining: demands for the use of 'emotional labour'. Employees are asked to evoke emotional reactions in clients or customers that bring about sales or at least make the targets feel more satisfied. From waitresses, bar attendants, sales assistants, and customer sales representatives in call centres to air stewards, aged care workers, and child carers, employees work with what Arlie Hochschild called the 'managed heart'.[27] They may be required to 'put on a face' to boost sales, stressfully pretending to feel something they do not (Hochschild calls this 'surface acting'), like in a 'smile' campaign documented by Emmanuel Ogbonna[28] but seen many times over by bewildered customers of numerous firms. Or employees may actually embody, deep down, the emotions that are needed, for example in care work (Hochschild calls this 'deep acting'). Often these skills are associated with 'women's work'. Often they are seen as 'attributes' rather than 'skills'. Often, therefore, the jobs undergo 'undervaluation' and the workers are poorly paid for what the work requires.[29]

Other emerging jobs in the service sector, though, may be alienated from human interaction. The rise of internet sales has caught many storefront retailers off-guard, replacing shop visits with screen clicks. There are no book sales assistants in Amazon warehouses, where mobile technology monitors and directs workers to use the quickest route between two points: 'You're sort of like a robot, but in human form', said one manager to the *Financial Times*.[30] Not just emotionless labour, some jobs are thoughtless labour.

27 Arlie Russell Hochschild, *The Managed Heart: The Commercialization of Human Feeling* (Los Angeles: University of California Press, 1983, repr. 2003).

28 Staff were instructed to smile at all customers. Emmanuel Ogbonna, 'Organisation Culture and Human Resource Management: Dilemmas and Contradictions'. In *Reassessing Human Resource Management*, ed. P. Blyton and P. Turnbull (London: Sage, 1992), 74–96.

29 Sara Charlesworth and Fiona Macdonald, 'Employment Regulation and Worker-Carers: Reproducing Gender Inequality in the Domestic and Market Spheres?'. In *Women, Labor Segmentation and Regulation: Varieties of Gender Gaps*, ed. David Peetz and Georgina Murray (New York: Palgrave Macmillan, 2017), 79–96.

30 Sarah O'Connor, 'Amazon Unpacked'. *Financial Times*, 8 February 2013.

The changes in economic structure had other implications. Manufacturing had long been a source of employment for migrant workers in many countries, and so its decline caused particular problems for that workforce. Manufacturing, once seen as the heartland of unionism, now accounts for only a small proportion of unionists. Unionism has become white collar, like the workforce.

Flexibility

One person's flexibility is another person's insecurity. The mythology of the 'portfolio' career, as if somehow workers like to be shunted from industry to industry over their lifetime, often hides the fact that workers are treated as more disposable than before. Some, of course, may prefer changes of career, but for others career changes are a euphemism that is forced upon them by the impermanency of work.

Particularly in English-speaking countries, employers have become less hesitant about downsizing, and less reluctant to make big cuts. Yet research by Wayne F. Cascio showed that downsizing often results in lower morale, lower productivity, and worse performance, in part due to 'survivor syndrome' among those left behind, and employer expectations that somehow those left will make up, at least in part, for those departed.[31] It may be a contradictory strategy, but still a popular one. We've seen companies turning permanent jobs into casual jobs, shifting from direct employment into labour hire, converting employees to the status of dependent contractors, often to avoid union-negotiated pay and conditions.[32]

For some workers, nonstandard employment of this type is a means of gaining some control over their working lives. Nurses, for example, might choose labour hire as an alternative to the grind of rotating daily shift work or to avoid night work.[33] For other workers, though, it deepens

31 Wayne F Cascio, 'Downsizing: What Do We Know? What Have We Learned?'. *Academy of Management Executive* 7, no. 1 (1993): 95–104.

32 Max Chalmers, 'Cooped up Workers and Mystery Contractors: Major Chicken Supplier Roasted for Labour Exploitation'. *New Matilda*, 18 June 2015; Josh Bornstein, 'The Great Uber Fairness Fallacy: As a Driver, How Do You Bargain with an App?'. *Guardian*, 24 August 2015; Anna Patty, 'Cold Storage Company Blocked from Locking Workers out of Bargaining'. *Age*, 19 June 2017.

33 Barbara Pocock, Rosslyn Prosser, and Ken Bridge, *'Only a Casual…': How Casual Work Affects Employees, Households and Communities in Australia* (Adelaide: Labour Studies, School of Social Sciences, University of Adelaide, 2004), 91.

risk and insecurity. Risk is passed on to workers, many of whom are no longer 'employees' but now responsible for their own sick leave and injury insurance. It may also be a means of weakening worker organisation. In Australia, it appears that there is a wage premium (a plus) for casuals on high incomes, but a wage penalty for casuals on low incomes, with most receiving less than what the 'casual loading' suggests they would have if they obtained equivalent rewards to other workers with similar characteristics.[34]

For workers in lower-skilled occupations, or at least those outside professional or managerial occupations, insecurity is likely to outweigh choice. But it is not only the low skilled who find themselves marginalised this way. Besides the food retailing and hospitality sector, it is in education where casualisation is greatest.[35] We are not referring here to workers who left school early and can find no better work—we are talking about highly skilled workers with doctoral qualifications, who spend semester after semester doing 'sessional' or 'adjunct' tutoring, lecturing or administering of courses, some never quite sure when they will be paid, sometimes only knowing a week in advance that they will be teaching a semester but knowing with certainty they will get no holiday pay.

Maybe just like Pat. Those 'sliding doors' portraits at the beginning of this chapter were not extreme imaginations. The first was inspired by modern day USA. From there, reports have emerged in the *Chronicle of Higher Education* of adjunct (sessional) academic staff living in relatives' basements or homeless shelters.[36] The problems of the unaffordability of healthcare would be familiar to anyone who has spent time in the USA—a country whose health, education and minimum wage regimes seem to be admired by some countries' present policy-makers. Health insurance is a work-related issue. In America, unions battle hard to obtain it for their members, employers see cutting it as a means to make major cost savings; Canadian employers regard national health insurance as

34 Inga Laß and Mark Wooden, 'The Structure of the Wage Gap for Temporary Workers: Evidence from Australian Panel Data'. *British Journal of Industrial Relations* (2019). doi.org/10.1111/bjir.12458.

35 Robyn May, David Peetz, and Glenda Strachan, 'The Casual Academic Workforce and Labour Market Segmentation in Australia'. *Labour and Industry* 23, no. 3 (2013): 258–75.

36 Isaac Sweeney, 'Adjunct Emergency Fund'. *The Chronicle of Higher Education*, 2 August 2011, chronicle.com/blogs/onhiring/adjunct-emergency-fund/29317; Simone Pathe, 'Homeless Professor Protests Conditions of Adjuncts'. *PBS News Hour*, 31 March 2014, www.pbs.org/newshour/making-sense/homeless-professor-protests-conditions-adjuncts/.

a competitive cost advantage that attracts businesses across the border; and Australian unions negotiated the reintroduction of national health insurance as part of their 1983 Accord with the federal Labor government.

The second portrait was inspired by my time in Norway, with its more socially engaged public sector in health and other areas, where university vice chancellors are elected by staff and students and resist state attempts to impose new public sector management techniques on universities,[37] and where mutual trust is so high that parents routinely leave prams with sleeping babies outside shops and cafes while they go inside. You can get arrested for that in the USA.[38]

Time and resistance

As employment becomes more insecure, and as management strategy toughens, work also becomes harder. Through the twentieth century, workers gradually achieved shorter and shorter working weeks through various rounds of industrial action and advocacy.[39] Yet in the 1980s this started to change. Working hours for full-time workers increased through the 1990s. Surveys showed large numbers of workers reporting increases in how hard they had to work and in the pressure they felt at work.[40] They also showed increasing difficulties experienced by workers in balancing their work and family lives, and problems of work interfering in their personal lives.[41]

37 David Peetz, 'Aim for Gains, Not Profits'. *The Australian* Higher Education Supplement, 6 September 2006, 30; Tobias Schulze-Cleven and Jennifer R. Olson, 'Worlds of Higher Education Transformed: Toward Varieties of Academic Capitalism'. *Higher Education* 73 (2017): 813–31.

38 Raquel Laneri, 'I Went to Jail for Leaving My Baby Outside a Restaurant'. *New York Post*, 25 November 2017, nypost.com/2017/11/25/i-went-to-jail-for-leaving-my-baby-outside-a-restaurant/; Reuters, 'Swedish Woman Who Left Baby Outside Restaurant Investigated', 16 August 2011. www.reuters.com/article/us-restaurant-baby/swedish-woman-who-left-baby-outside-restaurant-investigated-idUSTRE77E62O20110815.

39 Jeffrey Helgeson, 'American Labor and Working-Class History, 1900–1945'. In *Oxford Research Encyclopedia of American History* (Oxford: Oxford University Press, 2016). oxfordre.com/americanhistory/view/10.1093/acrefore/9780199329175.001.0001/acrefore-9780199329175-e-330.

40 Francis Green, 'Why Has Work Effort Become More Intense?'. *Industrial Relations: A Journal of Economy and Society* 43, no. 4 (2004): 709–41; Department of Industrial Relations, *Enterprise Bargaining in Australia: 1994 Annual Report* (Canberra: AGPS, 1995); Griffith Work Time Project, *Working Time Transformations and Effects* (Brisbane: Queensland Department of Industrial Relations, 2003).

41 Department of Industrial Relations, *Enterprise Bargaining Report 1994*. Griffith Work Time Project, *Working Time*.

No small part of this reflected the changing regulation of working time. Hourly wages with premiums (extra payments) for unsocial hours and overtime became less common, and annualised salaries that 'incorporated' these things became more common. Employers no longer paid the full cost when employees worked extra hours. So, management could raise expectations, employees would absorb them, and the extra work would get done. Some universities, for example, regularly expected their staff to increase research outputs annually with 5 or 10 per cent compound growth.[42] If wages and premiums stayed in place, then employers might push for the introduction of rotating 12-hour shifts. Alternatively, employers might push for the abolition of time-related premiums.

But these are not processes that could continue indefinitely. Eventually, increases in work intensity or working hours become unsustainable in the face of organised and unorganised resistance by employees and the disappearance of goodwill by employees. So, too, resistance to increasing insecurity may grow, and be manifested in the same ways.

Inequality

In public debate, the rationale for the policy choices that have underpinned these changes in work has almost always been about improving economic wellbeing. You may not be made better off as a result of being more insecure, working harder or having less quality time with your family, it goes, but you're better off through the higher productivity that is brought about. The trouble is, there has not been a productivity dividend from all this.

Not all countries adopted the 'liberal market' model as enthusiastically as Australia or New Zealand. Generally speaking, it is the English-speaking countries that are most closely associated with the 'liberal market' model. But when we make long-run comparisons across OECD countries, we do not find evidence that productivity growth, or productivity levels, are consistently higher in market liberal economies than in 'coordinated

42 For example, Griffith University, *Annual Report 2014* (Brisbane: Griffith University, 2014), 126–39.

market' economies like Norway, Sweden, Germany or the Netherlands. (In fact, Norway has higher productivity levels than *any* of the English-speaking countries.)[43]

Where these economic models really make a difference is in the distribution of income, wealth and power. Inequality is higher in market liberal countries. Poverty is higher.[44] The top 0.1 per cent typically gets more—though nowhere more than in the USA—and the bottom half usually get less. As documented by Georgina Murray, Bill Carroll and others, a small proportion of (mostly) men really do occupy increasingly powerful positions.[45] In a 2006 interview in *The New York Times*, one of the world's richest men, Warren Buffett, said, 'There's class warfare, all right, but it's my class, the rich class, that's making war, and we're winning'.[46] He said that with good reason. Measured income and wealth inequality declined in Australia and other countries through much of the twentieth century, but they have increased since the mid-1980s.[47] In addition, there has been growing outrage that the wealthiest in society have been minimising or avoiding tax through complex transnational accounting devices.[48]

Other inequalities persist. The narrowing of the gender gap in earnings between men and women—it closed substantially between 1969 and the late 1980s—has slowed and, in some countries, reversed.[49] Progress in achieving more positive attitudes among the populace at large and within institutional settings seems to have been offset by a greater

43 David Peetz, 'Does Industrial Relations Policy Affect Productivity?'. *Australian Bulletin of Labour* 38, no. 4 (2012): 268–92.

44 Ibid.

45 Georgina Murray, *Capitalist Networks and Social Power in Australia and New Zealand* (Aldershot: Ashgate, 2006); William Carroll, 'The Corporate Elite and the Transformation of Finance Capital: A View from Canada'. *Sociological Review* 56, no. s1 (2008): 44–63.

46 Ben Stein, 'In Class Warfare, Guess Which Class Is Winning'. *New York Times*, 26 November 2006.

47 Thomas Piketty, *Capital in the Twenty-First Century* (Cambridge, MA: Harvard University Press, 2014); Anthony B. Atkinson and Andrew Leigh, 'The Distribution of Top Incomes in Australia'. *Economic Record* 83, no. 262 (2007): 247–61.

48 Oxfam Australia, *The Hidden Billions: How Tax Havens Impact Lives at Home and Abroad* (Oxfam, 2016); Javier Garcia-Bernardo et al., 'Uncovering Offshore Financial Centers: Conduits and Sinks in the Global Corporate Ownership Network'. *Scientific Reports* 7, no. 6246 (2017).

49 House of Representatives Standing Committee on Employment and Workplace Relations, *Making It Fair: Pay Equity and Associated Issues Related to Increasing Female Participation in the Workforce* (Canberra: House of Representatives, 2009); Workplace Gender Equality Agency, *Gender Pay Gap Statistics* (Sydney: WGEA, 2013); Gillian Whitehouse, 'A Cross-National Comparison of Gender Gaps'. In *Women, Labor Segmentation and Regulation: Varieties of Gender Gaps*, ed. David Peetz and Georgina Murray (New York and London: Palgrave Macmillan, 2017).

distancing between working women and the regulation that protects their interests.[50] Women continue to be undervalued when in female-dominated occupations, discriminated against when in male-dominated occupations, and excluded from the top echelons of business.[51] Recent migrants often find their skills and qualifications undervalued and end up in jobs that underutilise their skills. People with disabilities continue to encounter career barriers.

It is not as if the period before market liberalism was one without difficulties, and not just those associated with gender and other forms of segmentation. In the 1970s and early 1980s, a key problem was competition for economic surpluses—what economists like to call 'rents'. In an economy with many areas where product markets were poorly competitive, especially in relation to overseas-produced goods, there were opportunities for parts of both labour and capital to extract surpluses. This competition for surpluses became a spiral that heightened the problems of simultaneous unemployment and inflation. That is what prompted incomes policies in a number of countries, including Australia.

These days surpluses are still being extracted, but by different groups—essentially extremely high income earners, the chief executive officers, directors, and managers of top firms, parts of the finance sector, and the like.[52] The old problem of general inflation (and of responding to it) has been superseded by the narrower inflation of executive remuneration and of the incomes and wealth of the rich (especially the top 0.1 per cent), including through asset price bubbles.[53] Market liberal 'reforms' have not solved our economic problems or delivered an acceleration of our growth in wellbeing. They have just changed the problems, and in doing so made life more difficult for many workers.

50 Gillian Whitehouse, 'Unequal Pay: A Comparative Study of Australia, Canada, Sweden and the U.K'. *Labour & Industry* 3, no. 2–3 (1990): 354–71.

51 See Chapter 8.

52 David Peetz, 'An Institutional Analysis of the Growth of Executive Remuneration'. *Journal of Industrial Relations* 57, no. 5 (2015): 707–25.

53 Charles M. Elson and Craig K. Ferrere, 'Executive Superstars, Peer Groups and Overcompensation: Cause, Effect and Solution'. *Journal of Corporate Law* 38 (2013): 497–8.

Globalisation and the mega-trends

You may have noticed that I have barely used the term 'globalisation' in this chapter to describe the forces at work. It is easy to blame problems in the way we work on globalisation, as if some external, inevitable force is at work and nothing can be done about it. After all, globalisation is a major force. But globalisation—if we mean increasing trade and international communications—is neither good nor bad in itself. Its effects are complex and contradictory.

On the one hand, for example, increased trade through globalisation helps Third World countries industrialise and grow wages, employment and living standards.[54] On the other hand, globalisation increases uncertainty and puts increased pressure on companies to find new flexibilities with the associated pressure on security and wages that this implies.[55] The net effect of these two tendencies is not set in stone. It depends on the policy choices taken by states and the mobilisations by employers, unions and other parts of civil society that determine the conditions under which globalisation proceeds.

The rhetoric of 'free trade' is used by multinational corporations to pressure governments to relinquish powers to regulate environmental or workplace behaviour, through special clauses in 'free trade agreements'. Yet governments do not need to do that. It is a choice they make. Norway, for example, is more 'globalised' than Australia—trade is 49 per cent of Norway's GDP, compared to 34 per cent of Australia's[56]—but Norway places more emphasis on 'job quality' or what the International Labour Organization (ILO) calls 'decent work' than is shown in Australia, and its sovereign wealth fund refuses to invest in multinational companies that breach certain ethical standards.[57]

---

54 Ann Harrison, *Globalization and Poverty*. NBER Working Paper 12347 (Cambridge, MA: National Bureau of Economic Research, 2006).

55 Streeck, 'Uncertainties of Management'.

56 World Bank, 'Merchandise Trade (% of GDP)' (Databank, World Bank, 2014). data.worldbank.org/indicator/TG.VAL.TOTL.GD.ZS.

57 Andreas Bieler, 'Small Nordic Countries and Globalization: Analysing Norwegian Exceptionalism'. *Competition & Change* 16, no. 3 (2012): 224–42; Mikael Holter, 'Norway's $860 Billion Fund Drops 52 Companies Linked to Coal'. *Bloomberg*, 14 April 2016; Norges Bank Investment Management, *NBIM Quarterly Performance Report; First Quarter 2008* (Oslo: Norges Bank, 23 May 2008).

Globalisation is one of four 'mega-drivers of change' identified by the ILO that it says will shape the future of work. The other three are technology, demographics and climate change. Each of these is, in its own right, important enough to warrant that epithet of 'mega'. We will cover each of these through the book, but it is worth expanding on each, just a little, here.

Technological change is what everybody seems to focus on when they write about the future of work. There is no doubt that it will have a huge impact. Much of the discussion focuses on the numbers of jobs lost by technological change: Will my job be one of those gone? Will there be anything else available for me? What will I have to do? Will I have to become a freelancer or 'gig' worker, or follow a 'portfolio career'? These are all legitimate questions, but sometimes the discussion of the future of work descends to its being *only* about these things, and there being an inevitability about them. Sometimes this is for political purposes: jobs will go, so you *must* be flexible, and forget about all those unnecessary protections and rigidities associated with the old ways. But one of the themes of this book is that there are choices to be made, including about those things like flexibility and protections. Technology is *part* of the future, but it is not the *whole* of the future.

A second 'mega-driver of change' is demographics. Western countries, in particular, are 'ageing' as birthrates drop and life expectancies increase. Women have entered the workforce in substantial numbers since the 1960s. In most countries, participation by women is still less than by men and, perhaps surprisingly, the ILO does not expect the gender gap in labour force participation to narrow substantially over the coming 15 years across the globe, with small improvements in the Arab states and northern Africa (where the gap is huge) almost offset by small deteriorations in eastern Asia and sub-Saharan Africa (where the gap is already much smaller) and little change in OECD countries.[58] Migration can be expected to continue and, if anything, intensify—though it may face rising political barriers from the growth of nationalistic or ethnocentric political sentiment.[59] The political conflict that this may engender has the potential to shape

58 International Labour Organization, 'Gender Gap in Participation Rates Is Not Expected to Improve over the Coming 15 Years' (ILO, 2017). www.ilo.org/global/topics/future-of-work/trends/WCMS_545630/lang--en/index.htm.

59 International Labour Organization, 'Migration Is Likely to Intensify in the Future as Decent Work Deficits Remain Widespread' (ILO, 2017).

the policy response to rising inequalities at work, much as the emergence of Trumpism in the USA has strengthened the hand of capital against labour in that country.

The final 'mega-driver of change', and one of the principal reasons behind the intensification of migrant flows, is climate change. In Bangladesh alone, 27 million people live on land at risk from sea-level rise by 2050, and 10,000 hectares is lost each year to riverbank erosion.[60] Globally, '300 to 650 million people live on land that will be submerged or exposed to chronic flooding, by 2100, under current emission trends'.[61] Aside from the effects on migration and political tension, even if abated, climate change will affect productivity, work organisation and the nature of technology.[62]

The rest of this book

The rest of this book explores these issues in more depth, giving at least as much attention to the reality of work now as to the future of work. The next chapter (Chapter 2) examines globalisation, financialisation, neo-liberalism and power. What is globalisation? Has it peaked? Is it still happening? How does it affect work—what are the contingencies involved and how do they relate to work? How do we distinguish between it, financialisation and neo-liberalism? The chapter also discusses the key theories of power and how they relate to work, and asks: what are the trends and prospects in power and inequality at work?

The third chapter looks at past and current visions of the future and what they have said about work. The chapter, in part, examines how accurate or otherwise earlier popular predictions of the future have proved to be. What happened to all those predictions of increased leisure and short working weeks? Have trends on working hours and work intensification

60 Tribune Desk, 'Report: 27m Bangladeshis at Risk of Sea-Level Rise by 2050'. *Dhaka Tribune*, 27 August 2017, www.dhakatribune.com/climate-change/2017/08/27/report-27m-bangladeshis-risk-sea-level-rise-2050/.

61 Climate Central, 'New Analysis Shows Global Exposure to Sea Level Rise' (Climate Central, 2017). www.climatecentral.org/news/new-analysis-global-exposure-to-sea-level-rise-flooding-18066.

62 For example, Charis Palmer and Sunanda Creagh, 'Climate Change Linked to Declines in Labour Productivity'. *The Conversation*, 25 February 2013, theconversation.com/climate-change-linked-to-declines-in-labour-productivity-12407; John P. Dunne, Ronald J. Stouffer, and Jasmin G. John, 'Reductions in Labour Capacity from Heat Stress under Climate Warming'. *Nature Climate Change* 3 (2013): 563–6.

continued? What explains recent developments in these areas? What is the future of, and what are the influences on, work–life balance? And what does this tell us about how the choices that affect the future of work will be made? Many visions of the future have been seen in books, movies and songs. A TV series, *The Worst Jobs in History*, told us of some of the work people did in earlier centuries, John Steinbeck's *The Grapes of Wrath* told us about working life in the Great Depression, but how has literature treated work in the future? One classic futuristic scenario is that in George Orwell's *Nineteen Eighty-Four*. As a dystopian vision, Margaret Atwood's *The Handmaid's Tale* had some similarities to Orwell's book: showing how power was maintained through ideology and violence, but it also emphasised the use of rewards and divisions among the subordinated in maintaining power, and placed a greater emphasis on gender and its interactions with class. Dave Eggers's *The Circle* depicts the dystopian reality within a seemingly utopian workplace. Those last three are the focus of much of that chapter.

Chapter 4 considers trends in employment and how they will be affected by two of the 'mega-drivers of change' mentioned earlier—technological change through digitalisation, and demographic change—though with most emphasis on the former rather than the latter. On the supply side, it looks at things like the ageing and so-called 'feminisation' of the workforce. On the demand side, it looks at the sorts of jobs that will be created and destroyed by digital change. It will look at the veracity of competing claims about the future numbers of jobs. Will over 40 per cent of present jobs not exist, as estimated in a study by Oxford University?[63] Will robots eat your job? Is the job you're aiming for going to be obsolete? Or will the scenario be more like the 8 per cent of jobs estimated by the OECD as being lost to technological change?[64] What sorts of skills, if any, will be demanded? What will be the areas of growth and decline in the industries and occupations of employment?

Chapter 5 examines trends in management and effects on employees. It asks: What models of management strategy exist? What types of management strategy are growing or declining into the future? What illusions affect managers and how can managers respond? The chapter

63 Carl Benedikt Frey and Michael A. Osborne, *The Future of Employment: How Susceptible Are Jobs to Computerisation?* (Oxford: Department of Engineering Science, University of Oxford, 2013).

64 Melanie Arntz, Terry Gregory, and Ulrich Zierahn, *The Risk of Automation for Jobs in OECD Countries: A Comparative Analysis*. OECD Social, Employment and Migration Working Papers No. 189 (Paris: OECD, 2016).

will then turn to issues of control, previously raised in Chapter 3 and the discussion of Orwell. How is technology used to tighten or loosen control—in areas such as logistics, warehousing, retail and call centres? Hugh Willmott discussed modern corporate cultural control and monoculturism, treating Orwell's *Nineteen Eighty-Four* as analogous to management in the 1990s.[65] The 1960s psychology experiments by Milgram and Zimbardo showed the dangers of monoculturism, and Joel Bakan's *The Corporation* applied this to modern organisations.[66] How have views on corporate culture and culturism changed, and where are they heading? What is the role of dissent in organisations? Are the mistakes of the past being repeated now and will they be in the future?

Chapter 6 looks at how these intersect—that is, it looks at trends in work, taking account of changing management structures and strategies. It considers the forms of flexibility that are sought by employers, their origins and their effects on employees—for example, through their impact on security and insecurity. It looks at 'precaritisation' of work through the push for flexibility. It asks what aspects of digital change are affecting, and likely to affect, work and workplace relations? Are digital platforms fundamentally changing or destroying the employment relationship? Are we moving to a world of freelancers or the 'gig economy' ('Uberisation')? The chapter analyses these questions through the lens of 'not there' employment (the attempts by core capital to centralise profits and minimise costs and accountability, through such devices as contracting out, franchising and the use of digital platforms) and the seemingly surprising persistence of the employment relationship. It therefore examines the reasons, in the logic of capitalism, for employment's resilience.

The seventh chapter investigates employee responses and actions in the face of these strategies and changes. Management often seeks to reduce employee resistance and harness the inputs of employees by expanding employee voice, and there may be broader social objectives for enhancing voice. So, what are the differences between formal and informal forms of employee voice, between direct and indirect forms, and between management-constrained (conditional) and employee-controlled (independent) forms—and why do these matter? What are

65 Willmott, 'Strength Is Ignorance'; Orwell, *Nineteen Eighty-Four*.

66 Stanley Milgram, *Obedience to Authority* (New York: Harper & Row, 1974); Philip Zimbardo, 'Stanford Prison Experiment: A Simulation Study of the Psychology of Imprisonment'. 2005. www.prisonexp.org; Joel Bakan, *The Corporation: The Pathological Pursuit of Profit and Power* (London: Constable & Robertson, 2004).

the patterns and trends in different forms of employee voice? How are ideas about collectivism changing? What does this mean for the future of collectivism? What have unions done in response to their own decline? How does the 'gig' economy affect cooperative and collective action and trade union futures?

The eighth chapter examines the reality and future of women and segmentation at work. It will interrogate the situation of women in employment and whether and how it has altered. What is the segmentation of work into male and female jobs? What causes it? Has it broken down or solidified? What are so-called 'male' and 'female' jobs? What are the links to science, technology, engineering and mathematics (STEM) work (especially in information and communications technology)? How does gender relate to harassment, career exits and apparent labour shortages? What explains patterns and trends in gender gaps? Why is there an increasing emphasis on emotional labour, and how do patterns and trends in emotional labour relate to gender? What is the concept of 'intersectionality' and how does it relate to gender, ethnicity, age and other forms of disadvantage? What are the futures of gender gaps and of women at work?

Chapter 9 looks at ethics, sustainability and work. It will ask about the meanings of ethics and sustainability, their relationships to each other and the role of externalities in those concepts. It considers that final 'mega-drivers of change' in the world of work: climate change. What are the future effects of climate change on work and productivity? What are the barriers to sustainability? What is a 'just transition'? What are the future demands for sustainability and responses to climate change? How are they affecting, and will they affect, employees?

Chapter 10 discusses regulatory responses to changes in the world of work, particularly those arising from the shift towards 'not there' employment discussed in Chapter 6. Three angles on this are discussed. The first is the regulation of 'not there' employment. The second is the problem of noncompliance (sometimes referred to as 'wages theft'), the factors that promote it and the changing methods used in enforcement of labour standards. The third is the maintenance of labour standards in global value chains or global production networks. The chapter looks at the purpose of regulation, the different forms of regulation by the state, innovation in regulation, and the potential and limitations on those innovations, drawing on, for example, the response to the Rana Plaza collapse in Bangladesh. How can and will organisations respond to increasing pressures for codes of conduct and corporate social responsibility?

The final chapter talks about what this all means for society as a whole: What are the options available to us, and the choices that will be made, at the social level that will affect and be affected by the workplace? Will the future be one of neo-democracy, neo-liberalism or neo-totalitarianism? What choices will determine which of those it becomes? What policy decisions are necessary in an agenda for a liveable future?

Through this book, we identify the policy implications of the patterns and trends that are discussed. This chapter began with a 'sliding doors' moment that showed the stark differences in outcomes that may arise from critical decisions still to be taken. We will also consider what those decisions are, and what directions need to be taken. There are choices that need to be made about the directions of economic policy; and there are choices to be made about the rights of people at work.

2

Globalisation, financialisation and power

In the mid-1980s, I spent time as a ministerial adviser in Old Parliament House in Canberra, the capital of Australia. One day, the Expenditure Review Committee (ERC) of Cabinet (it determined the Budget) broke for lunch, and my boss, a member of that committee, asked me to walk with him through the Parliamentary Rose Garden. A few weeks earlier, the government had announced some seemingly esoteric and somewhat symbolic changes to the treatment of international capital flows.[1] These would have closed off some exemptions to interest-withholding tax (a tax payable on behalf of overseas lenders to Australian firms or residents, based on the interest paid on the loan); these were relevant to the then debate about takeover activity but somewhat symbolic in that Treasury saw them as the least bad way of dealing with the issue. After the announcement, the Australian dollar had slid on global financial markets, not just for a day but for several weeks—from US$67.8 on 1 July to US$57.3 when the ERC broke for lunch on 28 July.[2]

It was not the first time the Australian dollar had dropped over the preceding year—falling commodity prices had already taken their toll. However, some ministers now feared potential intervention by the International Monetary Fund.[3] There was clearly a sense of panic and it

---

1 Paul Keating, 'Interest Withholding Tax Exemptions'. News release, Canberra, 1 July 1986.

2 Jim Killaly, 'Fair Game: Is Australia Vulnerable or Getting Its Fair Share?'. *Journal of Australian Taxation* 19, no. 3 (2017): 1–194.

3 Paul Kelly, *The End of Certainty: The Story of the 1980s* (Sydney: Allen & Unwin, 1992), 207; Milton Cockburn, 'Beware Those IMF Minders: Walsh'. *Sydney Morning Herald*, 13 August 1986.

came through in that walk. ERC ministers had seen what the 'Reuters screen jockeys' (as the Treasurer called them) had done to the dollar in the morning, and felt powerless. The meeting resumed. At 3 pm that day, the Treasurer announced not only the reversal of the earlier withholding tax decision, but also a series of other measures aimed at liberalising investment flows.[4]

The announcement was universally applauded by press and financial commentators.[5] The dollar recovered. The deterioration in the exchange rate had owed more to inexperience with the floating exchange rate regime than to market fundamentals,[6] but there were to be no more attempts at tightening rules on investment flows. Instead, the government buckled down to the task of reducing the Budget deficit beyond market 'expectations', and any residual ideas of an expansionary fiscal policy were, for two decades, erased. This not only set the scene for economic policy and the erasure of barriers to neo-liberalism, it also set the scene for workplace policy over the next decade. Perhaps more than any other, this was the day improvements in the 'social wage'—government spending on health, education, housing and welfare that directly boosted workers' living standards—fell off the government priority list. Under the Accord with trade unions, the social wage had been near the top of that priority list,[7] but no more. Through the remainder of the 1980s savings were made to social wage programs, product markets were deregulated, 'competition policy' reforms were introduced, and public assets were privatised.[8] It all said a lot about financialisation, globalisation and power.

To explain developments in work and workplaces, and indeed in economies, since the 1980s, reference is often made to these concepts. The relationships between *globalisation*, *financialisation* and *neo-liberalism* are so strong that sometimes the concepts get conflated. Sometimes one gets the blame for what is rightly the responsibility of another. Sometimes the concepts end up as buzzwords or just thrown around as objects of

4 Paul Keating, 'Foreign Investment Policy Relaxations'. News release, Canberra, 28 July 1986.

5 Christopher James Pokarier, 'Politics of Foreign Direct Investment in Australia 1960–96' (PhD diss., The Australian National University, 2000), 205.

6 David Gruen, Brian Gray, and Glenn Stevens, 'Australia'. In *East Asia in Crisis: From Being a Miracle to Needing One?*, ed. Ross H. McLeod and Ross Garnaut (London and New York: Routledge, 1998), 207–23, cited in Pokarier, 'Politics of Foreign Direct Investment'.

7 Gwynneth Singleton, 'Corporatism or Labourism?: The Australian Labour Movement in Accord'. *Journal of Commonwealth and Comparative Politics* 28, no. 2 (1990): 162–82.

8 John Quiggin, 'Social Democracy and Market Reform in Australia and New Zealand'. *Oxford Review of Economic Policy* 14, no. 1 (1998): 76–95.

abuse. So in this chapter we look at what these concepts each mean, and what they explain. But before we do that, we look at *power*—what power is, how we observe it, and how it relates to these three concepts. We do this because, in the end, these three concepts are critical in shaping the power of workers and employers in the world of work.

Power

'Power tends to corrupt, and absolute power corrupts absolutely.' So said Lord Acton.[9] Acton was not just making stuff up. Experiments have shown that, compared with the powerless, the powerful condemn other people's cheating more, but also cheat more themselves; and that the powerful are more strict in judging other people's moral transgressions than in judging their own transgressions.[10] Even *illusions* of power make a difference: other experiments showed that environments that increase the space people command (such as larger desks) can inadvertently lead people to feel more powerful, and these feelings of power can cause dishonest behaviour such as stealing money, cheating on a test or committing traffic violations.[11]

However, power is not important simply because it induces bad behaviour. Power is an important object of study in understanding work. Power shapes who has resources and who goes without. Workers want more of it, management wants to keep what it has to and expand it. Power is an important part of what happens in the workplace.

How power is exercised: The faces of power

Power has been written about in several ways. Some authors have focused on the origins of power, and talk about 'power resources'. Some have looked at the way power is exercised as a way of identifying who has power. Thus, discussions about 'reputations' concerning power were succeeded by discussion about the 'faces' of power and what they tell us

9 Technically, he was John Emerich Edward Dalberg Acton, first Baron Acton (1834–1902).

10 Joris Lammers, Diederik A. Stapel, and Adam D. Galinsky, 'Power Increases Hypocrisy: Moralizing in Reasoning, Immorality in Behavior'. *Psychological Science* 21, no. 5 (2010): 737–44.

11 A Yap et al., 'The Ergonomics of Dishonesty: The Effect of Incidental Posture on Stealing, Cheating, and Traffic Violations'. *Psychological Science* 24, no. 11 (2013): 2281–89.

about who has power. Others have written about the effects of power. We refer to that in the latter half of this chapter, but before that we focus on the sources and manifestations of power.

The first face of power and decisions

Over half a century ago, Robert Dahl wrote *Who Governs?*, based upon a study of New Haven in Connecticut, USA.[12] He was inspired to conduct this research in response to two earlier books: C. Wright Mills's study of the power of people in key positions in the USA and a study by another 'elitist' theorist, Floyd Hunter, about reputations of power within a local community.[13] Dahl argued that one could not measure power on the basis of whether somebody was in a particular position, or had a reputation for power. Instead, the only way power was measurable was if the researcher examined actual decisions, to see whether the preferences of the ruling elite were expressed in the outcome of decisions. To test the theory, Dahl had constructed an important *definition of power*:

> A has power over B to the extent that he can get B to do something that B would not otherwise do.[14]

A and B could be individuals, groups or organisations.[15] It owed much to Max Weber's original definition, which, by one translation, was 'the possibility of imposing one's will upon the behaviour of another person'.[16]

Dahl's was a simple, theoretically coherent approach that satisfied 'Occam's razor',[17] but it had substantial limitations. For example, looking at workplace relations, assessing a simple thing like who 'won' a strike is actually quite hard, especially in Australia as strikes have been used to 'signal' power. This occurred through 'unconditional' strikes whose duration was predetermined at the commencement of action (and hence

12 Robert A. Dahl, *Who Governs? Democracy and Power in an American City*. Yale Studies in Political Science, 4 (New Haven: Yale University Press, 1961).

13 C. Wright Mills, *The Power Elite* (New York: Oxford University Press, 1956); Floyd Hunter, *Community Power Structure: A Study of Decision Makers* (Chapel Hill: University of North Carolina Press, 1953).

14 Robert A. Dahl, 'The Concept of Power'. *Behavioral Science* 2 (1957): 201–15.

15 The use of 'he' in this and subsequent quotes reflects the gender ideologies of the time.

16 Reinhard Bendix, *Max Weber: An Intellectual Portrait* (New York: Anchor Books, 1962), quoted in Isidor Wallimann, Nicholas Tatsis, and George V. Zito, 'On Max Weber's Definition of Power'. *Australian and New Zealand Journal of Sociology* 13, no. 3 (1977): 231–35. There are a number of different translations of Weber's original (German) definition, discussed in the paper by Walliman et al.

17 Occam's razor holds that, other things being equal, the simplest explanation to something should be preferred (as it is most easily tested). Attributed to the fourteenth-century English Franciscan friar William of Ockham.

it was never expected that the employer would immediately capitulate before the end of the strike).[18] The Bureau of Census and Statistics in Australia once attempted to identify the result of each strike in terms of whether the employer or workers won (its data suggested that the employer won the great majority of disputes) but it abandoned this in 1951, the findings not aligning with common perceptions of the outcomes of conflict or union power.[19] Ambit claims have historically played such a significant role in industrial relations in Australia that it is important to be able to look into the motivations of the parties, not just what is laid on the table. And any analysis of power cannot just look at a small part or snapshot of the decision-making process.

The second face of power and nondecisions

Dahl's definition of power was rigorous but inadequate. As Bachrach and Baratz noted,[20] Dahl had uncovered one face of power, but a second face of power was exercised when:

> A devotes his energies to creating or reinforcing social and political values and institutional practices that limit the scope of … consideration of only those issues which are comparatively innocuous to A.[21]

The first face of power is observed decision-making. The second face of power, *nondecision-making,* is sometimes referred to as 'controlling the agenda'. Nondecision-making is *not* about deciding not to act, or deciding not to decide. Procrastination is *not* nondecision-making. Nondecision-making is a process of creating a 'nondecision'—that is, of suppressing or thwarting a challenge to the values or interest of the decision maker that would arise if a particular matter came onto the agenda for decision-making. It may do this through 'suffocating' demands

18 David Peetz, 'Industrial Conflict with Awards, Choices and Fairness'. In *Rediscovering Collective Bargaining: Australia's Fair Work Act in International Perspective*, ed. Anthony Forsyth and Breen Creighton (New York: Routledge, 2012), 159–81.

19 Australian Bureau of Statistics data consistently suggested that employers won almost all disputes. Yet in published opinion polls in the second half of the twentieth century a plurality or, more commonly, a majority of Australians considered that unions had too much power. Commonwealth Bureau of Census and Statistics, *Labour Report* (Melbourne: various years). David Peetz, 'Sympathy for the Devil? Attitudes to Australian Unions'. *Australian Journal of Political Science* 37, no. 1 (2002): 57–80.

20 Peter Bachrach and Morton S. Baratz, *Power and Poverty: Theory and Practice* (New York: Oxford University Press, 1970).

21 Peter Bachrach and Morton S. Baratz, 'Two Faces of Power'. *American Political Science Review* 56, no. 4947–952 (1962).

for change before they are voiced, or preventing them from gaining access to the decision-making arena, or maiming or destroying them in the implementation phase.[22] Bachrach and Baratz identified several forms of nondecision-making, including using a norm, precedent, rule or procedure to squelch a threatening demand; using sanctions, force or violence to prevent demands from entering the political process (such as threats against activists); 'co-opting' critics (such as promoting activists up the ranks); or reinforcing or establishing additional procedures or barriers ('mobilising bias').[23]

The third face of power, unrecognised interests and hegemony

A few years later, Stephen Lukes sought to specify a third face of power.[24] He provided a much broader definition:

> A exercises power over B when A affects B in a manner contrary to B's interests.[25]

It followed that a third face of power existed. That involved the shaping of people's preferences so that neither overt nor covert conflicts exist; conflict is only latent. This placed a focus on analysing efforts to create particular attitudes or ideologies that maintain the position of those in power. Lukes asked:

> Is it not the supreme and most insidious exercise of power to prevent people, to whatever degree, from having grievances by shaping their perceptions … and preferences in such a way that they accept their role in the existing order of things, either because they can see or imagine no alternative … or because they see it as natural … or … divinely ordained and beneficial. To assume that the absence of a grievance equals genuine consensus is simply to rule out the possibility of false or manipulated consensus by definitional fiat.[26]

22 Bachrach and Baratz, *Power and Poverty*, 44.
23 Ibid.
24 Steven Lukes, *Power: A Radical View* (London: Macmillan, 1974).
25 Ibid., 27.
26 Ibid., 28.

This radical approach was closely related to the concepts of 'false consciousness' elucidated by Marx and of 'hegemony' discussed in more detail by Gramsci and, later, by Connell.[27] Lukes criticised the term 'false consciousness' as it 'sounds patronizing' but, really, it is talking about much the same thing as Lukes. Lukes conceded it was useful to refer to 'the power to mislead', and that Marx and his successors highlighted the third dimension of power by pointing to 'the capacity to secure compliance to domination through the shaping of beliefs and desires, by imposing internal constraints under historically changing circumstances'.[28] Gramsci used 'hegemony' to encompass influence, leadership and consent, as opposed to violent domination.[29] The state, to him, is force plus hegemony (which covers most of the ground of the three faces of power discussed here).

The problem with Lukes's approach was the difficulty in identifying the real interests as opposed to the expressed preferences of people.[30] In a second, much-expanded edition of his book, Lukes modified some of his positions, arguing, for example, that his initial analysis focused on the *exercise* of power, whereas power was a *dispositional* characteristic identifying an ability or capacity, which may or may not be exercised, and that it also needed to consider multiple and conflicting interests people may have.[31] He also commented that:

> Power's third dimension is always focused on particular domains of experience and is never, except in fictional dystopias, more than partially effective. It would be simplistic to suppose that 'willing' and 'unwilling' compliance to domination are mutually exclusive: one can *consent* to power and *resent* the mode of its exercise.[32]

Another writer on power—and much else—was Michel Foucault, a key figure in the 'postmodern' paradigm. He spoke of how power was not something possessed or able to be willingly used by particular individuals or classes, but rather refers to complex patterns of domination and

27 Antonio Gramsci, *Selections from the Prison Notebooks* (London: Lawrence and Wishart, 1971); Raewyn Connell, *Ruling Class, Ruling Culture* (Cambridge: Cambridge University Press, 1977).

28 Steven Lukes, *Power: A Radical View*, 2nd ed. (London: Palgrave, 2005), 49, 143–5.

29 Anne Showstack Sassoon, ed., *Approaches to Gramsci* (London: Writers and Readers Publishing Cooperative Society, 1982), 13.

30 A discussion of how these three different faces of power can be applied to understanding individual contracting and collective bargaining is contained in David Peetz, *Brave New Workplace: How Individual Contracts Are Changing Our Jobs* (Sydney: Allen & Unwin, 2006), 75–80 (and also 87, 114).

31 Lukes, *Power.*

32 Ibid., 150.

subordination that exist whenever social relations exist. To him, power produced subjects, 'normalising' them and forming their character. Norms become the 'soul'. The person who is the subject of power is 'constituted' through their subjection to power, power is ubiquitous and so everyone is in some way formed by the effects of power. It was not possible to be free of power, nor to judge between ways of life, and each society imposes its own 'regime of truth'.[33] For Lukes, Foucault posed no 'analysis of the extent to which the various modern forms of power he identified actually succeed, or fail, in securing the compliance of those subject to it'.[34] Others are less kind. The famous linguist Noam Chomsky hasn't 'a clue' what Foucault and other postmodernists mean in their writings.[35] Christina Cregan criticises postmodernists for producing a bourgeois ideology that is a 'critique of neo-liberalism for the purpose of preserving it … [I]ts concern is for cultural forms with no reference to an underlying infrastructure'.[36] In my view, there is some merit to these arguments but the potential relevance of postmodernism to genuinely understanding the realities and futures of work lies not in what it says about power, but in helping provide insights into aspects of language and discourse at work, for example through writers such as David Knights and Hugh Willmott,[37] some of which are discussed in Chapter 3.

Power, dependence and power resources

Other writers have focused on the sources of power, and this affects how they define it. For example, Keenoy and Kelly (1998) define power as 'the capacity to get someone or some people to do something they otherwise would not do' (very close to Dahl's definition) but they refer to 'power resources' that go beyond Dahl's focus and emphasise power in social relations rather than merely in decisions.[38] Their work should be seen in the context of resource dependency theory and power dependency

33 Michel Foucault, *Power/Knowledge: Selected Interviews and Other Writings 1972–77* (Brighton: Harvester, 1980), cited in Lukes, *Power.*

34 Lukes, *Power*, 98.

35 Chomsky cited in David N. Gibbs, 'Is There Room for the Real World in the Postmodernist Universe?'. In *Beyond the Area Studies Wars: Toward a New International Studies*, ed. Neil L. Waters (Hanover: Middlebury College Press, 2000): 11–28.

36 Christina Cregan, 'Book Review: Understanding Work and Employment: Industrial Relations'. *Journal of Industrial Relations* 46, no. 1 (2004): 137–40.

37 David Knights and Hugh Willmott, *Management Lives: Power and Identity in Work Organizations* (London: Sage, 1999); Hugh Willmott, 'Strength Is Ignorance; Slavery Is Freedom: Managing Culture in Modern Organizations'. *The Journal of Management Studies* 30, no. 4 (1993): 515–52.

38 Tom Keenoy and Di Kelly, *The Employment Relationship in Australia*, 2nd ed. (Sydney: Harcourt, 1998).

theory.[39] The core idea of this body of thought is that whoever controls resources has power over those who need access to those resources, such that (as explained by Nienhüser):

> the greater the dependency of actor B upon actor A, the more power actor A has over B; and the dependence of an actor B upon actor A is (1) directly proportional to B's amount of motivational investments in goals mediated by A and (2) inversely proportional to the availability of those goals to B outside the A–B relation.[40]

Thus workers in strategic positions in an industry (e.g. those holding specialist technical skills or a central role in a production process) have more bargaining power if they strike than low-skilled workers, because the company is more dependent upon their resources. This idea has been applied in theorisation about power in industrial relations.[41] You will often hear of particular workers possessing, or not possessing, 'labour market power'. Those who possess it have skills or knowledge that an organisation may need. Sometimes it might be 'external' labour market power—their skills are in high demand from many employers but in short supply. Many have extensive 'specific' knowledge—'corporate history'—that the employer they work for values and is dependent upon, even if other employers may not feel the same way. They possess 'internal' labour market power. Either way, whether they negotiate individually or bargain collectively, those with high labour market power will be in a better position to extract gains from their employer.

---

39 Jeffrey Pfeffer and Gerald R. Salancik, *The External Control of Organizations. A Resource Dependence Perspective* (New York: Harper & Row, 1978); Richard M. Emerson, 'Power-Dependence Relations'. *American Sociological Review* 27 (1962); Werner Nienhüser, 'Resource Dependence Theory—How Well Does It Explain Behavior of Organizations?'. *Management Revue* 19, no. 1–2 (2008): 9–32.

40 Nienhüser, 'Resource Dependence Theory'; Emerson, 'Power-Dependence Relations', 32, as explained in Nienhüser, 'Resource Dependence Theory', 13. Careful readers of the original texts will have noted a bit of letter switching here: powerless A in the original has now become powerful A, and vice versa with B, the opposite of their use in the original source. This is to maintain continuity with previous definitions in this chapter. My apologies to Professor Nienhüser for swapping the letters.

41 Mick Marchington, 'Shop-Floor Control and Industrial Relations'. In *The Control of Work*, ed. John Purcell and Robin Smith (London: Macmillan, 1979); see also Adrian Wilkinson et al., 'Total Quality Management and Employee Involvement'. *Human Resource Management Journal* 2, no. 4 (1992): 1–20; Jeffrey Pfeffer, *Power in Organizations* (Pitman, 1981); Beverly J. Silver, *Forces of Labor: Workers' Movements and Globalization since 1870* (Cambridge, UK: Cambridge University Press, 2003). The notion of power resources has been usefully deployed (with different elements) in the analysis of union power in Christian Levesque and Gregor Murray, 'Local Versus Global: Activating Local Union Power in the Global Economy'. *Labor Studies Journal* 27, no. 3 (2002): 39–65, and to the analysis of women's access to power within unions in Geraldine Healy and Gill Kirton, 'Women, Power and Trade Union Government in the UK'. *British Journal of Industrial Relations* 38, no. 3 (2000): 343–60.

The concept of power resource dependency is most closely related to the first and second faces of power discussed earlier: A can make decisions disliked by B, or prevent matters B wants from being determined, by using resources that B is dependent upon. The application to the third face of power is less obvious but still valid: if B is dependent on A (or on those who act in A's interests) for the resources that provide information, education or beliefs, then A clearly has power over B.

For Keenoy and Kelly, power resources are 'any means through which one actor can influence the attitude and behaviour of another'. These include state power resources (having influence or control over or through government, the judiciary or other state agencies); economic power resources (ownership of capital, land, skills in short supply, etc.); associational power resources (the ability to combine and exercise collective power—so collective bargaining is an attempt to turn low resource dependency by the other side into high resource dependency); and ideological power resources (the ability to successfully promote a set of ideas or values, to shape policy, strategy and social practice).[42] The last of these is closely linked to Lukes's third dimension of power and Gramsci's 'hegemony'; in effect, it identifies the resources used to exercise hegemony.

So, while the 'faces of power' approach looks at how power is *exercised*, the 'resources' approach looks at what it is that *gives power* to A or B in the first place. There are advantages from using both approaches, as one can tell you things that the other might not. For example, if an employer or union wins a dispute over an enterprise agreement, you know that is the first face of power but you still want to know which resources both sides used to produce that outcome. Another example: if a worker suddenly abandons a claim for restitution of some type, it might not be surprising in light of the employer's larger resources, but looking at Bachrach and Baratz's theorising on the second face of power may shine more light on: What happened? (Was the worker co-opted? Were they threatened? Were the rules changed? and so on.) Our interest in the rest of this chapter, however, is broader, as it concerns the big forces at work that have shaped, or at least allegedly shaped, power at work and its future.

42 Keenoy and Kelly, *Employment Relationship*.

The meanings of globalisation, neo-liberalism and financialisation

We now turn to the other key concepts of interest, beginning with three basic definitions.

Globalisation is the process by which an increasing proportion of *economic activity* has been occurring between or across nation-states, rather than within them. It is the trend towards increasing integration of trade and investment flows between nations. So, economic activity is often thought of in terms of trade in goods or services, but it is also conceived in terms of capital flows (i.e. flows of money between countries). It may also be thought of in terms of human flows—increased international passenger transport, for work or tourism purposes, or temporary or permanent migration, often for work purposes—but inevitably the flow of capital is much freer than that of labour.

Neo-liberalism is a term used, often pejoratively, to describe a set of *public policy* settings that prioritise participants in private markets over individual workers or citizens. The most common manifestations of it are policies for privatisation of public services or assets, deregulation of product or labour markets, and the running of public sector agencies along 'corporate' lines that promote financially expressed objectives or 'competition'. While it is normally seen as promoting free market solutions to economic problems in any circumstance, this interpretation is contested and we return to it shortly.[43]

Financialisation is the process by which increasing command over economic activity is taken by the financial sector—banks, insurance companies, hedge funds and other financial institutions. The preferences and decisions of these organisations play an increasingly important role in shaping the behaviour of the other economic actors in society.

Neo-liberalism is thus a policy process, while globalisation and financialisation are economic processes. Globalisation and financialisation, are both often seen as resulting from the policy decisions of neo-liberalism.

43 Because of its pejorative implications, writers like Quiggin had avoided the term 'neo-liberalism', instead preferring 'market liberalism'. But I (somewhat reluctantly) use 'neo-liberalism' because, as discussed later, it goes beyond 'market liberalism' into policies that are not necessarily 'market liberal'. So 'market liberalism' is a subset of 'neo-liberalism'.

Alternatively, and perhaps more often, neo-liberal policies are portrayed as being driven by the economic imperatives of globalisation ('If we don't do X, then globalised markets will force us to') along TINA-esque lines ('There Is No Alternative', being a line made popular by Margaret Thatcher of the UK in the 1980s).[44] However, the reality is a bit more complex than either of these depictions.

Globalisation and contingency

Globalisation has been the buzzword since the 1970s or 1980s. It has been used to provide justification for many policy moves, mostly aimed at liberalising markets in one way or another, or in providing more favourable terms for foreign investment. It has also been highly controversial—partly because of those policy justifications I mentioned, and partly because some people have questioned it as a concept.

For example, some note (persuasively) that globalisation has been going on since the major European powers established empires across the globe and shipped massive amounts of primary commodities from the colonies to the home country (and secondary manufactures in the other direction).[45] The Hanseatic League of the sixteenth century can be seen as an early example of cross-border governance of trade.[46] It is only technological developments, greatly increasing the velocity and hence potential volume of financial transactions since the 1980s, that have enabled globalisation to 'step up a gear'. Some argue that globalisation has passed its peak, and the trend to ever-greater global integration has slowed down. For example, renowned Canadian philosopher John Ralston Saul authored a book as long ago as 2005 called *The Collapse of Globalism.*[47] Since then, others have seen the global financial crisis, the 'Brexit' vote or the election of Donald Trump as signifying a reversal of the trend to globalisation.[48]

44 Claire Berlinski, *There Is No Alternative: Why Margaret Thatcher Matters* (New York: Basic Books, 2008).

45 Jeffrey A. Frankel, 'Globalization of the Economy'. In *Governance in a Globalizing World*, ed. Joseph S. Nye and John D. Donahue (Washington DC: Brookings Institution Press, 2000), 45–71.

46 Ingo Take, 'The Hanseatic League as an Early Example of Cross-Border Governance?'. *Journal of European Integration History* 23, no. 1 (2017): 71–96.

47 John Ralston Saul, *The Collapse of Globalism: And the Reinvention of the World* (London: Atlantic, 2005).

48 John Rennie Short, 'Globalization and Its Discontents: Why There's a Backlash and How It Needs to Change'. *The Conversation*, 29 November 2016.

Some people see the effects of globalisation as overwhelmingly good.[49] Some see them as overwhelmingly bad. Some (like Tony Blair) see globalisation as 'a force of nature' and 'a fact'.[50] The key point is: the effects are contradictory and contingent. Take, first, a pathway through the impact of globalisation on industrialisation. For many Third World countries, particularly in Asia, globalisation has enabled them to expand manufactured exports and thereby build up a manufacturing base. That is, globalisation has promoted industrialisation. Industrialisation has, in turn, promoted economic development and, as a result, *growth* in real wages, reductions in poverty and greater job security.[51]

Then, look at another pathway, through the impact of globalisation on competition. Globalisation leads to greater competition between international and domestic firms. Increased competition in turn puts pressure on firms to *reduce* wages and reduce the stability of jobs and thereby makes poverty alleviation harder. This is an opposite tendency to the one that I mentioned in the preceding paragraph. Regarding the impact on wages, job security and poverty, then, globalisation has contradictory effects.

But wait, there's more. Higher wages from that first pathway (through industrialisation) may lead firms to seek ways of offsetting their higher labour costs by getting more flexibility in how they deploy their labour. At the same time, increased competition (the second pathway) leads to considerable pressure for firms to find greater flexibility in how they deploy their labour. And so, on that point, both pathways are leading to the same outcome: a greater search for flexibility. And then the push for higher flexibility will lead firms to find ways of reducing wage costs and job security. So that reinforces the effects via competition, but moderates the effects via industrialisation, on those things.

Whether the net effect is that globalisation improves or worsens real wages, poverty and job security is an empirical question. But it is not one that is decided in isolation. This is because its effects are contingent on what

49 For example, Mark Vaile, 'The Practical Benefits of Globalisation and the New Economy'. Trade Minister's Luncheon, Business Club Australia, Darling Harbour, 22 September 2000. trademinister.gov.au/speeches/2000/000922_globalisation.html.

50 Blair, quoted in Ryan Bourne, 'Tony Blair Is Right—Globalisation Is a Fact Not a Choice'. CATO Institute, 1 March 2019, www.cato.org/publications/commentary/tony-blair-right-globalisation-fact-not-choice.

51 Though Harrison points to conditionality here. Ann Harrison, *Globalization and Poverty*. NBER Working Paper 12347 (Cambridge, MA: National Bureau of Economic Research, 2006).

parties do. For example, how much globalisation leads to industrialisation in any particular country will depend on the policies taken by the state in that country to encourage that outcome. How much industrialisation in turn leads to higher wages also depends on the policies of the state—if policies prohibit or inhibit active trade unionism, then higher real wages are much less likely to flow from globalisation, or at least they will flow more weakly.

Similarly, the actions of unions themselves influence how much industrialisation leads to higher wages (compliant or weakly organised unions would be less successful in obtaining wage increases for members than widely organised, activist unions). The state, even a totalitarian one, cannot ignore unions: the maintenance of hegemony requires that it makes 'certain compromises with them in order to gain their consent for its leadership in society as a whole',[52] though these compromises, as Gramsci points out, 'cannot touch the essential'.[53]

How much increased competition leads to pressure for more flexibility, and for lower wages, will also depend on the actions of governments and unions. It will also depend on the historically shaped 'culture' of a country, as 'culture' influences laws and corporate behaviour: in East Asian countries such as Korea and Malaysia, workers were less easily laid off during the Asian financial crisis, or given greater redundancy pay when they were laid off, than workers in many industrialised countries.[54] Indeed, at just about every step along the pathway, the link between globalisation and a particular outcome is contingent upon some third factor or factors.

So, globalisation has contradictory pressures on wages, unionism and poverty. It creates competitive pressures on employers for increased flexibility, but whether and how this is translated into practice is contingent on local factors, including the state, labour and cultural factors. 'Culture' limits globalisation's push for flexibility (e.g. in much of Asia, notions of hierarchy, paternalism and security promote resistance to increased flexibility). The effects of globalisation on employment relations are contingent, and the net effect depends on the interplay of a number of forces. Worker organisation influences resistance, as well as state and

52 Sassoon, *Approaches to Gramsci*, 13.

53 Gramsci, *Selections from the Prison Notebooks*, 161.

54 David Peetz and Trish Todd, *Globalisation and Employment Relations in Malaysia* (Bangkok: International Labour Office, 2000), www98.griffith.edu.au/dspace/bitstream/10072/7320/1/13955_1.pdf.

employer strategies. State strategies are also influenced by domestic considerations: the state relies increasingly on international capital, but it is constrained by the need for domestic legitimacy and stability, and even unions help shape that legitimacy. This is an example of the point made in the previous chapter: that the outcomes of the forces acting upon our futures are not things entirely outside our control, but instead depend on decisions that we, as societies, make.

Globalisation also has complex impacts on income distribution and inequality. Increased trade does not always lead to wider inequality, for example. Economic growth in Taiwan, Japan and Korea during the 1960s and 1970s was associated with reduced inequality, as it improved prospects for low-income individuals.[55] More recently, however, the trend *within* most countries (especially the USA, but also many others) has been for widening inequality.[56] At the same time, though, inequality *between* nations has, overall, reduced, mainly because of higher growth in low-income countries such as China and India than in the high-income countries of the OECD (though poor growth in Africa weakens the average performance of low-income countries). Hence the net pattern of changing inequality over the past two decades has been complicated.

Some of the best work on this has been done by Branko Milanovic, whose famous 'elephant chart' (so named because mapping income growth by income percentile resembled the shape of an elephant lifting its trunk) using over 500 income surveys showed that, since the 1980s, income growth has been highest for the middle and upper classes of Asia, especially China, and for the very highest income groups in Western countries, especially the USA; these groups occupy the middle and the top of the global income distribution.[57] Income growth is weakest for denizens of many African countries, who occupy the bottom end of the global income distribution, and for the Western working classes, again especially in the USA, who occupy around the 70th or 80th percentiles of the global income distribution. Thus trends in global income inequality

55 Wang Feng, *The End of 'Growth with Equity'? Economic Growth and Income Inequality in East Asia*. Asia Pacific Issues, 101 (Honolulu: East-West Center, June 2011).
56 Ibid.; Thomas Piketty, *Capital in the Twenty-First Century* (Cambridge, MA: Harvard University Press, 2014); Georgina Murray and David Peetz, 'Plutonomy and the One Per Cent'. In *Challenging the Orthodoxy: Reflections on Frank Stilwell's Contribution to Political Economy*, ed. Susan Schroeder and Lynne Chester (Sydney: Springer, 2013), 129–48.
57 Branko Milanovic, *Global Income Inequality by the Numbers: In History and Now*. Policy Research Working Paper 6259 (Washington DC: Development Research Group, World Bank, 2012).

are more complex and less adverse than trends in income inequality within individual nations, and this again reflects the complex and contingent nature of the effects of globalisation. It appears that the effects of globalisation on inequality are often 'overstated', as 'globalisation is simply the international manifestation of the swing towards neo-liberal policies of market-oriented reform that has taken place throughout the world since 1970. Increased inequality is the result of the neo-liberal reform program as a whole'.[58]

That said, survey data have limitations, not the least being the way in which very high incomes are reported in 'grouped' data, leading to a potential understatement of incomes at the top. The work of Thomas Piketty, whose book *Capital in the Twenty-first Century* reignited debate about inequality of both income and wealth, relied more on administrative data (mostly from tax returns), which did not suffer the 'grouped' data problem.[59] Analysis of administrative data across a large number of nations by several of his colleagues in the *World Inequality Report 2018* showed a different picture of trends in global inequality since 1980: still a greater rise for those in the middle—workers in 'emerging' countries—than for those in the 70th or 80th percentiles—working class people in advanced countries—but with all of these eclipsed by spectacular rises for the highest 0.01 per cent and especially the top 0.001 per cent.[60] The top 1 per cent captured 27 per cent of income growth over the period, while the bottom 50 per cent captured just 12 per cent. The resultant chart mapping income growth by income percentile was described by one person as more closely resembling the shape of the Loch Ness monster than an elephant.[61]

It is possible that this method also understates inequality, if the wealthy are able to lie to tax authorities by a greater amount than the less wealthy. Likewise, wealth inequality is understated by the use of tax 'shelters'.[62] So if the opportunities for doing so have increased, then the

58 John Quiggin, 'Globalisation, Neoliberalism and Inequality in Australia'. *Economic and Labour Relations Review* 10, no. 2 (1999): 240–59.

59 Piketty, *Capital in the Twenty-First Century.*

60 Facundo Alvaredo et al., *World Inequality Report 2018* (World Inequality Lab/WID.world, 2018); Dylan Matthews, 'The Global Top 1 Percent Earned Twice as Much as the Bottom 50 Percent in Recent Years'. *Vox*, 2 February 2018. www.vox.com/policy-and-politics/2018/2/2/16868838/elephant-graph-chart-global-inequality-economic-growth.

61 Matthews, 'The Global Top 1 Percent'.

62 This increased usage of shelters appears to have happened in several countries. Alvaredo et al., *World Inequality Report 2018*.

rise in inequality is understated. Changing inequality, then, has a complex pattern, with redistribution within the global working and middle classes but the starkest element being strong redistribution towards a very small, wealthy elite. Even if globalisation has been responsible for the redistribution within the global working and middle classes, the redistribution towards a very small, wealthy elite appears to reflect much more the effects of financialisation (and perhaps, as discussed below, neo-liberal policy).

Complexity is also seen in the writing, in 1986, of prominent industrial sociologist Steve Frenkel, who made five key points about workplace relations.[63] First, he said, contemporary workplace relations are reproduced and changed in the context of a set of constraining factors that only rarely permit these relations to be newly created from scratch. Second, three principal factors tend to shape dominant patterns of workplace relations: large enterprises, the labour movement and the state. Third, the basic pattern of workplace relations is mostly inscribed at critical historical junctures. Fourth, arising from such crises and consequential action by major collectives, there is a process of institutional change in the regulation of industrial conflict—the new accommodation structures are an important influence on the character of workplace relations. Fifth, across countries, there will be differences in the way the major collectives institutionalise conflict and workplace relations, but there are common threads in the experience arising from the rise of the large corporation, state intervention, and the tendency towards greater integration in the world economy. Those factors that shape workplace relations shape the reality and future of work.

The importance of large, rather than small, enterprises, as highlighted by Frenkel, is one reason why this book spends more time discussing developments and futures in large rather than small enterprises. The former are much more important in influencing policy-makers, and their own demands often affect the practices of smaller enterprises. The behaviour of a few owners or managers of large corporations could have reverberations throughout the economy; the behaviour of a few owners or managers of small businesses will likely disappear without trace in national economic affairs.

63 Stephen J. Frenkel, 'Industrial Sociology and Workplace Relations in Advanced Capitalist Societies'. *International Journal of Comparative Sociology* 27, no. 1–2 (1986): 69–86.

The growing unpopularity of globalisation has even been recognised by the OECD.[64] Globalisation is seen as increasing the power of capital and reducing the power of labour, but this is not always true. Sometimes the rhetoric of globalisation, and the TINA idea, shift power in that direction. But the real effects of globalisation are complex and vary between groups. It may, for example, reduce the power of the working class in the developed West, but increase it for the working class in developing countries, by virtue of changes in trade and employment patterns.

If somebody says 'X happened at the workplace because of globalisation', that is usually just part of the story—because globalisation has complex, contradictory and contingent effects on workplace relations. The state, unions, large employers and their agents all shape how globalisation affects workplace relations, work and inequality.

Neo-liberalism

At the core of economic policy in many countries since the 1980s has been neo-liberalism, which has also been described as 'economic rationalism', 'economic fundamentalism', 'economic liberalism' and 'market liberalism'.[65]

While neo-liberalism emerged as a dominant philosophy among elites in the late twentieth century, it is not a philosophy that ever attained widespread acceptance in the community at large.[66] For example, opinion polls have typically shown the majority of Australian voters support

64 Angel Gurria, 'Globalisation: Don't Patch It up—Shake It Up'. News release, Organisation for Economic Co-operation and Development, Paris, 6 June, 2017; Organisation for Economic Co-operation and Development, *Making Globalisation Work: Better Lives for All*. Key Issues Paper, Meeting of the OECD Council at Ministerial Level (Paris: OECD, 7–8 June 2017).

65 Michael Pusey, *Economic Rationalism in Canberra: A Nation-Building State Changes Its Mind* (Cambridge, UK: Cambridge University Press, 2003); Fred Argy, 'Beware of Economic Fundamentalism (or What Makes a Good Policy Adviser?)'. *Australian Review of Public Affairs Digest* (31 March 2003), www.australianreview.net/digest/2003/03/argy.html; Frank Stilwell, *Political Economy: The Contest of Economic Ideas* (Melbourne: Oxford University Press, 2002); John Quiggin, *Zombie Economics* (New Jersey: Princeton University Press, 2010). In specific national contexts, terms like 'Rogernomics' (New Zealand), 'Thatcherism' (UK) and 'Reaganism' (USA) have been used along with, internationally, the 'Washington Consensus'.

66 Michael Pusey and Nick Turnbull, 'Have Australians Embraced Economic Reform?'. In *Australian Social Attitudes: The First Report*, ed. Shaun Wilson et al. (Sydney: UNSW Press, 2005): 161–81; Shaun Wilson, Gabrielle Meagher, and Trevor Breusch, 'Where to for the Welfare State'. In *Australian Social Attitudes: The First Report*, ed. Shaun Wilson et al. (Sydney: UNSW Press, 2005): 101–21.

import quotas and oppose privatisation.[67] In the realm of industrial relations, sympathy towards unions has increased over the past three decades (despite major falls in union membership) and voters consistently opposed the 'WorkChoices' reforms of Australia's Howard government.[68]

Neo-liberal policies often involve replacing state regulation with markets, and these can be described as 'market neo-liberalism'. But this is not always the case. Sometimes state intervention merely changes or even increases. An example is the Australian WorkChoices legislation of 2006. It increased restrictions and penalties on unions undertaking industrial action, imposed major limitations on union officials' right to enter workplaces, took away many remaining powers of the independent tribunals, sought to make state jurisdictions redundant, abolished protection against unfair dismissal for the majority of workers, and enabled individual contracts to undercut most minimum provisions in awards without compensation. While on the one hand espousing the rhetoric of enabling employers and employees to determine enterprise-level outcomes for themselves absent of third-party intervention, its 1,388 pages of legislation, 414 pages of regulations, and 890 pages of explanatory memoranda—2,692 pages in total—sought to intervene in microlevel relations in a partisan fashion to an unprecedented degree. If an agreement contained provisions that the federal minister found objectionable—for example, provisions for unfair dismissal protections or union training—the parties were liable to heavy fines.

One corporate lobbyist likened it to the 'old Soviet system of command and control, where every economic decision has to go back to some central authority and get ticked off'.[69] Hence this variant can be described as 'Stalinist neo-liberalism', in stark contrast to 'market neo-liberalism'. There are many variants in between.[70] The common theme is not laissez-faire markets, but the rewriting of rules (market or otherwise) in favour of

67 Georgina Murray and David Peetz, 'Ideology Down Under and the Shifting Sands of Individualism'. In *Labour and Employment in a Globalising World: Autonomy, Collectives and Political Dilemmas*, ed. Christian Azais (Brussels: PEI Peter Lang, 2010); David Peetz, 'Are Collective Identity and Action Being Squashed by Individualism?'. In *Work and Identity: Contemporary Perspectives on Workplace Diversity*, ed. Shalene Werth and Charlotte Brownlow (New York: Palgrave, 2018).

68 Murray and Peetz, 'Ideology Down Under'.

69 Quoted in 'IR Laws like "Soviet-style command"', *Sydney Morning Herald*, 27 March 2006.

70 For some examples in Australian industrial relations, see David Peetz and Janis Bailey, 'Neoliberal Evolution and Union Responses in Australia'. In *International Handbook on Labour Unions: Responses to Neo-Liberalism*, ed. G. Gall, A. Wilkinson, and R. Hurd (Cheltenham: Edward Elgar, 2011), 62–81.

capital. So it is that even think-tanks that describe themselves as advocates of free market policies end up supporting interventionist policies that favour capital or conservative political parties.[71]

The class-based nature of neo-liberalism was most effectively articulated by geographer David Harvey, who described 'accumulation by dispossession'—a series of ways (other than through the exploitation of labour) in which value was taken from ordinary people under neo-liberalism and given to the wealthy owners of capital.[72] These included privatisation of public assets; laws that facilitated mergers and acquisitions, Ponzi schemes, foreclosures and other financial rorts; the creation and manipulation of crises to impose emergency 'structural adjustment programs' of the International Monetary Fund or the like (what Naomi Klein calls 'disaster capitalism' or 'shock therapy');[73] and redistribution through taxes and public expenditures. Harvey drew similarities between 'accumulation by dispossession' and what Marx had referred to as 'the so-called primitive accumulation' by which peasants had been dispossessed of their land and property prior to the full emergence of capitalism.[74]

Another meaning that is given to 'neo-liberalism' is more about ideas than policies—what Bloom and Rhodes call 'the extension of market-based values to all dimensions of human endeavour'.[75] Thus neo-liberalism promotes 'managerialism', meaning that 'the management of market-based organisations is the preferred way to manage all other types of organisations'.[76] As a belief system, according to these authors, neo-liberalism has two major tenets: market efficiency and individualism.[77]

71 For example, in Australia the Institute of Public Affairs, the most prominent neo-liberal think-tank, has supported government intervention on industry superannuation fund boards to make them less competitive with bank-owned funds, warned that 'Gay Marriage Could Reduce Freedom', supported a subsidised 'special economic zone' in part of Australia, pushed for culturally conservative policies on issues such as 'race' and crime, supported Brexit, lamented 'If Only Trump Were Australian' and that the government 'Must Learn From Breitbart', though most extensively it has advocated climate change denial, including by promoting brown coal and nuclear energy, opposing carbon trading schemes and criticising private banks for not lending to possible new coal mines. See various entries at www.ipa.org.au. Further information on think-tanks in various countries is in A. Salas-Porras and G. Murray, eds, *Think Tanks and Global Politics: Key Spaces in the Structure of Power* (Singapore: Palgrave Macmillan, 2017).

72 David Harvey, 'The "New" Imperialism: Accumulation by Dispossession', *Socialist Register* 40 (2004): 63–87. David Harvey, *The New Imperialism* (Oxford: Oxford University Press, 2003).

73 Naomi Klein, *The Shock Doctrine: The Rise of Disaster Capitalism* (Toronto: Knopf, 2007).

74 Karl Marx, *Capital: Volume 1* (London: The Electric Book Company, 1887, repr. 1998), Chapters XXVI–XXXII.

75 Peter Bloom and Carl Rhodes, *CEO Society: The Corporate Takeover of Everyday Life* (London: Zed, 2018), 19.

76 Ibid.

77 Ibid., 20.

On the surface, this meaning seems quite at odds to the policy regime described above, which can also encompass some non-market, authoritarian policy tendencies in the interests of capital. But shortly after, Bloom and Rhodes expand the meaning to encompass 'corporate values associated with authoritarianism, self-determinism and rationality'.[78]

Perhaps, though, this is not an expansion of meaning. Deferring to the logic of markets essentially involves deferring to the logic of power. Neo-classical economics (the theoretical foundation for neo-liberal policy ideas) has no way of accounting for power in market transactions: it allows for the potential that 'rents' (surpluses) might be extracted through monopoly positions, and uses this to justify the need for government monopoly services to be privatised, but has no formal role for power in private markets. So the outcomes of all market transactions become the neutral outcomes of the laws of supply and demand, which, while very important, do not tell the whole story of markets, and do not tell the role of power in explaining why, for example, workers in some industries might be victims of 'wage theft', and of why CEOs end up overpaid, according to a consensus across many countries.[79] There is, after all, nothing especially democratic about markets: while democracy is based (in theory at least) on 'one vote one value', in markets power increases proportionately with financial resources, and, in at least one telling, 'politics and democracy are simply a hindrance on the way to efficiency and competitive advantages'.[80]

What Bloom and Rhodes are talking about, then, is the ideology that supports the policy practices described here. The main reason for using the term in this book to describe a set of *policies* is simply that it is not an *ideology* that commands, or has ever commanded, majority support among citizens. While some aspects of it have had widespread support, others, as mentioned, have not, even while as a belief system it has been widely adopted by senior policy cadres in many governments[81]—though even then it battles against political realities. It is because neo-liberalism is more often manifest in policy behaviour than as popular ideology—and its role in policy behaviour is what has shaped the realities of work—that the former meaning is given to it here.

78 Ibid., 39.

79 David Peetz, 'An Institutional Analysis of the Growth of Executive Remuneration'. *Journal of Industrial Relations* 57, no. 5 (2015): 707–25.

80 Thomas Klikauer, 'What Is Managerialism?'. *Critical Sociology* 41, no. 7–8 (2015).

81 Pusey, *Economic Rationalism.*

Public policy in most countries, including but not only most developed countries, has been heavily influenced by neo-liberal ideas since the 1980s. However, the take-up of neo-liberal ideas has varied between countries. Even before the 1980s, there were major differences in the broad policy approaches that countries took, ranging from the very market-dominated USA to the interventionist states in Scandinavian countries. One way of characterising the differences in approaches has been the 'varieties of capitalism' literature.[82] The key writers on this topic, Hall and Soskice, originally suggested two key varieties: countries with a higher commitment to equality ('coordinated market economies', such as Germany, Sweden and Japan, with a stronger welfare net, higher protections for workers and a more unionised labour force) and countries with a higher commitment to the market—'liberal market economies', such as the USA and UK, with relatively low protections for workers and a low welfare safety net. Others have argued there is more of a continuum, with many nuances.[83]

The precise origins of neo-liberalism are debated, but the US Reagan government and the UK Thatcher government, which dominated the 1980s in their countries, are seen as driving forces. As important as real-world actions were, credit must also be given to developments in the economics profession itself, with Keynesian economics falling out of favour and monetarist economics, spearheaded by Milton Friedman, coming to dominate economics thinking and teaching at universities. In that sense, it may be better to date the origins of neo-liberalism to the collapse of the Bretton-Woods international currency agreement in 1971 or the OPEC oil price rise of 1973 and the subsequent widespread phenomenon of 'stagflation' (simultaneous high unemployment and inflation), as these undermined the credibility of Keynesian economics. Although monetarism as a serious body of theory has long disappeared (something of that name is no longer commonly taught), for a long time free-market theorising dominated economic thinking, as its mathematical elegance (regardless of real-world applicability) made for ready publications and the comforting belief that economists were studying a hard 'science' with simple rules that meant it could be treated as a serious academic discipline.[84] Dating its origins to the early 1970s also makes it

---

82 Peter A. Hall and David W. Soskice, *Varieties of Capitalism: The Institutional Foundations of Comparative Advantage* (Oxford: Oxford University Press, 2001).

83 Colin Crouch, *Capitalist Diversity and Change: Recombinant Governance and Institutional Entrepreneurs* (Oxford: Oxford University Press, 2005).

84 Quiggin, *Zombie Economics*.

easier to recognise that the violent coup in Chile, on 11 September 1973, was the beginning of the first nationally imposed neo-liberal regime. As a project in which, as Connell points out, global market relations aim to penetrate every sphere and become the dominant rationality of life, it also has major implications for the global South as a new development strategy, involving, as she also says, reshaping of class relations within the South and a reconstruction of global trade.[85] Neo-liberalism only gained ascendancy in the global North, however, with the Thatcher and Reagan governments of the 1980s.

Its solutions were found wanting, and it was totally discredited with the global financial crisis (the 'great recession') of the late 2000s, when financial markets, operating in the closest thing yet to a 'perfect' market with 'perfect information', entirely failed to predict the collapse of key financial products and indeed largely created the crisis themselves. As nothing rose to take the place of neo-liberalism, however, ideas discredited by the global financial crisis—such as the efficient markets hypothesis, the benefits of privatisation, and 'trickle down' notions—still underpin the thinking of many policy-makers. The ideas are, as John Quiggin argues, like zombies: 'neither alive nor dead'.[86]

To some extent, the rise of 'behavioural economics' (which seeks to integrate some of the lessons from psychology about irrational behaviour into economic modelling) has been a response, albeit only partial, to the gap between theory and reality. Yet, despite the fatal flaws, neo-liberal beliefs persist, zombie-like, in economic theorising and, more importantly, in public policy-making, evident especially in the strength of 'austerity' politics in Europe. This suggests that the endurance of neo-liberal ideas is not so much a result of their merit but of the groups in whose interests it is that these ideas persist.

This is not to deny that some market liberal policies have benefited labour by tackling the high transfer of income to parts of capital through former protectionist policies (e.g. reductions in tariffs on highly protected imports used by working-class consumers benefited them—this was a policy

85 Raewyn Connell, 'Understanding Neoliberalism'. In *Neoliberalism and Everyday Life*, ed. Susan Braedley and Meg Luxton (Montreal, QC, & Kingston, ON: McGill-Queen's University Press, 2010): 22–36; Raewyn Connell and Nour Dados, 'Where in the World Does Neoliberalism Come From? The Market Agenda in Southern Perspective'. *Theory and Society: Renewal and Critique in Social Theory* 43, no. 2 (2014): 117–38.

86 Quiggin, *Zombie Economics*.

initiated in Australia by the Whitlam government, well before the onset of neo-liberal policy dominance).[87] It would indeed be surprising if every market liberal policy from the 1980s onwards unambiguously favoured capital—this outcome would rely upon every policy initiative before the 1980s being to the advantage of labour, an unlikely outcome in the light of labour's inability to seize total control of the state apparatus through the post–World War II era. And some market neo-liberal policies that, in relative terms, favour labour (such as, in Australia, the 1985 introduction of capital gains tax and abolition of deductions for entertainment expenses) may even be seen as the concessions that capital must make, without touching 'the essential', to maintain hegemony.[88] Other liberal market policies that would benefit workers and society generally (such as a carbon price) may be strenuously resisted by parts of capital. More often than not, though, market liberal policies favoured capital and thus the neo-liberal project embraced the market agenda, except where that agenda produced the 'wrong' results.

Financialisation

Financialisation has been described by Palley as 'a process whereby financial markets, financial institutions and financial elites gain greater influence over economic policy and economic outcomes' such that financialisation 'transforms the functioning of economic systems at both the macro and micro levels'.[89] Financialisation did not create globalisation, but it ensured that the globalisation would operate in a particular way, enhancing the mobility and mobilising power of capital but restraining that of labour, leading to a structural shift in income distribution away from wages towards profits and executive remuneration.[90] As, globally, 'patient capital' was replaced by 'agile capital', the focus of share markets became increasingly short term and corporate managers increasingly focused on achieving short-term profit goals, growth through acquisitions

87 David Peetz, 'Protection and the Labour Movement'. *Journal of Australian Political Economy* 12/13 (1982): 62–73.

88 Sassoon, *Approaches to Gramsci*, 13; Gramsci, *Selections from the Prison Notebooks*, 161.

89 Thomas I. Palley, 'Financialization: What It Is and Why It Matters'. Working Paper No. 525 (Annandale-on-Hudson, NY: Levy Economics Institute, 2007), papers.ssrn.com/sol3/papers.cfm?abstract_id=1077923.

90 Frank Stilwell and Kirrily Jordan, *Who Gets What? Analysing Economic Inequality in Australia* (Cambridge: Cambridge University Press, 2007).

and mergers, and the booms in executive remuneration thereby brought.[91] The logic of financialisation was that 'perpetual restructuring' becomes the norm 'as firms seek ways of cutting costs and managing assets to meet capital market requirements'.[92]

Financialisation may be thought of as being mainly seen in the rising share of the finance sector in the economy.[93] However, it is often specifically about the rising share of *finance capital income* in the economy. It is often only financial capital, not workers in the finance sector, that has benefited from financialisation, and this has contributed to rising inequality.[94] The labour time (as measured by relative employment) taken up by the finance sector has changed little.[95] The widely recognised shift in income from labour to capital can be predominantly a shift in income to finance capital.

Greater emphasis on maximising short-term financial returns makes managers in industrial capital more focused on minimising costs, including by cutting labour costs such as wages and money spent on training or worker development. The more that opportunities were provided for profits by what Harvey called 'accumulation through dispossession'—that is, the more money could be made by mergers and acquisitions, privatisation or numerous other such devices—then the more pressure would in turn be placed on corporate managers to go further and faster down this cost-cutting path in the race for competitive short-term returns.

Financialisation and power

Not only is financialisation important for understanding trends in inequality, it is also important in understanding trends in the forces that shape work. I will first illustrate how resource dependency is central to the reproduction of power, then canvass trends in the power of labour and capital.

---

91 William Carroll, *The Making of a Transnational Capitalist Class* (London: Zed Books, 2010).

92 Paul Thompson, 'The Capitalist Labour Process: Concepts and Connections'. *Capital and Class* 100 (2010): 7–14.

93 Richard B. Freeman, 'It's Financialization!'. *International Labour Review* 149, no. 2 (2010): 163–83.

94 David Peetz, 'The Labour Share, Power and Financialisation'. *Journal of Australian Political Economy* 81 (2018): 33–51.

95 Ibid.

Power resources and credibility

A good approach to looking at the ways in which power is produced and reproduced is to ask how it is that some (but not all) discredited institutions maintain power. The financial ratings agencies—which assess the creditworthiness (likelihood of default) of various financial products or organisations offering them—made huge and repeated errors in the lead-up to the global financial crisis, consistently overestimating the creditworthiness of numerous securities, such as collateralised debt obligations. If any part of finance capital was to lose its position of power after the financial crisis, it would be the ratings agencies. In effect, ratings agencies were paid by bond issuers to give them a good rating.[96] One agency's defence, when sued, was that their assertions (that they used 'transparent and independent decision-making' to produce 'independent and objective analysis') were 'mere commercial puffery'.[97] Yet no one in the ratings agencies went to gaol for their role in the global financial collapse and their ratings continue to be influential—even among those who should know better.

Objectively, one would expect such institutions to have lost their influence. After all, if a government agency makes a major blunder, or an organisation that is accountable to government does so, their loss of credibility may be followed by their being seriously restructured or even abolished. Yet here we have an example of institutions that have survived with little damage despite being discredited. The ratings agencies operate in a market context, so we cannot blame the lack of market exposure for the problem.

A feature of such resilient organisations is that they control resources that others are dependent on and that others cannot get through alternative means. As part of this, they are not dependent on coordinated others (unlike, say, government agencies who destroy their own credibility, but who are accountable to a coordinated entity—the government). The ratings agencies could be subverted and replaced if governments and investors were internationally coordinated, but the latter lack the will or capacity to do so. Absent international coordination, governments

96 Jesse Westbrook, 'SEC Ratings Probe Reveals Conflicts in Grading Debt'. *Bloomberg*, 8 July 2008; Matt Stoller, 'S&P—"Our Ratings in the Mortgage-Backed Securities Area Were Not Venal"'. *Naked Capitalism*, 12 August 2011.

97 Kevin Drum, 'S&P Admits in Court That Its Ratings Are Ridiculous and No One Should Ever Take Them Seriously'. *Mother Jones*, 8 July 2013.

(and investors) rely on the informational and reputational resources controlled by ratings agencies, as flawed as they may be. This power can also be likened to Bachrach and Baratz's second face of power: the idea of replacing the ratings agencies is not on the agenda of any decision-making process, due to the reliance of decision makers on the resources possessed by those agencies and the lack of an institutional process (coordination) that could address it.

Power and workers

Two different trends can be seen in employees' ability to have more say at work. Both are influenced by financialisation. The first is the decline in union membership over the past three decades. It has fallen from around 30 per cent of employees across the OECD in 1985 to 17 per cent in 2015, and fell in all but three OECD countries over that time.[98] Unions were the workers' 'voice' at work. At times they forced managers to take account of, even accede to, what workers wanted. Lower union membership and lower union power mean less worker say at work. Internationally, high rates of union membership had been linked to lower inequality, and better gender equity.[99]

The second trend affecting employees' ability to have a say at work concerns how managers handle employees. It is about the appearance of power. Some managers are seen by employees as tightening their grip over them. Barcode measurement of warehouse task times, scan rates in supermarkets and timing of gaps between calls in a call centre are all illustrations of that. But some managers are seen as giving workers *more* say. It is hard to tell, but the latter group seems to outnumber the former. Quality circles,[100] open-door policies, consultative committees and the like promote that perception. Sometimes it is for real. Sometimes employers do it in order to discourage workers from joining a union. Often, though, it is a mirage,

98 Organisation for Economic Co-operation and Development, *Employment Outlook* (Paris: OECD, 2017).

99 Ünal Töngür and Adem Yavuz Elveren, 'Deunionization and Pay Inequality in OECD Countries: A Panel Granger Causality Approach'. *Economic Modelling* 38 (2014): 417–25; Jonas Pontusson, 'Unionization, Inequality and Redistribution'. *British Journal of Industrial Relations* 51, no. 4 (2013): 797–825; Bruce Western and Jake Rosenfeld, 'Unions, Norms, and the Rise in U.S. Wage Inequality'. *American Sociological Review* 76, no. 4 (August 2011): 513–37.

100 A quality circle is a group of employees (typically 6 to 12 from the same work area) that meets regularly to solve problems affecting its work area. Edward E. Lawler III and Susan A. Mohrman, 'Quality Circles after the Fad', *Harvard Business Review*, January 1985, hbr.org/1985/01/quality-circles-after-the-fad.

and only lasts until the next round of redundancies. Starbucks called its employees 'partners' until it sacked 685 of them.[101] Walmart calls its employees 'associates' unless they start using words like 'grievance' or 'seniority'—that could make them ex-'associates'.[102] We'll see more about this in Chapters 4 and 7. One can try to stop employees thinking about their rights as employees by calling them 'members' or something else, but that does not make much difference when the pink slips[103] go around. And therein lies the problem with management-driven initiatives to give employees more say at work. What the boss giveth, the boss can take away.

The problem goes deeper than this, in fact. Within the workplace, there are major concerns about working hours, work intensity, work–life balance, pressures on women, 'overemployment' and underemployment, demands on employees for flexibility, insecurity, micromanagement of time and managerial efforts to control 'culture'. Most would likely not be happening if power was shifting *towards* workers. Another sign of low worker power is the low rate of wages growth, along with the fall in the labour share of national income that is evident in around three-quarters of OECD countries for which data are available.[104] Whatever employers have voluntarily done about employee say, there is little doubt that the underlying trend is for less worker power in the workplace. But, as mentioned, internal and external labour market power available to some individual employees, and the associational power available to workers who collectively organise, mean that the power of labour is unevenly distributed: some still have considerable power, even if most have very little. The combined negative effects of financialisation on workers' power in turn would help explain an observed correlation between financialisation and inequality in the USA since 1970 and across the OECD since 1990.[105]

---

101 David Emerson, 'Starbucks Axes 61 Stores and 685 Jobs'. *Sydney Morning Herald*, 29 July 2008.

102 Militantcentrist, 'Union-Busting & You: Wal-Mart's Handy Guide to Preventing Union Organization'. *Daily Kos*, 25 September 2012. www.dailykos.com/stories/2012/9/25/1136113/-Union-Busting-You-Wal-Mart-s-Handy-Guideto-Preventing-Union-Organization.

103 Redundancy notices.

104 Jim Stanford, 'The Declining Labour Share in Australia: Definition, Measurement, and International Comparisons'. *Journal of Australian Political Economy* 81 (2018): 11–32.

105 Oscar C. Soons, 'Inequality and Financialization'. Senior Honors Projects. Paper 492, University of Rhode Island, 2016. digitalcommons.uri.edu/srhonorsprog/492?utm_source=digitalcommons.uri.edu%2Fsrhonorsprog%2F492&utm_medium=PDF&utm_campaign=PDFCoverPages. Pasquale Tridico, 'The determinants of income inequality in OECD countries'. *Cambridge Journal of Economics* 42, no. 4 (2018): 1009–42.

Power and capital

Before the global financial crisis, members of the financial elite openly spoke of the rise of 'plutonomy', an economy 'powered by the wealthy'.[106] This illustrated clearly how much more capital had prospered than labour. Yet, while over the past three decades labour has become weaker, it does not follow that employers everywhere have become more powerful. The actions of corporations now are increasingly driven by the movements in stock or share prices, and their results are assessed on quarterly results, making planning over longer time periods increasingly precarious and responding to social considerations more difficult. Hence firms with higher volatility in share prices are less likely, for example, to commit to mechanisms associated with action on climate change.[107] The main owners of stocks (especially in the USA, but also globally, including in Australia) are now finance capital.[108] So the decisions of finance capital to buy and sell shares shape corporate behaviour. Finance capital is increasingly becoming the 'core' of capital, into which a growing amount of profit is being funnelled. Much of capital outside of the finance sector is 'peripheral' to this activity.

This does not mean, however, that all capital outside finance (call it 'industrial capital')[109] is peripheral. Within most industries, the trend over the past three decades has been towards increasing concentration of power, with a higher proportion of sales accounted for by a small number of corporations.[110] It is not only due to financialisation. We see a tendency for some parts of capital (finance capital and large firms dominating industries) to experience a growth in power, while other parts of capital,

106 Ajay Kapur, Niall Macleod, and Narendra Singh, 'Plutonomy: Buying Luxury, Explaining Global Imbalances'. *Citigroup Equity Strategy Industry Note* (Citigroup Capital Markets, 2005), 16 October; Ajay Kapur, Niall Macleod, and Narendra Singh, 'Revisiting Plutonomy: The Rich Getting Richer'. *Citigroup Equity Strategy Industry Note* (Citigroup Capital Markets, 2006), 5 March.

107 David Peetz and Georgina Murray, 'Financialization of Corporate Ownership and Implications for the Potential for Climate Action'. In *Institutional Investors' Power to Change Corporate Behavior: International Perspectives, Critical Studies on Corporate Responsibility, Governance and Sustainability*, ed. Suzanne Young and Stephen Gates (Bingley, UK: Emerald, 2013), 99–125.

108 G. Murray and D. Peetz, 'The Financialisation of Global Corporate Ownership'. In *Financial Elites and Transnational Business: Who Rules the World?*, ed. G. Murray and J. Scott (Cheltenham: Edward Elgar, 2012); Georgina Murray and David Peetz, 'Restructuring of Corporate Ownership in Australia through the Global Financial Crisis'. *Journal of Australian Political Economy* 71 (2013): 76–105.

109 'Industrial' is the term used in the stockmarket for non-finance firms.

110 Murray and Peetz, 'Financialisation of Ownership'; Murray and Peetz, 'Restructuring Corporate Ownership'.

acting in response to the demands of those with growing power, exhibit less power—and often place pressure on labour in an attempt to maintain profitability in some form.

Just as there are divisions within industrial capital, so too there are divisions within finance capital. For example, some parts have an increasingly short-term orientation; others need to maintain or even increase their long-term orientation.[111] We will look more closely at this in Chapter 9, in the context of responses to climate change, but the purpose in raising it here is to point out that financialisation is also a nuanced phenomenon. Finance capital is also quite unlike labour in that it is not interested in collective action. Even on matters of common concern—like the future of the planet—climate-interested investors may sign statements demanding action from governments, but they will not act in unity to invest in, or divest from, anything.[112] To do so would be both unnecessary (finance capital does not need associational power) and inconsistent with the competitive ideology that permeates finance capital. However, finance capital following a common logic sometimes gives the false appearance of conscious collective behaviour.

One more point about financialisation needs to be made in this chapter, and it concerns the link to neo-liberalism. The greatest beneficiary of neo-liberal policies has been finance capital. Privatisation has principally enriched the investors (financiers) who were able to purchase the organisations or licences for running previous government services. Cuts in wages and conditions have benefited share prices and shareholders, who are predominantly finance capital. It is the interests of finance capital, not the external validity of any findings, that maintain the primacy of neo-liberal policy. The economics profession itself is suffering from a hostile takeover by the finance sector: academic commentators who appeared on the media in the 1970s to comment on economic news have long since been replaced by professional economists on the payroll of financial corporations; enrolments in university economics courses are in decline, subverted by 'management', 'business' and 'finance' studies; and the profession is reeling from criticism of its treatment of gender issues and

111 David Peetz and Georgina Murray, 'Conflicts within Transnational Finance Capital and the Motivations of Climate-Interested Investors'. In *Globalization and Transnational Capitalism in Asia and Oceania*, ed. Jeb Sprague (Routledge, 2015), 163–79.
112 Ibid.

female economists.[113] Several prominent studies by economists used to justify neo-liberal policies have been subsequently found to be on weak or even erroneous foundations, their publication seemingly reflecting 'confirmation bias' among editors and/or reviewers.[114]

The theoretical logic of market solutions is more threadbare than ever in the light of policy failings, but finance capital itself was not weakened by the financial crisis it created; if anything, centralisation within finance capital increased, at least right at the top.[115] The reproduction of that power has, itself, facilitated the continuing importance of neo-liberal policies. Hence, for example, European finance capital played a crucial role in the perpetuation of 'austerity' policy in that continent after the global financial crisis, despite the illogic of market solutions. This in turn had implications for pay and conditions in many European countries, particularly those near the Mediterranean. Neo-liberal policy ideas are important for maintaining the power of finance capital, and the power of finance capital helps explain why neo-liberalism remains important.

In the garden

Finally, let's go back to that walk in the Parliamentary Rose Garden. The issues that prompted it tell us a lot about what shaped the next three decades of policy and may shape it for years to come. Globalisation was the backdrop for what happened, but not the driving force. Finance capital had gained new power through the deregulation of financial markets over two years earlier. It intimidated a Labor government, perhaps unwittingly—we should not assume a conspiracy to undermine the dollar, and the erratic nature of financial markets probably owed more to inexperience than anything else. However, it created the illusion of collective punishment by finance that heightened the insecurity of those in Cabinet. The government responded by strengthening neo-liberalism

113 Justin Wolfers, 'Even Famous Female Economists Get No Respect'. *New York Times*, 11 November 2015; Alice H. Wu, 'Gender Stereotyping in Academia: Evidence from Economics Job Market Rumors Forum'. SSRN, August 2017. pdfs.semanticscholar.org/5eb3/f36b34a9d6379a4de6923ceed99a9bc22a77.pdf?_ga=2.156327803.1957153287.1567424486-1023833107.1567424486.

114 Servaas Storm, *Labor Laws and Manufacturing Performance in India: How Priors Trump Evidence and Progress Gets Stalled*. Working Paper No. 90 (New York: Institute for New Economic Thinking, January 2019), www.ineteconomics.org/uploads/papers/WP_90-Storm-Labor-Laws.pdf.

115 Murray and Peetz, 'Financialisation of Ownership'.

almost each year thereafter (for which it was later rewarded by the media and conservatives through being retrospectively called a great 'reforming government').[116] There was a sense of powerlessness in the government in the face of financial markets—as if it had no alternative. Whether there was a viable alternative to the announcements of late July 1986 is a moot point. But for many of the policies that followed there were almost certainly viable alternatives. No two governments follow the same policy paths, each makes decisions that affects how it responds to globalisation and financialisation. The future, too, will be shaped by those responses.

The future of globalisation, and indeed of capitalism around the world, is unclear. Several scenarios suggest themselves, including further market liberal policies, strengthening the role of markets and the hand of capital; more authoritarian policies favouring capital, possibly weakening the role of markets but strengthening the hand of capital; or a shift in power towards labour. In the rest of this book we will consider factors shaping the current realities of work and the choices that will be made from now, and that determine which of the potential futures becomes a reality—and revisit these scenarios in the final chapter.

116 Laurie Oakes, 'An Overlooked Hero of Reform'. *Daily Telegraph*, 20 June 2014; Troy Bramston, 'Hawke Model Could Serve as a Pick-Me-up for Next-Gen Labor'. *Australian*, 4 March 2013.

3

Visions of the future

As a child, I saw Stanley Kubrick's *2001: A Space Odyssey* at the cinema. I was captivated by so many aspects of it—the moon base, the idea of life from other planets, the self-aware computer HAL, the cryptic scene at the end—and the magnificent technology. In 33 years time we would commute to a space station, in a Pan American passenger craft, and then on to the moon. Well, 2001 has come and gone, Pan American went bankrupt, and we are almost no closer to commuting to the moon now than we were four years after *2001* was released, when NASA finished its Apollo program. Like many movies about the future, some of the predictions have been illuminating but many have been way out.

If there was one area where technology has failed miserably to live up to its promise, it is in that area of transport. The Concorde, a supersonic passenger plane that first flew in 1969, a year after *2001* was released (and one that bore some visual resemblance to the imagined Pan Am Orion III spacecraft in *2001*) has not been bettered in speed; indeed, the Concorde stopped flying altogether in 2003. In 1969, the Boeing 747 'jumbo jet' was also launched, and it looked like planes would get bigger and bigger, not just faster and faster. They did not. The only other 'jumbo-sized' plane to come into production was the Airbus A380 in 2005, and the future of jumbo-sized planes is now in doubt in the face of weak demand, possibly killed off by the economics of air transport (though the need for low-emissions flight might, ironically, lead one day to a resurgence of larger planes).[1] Indeed, economics has been at least as big a barrier as technology against the translation of grand transport ideas into something experienced by consumers.

On the other hand, the dark, ultimately malevolent onboard computer, HAL, continues to fascinate. We may have been slower than *2001* predicted in getting to artificial intelligence (AI) with HAL's capabilities, but Google, Amazon and Siri are bringing that spaceship's AI capabilities to your home now—and, soon, to your workplace. The favourable economics of digital change make further developments here almost inevitable.

2001 said a lot about the future—not just technology, but also humanity's relationship with other species. It said very little about future society (aside from the commercialisation of space travel). In this chapter, we want to look at some earlier visions of the future, but we want to focus on what they say about society and what that suggests about work. Many of these visions have been seen in books, movies and songs. From the fiction side, we will focus on three main literary works, all of which have been adapted for the screen. There are many stories written about futures, and we cannot cover them all. All involve predictions of technology and society, varying in their emphasis on each. The ones I have chosen are all relevant to issues of control, class and oppression. They are not all directly about work, but through their views on society we can see things about work.

The first is George Orwell's *Nineteen Eighty-Four*, widely considered one of the best novels of the twentieth century, and first published in 1948.[2] The second is Margaret Atwood's *The Handmaid's Tale*, written over three decades after Orwell's book.[3] Both books were dystopian—they predicted nightmare futures as models that we should do everything to avoid. *Nineteen Eighty-Four* was turned into a movie three times, including a film starring John Hurt and Richard Burton, released in 1984 itself, that

---

1 Karl Kruszelnicki, 'Road Trip to Future Travel'. *Great Moments in Science*, Australian Broadcasting Corporation, 29 May 2018, www.abc.net.au/radionational/programs/greatmomentsinscience/lessons-from-first-road-trip/9795122. Hydrogen fuel would produce zero carbon emissions, but requires large storage volumes in planes, so some passenger space would need to make way for fuel space. On the demise of the A380 see Jasper Jolly, 'A380: Airbus to Stop Making Superjumbo as Orders Dry Up'. *Guardian*, 14 February 2019, www.theguardian.com/business/2019/feb/14/a380-airbus-to-end-production-of-superjumbo.

2 George Orwell, *Nineteen Eighty-Four: A Novel* (Harmondsworth: Penguin, 1949; repr., 1976).

3 Margaret Atwood, *The Handmaid's Tale* (London: Vintage, 1986).

was faithful to the book. There were also numerous stage productions. *The Handmaid's Tale* was turned into a widely watched TV series released in 2017, similar but not identical to the book. Three decades after Atwood wrote *The Handmaid's Tale*, Dave Eggers wrote *The Circle*, a very different book, about a large tech company that could almost be considered utopian by many of its employees.[4] It, too, was made into a movie, released in 2017, which followed closely the first half of the book but diverged widely in the second, such that the ending was almost the opposite of that in the book. While Eggers's book subtly highlighted the sinister side of this utopia, and had a suitably dark ending, the movie ended on a bizarrely positive note that somewhat missed the point. It was not a great box-office success.

Of course, predictions are made not just in fiction but in nonfiction as well, and in a chapter about visions of the future we must also consider these. We will also examine how accurate or otherwise earlier popular predictions of the future, by politicians, writers and futurists, have proved to be, particularly in relation to work. What happened to all those predictions of increased leisure and short working weeks? Have trends on working hours and work intensification continued? What explains recent developments in these areas? What is the future of, and what are the influences on, work–life balance? And what does this tell us about how the choices that affect the future of work will be made? We will start with these, and then move on to more literary futures.

Futures of work and leisure

If ever there was a need, in studies of work, for the somewhat hard-to-source maxim, 'It's dangerous to make predictions, especially about the future',[5] it is in relation to working time and leisure. John Maynard Keynes was not alone in predicting that increased productivity would see the average working week drop to 15 hours or so.[6] A series of academic or professional predictions issued in the 1960s and 1970s foresaw that

4 Dave Eggers, *The Circle* (New York: Vintage, 2013).

5 Although it has been attributed to people ranging from Neils Bohr to Samuel Goldwyn and even Yogi Berra, it appears to have originated from an unknown Dane, probably a parliamentarian, in the 1840s. Garson O'Toole, 'It's Difficult to Make Predictions, Especially About the Future'. Quote Investigator, 20 October 2013. quoteinvestigator.com/2013/10/20/no-predict/.

6 John Maynard Keynes, 'Economic Possibilities for Our Grandchildren'. In *Essays in Persuasion* (London: Palgrave Macmillan, 1930; repr., 2010).

working time would consistently drop, and a number predicted a working week of between 20 and 30 hours by the year 2000.[7] In the same era, some authors wrote of a forthcoming 'age of leisure', though they did not necessarily refer to quantitative forecasts of working hours to do so.[8] Such claims occasionally, but less commonly, resurface in the context of current technological projections.[9]

Hours of work

Needless to say, the working week did not shorten in the huge way anticipated by some of those predictions. In countries where average total working hours reduced, it arose from the growth of (mostly female-dominated) part-time employment, unrelated to technology effects. Reductions in average hours for *full-time* workers were harder to come by. Australia was one of those countries in the industrialised world that experienced increased working hours for full-time workers at the end of last century.[10] Part of this trend was an increase in the proportion of employees working unpaid overtime. An important feature of Australian work-time practice is the high proportion of employees working extended or long hours. Based on a comparison of nine OECD countries, Jacobs and Gerson found that Australia had the highest proportion of workforce working more than 50 hours per week.[11] A number of countries regulated maximum actual hours of work, but Australia did not. The trend was most marked in the 1990s. By the beginning of the next decade, mild-mannered researchers were pondering 'with the growing levels of stress and distress that are associated with the changes to labour utilisation that are favoured by employers, we have to wonder whether these trends are

7 Mary A. Holman, 'A National Time-Budget for the Year 2000'. *Sociology and Social Research* 46, no. 1 (1961); Herman Kahn and Anthony J. Wiener, *The Year 2000: A Framework for Speculation on the Next Thirty-Three Years* (New York: Macmillan, 1967); Michael Dower, 'The Fourth Wave: The Challenge of Leisure'. *The Architect's Journal* (1965): 123–90; J. Fourastié, *Les 40,000 Heures* (Paris: Editions Gonthier, 1965); M. Kaplan, *Leisure: Theory and Policy* (New York: Wiley, 1975). All cited in Anthony James Veal, 'The Leisure Society I: Myths and Misconceptions, 1960–1979'. *World Leisure Journal* 53, no. 3 (2011): 206–27.

8 Veal, 'Leisure Society'.

9 Matt Novak, 'Bullshit Article About Bullshit Automation Promises Bullshit Life of Leisure'. *Gizmodo*, 16 October 2017, paleofuture.gizmodo.com/bullshit-article-about-bullshit-automation-promises-bul-1819515685.

10 Iain Campbell, 'Extended Working Hours in Australia'. *Labour and Industry* 13, no. 1 (2002): 91–110.

11 Jerry A. Jacobs and Kathleen Gerson, 'Overworked Individuals or Overworked Families?'. *Work and Occupations* 28, no. 1 (2001): 40–63.

sustainable'.[12] Since then, Australian Bureau of Statistics (ABS) data on average hours worked by full-time employees have suggested that the trend stabilised or partially reversed over the subsequent decade. The average full-time working week rose from 44.5 hours in February 1979 to 46.5 hours in February 1998 in Australia, but gradually eased to 45.1 hours by February 2014.

Perhaps society approached a 'saturation point' regarding how many hours full-time employees can work in the context of their other responsibilities; perhaps this was also a result of a relative stabilisation, for a while, in union membership (after a long period of decline) and hence power relations in the workplace. Resistance grows, both organised—through unions and industrial action—and unorganised, through absenteeism, quitting, losses in loyalty, problems in quality of output, even possibly sabotage. The employee goodwill or 'organisational citizenship' that firms come to expect and indeed rely upon (often without realising it) may disappear. It's in this context that *employee* demands for greater flexibility in behaviour by employers (flexibility *for* employees) have expanded. Some workers have the labour market power to achieve this; many do not.

One interesting aspect, found in a study of employees in 13 Queensland organisations undertaken in 2002 by the Griffith Work Time Project, was that increasing hours were disproportionately concentrated among employees who were not compensated for them.[13] Thus increased hours were reported by 39 per cent of employees who *never* received overtime rates of pay for working extra hours, but by just 25 per cent of employees who received overtime rates *at least some* of the time. Long hours were also associated with other forms of weak regulation of working hours (absence of time off, absence of rostered days off or 'penalty rates') and management-driven workplace cultures that promoted long hours.[14]

12 David Peetz, Cameron Allan, and Michael O'Donnell, 'Are Australians Really Unhappier with Their Bosses Because They're Working Harder? Perspiration and Persuasion in Modern Work' (paper presented at Rethinking Institutions for Work and Employment, Selected Papers from the XXXVIII Annual CIRA Conference, Quebec, 26–28 May 2001).

13 Griffith Work Time Project, *Working Time Transformations and Effects* (Brisbane: Queensland Department of Industrial Relations, 2003).

14 Ibid.; David Peetz et al., 'Race against Time: Extended Hours in Australia'. *Australian Bulletin of Labour* 29, no. 2 (2003): 126–42.

The pattern of increasing hours was associated with simultaneous overemployment and underemployment. Many full-time workers still want fewer hours, while many part-time workers (especially casuals) want more hours, and many people without work seek employment. The first group (want fewer hours) outnumber the second group (want more hours) in aggregate, in both sexes, and among employees working 40 or more hours per week.[15] Over the years, though, the proportion of all workers wanting more hours has increased as the incidence of part-time work has increased (i.e. an increasing number of people are put into part-time work when what they wanted was full-time work). The ABS now publishes a time series on underemployment but not yet on overemployment.[16]

Instead of having more leisure time, working hours are increasingly interfering in traditional leisure days (Saturdays and Sundays), especially (but by no means exclusively) in the retail and hospitality industries. Public policy has facilitated this development, most recently in Australia with a reduction in 'penalty rates' (an addition to minimum hourly pay arising from the fact that an employee is working unsocial hours) for weekend and holiday workers in those two industries, commencing in 2017.[17] On the question of whether Sundays were worse for workers than Saturdays, the authors of a study from the Centre for Work + Life (CWL), using Australian Work and Life Index (AWALI) data, concluded: 'Those who work on Saturday and particularly Sunday have worse work life [sic] interference—an issue that is relevant to the current debate about penalty rates in Australia.'[18] Other Australian studies also showed that Sunday remained a day for family and civic activities, more so than Saturday or any weekday.[19]

15 Australian Bureau of Statistics, 'Employment Arrangements and Superannuation'. Canberra, 6361.0.

16 In Australian Bureau of Statistics, 'Labour Force, Australia'. Canberra, 6202.0.

17 Fair Work Commission, '4 Yearly Review of Modern Awards—Penalty Rates'. ([2017] FWCFB 1001, 2017), 23 February.

18 Natalie Skinner and Barbara Pocock, *The Persistent Challenge: Living, Working and Caring in Australia in 2014*. The Australian Work and Life Index 2014 (Adelaide: Centre for Work + Life, University of South Australia, September 2014), 1.

19 Lyn Craig and Judith E. Brown, 'Weekend Work and Leisure Time with Family and Friends: Who Misses Out?'. *Journal of Marriage and Family* 76, no. 4 (2014): 710–27; Michael Bittman, 'Sunday Working and Family Time'. *Labour and Industry* 16, no. 1 (2005): 59–81; David Peetz, Scott Bruynius, and Georgina Murray, 'Choice and the Impact of Changes to Sunday Premiums in the Australian Retail and Hospitality Industries'. *Journal of Industrial Relations* (2019), doi.org/10.1177/0022185618814578.

In some industries, particularly mining, there has been a move away from eight-hour work days back to standardised, rotating 12-hour shifts with a resultant working week of well over 38 hours.[20] Unused machines 'represent during the time they lie fallow, a useless advance of capital' and so using labour 'during all the 24 hours of the day' is, therefore, an 'inherent tendency of capitalist production'.[21] In countries with penalty rates and overtime to be taken into account, rotating 12-hour shifts pay well. However, a qualitative study showed they were associated with fatigue; irregular sleep; interruptions to family life; an increasing burden put on the (mainly female) non–shift working partner, especially where there are children in a family; increased stress on family relationships; pressure on community and sporting life in mining towns; and the growth of contractor-based fly-in fly-out 'long distance commute' workforces.[22] A study of over 2,000 mine and energy workers (mostly coal miners) found that half were working more hours than they would prefer, even after taking into account how that would affect their income and other activities, while 39 per cent were working the number of hours they would prefer and just 11 per cent were working fewer hours than they wanted.[23] The Griffith Work Time Project also illustrated both the role of tighter control and how employees internalised pressure on working hours. Among employees who reported no change in their say over how many hours they worked, only 23 per cent reported increased hours. But increased hours were reported by 51 per cent of those who said that their say in how many hours they worked had gone *down*—and by 58 per cent of those who reported that their say over how many hours they worked had gone *up*![24]

---

20 Kathryn Heiler and Richard Rickersgill, 'Shiftwork and Rostering Arrangements in the Australian Mining Industry: An Overview of Key Trends'. *Australian Bulletin of Labour* 27 (2001): 20–42.

21 Karl Marx, *Capital, Volume 1* (London: The Electric Book Company, 1887; repr., 1998), 369.

22 Georgina Murray and David Peetz, *Women of the Coal Rushes* (Sydney: UNSW Press, 2010).

23 David Peetz, Georgina Murray, and Olav Muurlink, *Work and Hours Amongst Mining and Energy Workers* (Brisbane: Centre for Work, Organisation and Wellbeing, Griffith University, 2012).

24 Griffith Work Time Project, *Working Time*, 24.

Thus there were, in effect, two paths to increased hours: one involving tighter direct control over employees' hours, and one involving a loosening of direct control and replacing it with internalisation of the need to work longer hours to 'get the job done'.[25] Employees internalised pressure to work long hours, often for reasons associated with 'long hours' organisational cultures, and the hegemonic power of ideas associated with 'working hard to get ahead' (or even to retain one's job!) so employees with higher say in their working hours paradoxically tended to work more, not fewer, hours. This is consistent with evidence from an earlier survey, which showed that work intensification could be achieved either by tightening managerial prerogative *or* by increasing employee control,[26] and with a qualitative study by Barker of work intensity in 'concertive' firms.[27] That is, the two paths to work intensification involve either stricter managerial direct control or less direct managerial control in order to achieve greater indirect managerial control.

Work intensity and work–life interference

Evidence for work intensification has indeed been found in many studies in multiple countries over several decades.[28] Work intensification can be a way that firms can adjust their labour inputs.[29] It may accompany greater functional flexibility[30] or numerical flexibility[31]—indeed, these forms of flexibility (both discussed in Chapter 6) may cause work intensification. It can be achieved through such simple mechanisms as speed-up of the production line, an increase in the target number of 'swipes' expected

---

25 Ibid.; Peetz et al., 'Race against Time'.

26 Peetz, Allan, and O'Donnell, 'Are Australians Really Unhappier'.

27 James R. Barker, 'Tightening the Iron Cage: Concertive Control in Self-Managing Teams'. *Administrative Science Quarterly* 38, no. 3 (1993): 408–37.

28 Francis Green, 'Why Has Work Effort Become More Intense?'. *Industrial Relations: A Journal of Economy and Society* 43, no. 4 (2004): 709–41; Brigid van Wanrooy et al., *Australia at Work: In a Changing World* (Sydney: Workplace Research Centre, University of Sydney, November 2009).

29 Cameron Allan, Michael O'Donnell, and David Peetz, 'More Tasks, Less Secure, Working Harder: Three Dimensions of Labour Utilisation'. *Journal of Industrial Relations* 41, no. 4 (1999): 519–35.

30 Anna Pollert, ed. *Farewell to Flexibility* (Oxford: Basil Blackwell, 1991); Michael O'Donnell, 'Empowerment or Enslavement? Lean Production, Immigrant Women and Service Work in Public Hospitals'. *Labour and Industry* 6, no. 3 (1995): 73–94.

31 Gareth Rees and Sarah Fielder, 'The Services Economy, Subcontracting and the New Employment Relations: Contract Catering and Cleaning'. *Work, Employment and Society* 6, no. 3 (1992): 73–94.

from a checkout operator,[32] 'downsizing' of an existing workforce[33] or computer-based monitoring of employees.[34] Increasingly, digitalisation is seen as driving work intensification.[35]

Working hours and work intensification have implications for what Skinner and Pocock call 'work–life interference'—inviting us to turn the well-rehearsed concept of work–life balance on its head.[36] Barbara Pocock is one of the leading writers on work–life issues and for some time headed the Centre for Work + Life (CWL) at the University of South Australia.[37] With Natalie Skinner she examined, in Australia, the Fair Work Act's 'right to request' (RTR) that was introduced in January 2010. This enabled certain employees to request changed working arrangements (to help them care for their child). These arrangements could include different start and/or finish times, shorter hours and a changed location of work. But it was merely a 'right to request', not a 'right to have'. Employers were able to refuse requests on undefined 'reasonable business grounds'. There was no appeal from the employer's decision. The right in itself was a step forward in promoting employee-centred flexibility and work–life balance, and echoed legislation in various European countries, especially the Nordic countries.

The Australian legislation, however, was 'generally weaker' than that in other countries,[38] restricting eligibility to a small group, and making it easy for employers to refuse a request. Employers appeared to reject

32 Ern Reeder, 'The Fast Food Industry'. In *Technology and the Labour Process*, ed. Evan Willis (Sydney: Allen and Unwin, 1988), 150–1.

33 Wayne F. Cascio, 'Downsizing: What Do We Know? What Have We Learned?'. *Academy of Management Executive* 7, no. 1 (1993): 95–104.

34 Christopher Wright and John Lund, 'Best Practice Taylorism: "Yankee Speed-up" in Australian Grocery Distribution'. *Journal of Industrial Relations* 38, no. 2 (1996): 196–212.

35 See Michael Bittman, Judith E. Brown, and Judy Wajcman, 'The Mobile Phone, Perpetual Contact and Time Pressure'. *Work Employment and Society* 23, no. 4 (2009): 673–91; and Judy Wajcman, 'Life in the Fast Lane? Towards a Sociology of Technology and Time'. *British Journal of Sociology* 59, no. 1 (2008): 59–77, which discuss the ethics of this trend, and some of the theoretical issues of the time/technology/work intensification nexus.

36 Natalie Skinner and Barbara Pocock, 'Flexibility and Work–Life Interference in Australia'. *Journal of Industrial Relations* 53, no. 1 (2011): 65–82.

37 Barbara Pocock, *The Work–Life Collision* (Sydney: Federation Press, 2003); Barbara Pocock, *The Labour Market Ate My Babies* (Sydney: Federation Press, 2006); Barbara Pocock, Sara Charlesworth, and Janine Chapman, 'Work–Family and Work–Life Pressures in Australia: Advancing Gender Equality in "Good Times"?'. *International Journal of Sociology and Social Policy* 33, no. 9/10 (2013): 594–612; Barbara Pocock and Natalie Skinner, *The Australian Work and Life Index (AWALI)* (Adelaide: Centre for Work + Life, University of South Australia, 2009).

38 Sara Charlesworth and Iain Campbell, 'Right to Request Regulation: Two New Australian Models'. *Australian Journal of Labour Law* 21, no. 2 (2008): 1–14.

applications for flexible work by men more often than by women, which might seem good for women at first glance but it reinforces traditional notions of the domestic division of labour and traditional notions of who should be demonstrating the flexibility.[39] More broadly, institutional arrangements and employing organisations make it difficult, especially for women, to make transitions between work and care,[40] and most organisations make a cost–benefit analysis of the value to the employer of providing family-friendly working conditions.[41]

Overall, the promise of increased leisure in the face of new technology has not been realised. One factor behind that failure was simply that productivity growth did not proceed as expected. Globally and in Australia, productivity growth has slowed since the introduction of market liberal reforms in most countries in the 1980s and beyond. But the bigger factor has been that social forces have panned out differently to what those making the projections appeared to anticipate. Workers have not had the collective power to ensure that higher productivity is translated into greater leisure. Indeed, worker organisation has declined. Moreover, regulation has tended to soften, again reducing the need for higher productivity to be translated into fewer working hours. Management has not sought to reduce the number of hours worked by full-time employees, instead finding advantage in increasing them (it saves on recruitment costs), while flexibly deploying casual, part-time labour. An increased supply of part-time labour (particularly from women with children (re-)entering the workforce) has made this easier for employers to do.

This tells us that accurately anticipating social forces and social trends will be at least as important in envisaging the future of work as will be accurately anticipating the broad types of technology to be introduced or their productivity effects. So, as we move to that part of this chapter that is based on literary sources, our focus is not really on those works that make

39 Natalie Skinner, Claire Hutchinson, and Barbara Pocock, *The Big Squeeze: Australian Work and Life Index 2012* (Adelaide: Centre for Work + Life, University of South Australia, 2012), 37; Glenda Strachan et al., *Work and Careers in Australian Universities: Report on Employee Survey* (Brisbane: Centre for Work, Organisation and Wellbeing, Griffith University, October 2012), 27, www.griffith.edu.au/__data/assets/pdf_file/0024/88125/Work-and-Career-Report-on-Employee-Survey_Final-v2.pdf; Georgina Murray, David Peetz, and Olav Muurlink, *Women and Work in Australian Mining* (Brisbane: Centre for Work, Organisation and Wellbeing, Griffith University, 2012), 5.

40 Barbara Pocock, 'Work/Care Regimes: Institutions, Culture and Behaviour and the Australian Case'. *Gender, Work & Organization* 12, no. 1 (2005): 32–49.

41 Belinda H. Reeve et al., 'Regulation, Managerial Discretion and Family-Friendliness in Australia's Changing Industrial Relations Environment'. *Journal of Industrial Relations* 54, no. 1 (2012): 57–74.

predictions or comments about technology and productivity. Instead, we want to focus on those that comment on social forces—and these need not even be explicitly about work.

Lessons from literature

Turning to fictional literature is something we do not do just for the fun of it. It is not merely about the rights and wrongs of imaginaries. It allows us to speculate on possible outcomes from our current conditions through several mechanisms. We can see contemporary commentaries on social, economic and other realities, placed in a futuristic context. We see scrutiny and satire about the human condition. We see ideas about our ongoing social struggles to maintain individual integrity and kindness in work in the face of economic struggles for power and control. We are invited to free our creative thinking to look at alternative futures. We might hear a message of alarm about the dangers at work. 'Predictions' from literature might be warnings of what is to be avoided, rather than expectations of what is to come.

There is also a healthy precedent for this approach. One of the most interesting reads on management is David Knights and Hugh Willmott's *Management Lives*,[42] which takes as its foundation four very different novels that illustrate the role of identity, insecurity, power and inequality in the management experience. The novels: are David Lodge's *Nice Work*; Kazuo Ishiguru's *The Remains of the Day*; Tom Woolfe's *The Bonfire of the Vanities*; and Milan Kundera's *The Unbearable Lightness of Being*. Like those we focus on here, all were subsequently transformed into movies or TV series. Knights and Willmott chose this approach because novels illustrated the issues they wanted to focus on, and are valued by readers because of the relevance they have to their own lives, potentially demonstrating the connection between theoretical concepts and personal experience.[43] None of the four were centrally about 'management', though Lodge's *Nice Work* probably came closest, while Ishiguru's *The Remains of*

42 David Knights and Hugh Willmott, *Management Lives: Power and Identity in Work Organizations* (London: Sage, 1999).

43 Alessia Contu and Hugh Willmott, 'The Docudrama: A Situated Learning Experience'. In *Innovations in Teaching Business and Management*, ed. Christine Hockings and Ian Moore (Birmingham: SEDA Publications, Staff Educational and Development Association, 2001), 95–109.

the Day and Kundera's *The Unbearable Lightness of Being* are on seemingly unrelated topics, but used to illustrate the issues of identity and insecurity that were relevant to understanding management.

But first a spoiler alert: if you do not want to find out what happens in *Nineteen Eighty-Four*, *The Handmaid's Tale* and *The Circle* here, put this down and first read those books instead.

Nineteen Eighty-Four

One classic futuristic scenario is that found in Orwell's *Nineteen Eighty-Four*. Written in 1948, the book tells the story of Winston Smith, a minor functionary in the totalitarian one-party state that is Oceania, one of only three countries in the world. The first part of the book concerns Smith's daily life in the Party and the state (he rewrites old news stories to make them consistent with the Party line), his writing a diary (which is itself 'thoughtcrime'), and meeting and having an affair with a woman from the Party, culminating in their capture. The second part describes his internment and torture by the 'Ministry of Love' until he finally relents and comes to love 'Big Brother', the head (if he exists) of the Party and state.

You have probably heard from time to time the adjective 'Orwellian' applied to something, usually undesirable—such as excessive surveillance or monitoring of people, or attempts by governments or corporations to exercise control over people's thinking. That adjective is used because Orwell described (very critically) his futuristic vision of what surveillance and control may come to look like. The activities of the National Security Agency (NSA), for example, are often described as 'Orwellian'. I am not sure that he would really appreciate his name being used that way, but that is the way that language has evolved. Some people would describe the use of cameras in every imaginable location in the house in the TV franchise *Big Brother* as being 'Orwellian' and they would be correct—the title for the franchise coming directly from the chief autocrat in *Nineteen Eighty-Four*. I doubt that Orwell would have approved of the *Big Brother* series.[44]

44 There was another British TV show, from 1970, also called *Big Brother*. This mini-series of six one-off plays, created by Wilfred Greatorex, drew a number of scenarios that were intentionally dystopian. IMDb, 'Big Brother'. Movies, TV & Showtimes. www.imdb.com/title/tt1236228/.

Although the book was not written explicitly about work—Orwell was warning against the dangers of totalitarian tendencies in society as a whole—in 1993 British academic Hugh Willmott wrote a seminal article that compared modern corporate culturism to the techniques used by the ruling party in *Nineteen Eighty-Four*.[45] To understand this argument, we first need some context about what culture is. We can think of it as 'a way of seeing things that is common to many people'[46] or, more precisely, 'the set of shared, taken-for-granted implicit assumptions that a group holds and that determines how it perceives, thinks about and reacts to its various environments'.[47] These definitions—from organisational studies—highlight that culture involves ideas and assumptions that influence how we see situations, think about them and react to them. The three main elements of any culture are: the basic assumptions that it embodies (about what *is*), the values (regarding what *ought* to be), and the culture's artefacts and creations (such as stories, myths, rituals, ceremonies, symbols, language and behavioural norms).[48] Despite what some managers say (and, at times, want), most organisations are not 'monocultural'. In other words, there is not just one culture at the workplace. There are various subcultures within organisations. Schein, for example, argued for three subcultures: 'operators', 'engineers' and 'executives'.[49] It may be an overgeneralisation but it is fair comment in as much as it draws attention to diversity of culture within organisations.

So culturism is the attempt by management to create specific organisational cultures reflecting management's objectives. When we discuss 'culturism', we are talking about attempts by management to shape employee beliefs. In recent decades senior managers have often consciously attempted to create a particular type of culture at the workplace. Some scholars are highly critical of management attempts to introduce cultural change. For instance, Mabey and Salaman argued that 'the focus on "cultural change" … is often an attempt to impose a consensual, unitarist conception of the organisation on all employees, and thus to gain their commitment'.[50]

45 Hugh Willmott, 'Strength Is Ignorance; Slavery Is Freedom: Managing Culture in Modern Organizations'. *The Journal of Management Studies* 30, no. 4 (1993): 515–52.

46 Diana C. Pheysey, *Organisational Cultures: Types and Transformations* (London: Routledge, 1993).

47 Edgar H. Schein, 'Culture: The Missing Concept in Organization Studies'. *Administrative Science Quarterly* 41, no. 2 (1996): 229–40): 236.

48 Edgar H. Schein, *Organisational Culture and Leadership* (San Francisco: Jossey-Bass, 1986).

49 Schein, 'Culture: The Missing Concept in Organization Studies', 236.

50 Christopher Mabey and Graeme Salaman, *Strategic Human Resource Management* (Oxford: Blackwell, 1995), 290.

Jaynes studied the New Zealand division of a multinational bank. He found that the deliberate creation of a sales culture reflected 'a strong unitarist approach in which the goals of management and employees are viewed as shared. This disguised management's vested power structure in a veil of neutrality and cohesion'.[51] The changes brought about were 'largely effective in achieving the desired transition of the workplace culture toward a sales and customer focus'. Employees were seen to 'internalise the culture change, unaware of their objectification and subjugation by management'.[52] Culture was thus a form of employee control.

The central element of Willmott's article was the comparisons he drew between the practices of culturism and the notions of 'newspeak' and 'doublethink' expounded in *Nineteen Eighty-Four*. Hence the main title of his article was 'Strength is Ignorance; Slavery is Freedom', inverting two of the three slogans of *Nineteen Eighty-Four*'s Ministry of Truth (responsible for propaganda). He argued:

> In the ideal-typical bureaucratic, rule-governed organisation, employees are at least permitted to think what they like so long as they *act* in a technically competent manner … in organisations with a strong corporate culture, such 'disloyal' communication is at best strictly coded if it is not entirely tabooed.

He then quoted early management gurus Peters and Waterman: 'you either buy into their norms or you get out'.[53] According to Willmott, the 'guiding aim and abiding concern of corporate culturism is to win the "hearts and minds" of employees, to define their purpose by managing what they think and feel, and not just how they behave'.[54] In this way, Willmott considered culturism was a 'totalising' management attempt to design the normative framework of work.[55] Management seeks to develop and sustain this culture by careful recruitment and promotion of employees who accept the core values of the organisation.[56]

---

51 Stephen Jaynes, 'The Control of Workplace Culture: A Critical Perspective'. Paper presented at Current Research in Industrial Relations conference, Brisbane, 1997, 182–9.

52 Ibid., 188–9.

53 Thomas J. Peters and Robert H. Waterman, *In Search of Excellence* (New York: Harper & Row, 1982), quoted in Willmott, 'Strength Is Ignorance', 528.

54 Willmott, 'Strength Is Ignorance', 516.

55 Ibid., 524.

56 Ibid., 534.

Willmott made repeated allusions to the world of Orwell's *Nineteen Eighty-Four*: 'Like the party member in Oceania, the well-socialised ... corporate employee "is expected to have no private emotions and no respites from enthusiasm ... the speculations which might possibly induce a sceptical or rebellious attitude are killed in advance by his ... inner discipline"'.[57] He drew parallels between practices of culturism and several concepts in Orwell's book. One was the relevance of *newspeak,* the official language of Oceania, designed to help shape thought in particular ways. We see the relevance of newspeak in how some corporations seek to exclude particular messages from entering employee consciousness. In Walmart, if 'associates' (their newspeak term for employees) are 'using union terms such as arbitration, grievance and seniority', managers are under instruction to ring the 'Union Hotline'.[58]

Language is therefore important in all this. Euphemisms like 'associate', 'member' and 'partner' in place of 'employee' help ensure, as Syme (the newspeak documenter in *Nineteen Eighty-Four*) would say, that 'the range of consciousness [becomes] always a little smaller'.[59] Syme observed, 'it's a beautiful thing, the destruction of words', and later Orwell remarked that the Party aimed to 'diminish the range of thought ... by cutting the choice of words down to a minimum'.[60] The use of the term 'associates' by Walmart, 'Servo' (a pseudonym for another corporation)[61] and several other corporations (or, in the case of the term 'partners', Starbucks)[62] for what are, at law, employees is intended to shape thinking and expectations towards a framework with its own internal logic—away from one in which workers might seek to obtain the rights that come with being an employee and join a collective organisation for employees.

Another relevant concept is that of *doublethink*—the power of holding two contradictory beliefs in one's mind simultaneously, and accepting both of them.[63] According to Willmott, 'culturism endeavours to secure control by managing the impression of respecting the distinctiveness and individuality of each employee ... enabl[ing] an idea—such as autonomy—

57 Ibid., 541, citing Orwell, *Nineteen Eighty-Four*, 220.

58 Wal-Mart Stores Inc., 'A Manager's Toolbox to Remaining Union Free' (unpublished company document, 1997).

59 Orwell, *Nineteen Eighty-Four*, 45.

60 Ibid., 242.

61 Diane Van den Broek, 'Human Resource Management, Workforce Control and Union Avoidance: An Australian Case Study'. *Journal of Industrial Relations* 39, no. 3 (1997): 332–48.

62 David Emerson, 'Starbucks Axes 61 Stores and 685 Jobs'. *Sydney Morning Herald*, 29 July 2008.

63 As discussed in Chapter 11, this is very close to the concept of cognitive dissonance.

to be repudiated while simultaneously laying claim to its reality'.[64] This phenomenon is manifested in many organisations that proclaim how they treat all employees 'as individuals' while simultaneously insisting they 'fit' with the culture of the organisation and pursue its collective, corporate wellbeing.[65] (You may have also encountered the concept 'doublespeak' and wondered if it came from *Nineteen Eighty-Four*. Although it combines those two previous concepts, it was actually coined some time later by William Lutz to refer to 'language that pretends to communicate but really doesn't … that makes the bad seem good … that avoids or shifts responsibility … that conceals or prevents thought'.)[66]

Willmott also refers to *crimestop*—'the faculty of stopping short as though by instinct at the threshold of any heretical thought'.[67] He separately adds that 'the sense of certainty associated with the cultural "uniformity" required by Big Brother can be highly appealing … [as providing] freedom from insecurity … Managers, no less than their subordinates, may welcome the absence or removal of ideas, people and situations that challenge or disrupt the immersion of self in corporate identity'.[68]

So, how well has *Nineteen Eighty-Four* predicted our future, or indeed the future of work? Such books are meant as warnings, not predictions, and their 'failure' to come true might reflect the success of the author's warnings. As it is, the real world in the year 1984 did not match, in detail, the world depicted in the book of that title, and neither does the world of today. That said, the emergence of electronic surveillance, including by state bodies such as the NSA and various state and private organisations in China,[69] has turned out to be at least as effective, perhaps more so, than that portrayed in Orwell's book. As to the workplace, the pervasiveness and violence of *Nineteen Eighty-Four*'s Ministry of Love cannot be compared with the control exercised in decollectivising firms. The relevance is

64 Willmott, 'Strength Is Ignorance', 526.

65 David Peetz, *Brave New Workplace: How Individual Contracts Are Changing Our Jobs* (Sydney: Allen & Unwin, 2006).

66 William Lutz, 'The World of Doublespeak'. *USA Today* 119, no. 2544 (1990): 34–36, which reproduced part of William Lutz, *Doublespeak*, 1st ed. (New York: Harper & Row, 1989).

67 Willmott, 'Strength Is Ignorance', 526.

68 Ibid., 536.

69 Matthew Carney, 'Leave No Dark Corner'. *ABC News*, 18 September 2018, www.abc.net.au/news/2018-09-18/china-social-credit-a-model-citizen-in-a-digital-dictatorship/10200278. These trials are leading to a national system of 'social credit' rating by 2020. René Raphael and Ling Xi, 'Discipline and Punish: The Birth of China's Social-Credit System', *Nation*, 23 January 2019, www.thenation.com/article/china-social-credit-system.

more in that, as Willmott points out, modern culturism focuses not so much on what employees do (the focus of rule-governed bureaucratic organisations) as on what employees think. One of the biggest constraints is that 'unlike the fictional world of Oceania, corporate employees are exposed to, and constituted by, other relations and discourses'[70] as they have a life outside the organisation. So we should examine closely the directions that corporate control of people's *lives* is taking. For that, we will look at Dave Eggers's book, *The Circle*, but before that we turn to a more gendered dystopia in *The Handmaid's Tale.*

The Handmaid's Tale

Margaret Atwood's *The Handmaid's Tale* tells the story of a woman, Offred, in a dystopian society (formerly the USA, but now known as Gilead following a violent takeover by a group of armed fundamentalist males). It had been brought to crisis by a plummeting birth rate and disappearing fertility due, presumably, to an environmental crisis. Offred, being fertile, is part of a subjugated class of women ('handmaids') that are ritually violated for the purpose of making them pregnant, in order to deliver a baby for a high-status male. These males have infertile 'wives' who have higher status than the handmaids but must participate as effective bystanders in the 'ceremonies' in which their husbands attempt to impregnate the handmaids. The handmaids are depersonalised, their names simply reflecting which male owns them at a particular time (hence Offred is 'of Fred'). They wear uniforms very reminiscent of a nun's habit, but red and white. Their sole purpose is to have babies. Those women who are neither wives nor handmaids (nor performing some other essential role, such as the 'Aunts' who control the handmaids, much like matrons in a boarding school) are declared to be 'unwomen' and banished to work and possibly starve to death in toxic and fatal distant lands (the Colonies).[71]

Written in the first person, the story shifts back and forth between the present travails and the previous life of Offred (we are not told her real name) with her husband, presumed murdered while they attempted to

70 Willmott, 'Strength Is Ignorance', 535.
71 Atwood, *Handmaid's Tale*, 20.

escape to Canada, and her child, long since taken from her. The story ends inconclusively, with Offred about to enter a space in which she either would escape or be captured, tortured and killed.[72]

After the end of the first-person story, however, Atwood adds an epilogue, set in an academic convention decades later, during which it is apparent that Gilead had fallen and some semblance of sense has returned. In that respect, *The Handmaid's Tale* can be considered to be a more optimistic book than *Nineteen Eighty-Four*, as there is some end to the misery, though even then we do not find out what happened to Offred. (This epilogue is not part of the TV series, which had to find a different means to bring about a form of ambivalent optimism.)

There are many similarities to *Nineteen Eighty-Four*. Power is maintained through the combined use of ideological force and violence. There are hangings of dissidents at 'the Wall',[73] just as traitors are hanged in *Nineteen Eighty-Four*, though in Gilead many hangings occur as a result of violations of fundamentalist norms about women's roles (particularly by abortionists) that may have occurred even before Gilead was created: 'it's no excuse that what they did was legal at the time: their crimes are retroactive'.[74] However, Atwood also emphasised the use of rewards and divisions among the subordinated in the techniques used by the powerful to maintain power. For example, every so often there is a 'particicution ceremony', in which handmaids are allowed (or required) to execute, usually by stoning, a male found to have broken a law that would also evoke the emotions of the handmaids. It is reminiscent of the 'two minutes hate' at the beginning of *Nineteen Eighty-Four*, but more focused on generating release of frustration and vicarious revenge for the participants, and so more hands-on. Conformity to the system is encouraged by little rewards that are given to the most compliant of the handmaids. Clever exploitation of divisions and a lack of solidarity between oppressed groups enable Gilead's ruling elite to win. Those divisions persist (e.g. between the handmaids and the Aunts) and help perpetuate the system.

72 A second series of the TV version takes off from here. Its storyline goes beyond that in the book, but Atwood was heavily consulted in this and its production. In this second series we find out Offred's real name, the fate of her husband, and her story after the last scene in the book.

73 Atwood, *Handmaid's Tale*, 42.

74 Ibid., 43.

As in *Nineteen Eighty-Four*, there is a network of spies and informers, in Gilead called 'Eyes'. Offred cannot be sure who is an Eye, and even at the end we are left wondering whether her lover, Nick, is an Eye who will arrest and torture her, or a dissident who will enable her to escape. In both books, continuing war is a theme. Oceania is constantly at war with one of the other two countries, Eastasia or Eurasia, and always in alliance with the other. The fight against the enemy is a rallying cry for patriotic servitude to the state and party. There is also the constant battle against the internal enemy, Goldstein, whose existence is dubious. In Gilead 'the war is going well',[75] but it appears to be mainly an internal war against insurgents and heretics, though it features heavily on the news.

Also similar to *Nineteen Eighty-Four* is the role of ideology and conformity. Much of what Willmott wrote about work and cultural control could be applied to *The Handmaid's Tale* as well as to *Nineteen Eighty-Four*. The culture in *Nineteen Eighty-Four* is strongly shaped by support for the ruling party, and for the wars being prosecuted against external and internal enemies. In *The Handmaid's Tale* that ideology is dominated by support for the ideals—that women exist to procreate (the handmaids) or to enhance the status of men (the wives and occasional babies), that women must adhere to very strict rules concerning who they talk to, what they talk about and do in public, and so on. Support for these ideas forms the basis of support for the system in Gilead. In some ways it might be seen as more viable than the dominant ideology in Oceania, but the suffering and humiliation of the handmaids makes the contradiction between ideology and practice very apparent, not least because many of the handmaids had a memory of what life was like before the overthrow of the US government, when they had jobs, among other things. A potential resistance network, though shadowy and obscure to Offred, is given more prominence in Atwood's world than in Orwell's. If Willmott were to write about Atwood's book, the contradiction between ideology and lived experience in Gilead, though more extreme than that faced by modern corporate workers, could better encapsulate the role of culture than analogy with Orwell's. In Gilead, workers are indeed 'exposed to, and constituted by, other relations and discourses',[76] as they had a life not outside but *before* the existing regime—and they are more exposed to alternatives by such mechanisms as visiting tourists or rumours of

75 Ibid., 29.
76 Willmott, 'Strength Is Ignorance', 535.

life in Canada. This is a better analogy with corporate culturism than provided by *Nineteen Eighty-Four* (though, again, the violence in Gilead has nothing comparable in modern culturism).

Unlike *Nineteen Eighty-Four*, *The Handmaid's Tale* has an obviously strong orientation towards gender—though it also looks at its interactions with class. In some ways, *The Handmaid's Tale* could be seen as a feminist version of *Nineteen Eighty-Four*. That, however, would downplay its separate significance. Certainly, *Nineteen Eighty-Four* paid no regard to gender issues, while *The Handmaid's Tale* placed them front and centre.

What is particularly striking about the storyline is the portrayed reversal of gains that had been made by women through the twentieth century (when the book was written). Atwood contrasts the victories many women had in the 1960s and 1970s with their fate in Gilead. The point is really to demonstrate that the successes achieved by women in the move closer towards equality are fragile, and could be undone as long as women remain excluded from centres of power. The lessons for work are not just about women. They suggest that any apparent gains that do not result in a major shift in power are also susceptible to reversal. Thus while many managers encourage participation by employees in decision-making (discussed in Chapters 2 and 7), this remains in place entirely at the whim of management, and can be easily taken away.

Atwood's book probably also has a more nuanced view of class than Orwell's. In *Nineteen Eighty-Four* the 'proles', as they are described, are barely discussed. Winston Smith ruminates that they are the only hope for the future, but gives no hint as to how or why any change might come from them. It seems the only glimmer of light in Oceania as, for the inner and outer circles of Party officials (Smith is part of the outer circle), Party control is complete. So it is also a bit of a puzzle as to why the Party gives so little focus to the proles (or why Orwell does likewise). Atwood goes into considerable detail as to the roles of different classes. While women of all classes are clearly oppressed by the theocracy that rules, the majority of men are also oppressed by the social order, and are subject to the same potentially violent control and punishment as the women are.

The Circle

Dave Egger's *The Circle* is probably the most important book written about a (fictional) workplace since the turn of the century. Set in the near future, it tells the story of Mae, a young woman working at a large 'tech' company, called The Circle, that occupies the market space presently occupied by Google and Facebook. She has the appearance of being in the dream job—in 'the hottest company on the planet'[77]—but, as the reader, we know it is not as it seems. Part of the brilliance of Eggers is not to write the book, as so easily could have been done, as a story of Mae's gradual growing horror at the reality of her situation and the evil managers she encounters in her bid to escape. Rather, he depicts Mae as someone who, while initially disturbed by some of the things she encounters, gradually embraces the corporation and everything it stands for. Indeed, she is eventually repulsed by the warnings of corporate excesses proffered by one of the firm's three founders, and finally betrays him. Along the way she also alienates herself from her parents and inadvertently causes the death of her ex-husband, though she blames that, in effect, on his antisocial rejection of all the good that The Circle offers.

The Circle has several important themes. One is monopolisation. The corporation is depicted as having 90 per cent of the search market, 88 per cent of email and 92 per cent of text servicing.[78] It grows ever stronger. A second theme is performance management. As soon as Mae starts her job in Customer Engagement, she is measured by the ratings customers give her, remarkably high benchmarks are set and expected of her, and she obsesses about achieving them. Later, she is told of the need to achieve a high 'conversion' rate (how many people buy products she mentions) and 'retail raw' (the value of consumer purchases of products she mentions).[79] Eventually, Mae offers the view that 'humans can measure all things'.[80] She comes to dislike life off-campus, with its homeless people, unnecessary problems that were correctable through 'simple enough algorithms', and the attendant 'chaos of an orderless world'.[81]

77 Eggers, *The Circle*, 73.
78 Ibid., 174.
79 Ibid., 249–52.
80 Ibid., 338.
81 Ibid., 373.

We also see the role of cultural control, especially through social activities. Mae is counselled early for not participating enough in social activities sponsored by the corporation, and the HR managers ask if it is because she does not like working there, or suggest she is being selfish. An algorithm generates an indicator of social participation, the PartiRank, which is taken seriously and Mae spends late nights trying to improve her PartiRank. It measures attendance at the parties, brunches or other events organised by The Circle or 'Circlers' (employees), but also interactions via social media. Two pages of Eggers's book detail the many performance indicators Mae tries to influence in order to improve her PartiRank.[82] Social media engagement helps drive monetisation of the Circlers' work, and is one of the main sources of work intensification, judging by how many screens it adds to Mae's desk.[83] *The Circle* makes no mention of Orwell's 'doublethink', but it is in effect what Mae practises when she objects to invasions of her privacy—especially over sexual matters[84]—arising from the policies of The Circle ('we don't delete here'),[85] yet she increasingly endorses the objectives of the corporation.

Another theme is the contradiction in the rhetoric of 'transparency' and its use in ensuring surveillance. Each new technology and process of the corporation leads to greater surveillance, either of employees or of citizens more generally. Participants are pressured to participate in the interests of transparency: 'If you aren't transparent, what are you hiding?'[86] In Orwell's *Nineteen Eighty-Four*, the ruling party had three paradoxical slogans, depicted thus:

WAR IS PEACE
FREEDOM IS SLAVERY
IGNORANCE IS STRENGTH

In *The Circle*, Eggers presents three slogans that arise from an onstage interview Mae performs, in the same format as Orwell's, and, in the storyline, projected onto a screen on stage. They draw on Mae's own words:

SECRETS ARE LIES
SHARING IS CARING
PRIVACY IS THEFT[87]

82 Ibid., 194–5.
83 Ibid., 96, 252.
84 Ibid., 204–6.
85 Ibid., 206.
86 Ibid., 241.
87 Ibid., 305.

They are not all paradoxes in the same way as Orwell's, but rather plausible in the context, even if objectively false. They are also explicitly focused on issues of 'transparency'. The rhetoric of transparency becomes the basis for a totalitarian, corporate-controlled workplace and society.

Indeed, each transgression of personal liberty through heightened surveillance is brought about by a technology that plans to improve the lives of people: protecting children from deviants, protecting adults from crime, advancing human rights or democracy, enhancing the lives of disabled people, or even making it easier to decide which beach to go to. The mechanisms in place or proposed include cameras located almost ubiquitously, in locations or even on people; chips implanted under the skin, even in bones; sensors in communities to detect and locate 'strangers' in houses; even sensors in houses to detect sudden, 'violent' movements.

The book ends with Mae wondering what her friend, Annie, hospitalised and in a coma, is thinking—and considering it an affront and a deprivation that neither she nor anyone else could know. 'The world deserved nothing less' than to know her thoughts 'and would not wait'.[88]

Another idea is the importance of information. On the one hand, 'to know we must share';[89] on the other, says one of the founders, 'if you can control the flow of information, you control everything'.[90] This is linked to a key theme: the great power of large corporations in such sectors ('How can anyone rise up against the Circle if they [The Circle] control all information and access to it?'). This power is also shown by what happens to dissent. A Senator seeks to break up The Circle, but she is later under investigation for 'all kinds of weird stuff' after things were 'found on her computer'.[91] One of the company's founders later tells Mae that this is 'about the hundredth person' the company has done that to.[92] Eventually all politicians succumb to pressure to become 'transparent'—to have a body camera attached to them to track their every move and broadcast it live via The Circle to the world. The rhetoric of democratisation disguises increased centralisation of power in the hands of corporate leaders.

88 Ibid., 497.
89 Ibid., 151.
90 Ibid., 487.
91 Ibid., 207.
92 Ibid., 488.

The 'completion of the Circle' turns out to be the prospect of The Circle taking over the voting process for elections, such that one company chief says 'it might even eliminate Congress'.[93] Another warns Mae, to no avail, of a 'totalitarian nightmare'.[94] One of the last scenes is in the aquarium on the company's campus, in which tuna, a rare octopus, scarce and beautiful seahorses and a shark, all from the Marianas Trench, are brought together ('reunited') in a single tank, 'so they can coexist and create a more natural picture'.[95] In a metaphor for the corporation, the shark eats everything else. To emphasise the metaphor, one of the founders refers to The Circle as the 'shark that eats the world'.[96]

Eggers also emphasises the *absence* of evil in driving the descent into totalitarianism. While O'Brien, the chief torturer in *Nineteen Eighty-Four*, is clearly an evil character, most people in *The Circle* are not, with the possible exception of one of the firm's founders (Stenton, who is probably greedy for money and power). There is certainly not the overtly oppressive bureaucratic apparatus of *Nineteen Eighty-Four*. Instead, the second founder was just 'trying to make the web more civil', while the third is like 'an eccentric adjunct professor somewhere' with naive views about openness.[97] Winston Smith in *Nineteen Eighty-Four* was tortured into submission, but Mae is gradually captured by the ideology that flows almost inevitably from the nature of the company. She is horrified by the thought that 3 per cent of Circlers voted no to the question 'Is Mae Holland awesome or what?', showing tendencies towards authoritarian, vengeful behaviour herself but eventually concluding she has to 'win them over'.[98] In placing less reliance on overt and pervasive authoritarianism to tell its story, *The Circle* is more persuasive than *Nineteen Eighty-Four*, and less subject to the criticism that no corporation is as ubiquitous, persuasive or violent as Orwell's Ministry of Love.

The technology discussed in *The Circle* is not surprising. It all seems plausible given current developments. Some companies are already inserting chips into employee bodies,[99] and the US military is working

93 Ibid., 395.

94 Ibid., 486.

95 Ibid., 474.

96 Ibid., 484.

97 Ibid., 485, 489.

98 Ibid., 408–19.

99 Maggie Astor, 'Microchip Implants for Employees? One Company Says Yes'. *New York Times*, 25 July 2017; Rory Cellan-Jones, 'Office Puts Chips under Staff's Skin'. *BBC News*, 29 January 2015.

on an implant to allow humans to directly interface with computers—that is, to benefit people with aural and visual disabilities.[100] Even the closing sequence, in which Mae demands to know her friend's thoughts, anticipates developments likely to arise in neural link technology.[101] If anything, the book understates the capacity for technological change to be used for surveillance purposes. A founder makes the comment that one of their problems is that 'even when there are cameras everywhere, not everyone can watch everything',[102] but soon artificial intelligence (AI) will make it possible for thousands of cameras to be monitored effectively by a single bot. If there is a criticism to be made of Eggers's view of the future, it is that it ironically makes future technology seem too limited by human frailties and takes not enough account of the power of algorithms and AI.

In the world of dystopian fiction, *The Circle* has fewer evil characters, less overt suppression and less malevolence than the other works featured here and indeed almost all other dystopian works—so much so that the Hollywood treatment of it gives the movie a happy ending (in which Mae chooses to reveal to a huge audience the dark secrets of the company's founders, leading the Tom Hanks character to say 'we are so f—ked'). Yet, as a book, *The Circle* is also the most realistic of the dystopian genre, especially in its musings about the future of work. It is therefore perhaps the scariest of them all. That said, it points to the importance of critical choices in shaping the future. Mae's decision to ignore the urgings of one of the company's founders, including to publicise a document on 'The Rights of Humans in a Digital Age', was crucial in enabling The Circle to continue along its shark-emulating path. Perhaps the Hollywood ending points to what outcomes could have been if the more difficult choices, those that move us away from path dependency, had been taken.

100 Ryan Browne, 'U.S. Military Spending Millions to Make Cyborgs a Reality'. *CNN*, 7 March 2016.

101 Eggers, *The Circle*, 497. Guardian, 'Elon Musk Wants to Connect Brains to Computers with New Company'. *Guardian*, 28 March 2017. See also Antonio Regalado, 'With Neuralink, Elon Musk Promises Human-to-Human Telepathy. Don't Believe It'. *MIT Technology Review*, 22 April 2017. Annalee Newitz, 'Scientists Just Invented the Neural Lace'. *Gizmodo*, 17 June 2015, www.gizmodo.com.au/2015/06/scientists-just-invented-the-neural-lace/; Jia Liu et al., 'Syringe-Injectable Electronics'. *Nature Nanotechnology* 10 (2015): 629–36; Bryan Johnson, 'Kernel's Quest to Enhance Human Intelligence'. *Medium*, 20 October 2016, medium.com/@bryan_johnson/kernels-quest-to-enhance-human-intelligence-7da5e16fa16c.

102 Eggers, *The Circle*, 426–7.

Conclusions

We have looked at two broad issues here relating to work—working hours and culturism—as well as some others, but we have done so through quite different predictive lenses: the forecasts made up to half a century ago about the direction working time would take, and the storylines of authors of fiction that both pre- and post-dated those forecasts, about cultural management and control. In doing so, we also touched on such issues as gender, performance management and, of course, power. All of this constitutes 'visions of the future'. Some of those visions border on the idyllic (how else would one describe a world of extreme leisure), others are more like nightmares—and some that look idyllic on the surface (such as the workplace in The Circle) turn out to be nightmares, though not necessarily in the way we expected. To use a Gramscian typology, the powerful in all three books used hegemony to maintain control, but in *Nineteen Eighty-Four* and *The Handmaid's Tale* force was also heavily relied upon, while *The Circle* was ultimately a story of hegemonic control without even an evil mastermind behind it all.

Those different fictions, we must also acknowledge, say very different things about choice and agency. In *Nineteen Eighty-Four* choice is virtually futile, as the Party will always win—at least, as far as the experience of the protagonists indicates. In *The Handmaid's Tale*, choice operates at an individual level, and Offred's individual act of rebellion, facilitated through a collective resistance network, might just liberate her. We don't know whether it does, but we do know that, in the end, Gilead falls. In *The Circle*, choice is central, and there are critical junctures—'this is the moment where history pivots'[103]—where decisions by the players have a monumental effect not only on themselves but on others as well. In effect, these are policy decisions that affect the future, not just decisions about their own welfare. The movie is less plausible than the book, but the two combined are still useful in showing the nature and effect of choices. The two together are a bit of a 'sliding doors' experience, like that in Chapter 1.

103 Ibid., 403.

The problem with many of those forecasts of working time and leisure, mentioned in the early part of this chapter, was that they did not, or could not, take account of society's choices that would be made and the social forces that would emerge. The prognosticators assumed one set of doors would open, but it turned out very different ones opened, leading down a very different track. In the rest of this book, we will see how social choices and social forces interact with technology and markets to produce possible futures of work.

4

Digitalisation and the jobs of the future

Mae's eventual job in *The Circle* was essentially to monetise the influence she had through her social media platform. We presently call this an 'influencer'.[1] It was a job that really did not exist a few decades ago. The closest thing may have been how sports stars and TV celebrities made large amounts of money by endorsements of products—they were a kind of 'influencer', but their main job was something else. Over years, technological changes had enabled the creation of this job.

We saw in Chapter 3 the potential role of technology, through both *Nineteen Eighty-Four* and *The Circle*. The authors of both books tried to imagine technologies of the future and how they would be used, but in neither case wrote beyond the realms of possibility. In all probability, the technologies seemed all too real in each of the three books featured in that chapter. Importantly, it was the social order that shaped how technology would affect people's lives.

Popular interest in the future of work, however, often centres around how technological change will affect the types of jobs we do. So let us look at that. In this chapter, we look at trends in employment and how they will be affected by two of the 'mega-drivers of change' mentioned earlier: technological change through digitalisation, and demographic change. On the supply side, we consider the 'ageing' and so-called 'feminisation' of

1 Though some prefer 'content creator'. Ben Bryant and Moya Lothian-McLean, 'How "Influencer" Became a Dirty Word'. *BBC*, 23 February 2019, www.bbc.co.uk/bbcthree/article/61d019b6-fd08-4da5-aaf8-b28faf17e616.

the workforce. We will see that demographic changes affecting workplaces include workforce ageing and growing female labour force participation. On the demand side, we look at the sorts of jobs that will be created and destroyed by technical change. We also consider the veracity of competing claims about the future numbers of jobs. Will over 40 per cent of present jobs not exist, as allegedly estimated in a study at Oxford University?[2] We look at the areas of growth and decline in the industries and occupations of employment, and the levels of skills, if any, that will be demanded. There are major industrial changes (such as the decline of manufacturing) and occupational changes (the shift to 'white collar' work, including professional employment). We also mention six 'disruptive technologies' identified by the International Labour Organization (ILO) as affecting the world of work. So, the demand side dominates this chapter. We finish with a discussion on the implications for trends in inequality and ethics.

External forces for change in the workplace

The ILO, in one of its publications, identified four major forces for change in the workplace: demographic change; technological change; globalisation; and climate change.[3] To these might be added another matter frequently raised by the ILO: changes in the employment relationship,[4] which we cover in Chapter 6.

We discussed globalisation in Chapter 2, and we will discuss climate change in Chapter 9. Demographic change refers to changes in the characteristics of workers themselves. Technological change may affect what employers produce (their industries), what employees do (their occupations), and the organisation of work including the employment relationship itself. So we will cover demographic changes first.

2 Carl Benedikt Frey and Michael A. Osborne, *The Future of Employment: How Susceptible Are Jobs to Computerisation?* (Oxford: Department of Engineering Science, University of Oxford, 2013).

3 International Labour Office, *Future of Work. Inception Report for the Global Commission on Work* (Geneva: ILO, 2017).

4 International Labour Office, *A Challenging Future for the Employment Relationship: Time for Affirmation of Alternatives?* Future of Work Centenary Initiative, Issue Note Series No. 3 (Geneva: ILO, 2017).

Demographic changes

On the supply side, there are two important forces to consider: an ageing and maybe a 'feminising' workforce.

An 'ageing' population

We are all getting older, of course (well, you are, anyway). But this term refers to the tendency for the workforce's share occupied by young workers to decline, while the share of older workers increases. The former phenomenon is due to gradually declining birth rates, and the latter phenomenon reflects a trend for workers to retire later (particularly since the mid-1990s) and for women workers, in particular, to return to the workforce in growing numbers after their children have gone to school, or left home. So the average 'age' of the workforce, arithmetically, increases.

This trend is expected to continue, across all developed nations, though it is less a phenomenon in Australia than in most other advanced developed nations (in no small part due to immigration and a higher birth rate).

This creates some dilemmas for policy-makers. For a long time, governments were encouraging early retirement, on the rationale that retiring early would create 'room' for younger people entering the workforce. Now they worry about the implications for public finances, and how the workforce would be able to pay for aged care without raising taxes (as if taxation levels were set at some constant, which rather ignores the great cross-national variations in tax rates).

A common response is to lift retirement ages. At a number of levels this makes sense. Fewer jobs are manual. But what about those workers who have spent their lives in manual jobs? Increasing life expectancy reflects falling deaths from disease and accidents in working-age people, but it does not make postponing retirement any easier for workers whose bodies are, for work-related purposes, worn out by the time they hit their mid-60s. Some have been in low paid jobs. This makes an argument for easier access to disability pensions, but the trend has been in the opposite direction, in order to reduce public spending. Those with low capacity are being asked to pay for demographic changes from which they have not benefited.

Governments urge employees to work longer, but have so far found no effective antidote to employer discrimination against older workers. Age discrimination in employment is widespread, evident in data on post-redundancy experiences, for example, and very difficult to detect.[5] The problem may not be an insufficient number of prime-age workers but an insufficient number of workers that employers are willing to accept.

Changing female participation

I have already mentioned that women in developed countries are returning to the workforce in growing numbers after their children have gone to school, or left home. So it is in the 35-and-above age groups that increases in women's labour force participation over the last two or three decades have been greatest. But women are also increasing their participation amongst some lower age groups as well, when children are younger (or not yet born).

Much, but not all, of this supply of female labour has been people looking for part-time hours, as the domestic division of labour means that it is women, rather than men, who are expected to provide primary care for children, including after-school hours.

But while the 'ageing' of the population is expected to continue, across all developed countries, the projections for female participation are less uniform. The ILO commented:

> the global gap in participation rates between women and men stood at more than 26 percentage points in 2016—a figure which is close to or exceeding 50 percentage points in Arab States, Southern Asia and Northern Africa. Looking ahead to 2030, based on current trends, there is little or no improvement expected in the gender gap at the global level.[6]

5 Mark Wooden, 'The Impact of Redundancy on Subsequent Labour Market Experience'. *Journal of Industrial Relations* 30, no. 1 (1988): 3–31; Linda Walley, Margaret Steinberg, and David Warner, *The Mature Age Labour Force*. Workforce Strategy Unit, Employment Taskforce, Monograph series No. 2 (Brisbane: Department of Employment, Training and Industrial Relations, May 1999); Chris Kossen and Cec Pedersen, 'Older Workers in Australia: The Myths, the Realities and the Battle over Workforce "Flexibility"'. *Journal of Management & Organization* 14 (2008): 73–84.

6 International Labour Organization, 'Gender Gap in Participation Rates Is Not Expected to Improve over the Coming 15 Years'. ILO, 2017, www.ilo.org/global/topics/future-of-work/trends/WCMS_545630/lang--en/index.htm.

Female labour force participation is high in very poor countries. It is lower in middle-income countries, and higher again in high-income countries.[7] A very stylised way of explaining this would be to say that, in very poor countries, most women work since household incomes are so low. As incomes rise, for example through industrialisation, women can leave the workforce and focus on childcare, and it may seem rational in a sense to do so as men typically receive higher pay (hence, for example, female labour force participation in China has been declining for at least two decades).[8] As national incomes rise, and institutions supporting women in the workforce improve (e.g. state-subsidised childcare or maternity leave entitlements), women re-enter the workforce and participation rises again.[9]

It is an overly simplistic story because there are very large divergences in female labour-force participation among countries with similar levels of economic development, reflecting such matters as the availability and acceptance of education for women (which reduces participation among the young, but increases it among older women by increasing incomes) and dominant norms about working women. Educational norms help us understand, for example, the very high gender gaps in labour participation in some of the regions mentioned above.

Industrial changes

Over the past four decades, manufacturing has been in relative decline in developed countries. Between 1970 and 2013, manufacturing jobs' share in total employment fell from 24.3 per cent to 11.9 per cent across the OECD.[10] The 'services' sector—a term used to describe anything that isn't primary (agriculture, forestry, fishing or mining) or secondary (manufacturing) industry, so it is not all that useful—has increased its share of employment.[11] Within the services sector, health, community and aged care has grown substantially and is now the largest employer. By 2030, 'healthcare and social assistance' is likely to be close to 15 per cent

7 Sher Verick, 'Female Labor Force Participation in Developing Countries'. *IZA World of Labor* 87 (2014): 1–10.

8 Statista, 'Female Labor Participation Rate in China from 2007 to 2017'. Statista, 2019, www.statista.com/statistics/252721/female-labor-force-participation-rate-in-china/.

9 Verick, 'Female Labor Force Participation'.

10 Organisation for Economic Co-operation and Development, *Knowledge Economies: Trends and Features*. OECD Science, Technology and Industry Scoreboard 2015 (Paris: OECD, 2015).

11 Ibid.

of Australian employment, and manufacturing, accounting for a quarter of the workforce in the 1960s, will be less than 5 per cent.[12] The trend may be less pronounced, but it will be in the same direction, in most industrialised countries.[13]

Occupational changes

There has been a long-term decline in 'blue collar' or 'manual' work, mirrored by an equivalent increase in 'white collar' or 'non-manual' work. For example, in Britain, the blue collar share of jobs fell from 62 per cent in 1961 to 41 per cent in 1991 and a mere 29 per cent in 2006.[14] This is despite the fact that some jobs classified as being in the 'services' sector are 'blue collar' jobs in construction or utilities. Among 'white collar' work, professional occupations have particularly grown, including medical professions such as doctors, nurses and associated health professionals.

The emphasis has been more on jobs requiring higher level or creative skills. So in 1996, Australian employment of photographers and, on the other hand, photographic designers and printers, were both around 8,000; by 2014 the former group was more like 12,000, the latter group almost disappeared. In 2001 there were almost 30,000 graphic designers and almost 30,000 printers and graphic press workers; by 2014 there were close to 50,000 of the first group and 20,000 of the second.

Between 2003 and 2012 the greatest increase in employment was in the jobs requiring the highest skill levels (employment in occupations with 'skill-level 1' grew by 38 per cent, and 'skill-level 2' grew by 32 per cent, compared to 10 per cent, 18 per cent and 6 per cent respectively amongst skill levels 3, 4 and 5).[15]

12 Katherine Barnes and Peter Spearritt, eds, *Drivers of Change for the Australian Labour Market to 2030* (Canberra: Academy of the Social Sciences in Australia, 2014).

13 Even in Germany, the OECD's largest manufacturer, the share of manufacturing in employment fell from 33 per cent in 1970 to 18 per cent in 2013. Organisation for Economic Co-operation and Development, *Chapter 1. Knowledge Economies: Trends and Features*.

14 Learning and Skills Council, *Skills in England 2007 Volume 2: Research Report* (Coventry: LSC, 2007); Mike Savage, 'Individuality and Class: The Rise and Fall of the Gentlemanly Social Contract in Britain'. In *Social Contracts under Stress: The Middle Classes of America, Europe, and Japan at the Turn of the Century*, ed. Olivier Zunz, Leonard James Schoppa, and Nobuhiro Hiwatari (New York: Russell Sage, 2002): 47–65.

15 Kirsten Woyzbun, Susan Beitz, and Katherine Barnes, 'Industry Transformation'. In *Drivers of Change for the Australian Labour Market to 2030*, ed. Katherine Barnes and Peter Spearritt (Canberra: Academy of the Social Sciences in Australia, 2014), 17–34.

CSIRO researchers analysed employment patterns of occupations since the 1980s and found that jobs involving 'people skills' grew most rapidly, jobs working with machines or doing manual work declined the most in numbers, and knowledge and service occupations grew about average (though, within knowledge occupations, those involving the highest skills grew most rapidly, while those involving the lowest skills grew least rapidly).[16]

Global value chains

A major phenomenon, by which firms have incorporated changes in technology and management systems into their production structures, has been the growth of global value chains (also referred to as 'global supply chains' or even 'global value networks'). For example, Woyzbun, Beitz and Barnes showed the many countries involved in the construction of a Boeing 787 Dreamliner, including:

- the engines from Rolls-Royce in Derby, UK, and GE in Evendale, Ohio, USA
  - but the engine covers ('nacelles') from Goodrich in Chula Vista, California, USA
- the wing from several countries including:
  - the main part of the wing from Mitsubishi in Nagoya, Japan
  - the wing tips and flap support fairings from KAL-ASD in Busan, Korea
  - the leading edge from Spirit in Tulsa, Oklahoma, USA
  - the fixed trailing edge from Kawasaki in Nagoya, Japan
  - the moveable trailing edge from Boeing in Melbourne, Australia
  - the centre wing box from Fuji in Nagoya, Japan
- the fuselage also from several countries:
  - the forward fuselage from Spirit in Wichita, Kansas, USA
  - the mid-forward fuselage from Kawasaki in Nagoya, Japan
  - the centre fuselage from Alenia in Grottaglie, Italy

16 Stefan Hajkowicz et al., *Tomorrow's Digitally Enabled Workforce: Megatrends and Scenarios for Jobs and Employment in Australia over the Coming Twenty Years* (Brisbane: CSIRO, 2016).

  - the aft fuselage from Boeing in Charleston, South Carolina, USA and from KAL-ASD in Busan, Korea
  - the passenger doors from Latecoere in Toulouse, France
  - the cargo access doors from Saab in Linkoeping, Sweden
- as for the tail:
  - the horizontal stabiliser from Alenia in Foggia, Italy
  - the tail fin and tail cone from Boeing in Frederickson and Auburn, respectively, both in Washington, USA
- and when you land:
  - the main landing gear well from Kawasaki in Nagoya, Japan
  - the landing gear doors from Boeing in Winnipeg, Canada
  - the landing gear from Messier-Dowty in Gloucester, UK.[17]

In the manufacture of mobile phones and other digital devices, Apple only employs a small fraction of the more than 700,000 people who are part of its global value chain.[18]

Global value chains are the most efficient way for a major corporation to maximise profits. Especially when production is undertaken in less developed countries, they provide low costs while still enabling the corporations to maintain control over the production process but avoid accountability for poor behaviour (low wages, bad or hazardous working conditions) overseen by managers within that production process. It is thus both controversial and accepted as the normal way of doing things. We look again at global value chains (and the broader employment model of which it is a part, referred to as 'not there' employment) in Chapter 6.

Global ('transnational') corporations are, in turn, commonly owned by clusters of international financial institutions. A global corporation must have a formal headquarters in a physical location somewhere, and its managers and directors all have some geographical home, but chains of command and ownership rely less and less on geographic ties. Hence researchers increasingly talk of a transnational capitalist class[19] and of

17 Woyzbun, Beitz, and Barnes, 'Industry'.

18 International Labour Office, 'Changing Nature of Work in the 21st Century: Technology at Work' (Geneva: ILO, 2017).

19 William I. Robinson and Jerry Harris, 'Towards a Global Ruling Class? Globalisation and the Transnational Capitalist Class'. *Science and Society* 64, no. 1 (2000): 11; Georgina Murray and John Scott, *Financial Elites and Transnational Business: Who Rules the World?* (Cheltenham: Edward Elgar, 2012).

individual beneficiaries' minimal contributions to any state revenues, due to the use of tax havens to avoid what were once considered to be civic responsibilities.[20]

The future of employment growth

What are the jobs of the future? There are short-term trends to consider—for which the recent path is a reasonable guide—and there are longer-term trends, which are necessarily harder to pick and dependent on a range of technological, social and economic developments. So we look first at the short term, before considering new technology and what that might mean for the longer term.

Employment growth in the near future

A reasonably representative indication of industrialised countries generally might be found in the employment projections of Australia's Department of Jobs and Small Business. It projects employment growth five years ahead, based on fairly sophisticated extrapolations from the recent past and information at hand about likely developments, and in 2017 it projected that, by 2022, the fastest employment growth was expected to occur in the healthcare and social assistance industry (with 16 per cent total growth in employment) followed by professional, scientific and technical services (13 per cent), and education and training (12 per cent). Industries expected to show an absolute fall were electricity, gas, water and waste services (by 7 per cent); manufacturing (4 per cent); and agriculture, forestry and fishing (1 per cent). The biggest contribution to employment growth was also expected to come from the healthcare and social assistance industry, which was expected to add a bit over a quarter of net new jobs. Essentially, this reflects expectations that lots of people are going to get old over the next few years.

20 Anthony Van Fossen, 'Money Laundering, Global Financial Instability, and Tax Havens in the Pacific Islands'. *The Contemporary Pacific* 15, no. 2 (2003): 237–75; Oxfam Australia, *The Hidden Billions: How Tax Havens Impact Lives at Home and Abroad* (Oxfam, 2016); Javier Garcia-Bernardo et al., 'Uncovering Offshore Financial Centers: Conduits and Sinks in the Global Corporate Ownership Network'. *Scientific Reports* 7 (2017); Facundo Alvaredo et al., *World Inequality Report 2018* (World Inequality Lab/WID.world, 2018).

The *occupational* group with the largest growth rate was expected to be community and personal service workers (19 per cent), while the worst job prospects were for clerical and administrative workers (just 2 per cent growth). That said, these were averages only, and within each of these occupational groups there was lots of variation. For example, among professionals, the fastest growing profession at the more disaggregated level (audiologists and speech pathologists or therapists) had projected employment growth of 32.6 per cent, while at the other end the worst (surprisingly, ICT sales professionals) was projected to face an employment fall of 11 per cent. The fastest growing occupation at this level of disaggregation was aged and disabled carers (47 per cent), who would also provide the biggest contributions to projected employment growth, while other major contributions were expected to come from registered nurses, child carers and general sales assistants. At the other end of the scale, it looked like there could be a lot of displaced secretaries, farmers, accounting clerks, bookkeepers, checkout operators, technical sales representatives and people in several manufacturing occupations.

And what about skill levels? Generally speaking, in the past technological change has tended to have greater impacts on low-skilled than high-skilled jobs, but is that what is projected over the next five years? Those same Australian projections indicated that the fastest employment growth rate, and the greatest contribution to employment, was still expected to be made by the highest skill-level group (skill-level 1). The next highest growth rate is among skill-level 2. But, interestingly, skill-level 4 (the second lowest) is projected to have considerably faster growth than skill-level 3 (the middle skill-level, which was expected to be the worst of all five groups). The biggest factor in the expected growth of skill-level 4 is the growth in aged and disabled carers, which, in Australia, will be promoted by the National Disability Insurance Scheme but is really an integral feature of most industrialised countries' employment futures. So it is not a uniform picture. That said, there was tremendous variation between the occupations that make up each skill level. European data also suggests that employment growth will, on average, be strongest in the high-skilled occupations but that, as some jobs requiring high skills are at risk of being automated, highly educated workers might also face increased competition on the labour market.[21] In short, with some caveats,

21 Cornelia Suta, Luca Barbieri, and Mike May-Gillings, 'Future Employment and Automation'. *Quaderni Fondazione G. Brodolini: Studi e Ricerche* 61 (2018): 17–43.

future employment prospects were not so much a question of 'how skilled you are likely to be' but 'in what area you have (or you can obtain) skills'. The European target strategy target of 25 per cent of people 'engaging in learning throughout their lives by 2025' may be insufficient.[22] The variability of experiences over time also tells us that adaptability is going to be very important as well, perhaps more important than the specific area in which people have skills.

Recent developments in technology

Over the past half-century, several developments in technology have significantly affected the workplace. These include computer chips; word processing, spreadsheets and personal computing; communication technology (mobile phones); automation and robots; the internet; and barcodes and scanning. In recent years, there has been considerable excitement about the role of technology in the future of work, including whether or not this will lead to a net loss of jobs and, if so, by how many; and, to a lesser extent, what impact it will have on the way work is organised.

The ILO has identified six 'disruptive' technologies.[23] These are:

- the 'internet of things'—a network of physical objects that have an IP address and internet connectivity and communication;
- 'big data'—a massive volume of structured or unstructured data, sometimes derived from commercial or personal transactions to predict behaviour or drive complex algorithms for such functions as language translation;
- 'cloud computing'—a network of remote servers to store, manage and process data, used instead of local computers;
- robotics—goods- or service-producing computers that, mechanically, behave in some way like humans would; by 2018 an estimate is that there will be 1.3 million robots in factories (though few of those look remotely human);

22 Ibid., 40.

23 Kai Hsin Hung, 'Tech@Work: Top 6 Disruptive Technologies You Should Know'. ITCILO, International Labour Office, 25 July 2016.

- 3D printers—creating three-dimensional objects based on computer programs;
- machine learning—giving computers the ability to learn autonomously, without being explicitly programmed (creating what is known as artificial intelligence).

The last three of these in particular have the potential to make many jobs, perhaps even industries such as manufacturing, obsolete. The 'internet of things', 'big data' and 'cloud computing' will affect how we work, but robotics, 3D printing and machine learning will affect both how we do our work and how many jobs there will be. Some alarmist predictions have been made, including one discussed below that 47 per cent of US jobs would be rendered obsolete by technical change. Regardless of any exaggeration, artificial intelligence means that it is no longer just routine jobs that are threatened by new technology.

How many jobs in the longer term?

Each year many new jobs are created, while many others are destroyed as firms downsize or close. The figures you see in the news each month, about how many jobs were 'created' (or 'lost') in the economy, are just net figures, disguising some large gross movements in both directions.

Some jobs will be easy to replace with machines, once artificial intelligence (AI) is more developed. Some jobs, particularly many involving emotional labour or creativity, will be much harder to replace. There are two main estimates that have been made of the number of jobs that will be eliminated by new technologies, AI and automation. The first one, which received a lot of publicity, came from two Oxford researchers, Frey and Osborne,[24] and was published in 2013. It found that 'around 47 per cent of total US employment is in the high risk category'. Their method was essentially to get an expert panel to look at 70 occupations, assign them into the 'automatable' (their term) or 'not automatable' categories, look at the characteristics or tasks of those jobs and, using US data, estimate the probability of automation of the other 632 US occupations for which they could get data.

24 Frey and Osborne, *Future of Employment.*

The alternative view, put by three German researchers writing a study for the OECD[25] and published in 2016, looked at data about individual jobs, not whole occupations, and concluded that 'on average across the 21 OECD countries, 9 per cent of jobs are automatable', and the figure was the same for the US. In effect, they took as their starting point Frey and Osborne's estimates for occupations but then applied those data to what individual employees said about their own work in another survey.

My own view is that Frey and Osborne's very large numbers do not tell us anything about how many *jobs* are going to be displaced, because *occupation* is too broad a category. The OECD researchers are probably a little closer to the mark, but substantial gross job losses seem likely. Neither, however, really tells us about how much unemployment will be created by technological change, for two main reasons.

The first is that these estimates do not (and usually cannot) take account of the *cost* of new technology. New technology has meant a proliferation of automatic car washes, but many car washes are still labour-intensive, because those machines are very expensive, and often people are cheaper. A while ago I came across a cartoon featuring two nurses and a robot 'nurse': one human nurse turns to the other and says 'He's being returned to the supplier. It turns out that his running costs are higher than our wages'.[26] That is before even taking account of the capital costs of new technology. We have the technology for commercial supersonic aircraft that would take us to the other side of the world in less than half a day. It would push workers in many airlines out of a job. We have had it for half a century. We do not do it because it is just too expensive to do what we would need to do.

The second reason, why those studies do not tell us how much unemployment will be created by technological change, is that they do not attempt to take account of how many new jobs will be created. Suppose technological change means a robot can now produce a toaster for half the price of one made previously. Most of those people previously making toasters would not be employed any more—or at least when they leave they would not be replaced. But because the toaster is cheaper, we as consumers now have money to spend on something else, not just

25 Melanie Arntz, Terry Gregory, and Ulrich Zierahn, *The Risk of Automation for Jobs in OECD Countries: A Comparative Analysis*. OECD Social, Employment and Migration Working Paper No. 189 (Paris: Organisation for Economic Co-operation and Development, 2016).

26 View the cartoon at agedcaresite.wordpress.com/2015/01/27/aged-care-terminators/.

a toaster, that we did not have before. This 'new consumption' effect in turn will create more jobs. It is a more important effect than that arising from the fact that some people will be used to make the new machines. New technology results in the loss of some (perhaps many) jobs, and their partial, perhaps complete, replacement with other jobs, the net effect being on average less repetitive work requiring more skill—that is, the liberation of many workers from 'drudgery'. New jobs are created largely because people have more money to spend on consumption and buy things they did not buy before.

That said, some newly created jobs (empirically, a minority) involve less skill than previously (so there is no 'liberation' there); and some workers are not employed in the new jobs—they lack the 'skills' or location necessary for such employment, creating what is called 'structural unemployment'. The net effects of all this on the number of jobs is a bit uncertain. In particular, it depends on who saves money as a result of technological change—a point I will come back to shortly.

Bursts of technological change since the beginning of the industrial revolution over two centuries ago are not what has not led, in itself, to mass unemployment and depression. We certainly have experienced periods of mass unemployment, but these were not due to technology; they were due to the cycles and crises of capitalism and the failures of government macroeconomic management.[27] Whether an economy ends up with 'full employment' after a period of technological change depends much more on whether the state can ensure adequate demand (including through fiscal and monetary policy, and through enabling the benefits from productivity improvements to feed into consumer demand) and on whether the state can ensure retraining and re-employment of structurally affected workers than it does on the rate of technological change. Periods of structural unemployment also tell us that governments need to be active in training and retraining displaced workers for future skills, because the market will not do it, left to itself.

It is common to think of the rate of technological change as being unusually high at the moment, and to suggest, by that logic, that the past pattern (of new jobs replacing old ones) would not be repeated. However, to quantify the effects of technological change you look at productivity

27 John Maynard Keynes, *The General Theory of Employment, Interest, and Money* (Macmillan: London, 1936); Ernest Mandel, *Late Capitalism* (London: New Left Books, 1972).

growth—and productivity growth in most OECD countries peaked in the postwar era of full employment. It has declined each decade since the 1970s—that is, the pace (or at least the effect on labour demand) of technological change has been in medium-term *decline*.[28]

There is not much point in predicting in great detail *what* we will spend our extra money on and so what jobs will be created. History is littered with unfulfilled predictions about future technologies and jobs; though I suspect we can be confident that projections that the biggest employment growth will be among health professionals, followed by carers and aides, and business, human resource and marketing professionals, are roughly on the mark.[29]

But still, many people are interested in the jobs likely to disappear, even if others will likely be created in their place. Structural unemployment will almost certainly occur, affecting individuals and regions. That is because the jobs that are lost will involve different skills to the jobs that are created, and the people who lose jobs may not have, or live in an area where they can obtain, the skills that are needed to occupy the new jobs that are created.[30] The more people lack, and cannot obtain, those skills, the fewer new jobs will be created, because inflation will start to increase at a lower level of economic activity and governments will be reluctant to allow the economy to expand at a rate that permits inflation to expand above some desirable level.

So the first big constraint on economies' ability to create new jobs in response to technology's destruction of other jobs will be where the public money goes—that is, the willingness and ability of governments to spend money on effective structural adjustment programs. These are programs that retrain people who lose, or never get, jobs as a result of new technology, and help establish new enterprises, often new industries, in regions where those people live. The problem is that one of the tenets of neo-liberalism has been to reduce public spending, a tenet that runs counter to this need for structural adjustment expenditure.

28 Organisation for Economic Co-operation and Development, 'OECD Productivity Database' (spreadsheet) (Paris: OECD, 2006).

29 Department of Jobs and Small Business, '2018 Employment Projections'. Department of Jobs and Small Business, 2018, lmip.gov.au/default.aspx?LMIP/EmploymentProjections.

30 Sarah O'Connor, 'Robot Shock Threatens the Most Vulnerable Communities'. *Financial Times*, 19 September 2017.

A number of governments in industrialised countries have put resources into 'active labour market policies' that go part way in this direction. One of these was Denmark, from where the term 'flexicurity' emerged to describe programs that combined 'flexibility' (for employers—it was easy to lay off workers) and 'security' (i.e. displaced workers had easy access to income support and retraining programs), an approach that earned the enthusiastic support of the OECD. But, over time, there was more emphasis placed on the 'flexi' part, and spending on those programs that promoted 'security' was cut back. Now the term 'flexicurity' is associated in many minds with the promotion of greater flexibility and *in*security. There are many examples of creative approaches that have been taken in the past to adjust to the structural loss of jobs,[31] but it will take a radical change in approach by many governments to adequately respond to the digital changes that lie ahead.

The second big constraint on economies' ability to create new jobs in response to technology's destruction of other jobs will be where the private money goes—that is, who saves money as a result of technological change. For much of the postwar period in the twentieth century, the gains from productivity growth were fairly evenly shared between capital and labour, so no major change in the distribution of income happened. In recent years, though, as a result of the changing balance of power, the gains from productivity growth—that is, the gains from new technology—have been absorbed mostly by capital, by high-income earners. This has been most evident in the USA, where since the 1980s productivity has grown substantially, but real median wages have been stagnant, so profits have soared and income has been redistributed to the wealthy: most of the increase in inequality has been due to a rising share of the top 0.1 per cent.[32]

That rather fortunate scenario I painted earlier, about what happens when a robot starts making toasters, depends on what happens to the price of the toaster after the robot has made it. If the full benefit of that productivity gain is passed on as lower prices, then all those savings will be available to be recycled in continuing demand. Alternatively, if wages for the remaining toaster workers go up by a significant amount, then again maybe all those productivity gains can be recycled in continuing demand.

31 John Buchanan et al., *Facing Retrenchments: Strategies and Alternatives for Enterprises* (Canberra: Department of Education, Employment and Training/AGPS, 1992).

32 Joseph E. Stiglitz, 'A Rigged Economy'. *Scientific American*, 1 November 2018.

But what happens if the corporation increases its share of income as a result of this change? Prices might go down, but not all the way; wages might even go up a bit, but not enough to account for all the productivity gain; and the capitalist then pockets the rest. Maybe it will be reinvested, or maybe paid out as dividends. If the latter, the new demand might not be enough to offset the loss of jobs.

The problem for job creation is that the wealthy are less likely than lower income earners to spend their money in a way that will create jobs—they have what economists call a considerably lower marginal propensity to consume. They are more likely to save additional money they receive by putting it into financial assets, perhaps as savings in a Cayman Islands account, or status goods such as artworks,[33] of which the increase in value leads to no new jobs being created. By contrast, lower income earners are more likely to spend additional money on consumption items, the production of which leads to other people being employed. In the extreme case, if all the income generated by new technology were to be spent on artworks, then almost no jobs would be created to offset the gross loss of jobs. In reality, not all money flowing to the rich is lost in this way—some 'conspicuous consumption' creates some jobs—but if the benefits of digital change flow much more to the rich, then insufficient jobs will be created to offset those lost by new digital technology. When Citigroup economists sought to explain the growth of income inequality in favour of the group they called the 'plutonomists' or the 'uber-rich', the first of the six drivers they listed was 'an ongoing technology/biotechnology revolution'.[34] Their emphasis, unfortunately, was on the benefits to investors of buying shares in the companies that produced conspicuous-consumption goods.

A solution sometimes offered to this conundrum is to create a universal basic income (UBI). This is discussed more in Chapter 11; here we just observe that it would not stop the high growth in incomes and expenditures of the wealthy alluded to by the Citibank economists, though it may have other effects.

---

33 Thorstein Veblen, *The Theory of the Leisure Class: An Economic Study of Institutions.* (London: George Allen & Unwin, 1925; repr., 1970).

34 Ajay Kapur, Niall Macleod, and Narendra Singh, 'The Plutonomy Symposium—Rising Tides Lifting Yachts'. Citigroup Equity Strategy Industry Note (Citigroup Capital Markets, 29 September 2006), 7; Ajay Kapur, Niall Macleod, and Narendra Singh, 'Plutonomy—Buying Luxury, Explaining Global Imbalances. Citigroup Equity Strategy Industry Note (Citigroup Capital Markets, 16 October 2005), 9.

Much of the debate about the number of jobs displaced by new technology misses what else we could be focused on, particularly when examining work. Technological change has often been used to increase managerial or owner control (e.g. through barcodes, computer timing in call centres or apps in the 'gig economy'). This has often also enabled management to increase its control over the timing of labour—and more casual or labour hire employment—but there is little new, historically, about this. It harks back to the way labour was used, including through piece rates and contract labour, in the early parts of the industrial revolution or even in the nineteenth century.[35] And some technologies may have reverse effects (e.g. social media may have facilitated collective action).

Technological change in itself is neither malevolent nor benign. What matters is the social context within which it exists and the use to which it is put. The application of Einstein's theories of special and general relativity led to many lives being saved through new medical diagnostic and treatment procedures, but hundreds of thousands dying in Japan. The geospatial tracking that this theory made possible also makes it easier for us to find our way to the location of bookstores, but easier for trucking companies to monitor and control their workers—though also easier for the European Commission to enforce safe driving practices by truck drivers. Computers have made aspects of the lives of academics like me better, in as much as they enable research that could not be done in the past, but they have also led to surveillance and work intensification for workers in many industries like warehousing, call centres and even higher education. So the issues about technology and the future of work are more about the implications for power, control and equality or inequality. We will look at this issue in more detail in chapters to come. But first, we look more closely at the jobs that indeed might be under threat.

Which jobs?

The best publicly available data on jobs at risk from technological change come from the Frey and Osborne (2013) study mentioned earlier. So Table 4.1 lists the expected 'automatability' of occupations, using the US occupational classification system,[36] for the 20 least susceptible and (below them) the 20 most susceptible to automation among those

35 Simon Deakin, *The Comparative Evolution of the Employment Relationship*. Centre for Business Research, Working Paper No. 317 (Cambridge, UK: University of Cambridge, December 2005).
36 This classification system is not the same as that used in Australia.

300 occupations large enough to have their size estimated by gender in the US regular common population survey. It also shows the estimated size of employment of that occupation, based on data from the US Current Population Survey (CPS).[37]

Table 4.1: Risk of automation, US occupations, ranked by probability of automation

	Employment ('000)	Risk of automation
Low risk		
First-line supervisors of mechanics, installers and repairers	253	0.3%
Occupational therapists	122	0.4%
Lodging managers	156	0.4%
Dieticians and nutritionists	114	0.4%
Physicians and surgeons	1,079	0.4%
Psychologists	187	0.4%
Elementary and middle-school teachers	3,268	0.4%
Dentists	159	0.4%
First-line supervisors of police and detectives	95	0.4%
Medical scientists	161	0.5%
Counsellors	853	0.5%
Human resources managers	327	0.6%
Recreation and fitness workers	480	0.6%
Training and development managers	63	0.6%
Speech/language pathologists	141	0.6%
Computer systems analysts	554	0.7%
Social and community service managers	390	0.7%
Medical and health services managers	671	0.7%
Preschool and kindergarten teachers	712	0.7%
Secondary school teachers	1,039	0.8%
High risk		
File clerks	182	97%
Payroll and timekeeping clerks	129	97%
Counter and rental clerks	109	97%
Crushing, grinding, polishing, mixing and blending workers	72	97%

37 Bureau of Labor Statistics, CPS Tables, Table 11: Employed persons by detailed occupation, sex, race, and Hispanic or Latino ethnicity (Washington DC: BLS, 2019).

	Employment ('000)	Risk of automation
Credit authorisers, checkers and clerks	55	97%
Driver/sales workers and truck drivers	3,506	98%
Bookkeeping, accounting and auditing clerks	1,089	98%
Inspectors, testers, sorters, samplers and weighers	793	98%
Shipping, receiving and traffic clerks	623	98%
Claims adjusters, appraisers, examiners and investigators	350	98%
Tellers	306	98%
Packaging and filling machine operators and tenders	292	98%
Insurance claims and policy processing clerks	237	98%
Parts salespersons	130	98%
Order clerks	107	98%
Models, demonstrators and product promoters	61	98%
Data entry keyers	267	99%
Tax preparers	107	99%
Insurance underwriters	104	99%
Telemarketers	58	99%

Source: Frey and Osborne (2013) and US CPS Table 11.

In brief, it shows that several health-related professions, some types of managers or supervisors and even HR managers, appear pretty immune from replacement by machines. On the other hand, telemarketers, insurance underwriters, tax preparers and data entry keyers look, on this method, pretty doomed.

Despite the size threshold, the list contains many small occupations. So if we want to work out what sorts of workers are most likely to need to take-up resources for retraining, we could consider the data another way. Table 4.2 does that, by linking the danger of automatability to CPS employment estimates. The last column of Table 4.2 multiplies those numbers together, to give the expected 'employment risk' of an occupation, which can be thought of as the statistically expected number of people in an occupation displaced by technology, following the methodology of Frey and Osborne. The important thing is not the absolute value of the 'employment risk' since, as I mentioned, I think Frey and Osborne have overestimated the probability of automation. Rather, it is more useful to approach the last column in the table as indicating something about the *relative* numbers of workers at risk in an occupation. Even then, we should be very cautious in interpreting these numbers, as they fail to account for any differences in the costs of automation between occupations. So it is a rough guide, at best. Moreover, the risk of automation takes no account of the likely growth or decline in employment in a particular occupation due to other demand-related factors operating in product markets, especially the changing consumer behaviour as more consumption is freed by cheaper goods arising from new technology—an effect that is almost impossible to try to estimate with any certainty for all but a very short period ahead.

Table 4.2: Risk of automation, US occupations, ranked by size of employment risk

	Employment ('000)	Risk of being automated	Expected 'employment risk'
Driver/sales workers and truck drivers	3,506	0.98	3,436
Cashiers	3,253	0.97	3,155
Retail salespersons	3,235	0.92	2,976
Secretaries and administrative assistants	2,769	0.96	2,658
Waiters and waitresses	2,016	0.94	1,895
Cooks	2,079	0.83	1,726
Construction labourers	1,946	0.88	1,712
Accountants and auditors	1,804	0.94	1,696
Labourers and freight, stock and material movers, by hand	1,930	0.85	1,641
Janitors and building cleaners	2,307	0.66	1,523
Customer service representatives	2,494	0.55	1,372
Office clerks, general	1,271	0.96	1,220
Receptionists and information clerks	1,267	0.96	1,216
Managers, all other	4,398	0.25	1,100
Sales representatives, wholesale and manufacturing	1,264	0.85	1,074
Bookkeeping, accounting and auditing clerks	1,089	0.98	1,067
Maids and housekeeping cleaners	1,527	0.69	1,054
Personal care aides	1,365	0.74	1,010
Stock clerks and order fillers	1,525	0.64	976
Carpenters	1,351	0.72	973

Source: Calculated from Frey and Osborne (2013) and US CPS Table 11. Column 4 is column 2 multiplied by column 3.

Still, it is noteworthy that drivers (including truck drivers) are at the top of the list, due both to the large number in the occupation and the high risk of automation, followed by cashiers, retail salespersons, secretaries and administrative assistants, and then waiters and cooks.

What does this all mean for the future of jobs and careers?

There are a couple of ways that this sort of information may be used by people to predict the future. One is to extrapolate from existing trends. The second is to use your imagination.

There is a logic to the first. What can we know about other than what we know about? And for short to medium term trends, it's not a bad way to go. In effect, that is what government bureaucrats do in making projections, often in a rather sophisticated way and taking a little account of things that may make them think the current direction may be disrupted in some way. But even this can be difficult. Circumstances can change rapidly. For example, Ibis World in 2015 forecast 9 per cent growth in employment in black coal over the period from 2015–16 to 2020–21. By April 2016, Ibis World had revised its 2020–21 employment forecast downwards by 5.5 per cent, to growth of just 2.8 per cent.[38] Around this time, forecasts by the Australian Department of Employment were for a 20 per cent decline in employment in the coal industry by 2020.[39] Two years later and the five-year forecast by that department was for a decline of just 7.6 per cent. While the long-term prospects for coal mining are pretty clear (i.e. there aren't any), in the short to medium term they are very volatile, dependent in no small part on coal prices and on who does the numbers.

The further you look ahead, the less useful the present is as a guide to the future. This is especially the case in employment because technology is hard to predict and changing consumption patterns are even harder to predict. Some factors are evidently important, such as the ageing population and the increasing demands that will be put onto care workers.

---

38 IBIS World, 'Competitive Landscape'. Australia Industry Reports: Black Coal Mining, 2015; IBIS World, *Black Coal Mining in Australia*. IBISWorld Industry Report B0601 (Melbourne: IBIS World, 2016).

39 Department of Employment, 'Employment Projections', Canberra, lmip.gov.au/default.aspx?LMIP/EmploymentProjections.

In the short to medium term, it is very clear this will be a major area of growth. But in the long term? Robots are being developed to provide care in various forms for older people. Will people want these? Will they be economic? Will models of funding encourage or discourage providers from deploying them?

On the other hand, what about jobs in new technology—like computer designers and programmers? If technological change is going to be so rapid and important, would not that be the place to be? Maybe, but remember that ICT sales professionals had one of the greatest employment declines projected to 2022. Computer systems analysts may be hard to replace with machines, but some people argue that computer programming will eventually be done by other computers, once AI becomes more advanced. Computer industries and occupations are likely to become strategically important, but they need not be numerically important to do that. It is probably true to say that caring occupations will be very important in the long term, but *how* important is harder to estimate.

One of the major projects looking at the future of employment has been undertaken by Australia's Commonwealth Scientific and Industrial Research Organisation (CSIRO) which, although specifically about that country, had implications for many other developed countries.[40] Going more on imagination than extrapolating trends in numbers, CSIRO speculated about six new jobs that may emerge, which they described as:

- bigger big-data analysts;
- complex decision support analysts (reflecting a move from 'big data' to 'big decisions' and 'an explosion of choice');
- remote-controlled vehicle operators (for drones, trucks, boats, etc.);
- customer experience officers (for mostly virtual shoppers);
- personalised preventative-health helpers (like personal trainers but in preventative health);
- online chaperones (in cybersecurity, management of online identities, responding to online bullying etc.).[41]

40 Hajkowicz et al., *Tomorrow's Digitally Enabled Workforce*.

41 Ibid., 76–82.

Interestingly, despite it being a scientific organisation, the CSIRO's report did not overly emphasise the growth of work related to scientific, technological, engineering or mathematical (STEM) fields in the future. While arguing that STEM skills would 'certainly be in demand', the report asserted that:

> our aging population means that the healthcare and aged care sectors will be the largest employers and thus most workers will need some hybrid of technical, business, creative and interpersonal skills. Although development of 'soft' skills in students is on the agenda of some tertiary education providers today, development and integration of specific programs in collaboration with employers might still be needed to ensure graduates are prepared for future workplace needs.[42]

A lot of scary or at least overblown stories are written about future jobs, with authors sometimes breathlessly exclaiming that 50 per cent of jobs studied for at university will disappear by some date (I have not been able to track down the original source, but if it is the Frey and Osborne research it is a misrepresentation of their findings) or that the top in-demand jobs now did not exist in the early 2000s (Really? No aged care workers?). Still, when you peel away the overblown rhetoric, there are sometimes useful indications, at least on the *type* of skills that will be in demand (not the specific skills themselves) and the implications these have for educational curricula and what some call 'employability'. These appear likely to be skills (or perhaps better expressed, *competencies*) relating to creativity, problem-solving, collaboration, cooperation, resilience, communication, complex reasoning, social interaction and emotional intelligence. They include empathy-related competencies such as compassion, tolerance, intercultural understanding, pro-social behaviour and even social responsibility.[43] Some of these are what universities used to call 'critical thinking', but there are also many social skills as well on that list. While ICT skills are likely to be important, they are unlikely to be sufficient on their own.

One other point about education is worth making. Education serves multiple purposes. It serves as a creator of skills and knowledge (human capital). It also serves, though, as a signalling device for employers.[44]

42 Ibid., 88.

43 Phil Lambert, 'The Future of Work and Skills'. *Professional Educator* 17, no. 2–3 (2017): 15–17; Hajkowicz et al., *Tomorrow's Digitally Enabled Workforce*.

44 Luisa Rosti, Chikara Yamaguchi, and Carolina Castagnetti, 'Educational Performance as Signalling Device: Evidence from Italy'. *Economics Bulletin* 9, no. 4 (2005): 1–7.

There are many jobs people obtain for which their university education has not really provided prerequisite knowledge; they learn on the job how to do it or attend short, tailored courses. But the holding of a university degree signals to the employer that the successful applicant is capable of learning and (if highly credentialed) is more capable or suitable than other applicants.[45] In India, for example, a degree is a standard requirement for a call centre worker, not because the work requires a degree, but because of what possession of a degree signals.

Employers might raise or lower their demands of applicants, depending on how tight or loose the labour market is: one year they might demand a postgraduate qualification for a job, the next year (when labour is in shorter supply) they might be happy with an undergraduate degree. All the while this job might not really require a degree, just someone who is capable of learning how to do it. This process is called *credentialism* and, as the proportion of people in the workforce with degrees increases, is likely to lead over time to the bars on jobs being raised incrementally higher. So even if middle-skill jobs are in declining demand, the credentials required to get a job at that or even lower levels might increase over time. In that sense, choosing exactly the right field for a degree may be less important than simply doing one. As complexity of work increases and skill demands rise, employers will demand a more educated workforce (and continue to complain that it is not 'work ready') regardless of the desirability or ability of any education system to anticipate the skill needs of the future.[46]

Technological change, inequality and ethics

How has past and current technological change related to inequality? In the long run, new technology leads to higher living standards via higher incomes, which can be fought over by capital and labour. To what extent wage increases have occurred has depended on the relative bargaining power of labour and capital, which was approximately balanced in the immediate postwar era (in that the benefits of productivity growth were roughly evenly shared between labour and capital in that period). More

45 This point is also made with regard to trade qualifications by Phillip Toner, 'Long Run Shifts in the Industry and Workforce Structure of the Australian Construction Industry: Implications for a Sustainable Labour Supply'. Paper presented at Reworking Work: AIRAANZ 2005, Sydney, 503–9.
46 See also John Quiggin, 'In Praise of Credentialism'. *Inside Story*, 27 February 2017.

recently, the low rate of wages growth,[47] despite a fairly average rate of productivity growth, suggests that the balance of power has favoured capital since the 1980s. This is most obviously the case in the USA, where real median wages have been virtually frozen since the mid-1980s,[48] but is true to a lesser extent in many OECD countries, which have seen a decline in the labour share of national income.[49] Hence the rise of what is often called 'neo-liberalism' has been associated with a decoupling of wages and productivity.[50]

So, *if* the rate of technological change accelerates, then there could be more opportunities to depress wages, because there will be more opportunities to replace existing workers with machines and low bargaining power for workers in seeking to capture the productivity gains from that technology. Moreover, if capital captures most of the gains from job-displacing technology and spends it on conspicuous consumption goods or 'saves' it, maybe in an offshore tax haven,[51] then most likely insufficient new jobs will be created to offset job losses. If the state is unwilling (perhaps under pressure from capital) to devote the resources necessary to respond to the geographic and occupational structural issues, then structural unemployment will likely rise. However, technological change itself does not drive widening (or narrowing) inequality. Technological change has been going on for over two centuries.[52] There seems little new about it and, as shown in the productivity data, there has been no acceleration of it since the 1980s. If now the benefits of technological change are being disproportionately distributed to capital, we need to consider why that is happening and what has changed in recent decades.

---

47 Jim Stanford, 'The Declining Labour Share in Australia: Definition, Measurement, and International Comparisons'. *Journal of Australian Political Economy* 81 (2018): 11–32.

48 Frank J. Lysy, 'Why Wages Have Stagnated While GDP Has Grown: The Proximate Factors'. An Economic Sense, 13 February 2015, aneconomicsense.org/2015/02/13/why-wages-have-stagnated-while-gdp-has-grown-the-proximate-factors/.

49 Luci Ellis and Kathryn Smith, *The Global Upward Trend in the Profit Share*. BIS Working Paper No. 231 (Basel: Bank for International Settlements, July 2007); Damien Cahill, *The End of Laissez Faire? On the Durability of Embedded Neoliberalism* (Cheltenham: Edward Elgar, 2014).

50 Matt Cowgill, *A Shrinking Slice of the Pie* (Melbourne: Australian Council of Trade Unions, March 2013); Joe Isaac, 'Why Are Australian Wages Lagging and What Can Be Done About It?'. *Australian Economic Review* 51, no. 2 (2018): 175–90.

51 Facundo Alvaredo et al., *World Inequality Report 2018* (World Inequality Lab/WID.world, 2018); Thomas Piketty, 'Panama Papers: Act Now. Don't Wait for Another Crisis'. *Guardian*, 10 April 2016.

52 For example, Ruth Schwartz Cowan, *A Social History of American Technology* (Oxford: Oxford University Press, 1997); Joel Mokyr, 'Long-Term Economic Growth and the History of Technology'. In *Handbook of Economic Growth*, ed. Philippe Aghion and Steven N. Durlauf (Amsterdam: Elsevier, 2005), 1113–80.

It does not follow, though, that technology plays no role. Probably the way in which this issue has been highlighted most has been through the emergence of the so-called 'gig economy'. It refers to the use of technological platforms, created by companies like Uber, Airtasker, Deliveroo and so on, to arrange for the hiring of workers to do one-off tasks or, as they have been called for ages in the music industry, 'gigs'. Ostensibly these jobs are mostly performed not by employees but by independent contractors. By doing this, these organisations are able to pay these workers less than their entitlements as employees. But here the technology enables a particular form of work organisation to be reinforced. We will look at this in more detail in Chapter 6.

Technology and ethics

The preceding discussion raises many ethical issues. Should technological advances be permitted or encouraged if they lead to people losing jobs, even if the rest of society benefits through higher living standards? What obligations does society have to people who are displaced, and how much should it contribute to their retraining or welfare?

The ethical implications for work itself are wider. Computers enable the use of complex algorithms to facilitate decisions, on matters ranging from identifying the best person for the job or a promotion or a position in an educational institution, to the best performer in the job, to who should be targeted for counselling or dismissal. Yet algorithms are not neutral or unbiased: there are many examples of discrimination being unexpectedly built in to decision-making processes through the use of algorithms, as documented in Cathy O'Neill's aptly named book *Weapons of Math Destruction*.[53]

AI utilises the most complex algorithms—algorithms that 'learn' through experience and so change their behaviour. Universities are trialling an AI bot (at Griffith University it is called 'Sam') to deal with student queries. As it has more interactions with students, it will learn how to deal with more and more complex issues without the need to refer them on to a human. The more complex the algorithm, the harder it is to identify a source of discrimination, or even to identify its existence. Sometimes discrimination becomes too obvious. 'Tay', Microsoft's chatbot, had to be

53 Cathy O'Neill, *Weapons of Math Destruction: How Big Data Increases Inequality and Threatens Democracy* (New York: Crown Publishing Group, 2016).

shut down within a day after it started volunteering racist rants that it had 'learned' from other Twitter users. There were some major ethical issues there.[54] While Tay's adventure off the rails amused some, it demonstrated the potential damage that could arise when AI has significant control over something but lacks ethical guidance. More concerning still may be AI tools in the hands of individuals or organisations actively seeking to enrich themselves in ways that have little concern for the rights or privacy of individual workers, consumers or citizens.

Accordingly, some have sought to promote international standards on robotics and AI, for example through an international code of ethics. In 2010 a group of the world's leading AI and robotics researchers drafted a set of 'Principles of robotics: Regulating robots in the real world'.[55] It was more wide-ranging than Isaac Asimov's three fictional 'laws for robots',[56] but driven by the same need to find a resolution to the complex ethical issues arising from AI. There have been special editions of journals looking at the question of how to build ethical design into AI systems: if you cannot be certain of being able to push the 'big red button' (the switch that enables you to turn off an AI device before it becomes maliciously self-aware), then is it possible to design ethical programming into an integrated part of the AI system, without the system knowing about it?[57] Most recently, there has been work done by the Institute of Electrical and Electronics Engineers (IEEE) and the IEEE Standards Association, working towards an ISO standard that would incorporate ethical principles in the design of AI. But how would that work? How could it be made foolproof? How could ordinary citizens be given the capability to control the use by others of their personal information, histories or behaviours? And what would happen if not everyone incorporated such design principles into their AI systems? What of the 'biohackers' who eschew hospitals, universities and regulatory institutions, using backyard workshops and linking with

54 Elle Hunt, 'Tay, Microsoft's AI Chatbot, Gets a Crash Course in Racism from Twitter'. *Guardian*, 24 March 2016, www.theguardian.com/technology/2016/mar/24/tay-microsofts-ai-chatbot-gets-a-crash-course-in-racism-from-twitter.

55 It was initially released in 2011 then published as a journal piece as Margaret Boden et al., 'Principles of Robotics: Regulating Robots in the Real World'. *Connection Science* 29, no. 2 (2017): 124–29.

56 Isaac Asimov, *I, Robot* (New York: Gnome Press, 1950).

57 Thomas Arnold and Matthais Scheutz, 'The "Big Red Button" Is Too Late: An Alternative Model for the Ethical Evaluation of AI Systems'. *Ethics and Information Technology* 20, no. 1 (2018): 59–69; Iyad Rahwan, 'Society-in-the-Loop: Programming the Algorithmic Social Contract'. *Ethics and Information Technology* 20, no. 1 (2018): 5–14; Peter Vamplew et al., 'Human-Aligned Artificial Intelligence Is a Multiobjective Problem'. *Ethics and Information Technology* 20, no. 1 (2018): 27–40.

body piercers to implant forms of computer technology into their own bodies?[58] What of rogue states or corporations who failed to follow the ethical guidelines? As Moshe Vardi pointed out, the dramatic reductions in automobile deaths over the last century arose from regulation, not ethical design of cars. Regulation should be determined by ethics, but not vacate the field in favour of it.[59] But how would such regulation operate? Vardi proposes, as first steps, some simple regulations promoting things like transparency of code,[60] but there are big issues that require a lot of thought and action.

And so there is also the question of the ethics of human interaction with AI. Suppose the key ethical issues are not in how the algorithms are designed but in how humans use them—especially when, as seems inevitable, digital technology is integrated with human biology.[61] We will not just have to consider AI machines that can be programmed to kill, or with the side-effect of killing, but also humans who, equipped with AI, can do those things.

These are real 'sliding doors' issues. The life-and-death matter of machines that can kill is just an extreme example of the outcomes of choices to be made. In the face of these, the choices we make about what courses to study or what careers to pursue might seem minor—but they are not. Organisations face real ethical issues that must be addressed. What of the use of predictive technology that can anticipate whether a person will 'work out' in a job? Is it ethical to hire or not hire someone on the basis of such predictions, bearing in mind that many such predictions may contain gender- or race-based biases?[62] What if that technology can 'learn'

58 Lauren M. Britton and Bryan Semaan, 'Manifesting the Cyborg Via Techno Body Modification: From Human–Computer Interaction to Integration'. Paper presented at CHI 2017—Proceedings of the 2017 ACM SIGCHI Conference on Human Factors in Computing Systems, Denver, 2017, 2499–510.

59 Moshe Y. Vardi, 'Cars Are Regulated for Safety—Why Not Information Technology?'. *The Conversation*, 22 March 2019, theconversation.com/cars-are-regulated-for-safety-why-not-information-technology-111415.

60 Ibid.

61 Guardian, 'Elon Musk Wants to Connect Brains to Computers with New Company'. *Guardian*, 28 March 2017; Antonio Regalado, 'With Neuralink, Elon Musk Promises Human-to-Human Telepathy. Don't Believe It'. *MIT Technology Review*, 22 April 2017. See also Annalee Newitz, 'Scientists Just Invented the Neural Lace'. *Gizmodo*, 17 June 2015, www.gizmodo.com.au/2015/06/scientists-just-invented-the-neural-lace/. Jia Liu et al., 'Syringe-Injectable Electronics'. *Nature Nanotechnology* 10 (2015): 629–36; Bryan Johnson, 'Kernel's Quest to Enhance Human Intelligence'. *Medium*, 20 October 2016. medium.com/@bryan_johnson/kernels-quest-to-enhance-human-intelligence-7da5e16fa16c.

62 O'Neill, *Weapons of Math Destruction*.

as a person spends more time at work (as it will), and the employee does something that changes the prediction from 'will work out' to 'will not work out'? Is it ethical to fire them? What if that prediction is based on a new expression of social or political views that are out of step with those of the management? If corporations won't make ethical decisions, who should, and how? In the next chapter, we will see how some of these issues for management have been, and perhaps could be, manifest.

5

Management, culture and control

In the 1990s I was a senior executive in the Australian public service. One evening, at a dinner at a departmental 'retreat' for senior managers, I sat next to the man who had just been the keynote speaker. He was the human resource manager for a large, new company that was operating at the cutting edge of technology. He did not know me or my job, just that I was a senior executive. My departmental job had involved, among many things, overseeing a survey on collective bargaining (there had just been major policy reforms) sent to over a thousand randomly selected companies. His company was one of the few at the time with a nonunion collective agreement, and the response rate among them was much lower than among other companies. Without prompting, he told me he had received a survey from my department. ('Oh, really?') Yes, but he could not allow it to be distributed among the associates—his word for employees. ('Why was that?') It contained the word 'bargaining', something that implied conflict, and that wasn't really an idea he wanted his associates exposed to.

It was an intriguing conversation from an otherwise tedious evening, one that told me more than so many studies that had been done with management's permission. Understanding what was behind that helps us understand the managerial forces shaping the direction that future work will take. The previous chapter told us about the types of *jobs* that have been growing, and declining, in recent times, how technology is affecting many jobs and how many are likely to be partly or fully replaced by automation. But by extrapolating from current information about jobs and technology, we only get part of the picture of the future of *work*.

We also saw that the future depends on future technologies, about which our current knowledge is largely inadequate, and on future consumption patterns, about which we know very little. It also depends on future management behaviours about whether to invest in certain technologies (and we spoke quite a bit in the previous chapter about the economics of technology, which shape such investments) and how to use the technologies that they possess or purchase. Before we understand about management behaviours in the future, we need to know about the realities of management behaviour now.

There are many realities, many different ways in which management behaves. We must understand the importance of the function of control to management, and some of the key developments in the exercise of managerial control. In doing so, we must refer back to the concept of culturism that featured in interpretations of some of the visions of the future discussed in Chapter 3.

Different elements of management strategy or style

In studying the current realities of work, we need to consider the main ways of managing employees. How this is undertaken is referred to as management style or management strategy. Both terms are used almost interchangeably in the literature.

Views on the meaning of strategy range from 'rational conscious planning' to what Mintzberg referred to as something best 'seen as a pattern in a stream of decisions'.[1] To Bray and Littler, strategy referred to 'the modus operandi of managing labour' and was 'a useful method of modelling organisational processes irrespective of the coherence, or otherwise, of the managing director's consciousness'.[2]

1 Henry Mintzberg, 'Strategy Formulation as a Historical Process'. *International Studies of Management & Organization* 7, no. 2 (1977): 28–40. See also Margaret Gardner and Gillian Palmer, *Employment Relations: Industrial Relations and Human Resource Management* (Melbourne: Macmillan, 1992).

2 Mark Bray and Craig R. Littler, 'The Labour Process and Industrial Relations: Review of the Literature'. *Labour & Industry* 1, no. 3 (1988): 551–87.

So 'management style' is probably a more accurate term than 'management strategy' as, for many, strategy implies a plan or coherent pattern of action. It is often difficult to discern that there is a clear strategy shaping management behaviour, even in retrospect. Implicit strategy may be inferred from actions rather than explicitly specified in a plan. The term 'management style' denotes a pattern or approach to labour management without implying a conscious or unconscious plan. That said, as mentioned, we use the terms interchangeably as we follow the lead of Mintzberg and of Bray and Littler in not requiring explicit coherence in a strategy.

It appears that there are three dimensions, which we discuss in turn, into which management style can be categorised:

- high trust versus low trust styles;
- collective versus individualising styles;
- structured versus unstructured styles.

Other dimensions, referred to in some of the literature, mostly fit into one of the three above.

1. High-trust and low-trust approaches

One of the most common dimensions of management style is the degree of 'trust' exhibited by management towards employees.

Chris Wright identifies low-trust and high-trust approaches to labour management.[3] The *coercive, 'low-trust' approach* is characterised by low worker autonomy, close supervision and strong discipline such that workers are treated as a commodity and are forced to comply with management commands. For example, staff at a Tesco warehouse had to wear digital armband devices that constantly monitored their performance, and some Irish warehouse workers said they got lower scores on a rating system if they keyed in that they went to the toilet or took a break.[4]

3 Christopher Wright, *The Management of Labour: A History of Australian Employers*. Australian Studies in Labour Relations 4 (Melbourne: Oxford University Press, 1995).

4 Anne-Marie Walsh, 'Tesco Staff Forced to Wear Arm Monitors That Track Work Rate'. *Irish Independent*, 11 February 2013, www.independent.ie/irish-news/tesco-staff-forced-to-wear-arm-monitors-that-track-work-rate-29060257.html.

The *consensual, 'high-trust' approach* occurs where there is mutual trust between the parties, and workers are treated by management as a 'resource', not a commodity (so, yes, being treated like a 'resource' in this context is a relatively good thing). Management aims to develop and nurture employee talent by giving workers autonomy at work to make decisions and fully use their skills and abilities.

Christopher Wright examined high- versus low-trust management style in three areas of the employee–employer relationship: [5]

- 'employment relations'—e.g. human resource (HR) arrangements such as recruitment, training, rewards;
- 'work relations'—how management organises the technical and social aspects of work;
- 'industrial relations'—how employers manage organised labour, and deal with unions and with bargaining (though this last one is better located under our second dimension, discussed below).

Wright noted that it was difficult to discern a common pattern of Australian employer behaviour. He also found that there was no single management style among Australian employers. Instead, there were inconsistent patterns of management style, not only *between* firms but even *within* firms. Wright argued that employers' approaches to the management of labour have been complex and contradictory at times: 'Australian employers have adopted elements of both high-trust and low-trust strategies simultaneously within the same organisation, and sometimes in relation to the same groups of employees.'[6] At some points in history, employers have tended to favour elements of the high-trust approach, only to abandon them later. Also, for some groups of employees, employers adopt elements of both the high and the low-trust approach to labour management. (More recently, Wright and colleagues have looked at the role of management consultants in spreading key ideas through managerial ranks across businesses—and the gradual demise of this group, as managers themselves internalise many of the ideas and methods propagated by management consultants and take on some of the characteristics of what the researchers call 'management as consultancy'.)[7]

5 Wright, *Management of Labour*, 6.

6 Ibid.

7 Andrew Sturdy, Christopher Wright, and Nick Wylie, *Management as Consultancy: Neo-Bureaucracy and the Consultant Manager* (Cambridge, UK: Cambridge University Press, 2015).

The management literature suggests that, to some extent, there may have been a net shift in emphasis from lower trust to higher trust management styles, often associated with the word 'empowerment', although there are many counter-examples.[8]

Other analysts have developed comparable typologies of management strategies or styles. Although these typologies differ in their precise content and definition, they all establish some form of 'black hat'/'white hat' contrast that relates in part at least to high trust and low trust. Andrew Friedman, for example, distinguished between 'direct control' (management try to reduce the responsibility of individual workers by close supervision and by setting out in advance and in great detail the specific tasks allocated to each worker) and 'responsible autonomy' (managers try to emphasise the positive aspects of labour capacity, namely its malleability, so that workers are granted responsibility and status, supervision is restricted, loyalty is rewarded etc.). The choice taken was seen as depending on the degree of competition in labour markets and product markets.[9]

Michael Burawoy, one of the major living sociologists, created a three-way classification, involving 'despotic control' (direct control), 'hegemonic control' (more sophisticated methods relating to bureaucratic control)[10] and 'hegemonic despotism'. The last meant the fear of being fired was replaced by the fear of capital flight, plant closure, the transfer of operations and disinvestment—enhanced power of capital was associated with new management practices such as 'quality of working life' programs and quality circles that attempt to mobilise consent for increased productivity.[11]

In Australia, authors such as Curtain and Mathews, and Boreham, Hall and Harley identified two types of workplace reform strategies available to organisations to enhance profit in the context of change.[12] The first

8 Rosabeth Moss Kanter, 'Leadership and the Psychology of Turnarounds'. *Harvard Business Review* (June 2003).

9 Andrew L. Friedman, *Industry and Labour* (London: Macmillan, 1977).

10 Bureaucratic control is discussed in the next section, on 'Conflict over control'.

11 Michael Burawoy, *Manufacturing Consent* (Chicago: University of Chicago Press, 1979); Michael Burawoy, 'Between the Labor Process and the State: Changing Face of Factory Regimes under Capitalism'. *American Sociological Review* 48 (1983): 587–605.

12 Richard Curtain and John Mathews, 'Two Models of Award Restructuring in Australia'. *Labour and Industry* 3, no. 1 (1990): 58–75; Paul Boreham, Richard Hall, and William Harley, 'Two Paths to Prosperity? Work Organisation and Industrial Relations'. *Work, Employment and Society* 10 (19886): 449–68.

was a 'cost minimisation' approach, focused on achieving numerical flexibility in labour costs or employee numbers. The second was a 'productivity enhancement' approach, focused on improving functional flexibility of labour—emphasising skills acquisition, multiskilling, flexibility in work assignments, quality and devolution of authority. Cost minimisation reflected the logic of managerialism, with emphases on auditing, casualisation, managerial control and work intensification.[13] It was a type of 'low-trust' approach. Productivity enhancement, on the other hand, included quality enhancement, investment in training and the creation of 'high performance work systems'.[14] It was a more 'high-trust' approach. The literature often highlights the contradictory nature of these two paradigms. These two strategies, pursued properly, would seem to be mutually exclusive.[15] Each represents one of the two opposite paths to longer hours or work intensification.[16] Nonetheless, a number of firms attempt to pursue both strategies, and so might be called 'mixed strategists'.[17] You may have experienced this yourself. While management may apply different strategies to different parts of its workforce (which is not so surprising), it sometimes also tries to apply different, contradictory strategies to the same workers.

In these various dichotomies we see the dual nature of, and tensions in, the control relationship. The first is tension for management: between treating labour as a commodity and as a continuing social relationship. The second is tension for labour: between resistance to subordination and exploitation, and the maintenance of economic relationships including, critically, the viability of the employer.[18]

13 For an example, see Oliver Wright, 'Join Ryanair! See the World! But We'll Only Pay You for Nine Months a Year'. *Independent*, 16 May 2013, www.independent.co.uk/news/uk/home-news/join-ryanair-see-the-world-but-well-only-pay-you-for-nine-months-a-year-8619897.html.

14 Bill Harley, Belinda C. Allen, and Leisa D. Sargent, 'High Performance Work Systems and Employee Experience of Work in the Service Sector'. *British Journal of Industrial Relations* 45, no. 3 (2007): 607–33.

15 Richard E. Walton, 'From Control to Commitment in the Workplace'. *Harvard Business Review* 85, no. 2 (1985): 77–84.

16 See, for example, Chapter 3.

17 David Peetz et al., 'Workplace Bargaining in New Zealand: Radical Change at Work'. In *Workplace Bargaining in the International Context*, ed. David Peetz, Alison Preston, and Jim Docherty, Workplace Bargaining Research Project (Canberra: Department of Industrial Relations and Australian Government Publishing Service, 1993). See also Peter Boxall and Peter Haynes, 'Unions and Non-Union Bargaining Agents under the Employment Contracts Act 1991: An Assessment after 12 Months'. *New Zealand Journal of Industrial Relations* 17, no. 2 (1992).

18 Peter Cressey and John MacInnes, 'Voting for Ford: Industrial Democracy and the Control of Labour'. *Capital and Class* 11 (1980): 5–33.

Within management that tension between treating labour as a commodity and as a continuing social relationship often leads to managers *saying* they want a continuing social relationship but *behaving* in a manner consistent with its treating labour as a commodity. That is, a large gap between rhetoric and reality emerges. Some organisations portray themselves as based on 'high trust' or 'commitment' but behave otherwise. Some organisations, aiming to promote commitment and loyalty at the same time, take a hard line against dissent,[19] especially in seeking to exclude unionism. Certain managements will try to resolve this contradiction by trying to engage in some form of 'cultural' control, whereby substantial effort is put into ensuring employees have the 'mindset' that enables them to be persuaded that the workplace really is a high-trust environment, while simultaneously exercising considerable control over those employees. This is particularly common where management adopts particular positions on the two other dimensions of management strategy. So we will discuss those first before returning to this issue of attempted cultural control or 'culturism'.

Changing technology itself has potentially mixed effects. On the one hand, it makes communication easier, which may facilitate higher trust approaches, as it makes it easier in principle for the wishes of employees to be known to managers, and for groups of workers to autonomously and coherently make decisions. It may be easier to work from home, enabling employees to better juggle work–life balance issues and for managers to be less obsessive about attendance. On the other hand, if it is easier for people to work from home it is easier to give them extra things to do *at* home (or in the park, on the beach, etc.). It makes it easier for managers to monitor what workers are saying to each other. It makes it easier to count things, and the metrification of work is one of the major tools of the low-trust manager.

In *The Circle*, the work environment seemed very high trust on the surface but the ability of managers to count almost everything Mae did, and to quantify each aspect of her worth, turned it into a very low-trust environment in reality. This dual capability of technology is mirrored in the dual directions that management trust appears to be taking, though

19 Diane Van den Broek, 'Human Resource Management, Workforce Control and Union Avoidance: An Australian Case Study'. *Journal of Industrial Relations* 39, no. 3 (1997): 332–48; David Peetz, *Brave New Workplace: How Individual Contracts Are Changing Our Jobs* (Sydney: Allen & Unwin, 2006); Dennis Tourish, David Collinson, and James R. Barker, 'Manufacturing Conformity: Leadership through Coercive Persuasion in Business Organisations'. *M@n@gement* 12, no. 5 (2009): 360–83.

for many, as in *The Circle*, the appearance of higher trust may actually be deceptive. By contrast, the environments in both *Nineteen Eighty-Four* and *The Handmaid's Tale* both appeared very low trust from early on.

2. Collective and individualising approaches to employee management

A second way of categorising management style is the extent to which management adopts 'collective' or 'individualising' approaches to dealings with employees. We can think of this dimension as a single scale with both 'collective' and 'individualising' denoting each end of the scale.

Organisations that adopt an 'individualising' approach are commonly antiunion. By our definition, they are the opposite of collectivist (where managers respect the rights of employees to be represented by unions). Individualising managers often endeavour to exclude unions from the workplace so that management can maintain a direct relationship with workers. Managers that adopt this approach could be said to have a unitarist view of work. Managers with a pluralist perspective, by contrast, will more likely support or at least tolerate a collectivist approach.

Not all pluralist managers will work in collectivist workplaces. This is because, for collectivism to exist, employees must have some organisation. A workplace or organisation may be too small for this to happen, or the union itself may be absent or not well enough organised, or the industry too difficult to organise. Some small firms might end up adopting what appear to be nonunion, low-wage or exploitative strategies because of their dependence on larger organisations and subordination to a competitive environment.[20] Most small businesses are not unionised, regardless of the philosophies of their owners. We should not infer, from the discussion here, that all managers are malevolent and opposed to employees organising themselves collectively.

Individualising strategies can be used with either low-trust or high-trust strategies. Earlier changes to industrial relations law, particularly under the New Zealand Employment Contracts legislation or the 2005 Australian 'WorkChoices' legislation (both now repealed), appeared to encourage the use of formalised individual contracting to reduce labour

20 Tony Dundon, Irena Grugulis, and Adrian Wilkinson, 'Looking out of the Black Hole: Non-Union Relations in an SME'. *Employee Relations* 21 (1999): 251–66.

costs and wages (i.e. the low-trust path). Individualisation through individual contracting often leads to inferior pay and conditions. However, individual contracting does not inevitably lead to this. Some employees will receive higher incomes under individualisation strategies, because of a nonunion premium offered by some employers to purchase a transfer of power and, sometimes, increasing productivity as a result.[21] Nonetheless, it appears that data showing poorer pay and conditions for workers on individual contracts such as Australian Workplace Agreements (AWAs)[22] reflect the inherently lower bargaining power of employees, by comparison to management, on individual contracts.[23]

It is very important to note that the term 'individualism' is often (mis)used to describe many different things, and in that context might imply a different meaning to the one I use here. For example, 'individualism' can mean to some the 'differentiation' of individual employees' employment contracts.[24] This is what Willie Brown and his colleagues refer to as 'substantive individualisation', but it is not what we are talking about here. Brown and friends were talking about significant differences between employees in a corporation with reference to their pay and other terms and conditions of employment. Substantive individualisation does not need to go with 'procedural individualisation'—that is, with individual contracting—as all individual contracts offered by a firm might be mostly identical.[25]

21 David Peetz and Alison Preston, 'Individual Contracting, Collective Bargaining and Wages in Australia'. *Industrial Relations Journal* 40, no. 5 (2009): 444–61.

22 Ellen Dannin, *Working Free: The Origins and Impact of New Zealand's Employment Contracts Act* (Auckland: Auckland University Press, 1997); Richard Mitchell and Joel Fetter, 'Human Resource Management and Individualisation in Australian Law'. *Journal of Industrial Relations* 45, no. 3 (2003): 292–325; Sarah Oxenbridge, 'The Individualisation of Employment Relations in New Zealand: Trends and Outcomes'. In *Employment Relations: Individualisation and Union Exclusion—an International Study*, ed. Stephen Deery and Richard Mitchell (Sydney: Federation Press, 1999), 227–50; Peetz and Preston, 'Individual Contracting'; E. Rasmussen and J. Deeks, 'Contested Outcomes: Assessing the Impacts of the Employment Contracts Act'. *California Western International Law Journal* 28 (1997): 275–96; Kristin Van Barneveld, 'Under the Covers: Negotiating Australian Workplace Agreements: Two Cases'. Paper presented at the Current Research in Industrial Relations conference, AIRAANZ, Adelaide, 4–6 February 1999.

23 For more on power under individual contracting, see Peetz, *Brave New Workplace*, 75–80, Chapter 4.

24 William Brown et al., *The Individualisation of Employment Contracts in Britain*. Employment Relations Research Series No. 4 (London: Department of Trade and Industry, 1998).

25 Ibid.

Other people may ascribe quite different meanings to the term. For instance, John Purcell used individualism to refer to the 'extent to which personnel policies are focused on the rights and capabilities of individual workers'. That is more like the high-trust/low-trust dimension. He saw this as a different dimension of management style to collectivism, which could coexist with individualism.[26] Finally, some researchers in social psychology treat individualism and collectivism as different but not diametrically opposed concepts, and use different survey questions to measure them.[27] For us, though, individualism and collectivism in employment relations are opposing points on a single continuum.[28]

Artificial intelligence and technology facilitate the surveillance of employees that makes it easier to thwart the collective organisation of employees, in much the same way as it makes it easier for dictatorial governments to maintain control over potentially dissident populations.[29] Workers in *The Circle* are increasingly monitored for their performance, in order to control them. Digital technologies also make it easier to fragment workforces (e.g. in 'platform economy' work), thereby making it harder for workers to collectively organise. On the other hand, similar technologies may provide the tools that unions themselves can use to facilitate collective organisation (discussed in Chapter 7). So the net effect of technological change on this second dimension depends on the choices that both sides make.

---

26 John Purcell, 'Mapping Management Styles in Employee Relations'. *Journal of Management Studies.* (1987): 205–23.

27 Carolina Gomez, 'The Relationship between Acculturation, Individualism/Collectivism and Job Attribute Preferences for Hispanic MBAs'. *Journal of Management Studies* 40, no. 5 (2003): 1089–105; Hatty C. Triandis and Theodore M. Singelis, 'Training to Recognize Individual Differences in Collectivism and Individualism within Culture'. *International Journal of Intercultural Relations* 22, no. 1 (1998): 35–47.

28 Peetz, *Brave New Workplace*, 10–11.

29 Troy Henderson, Tom Swann, and Jim Stanford, *Under the Employer's Eye: Electronic Monitoring and Surveillance in Australian Workplaces* (Canberra: Centre for Future Work, Australia Institute, 2018); Mike Allen, 'How Tech Fuels Authoritarians'. *Axios*, 12 August 2018, www.axios.com/big-tech-surveillance-authoritarianism-china-artificial-intelligence-2b91dedb-93a0-460c-a236-4a3bb7cf9c99.html.

3. Structure in management: A third dimension of labour management

A third way of categorising management is the degree of formalisation or structure in management procedures at the workplace. Formalisation or structured management refers to the extent to which management has developed systematic written policies and procedures for dealing with labour management issues. The opposite of a formalised system would be unstructured management where there are few set rules and managers deal with most matters on an ad hoc and informal basis.[30]

Structured management could involve some of: a formal grievance procedure; a formal disciplinary procedure; a performance management system; developed formal training system; occupational health and safety (OHS) committees; joint consultative committees; quality circles; and/or well developed policies on equal employment opportunity (EEO) and/or gender equity.

Overall, structured management is becoming more common. Part of this is due to the impact of regulatory changes in a number of countries such as unfair dismissal laws (that create a need for consistent disciplinary procedures); antidiscrimination and EEO laws (that create a need to manage equity at work); in some countries, changes in bargaining practices (e.g. in Australia the shift to enterprise bargaining, supported by laws, in turn generating a need for formal bargaining committees); and OHS law (in turn creating a need for OHS committees). Even beyond this legal pressure, management in many organisations is also gradually increasing other areas of structured management such as training, employee monitoring and grievance procedures. Technological change increases the potential for structure in management by increasing the opportunity for computerised record-keeping and counting and formalising things that previously may have been undocumented, for example in performance appraisals. This was seen very clearly in the burdensome performance metrics required in *The Circle*. So the trend towards more structure in management is likely to continue.

30 Ron Callus et al., *Industrial Relations at Work: The Australian Workplace Industrial Relations Survey* (Canberra: AGPS, 1991).

That said, low formalisation or low structure in management is common in small business, as these frequently do not have the resources for the specialist functions associated with formal structures. The industrial relations practices in small business are often quite distinctive.[31] While technological changes may facilitate the introduction of some more structure into small business management, it is hard to believe the gap between large and small businesses in the degree of structure would disappear. The opposite might be equally possible.

Conflict over control

Negotiations over new collective agreements may centre on wage increases or benefits—that is, resources. But they may also centre on procedural issues of managerial prerogative or control. As we know from Chapter 2, resources are an important influence on control. But conflict in the workplace may often be specifically about control itself.

In small organisations, the capitalist can directly supervise employment and payment; for Richard Edwards, this was 'simple control'.[32] Yet in *some* small organisations, as Andrew Friedman pointed out, workers can still have substantial levels of autonomy.[33] Regardless, as organisations grow in size, management's personal ties with workers are weakened and worker resistance may be more organised and more successful.

31 Phil Beaumont and Ian Rennie, 'Organisational Culture and Non-Union Status of Small Businesses'. *Industrial Relations Journal* 17, no. 3 (1986): 214–24; Ron Callus, Jim Kitay, and Paul Sutcliffe, 'Industrial Relations at Small Business Workplaces'. *Small Business Review* 7 (1992): 106–45; Joe Isaac, *Small Business and Industrial Relations: Some Policy Implications*. Industrial Relations Research Series No. 8 (Canberra: Department of Industrial Relations, 1993); Joe Isaac et al., *A Survey of Small Business and Industrial Relations*. Industrial Relations Research Series No. 7 (Canberra: Department of Industrial Relations, May 1993); Alison Morehead et al., *Changes at Work: The 1995 Australian Workplace Industrial Relations Survey* (South Melbourne: Longman, 1997); Rowena Barrett and Al Rainnie, 'What's So Special About Small Firms?'. *Work, Employment & Society* 16, no. 3 (2002): 415; Monder Ram and Paul K. Edwards, 'Praising Caesar Not Burying Him: What We Know About Employment Relations in Small Firms'. *Work, Employment and Society* 17, no. 4 (2003): 719–30; Adrian Wilkinson and Tony Dundon, 'Employment Relations in Smaller Firms'. In *Handbook of Employment Relations, Law and Practice* (4th ed.), ed. B. Towers (London: Kogan Page, 2003): 288–307; Grant Cairncross and Jeremy Buultjens, 'Enterprise Bargaining under the Workplace Relations Act 1996 in Construction and Hospitality Small Businesses: A Comparative Study'. *Journal of Industrial Relations* 48, no. 4 (2006): 475–88.

32 Richard C. Edwards, *Contested Terrain* (London: Heinemann, 1979).

33 Friedman, *Industry and Labour*.

Over time, according to Edwards, larger organisations have become able to develop *technological* and *bureaucratic control*—that is, to use technology and rule-making as structural forms of control. Internal labour markets, rules governing job specifications, and work practices are examples of bureaucratic controls.[34] Technology allows the employer to control the processes of work and the pace of work. One mechanism by which these two control processes were merged was through the spread of Taylorism, a management system developed early in the twentieth century, focusing on narrowing the division of labour and timing each step of the production process, and picked up most famously in Henry Ford's mass production factories.[35] Friedman described Taylorism and other unilateral forms of managerial control as *direct control.* However, labour is too difficult to control through consistently simple methods, and no 'single form' of control is adequate for all circumstances.[36] Various management tactics lead to matching employee responses, establishing a 'frontier of control' or an area of 'contested terrain' between labour and management.[37] They 'push back' against each other, and so the frontier of control can shift depending on the power resources of the parties. For example, managers may decide to introduce a system of incentive pay; employees may resist and press for specific rules to be emplaced; management may try to amend rules to achieve their prior objective; employees may 'work to rule' to maximise their incentive payment but undermine other management objectives; and so on.

Conflict 'arises over a range of issues including the organisation of work, the pace of work, defining the rights and responsibilities of each party, and how employees are to be incorporated into the labour process'.[38] Hence, 'the workplace becomes a battle ground, as employers attempt to extract the maximum effort from workers and workers necessarily resist their bosses' impositions'.[39] Management aims to reduce uncertainty by gaining optimal control of labour power in order to generate profit.[40]

34 Keith Townsend, 'Teams, Control, Cooperation and Resistance in New Workplaces' (PhD diss., Department of Industrial Relations, Griffith University, 2005), 14.

35 Taylorism was named after Frederick Winslow Taylor, the most famous proponent of what was called 'Scientific Management'. Unsurprisingly, the spread of systems of mass production with little or no variation became known as Fordism. Frederick Winslow Taylor, *The Principles of Scientific Management* (New York: Harper & Brothers, 1911).

36 Paul Thompson, *The Nature of Work: An Introduction to Debates on the Labour Process* (Hampshire: Macmillan, 1989), 133 (my emphasis).

37 Carter L. Goodrich, *The Frontier of Control: A Study in British Workshop Politics* (London: G. Bell and Sons, 1920); Edwards, *Contested Terrain.*

38 Townsend, 'Teams, Control', 14.

39 Edwards, *Contested Terrain*, 13.

40 Burawoy, 'Between Labor Process'.

What does the future hold for this mutual 'push back'? Since the 1980s, manufacturing and large retailing firms in particular have moved towards 'just in time' (JIT) production systems that minimise use of inventories and hence costs, but render large systems open to disruption by a small interruption. JIT has been facilitated by modern technologies including computer systems and barcodes. Digital technology gives both high-trust and low-trust approaches additional ammunition. It provides the means for greater future collaboration if that is wanted, but perhaps that is not what many managements will want. They may prefer to exercise greater control and supervision. Just as employees seek to exercise control over their work—the importance of job control is a recurring theme of organisational psychology[41]—so too do managers, and they are increasingly held accountable for what their subordinates do. That makes it pretty difficult for individual managers to resist the urge to control. JIT systems reduce cost but increase risk, and so managers seek to increase control to counter risk.

We should not underestimate the potential impact of artificial intelligence on human resource management. Increasingly, firms are using algorithms to help in recruitment, with potentially discriminatory results.[42] Some are, or will, use AI for terminations. A Californian software engineer was sacked, without sense or explanation, by a computer algorithm; the firm acknowledged the error but made him recommence employment at the cost of three weeks' lost pay, and the trust from his fellow workers.[43] The trusted, informal discretion of managers will defer to the structured, sometimes flawed logic of the algorithm. The danger of technological job-loss is overall less significant to workers as a whole than the threat posed by increased use of algorithmic management for decision-making, surveillance and control, and also (as we shall see in Chapter 6) the potential for greater use of 'not there' employment.[44]

41 For example, Deborah J. Terry and Nerina L. Jimmieson, 'Work Control and Employee Well-Being: A Decade Review'. In *International Review of Industrial and Organizational Psychology*, ed. Cary L. Cooper and Ivan T. Robertson (Chichester: John Wiley & Sons, 1999).

42 Cathy O'Neill, *Weapons of Math Destruction: How Big Data Increases Inequality and Threatens Democracy* (New York: Crown Publishing Group, 2016).

43 Monique Ross and Damien Carrick, 'A Robot Didn't Take Ibrahim's Job, but It Did Fire Him'. *ABC News*, 16 August 2018, www.abc.net.au/news/2018-08-14/ibrahim-diallo-man-who-was-fired-by-a-machine-law-ai/10083194.

44 Brishen Rogers, *Beyond Automation: The Law & Political Economy of Workplace Technological Change* (SSRN, 4 February 2019), doi.org/10.2139/ssrn.3327608.

The other important factor in take-up of technology is its cost. Businesses will usually not introduce technology that enables greater monitoring and control unless the investment is expected to pay off, and for small businesses in particular that means that it needs to be very cheap or have a high and obvious payoff. A technology would likely require very wide penetration across larger businesses before it became acceptable in small and medium enterprises because of the cost implications. It becomes hard to predict which will be adopted first across businesses: technology that facilitates cooperation, or technology that facilitates control. The cost of accompanying hardware may be critical. So will the cost of resistance, which would be higher for technology that facilitates managerial control. If unemployment or underemployment are high or it is otherwise easy to replace labour (there is a substantial 'reserve army' of labour),[45] resistance will be lower and the conditions will favour technology that facilitates managerial control.

Much of this debate about workplace control developed after Harry Braverman (formerly an American factory worker) published *Labor and Monopoly Capital* in 1974.[46] Developing a Marxist framework, he argued that Taylorism or Scientific Management comprised a form of managerial control that was aimed at reducing worker control and that, among other things, it led to the deskilling of workers. The focus in Braverman's work was on factory work, although manufacturing declined thereafter, but the influence Taylorism had spread well beyond manufacturing into areas such as vocational education.[47]

Braverman was criticised for not giving enough attention to how employees responded to managerial attempts at control.[48] The labour process is rarely characterised by unrestrained hostility and usually has at least some component of consent.[49] To some extent management and labour must adjust to each other's preferences and expectations. So when it comes to issues like the pace at which the work will be performed, the amount of work that will be performed, who performs particular

45 Karl Marx, *Capital, Volume 2* (London: The Electric Book Company, 1998), 427.

46 Harry Braverman, *Labour and Monopoly Capital: The Degradation of Work in the Twentieth Century* (New York & London: Monthly Review Press, 1974).

47 Lucy Taksa, 'The Cultural Diffusion of Scientific Management: The United States and New South Wales'. *Journal of Industrial Relations* 37, no. 3 (1995): 427–61.

48 For example, Burawoy, 'Between Labor Process'; Thompson, *The Nature of Work*.

49 Paul K. Edwards and Hugh Scullion, *The Social Organisation of Industrial Conflict* (Oxford: Basil Blackwell, 1985).

tasks and so on, labour commonly retains some control.[50] You cannot explain the cooperative nature that can be found in many workplaces, by the majority of employees, much of the time simply by referring to control and resistance on their own.[51] For Burawoy, the labour process is organised such that employees consider that they have choices, and this 'participation in choosing … generates consent'.[52]

Employees may create 'games' to counter the problems of repetitive work.[53] The British 'surviving work' website is an example of attempts to relieve the frustrations within *any* work.[54] The opportunity for workers to gain small victories through 'games' is seen as disguising the core disadvantage of workers under capitalism.[55] Burawoy talks about the 'games' that workers engage in as part of the wage–effort bargain. Many studies also refer to employee efforts to restrict work.[56] What used to be called the 'darg' was the accepted level of work effort, put in by employees, socially determined by informal work groups to which employees belonged.[57] They still do, but few call it the 'darg' any more. Employees may engage in what, to managers, is organisational misbehaviour but to themselves is a rational way of making work bearable and ensuring that everyone is able to get by—though some forms of misbehaviour may be frowned upon even by other employees.[58]

As per the title of Burawoy's most famous book, management 'manufactures consent'. Employees might 'make out' (reach an output target) and this achieves more than just higher earnings. There are benefits such as lower fatigue, overcoming boredom, and the 'social and psychological rewards of making out on a tough job'.[59] It is an example of the movement from coercion to consensual regimes in the labour process.[60]

---

50 Steven Tolliday and Jonathan Zeitlin, eds, *Between Fordism and Flexibility: The Automobile Industry and Its Workers* (New York: Berg, 1992).

51 Burawoy, *Manufacturing Consent.*

52 Ibid., 27.

53 Ibid.; Burawoy, 'Between Labor Process'.

54 survivingwork.org/.

55 Jim Kitay, 'The Labour Process: Still Stuck? Still a Perspective? Still Useful?'. *Electronic Journal of Radical Organisation Theory* 3, no. 1 (1997): 1–10.

56 Burawoy, *Manufacturing Consent*; Stephen Ackroyd and Paul Thompson, *Organizational Misbehaviour* (London: Sage, 1999); Donald Roy, 'Quota Restriction and Goldbricking in a Machine Shop'. *American Journal of Sociology* 57, no. 5 (1952): 427–42.

57 For example, at a central Queensland coal mine in the 1950s, 'The "Darg" for two mates was approx. 20 skips a day, and for this the average wage was between 35 & 40 pounds a fortnight'. Collinsville Memoirs [CD] (Collinsville, Qld: Collinsville Connect Telecentre, 2002).

58 Ackroyd and Thompson, *Organizational Misbehaviour.*

59 Burawoy, *Manufacturing Consent*, 85.

60 Thompson, *The Nature of Work.*

Burawoy, who worked in a factory for his research, surprisingly found himself 'breaking [his] back to make out … risking life and limb for that extra piece'.[61] He described how 'We participated and strategized our own subordination. We were active accomplices in our own exploitation'.[62] Thus the labour process framework concentrates very much on control, consent and resistance, and often portrays workers as aware of whether it is consent or resistance that better serves their interests, or some combination of both.[63] Management aims, in part, to persuade employees that consent, or even commitment, is in their best interests rather than resistance.[64]

So, will the future see employers more likely to offer, or employees more likely to seek, consent-based, consensual regimes? To consider this, we first need to look at the role of 'culturism' in management strategies and what it means for consent.

Culturism, dissent and control

In recent decades, management in some, mostly large, firms has sought to win the conflict about control—to achieve full 'consent'—by attempting to manage 'culture' in the organisation. This is often expressed as getting employees with the right 'mindset' or the right 'fit' into the organisation.[65] If employees have appropriate attitudes that support the objectives of the organisation and that are willing to subordinate other personal interests to that goal, then much conflict over control would disappear. Attempts to exercise such control are described as 'culturism', and this was the central focus of Hugh Willmott's article discussed in Chapter 3.[66] So here we consider the role of organisational 'culture' in maintaining consent and control in workplace industrial relations in the context of what might superficially appear to be 'high-trust' management styles and the problems they might bring, and the role of dissent in organisations. To do this, I return to what culture means.

61 Burawoy, *Manufacturing Consent*, xi.

62 Burawoy, 'Between Labor Process', 10.

63 David Knights and Darren McCabe, 'Ain't Misbehavin'?'. *Sociology* 34, no. 3 (2000): 421–36.

64 Townsend, 'Teams, Control', 14.

65 For example, the term 'mindset' is used by several of Van den Broek's interviewees at 'Servo', though it was also used approvingly in this context by the Business Council of Australia as far back as the 1980s. Van den Broek, 'HRM, Workforce Control', 340; Business Council of Australia, *Enterprise-Based Bargaining Units: A Better Way of Working*. Part 1 (Melbourne: BCA, 1989), 2.

66 Hugh Willmott, 'Strength Is Ignorance; Slavery Is Freedom: Managing Culture in Modern Organizations'. *The Journal of Management Studies* 30, no. 4 (1993): 515–52.

Culture and culturism

The word *culture* comes from 'the idea of cultivation, the process of tilling and developing the land'.[67] We saw in Chapter 3 how it is about 'the set of shared, taken-for-granted implicit assumptions that a group holds and that determines how it perceives, thinks about and reacts to its various environments',[68] and that *culturism* is the attempt by management to create specific organisational cultures reflecting management's objectives.[69] In recent decades senior managers have often consciously attempted to create a particular type of culture at the workplace, and this is what Willmott, discussed in Chapter 3, was railing against.[70] From the 1980s, numerous management gurus spoke of 'managing culture', 'managing myths' and 'creating meaning'—in effect, creating a form of intracorporate hegemony.[71] Despite the rhetoric of managerial consultants and motivational texts, research has been unable to demonstrate that a particular culture is part of a recipe for success. The link between culture and performance 'is a tenuous one, as only behaviour can affect performance, and culture is not the only determinant of behaviour'.[72] Some evidence suggests the direction of causality is the other way around: changing performance leads to a change in culture.[73] A study of nearly 200 organisations suggested 'strong' cultures did not aid performance, and indeed could be counterproductive if they were not 'contextually or strategically appropriate' and did not 'contain norms and values that can help firms adapt to a changing environment'.[74] (The term 'strong' in relation to culture suggests a common culture that is widely adopted and reinforced within the organisation, which those writing about it often suggest is a good thing, like the word 'strong' itself.)

---

67 Gareth Morgan, *Images of Organisation* (London: Sage, 1986), 112.

68 Edgar H. Schein, 'Culture: The Missing Concept in Organization Studies'. *Administrative Science Quarterly* 41, no. 2 (1996): 236.

69 Willmott, 'Strength Is Ignorance'.

70 Ibid.

71 Terence E. Deal and Allan A. Kennedy, *Corporate Cultures—the Rites and Rituals of Corporate Life* (Massachusetts: Addison-Wesley, 1982); Thomas J. Peters and Robert H. Waterman, *In Search of Excellence* (New York: Harper & Row, 1982).

72 Dianne Lewis, 'Five Years on—the Organizational Culture Saga Revisited'. *Leadership & Organization Development Journal* 23, no. 5 (2002): 280–87.

73 Randy G. Pennington, 'Change Performance to Change the Culture'. *Industrial and Commercial Training* 35, no. 6 (2003): 251–55.

74 John P. Kotter and James L. Heskett, *Corporate Culture and Performance* (New York: Free Press, 1992).

Anyway, management rarely controls culture totally. Organisation culture reflects corporate history and practices. Culture may reflect the national and community environment and the different occupations of workers. It may be driven by employees and the communities from where they come. It may reflect the strategies and cultures of unions who are represented among the workforce. And it may reflect the importance of service versus profit objectives (in some public sector or nonprofit organisations, the former prevails over the latter).[75]

The leadership of an organisation can attempt to drive cultural change. The chief executive officer (CEO) is often seen as shaping the culture of the organisation. However, it is very difficult to manipulate culture once it exists. Culture is a very complex social process in organisations. Many firms have tried to change corporate culture and failed. One study of 22 cases of attempted culture change programs found that 16 of them failed.[76] Perhaps the most potent force for cultural change, though, is critical junctures[77] encountered by the organisation. That is, critical incidents or events tend to signal a break with past practices and the adoption of new practices and ideas.[78] An organisation facing a crisis (such as looking down the barrel of financial oblivion) may make a radical shift from a low-trust to a high-trust strategy, or vice versa, with accompanying changes in culture if employees share the perspective of crisis.

Culturism and dimensions of management strategy

As already mentioned, culturism is often used by organisations who want to portray themselves as high-trust but practise low-trust management strategies—the contradiction between reality and rhetoric on the first dimension of management strategy. Culturism is also common where management adopts particular positions on the other two dimensions of management strategy.

75 Morgan, *Images of Organisation*, 131–2.

76 Kotter and Heskett, *Corporate Culture and Performance*, 83.

77 The term 'critical junctures' was used by the Colliers to examine political change in Latin America, but it can have broader application. Ruth Berins Collier and J. David Collier, *Shaping the Political Arena: Critical Junctures, the Labor Movement and Regional Dynamics in Latin America* (Princeton, NJ: Princeton University Press, 1991).

78 An example is ICI Botany (later Orica). See Tony Mealor, *ICI Australia: The Botany Experience* (Sydney: School of Industrial Relations and Organisational Behaviour, University of New South Wales, 1992).

On the surface, it might seem that culturism is a form of collectivism. In one sense it is, in that organisations are attempting to get employees to take a collectively focused view of their welfare—that is, one focused on the collective welfare of the organisation (usually a corporation, which is itself a collective of capital). Yet many culturist policies are aimed at undermining collectiv*ism* by undermining unionism. On the other hand, some organisations seek to promote cooperative relations with their unions and members.[79] If this is done with the support of union officials but not their members, or vice versa, it might lead to a split between union members and paid officials, and 'wildcat' actions by members or desertions from the union.

Perhaps more commonly, these days, organisations pursue antiunion culturist strategies to promote commitment to the organisation. These organisations assume that employee commitment to their union is inconsistent with employee commitment to the organisation. Interestingly, the assumptions behind this organisational perspective are not supported by research. Studies from the 1950s to recent times show that employees can possess 'dual commitment' to the organisation and to a union.[80] Indeed, there is a positive association between commitment to the organisation and commitment to a union. In other words, employees who are strongly committed to the union are likely to be strongly committed to the organisation. Not all studies show these findings, although a lot of them do. Very few studies find a negative relationship between union and organisational commitment.[81] Despite these findings, that commitment to the union and employer are positively related; some managers still

79 Ibid.

80 Ed Snape and Andy W. Chan, 'Commitment to Company and Union: Evidence from Hong Kong'. *Industrial Relations* 39, no. 3 (2000): 445–59; D.G. Gallagher, 'The Relationship between Organizational and Union Commitment among Federal Government Employees'. *Academy of Management Proceedings*. (1984): 319–23; Cynthia V. Fukami and Erik W. Larson, 'Commitment to Company and Union: Parallel Models'. *Journal of Applied Psychology* 69, no. 3 (1984): 367–71; Harold L. Angle and James L. Perry, 'Dual Commitment and Labor–Management Relationship Climates'. *Academy of Management Journal* 29, no. 1 (1986): 31–50; Edward J. Conlon and Daniel G. Gallagher, 'Commitment to Employer and Union: Effects of Membership Status'. *Academy of Management Journal* 30, no. 1 (1987): 151; Daniel G. Gallagher and Paul F. Clark, 'Research on Union Commitment: Implications for Labor'. *Labor Studies Journal* 14, no. 3 (1989): 52–71; John M. Magenau, James E. Martin, and Melanie M. Peterson, 'Dual and Unilateral Commitment among Stewards and Rank-and-File Union Members'. *Academy of Management Journal* 31 (1988): 359–76; Aaron Cohen, 'Dual Commitment to the Organization and the Union: A Multi-Dimensional Approach'. *Relations Industrielles* 60, no. 3 (2005): 432–54.

81 Roderick D. Iverson and Sarosh C. Kuruvilla, *Does Dual Commitment Underline Company and Union Commitment? An Application of Second Order Confirmatory Analysis*. Working Paper 67 (Melbourne: Centre for Industrial Relations and Labour Studies, University of Melbourne, 1992).

oppose unionism because unions are a counterculture that recognises that the interests of employee and employer may not be synonymous—even if employees are committed to the employer. Thus hegemony through cultural control in *Nineteen Eighty-Four*'s Oceania and in *The Handmaid's Tale*'s Gilead was aimed in part at preventing collective organisation against the ruling elites, not to improve efficiency but to maintain power. Even in *The Circle*, any collective organisation of employees, beyond those organising the countless work-related social activities, would have been frowned upon.

An early study that looked closely at nonunion culturism (before companies became too sensitive to allow such studies to happen) was that of 'Servo'—a pseudonym for a large Australian company studied by Diane Van den Broek.[82] Culture was created and reinforced through recruitment, induction and socialisation. Recruitment and selection were designed 'to select employees most likely to aspire to company-defined goals and objectives'. The idea was to avoid recruits with 'cultural baggage', and to select those from companies with the right 'mindset' or with little work experience. Induction workshops inculcated the Servo mission. Performance-related pay was used to discourage potentially disruptive behaviour. Servo was the company whose HR manager I met at the beginning of this chapter.

Several aspects of culturism at Servo served to undermine any potential for unionism developing. Employees with incorrect attitudes could be weeded out. Performance-based remuneration and teamwork played an important role in individualising employment relations by breaking down the potential for employees to mount collective action around issues of pay and working conditions. Management at Servo believed that seeking assistance from 'outside influences' such as trade unions reflected a failure on the part of employees. Regarding a proposed nonunion enterprise agreement, the 'internal management processes left many employees with the impression that undue managerial pressure was applied and that the agreement was a *fait accompli*', for example through employees feeling 'intimidated into acquiescence'. On this matter, group control was important: 'some team leaders [stipulated] that voting be carried out as a team'. This was 'not to suggest that Servo employees have not been willing partners', Van den Broek added: 'on the whole', the remaining

82 Van den Broek, 'HRM, Workforce Control'.

employees reacted favourably to Servo's HR policies although they were aware of the existence of coercion. Most employees 'were either unaware or uninterested in union activities or held the view that requesting union support would incite managerial hostility'.[83]

In some cases, firms have used individual contracts and individual performance appraisal and pay as means of attempting to change culture. The most prominent example of this strategy was CRA, later known as Rio Tinto, which through a combination of financial, cultural and legal devices managed to largely deunionise substantial parts of its workforce in metalliferous mining and smelting, though it faced much more substantial difficulties in coal mining, where a different union had coverage.[84] Companies that set out to avoid unions (or deunionise) shape the symbolic dimensions of their actions to attempt to create a culture that identifies certain individuals and forms of behaviour as 'in' and other individuals, groups (such as unions) and behaviours as 'out'. The former can be referred to as *inclusivist* and the latter as *exclusivist* actions.[85] That said, subsequent problems including the rejection of proposed nonunion agreements by several large, nonunionised Rio Tinto sites in Western Australia[86] illustrated the vulnerability of culturism as a technique of control.

Related to this, cultural programs combined with deunionisation and individualisation can be a means of paying staff poorly. For example, the Merivale hotel chain in Sydney, Australia, emphasised its 'family' culture to employees—one manager said, 'we're not selling food, we're not selling alcohol, we're selling a feeling', while the HR manager is called a 'people experience manager'—but it used a nonunion agreement that had expired six years previously to pay employees below-award wages.[87]

83 Ibid.

84 Peetz, *Brave New Workplace*, Chapter 5.

85 Ibid., 207.

86 Bradon Ellem, *Hard Ground: Unions in the Pilbara* (Port Hedland: Pilbara Mineworkers Union, 2004); Samantha Donovan, 'Rio Tinto Loses Appeal on Worker Agreements'. *ABC News Online*, 11 February 2012, www.abc.net.au/news/2012-02-11/rio-tinto-loses-appeal-on-work-agreements/3824636.

87 'Merivale Staff Say They Aren't Being Paid Properly', *7.30*, ABC, 12 November 2018, www.abc.net.au/7.30/merivale-staff-say-they-arent-being-paid-fairly/10490500; Workplace Express, 'FWC Kills Off "Zombie" Deals'. *Workplace Express*, 22 January 2019, www.workplaceexpress.com.au/nl06_news_selected.php?act=2&stream=1&selkey=57483 (subscription required).

Strongly culturist organisations tend to have a set of characteristics on the dimensions of management style. They depict themselves as high trust but frequently behave as low trust and seek a monoculture to facilitate control. They are mostly individualistic, as opposed to collectivist. And they are usually highly structured because they are commonly large, with the HR functions (often renamed) to support such an approach. In the 'stronger' forms of culturism they use formal elements of HR such as performance appraisal to reinforce the desired culture.

Culturism as control of employees

The use of culturism to promote individualisation brings us back to a paradox—culturism appears collective but often undermines collectivism. As Willmott says, culturist organisations often use the rhetoric of individualism while aiming to suppress individual diversity. The (in)famous Milgram experiments of the 1960s[88] help us understand why sophisticated individualising corporations put such emphasis on creating a monoculture in which employees are not exposed to dissenting ideas, as exposure to dissent enabled participants to defy the directions of authority figures.[89] They also therefore illustrate another aspect of the limits to culturism. A recent example of the points made (somewhat inadvertently) by Milgram, and by Zimbardo in the Stanford prison experiments, can be seen in the argument made by University of New South Wales psychiatrist Michael Dudley, concerning the organisational culture that developed within Border Force (the Australian immigration bureaucracy) and the private security corporations that are used to control asylum seekers in detention centres, mostly outside Australia. He wrote in *Australian Psychiatry* of how 'policies misuse helping professionals to underwrite state abuses and promote public numbing and indifference, resembling other state abuses in the "war on terror" and (with qualification) historical counterparts, e.g. Nazi Germany'.[90] It followed from earlier research he had published that focused on the culture of Nazi psychiatry.[91] The interest in the behaviour of Nazi officials was what initially motivated Milgram's interest in undertaking his experiments. The power of organisational

88 Stanley Milgram, *Obedience to Authority* (New York: Harper & Row, 1974).

89 Randall Morck, *Behavioral Finance in Corporate Governance—Independent Directors and Non-Executive Chairs*. Discussion Paper No. 2037 (Cambridge, MA: Harvard Institute of Economic Research, May 2004).

90 Michael Dudley, 'Helping Professionals and Border Force Secrecy: Effective Asylum-seeker Healthcare Requires Independence from Callous Policies'. *Australasian Psychiatry* (2016).

91 Michael Dudley and Fran Gale, 'Psychiatrists as a Moral Community? Psychiatry under the Nazis and Its Contemporary Relevance'. *Australian and New Zealand Journal of Psychiatry* 36 (2002): 585–94.

culture helps us understand what Hannah Arendt was talking about when she wrote of the 'banality of evil'.[92] Organisation culture makes what, in other circumstances, would be extraordinary seem ordinary, even banal.

Bad behaviour by banks led to a number of questions being asked, with a common official response being like this: 'the culture that we're building throughout the Commonwealth Bank … is one with the customer at the centre of what we do'.[93] Yet as one observer remarked, a monoculture was at the core of the problem: 'While the banks claim to want ethical cultures, in practice they are in the business of curtailing the very forms of critical questioning that allow ethical issues to be surfaced in the first place'.[94] Performance appraisal and payment systems that rewarded and prioritised sales reinforced this culture.

The issues surrounding monoculturism are not just about the ethics of it—they are also about its economic efficiency. Diversity is the antithesis of monoculturism. Measuring the impact of a diverse workforce on improved firm performance is difficult, but McPherson concluded that diverse employees have the potential to improve firm performance.[95] Research has generally (though not always) found that companies with a diverse workforce have improved organisational outcomes based on financial performance.[96] And in the end, the monoculture in banks described above, with the associated reputation cost, seems likely to see them losing customers and profit.

---

92 Hannah Arendt, *Eichmann in Jerusalem: A Report on the Banality of Evil* (New York: Viking, 1963).

93 Carl Rhodes, '"Command and Control" Banks Have Got Ethics and Culture All Wrong'. *The Conversation*, 18 March 2016. For an example of a 'toxic and unsafe culture', especially for women, at ANZ, see Jemima Whyte et al., 'Inside ANZ's Toxic Culture: The High-Octane World of Dealing Rooms'. *Australian Financial Review*, 15 January 2016. See also behaviour by a major insurance company owned by a bank in Adele Ferguson, Klaus Toft, and Mario Christodoulou, 'Money for Nothing'. *Four Corners*, Australian Broadcasting Corporation, 8 March 2016, www.abc.net.au/4corners/stories/2016/03/07/4417757.htm.

94 Rhodes, '"Command and Control" Banks'.

95 Mevyl McPherson, 'Workforce Diversity: Evidence of Positive Outcomes and How to Achieve Them. A Review of the Literature'. Paper presented at Labour, Employment and Work conference, Wellington, 2008.

96 Catalyst, 'The Bottom Line: Connecting Corporate Performance and Gender Diversity'. *Catalyst*, 2004; O.C. Richard, 'Racial Diversity, Business Strategy, and Firm Performance: A Resource-Based View'. *Academy of Management Journal* 43, no. 2 (2000): 164–77; C.W. Von Bergen, B. Soper, and J.A. Parnell, 'Workforce Diversity and Organisational Performance'. *Equal Opportunities International* 24, no. 3–4 (2005): 1–16; Robert A. Weigand, 'Organizational Diversity, Profits and Returns in U.S. Firms'. *Problems and Perspectives in Management* 5, no. 3 (2007): 69–83; Anne M. McMahon, 'Does Workplace Diversity Matter? A Survey of Empirical Studies on Diversity and Firm Performance, 2000–09'. *Journal of Diversity Management* 5, no. 2 (2010): 37–48; Thomas A. Kochan et al., 'The Effects of Diversity on Business Performance: Report of the Diversity Research Network'. *Human Resource Management* 42, no. 1 (2003): 3–21.

In one article, Dennis Tourish, David Collinson and James Barker[97] drew on works such as that by Willmott, as well as Barker's own study of concertive control at ISE electronics,[98] the Milgram experiments[99] and, in particular, an early study of Schein and colleagues.[100] The last-mentioned looked at the experience of US POWs during the Korean War, and sought to explain the (slow) conversion many of them experienced to the philosophies of their captors (also referred to as 'Stockholm Syndrome', named after the reactions of hostages in a Swedish bank robbery and becoming prominent due to the events surrounding kidnapped heiress Patricia Hearst, in which she was said to have become sympathetic to her captors' aims). Tourish and colleagues draw a number of analogies between the techniques used on the POWs and the techniques used by corporate culturists, in particular use of what they call 'coercive persuasion' to ensure conformist behaviour within organisations.[101]

Yet although Willmott, as discussed earlier, was highly critical of culturism, he was not entirely pessimistic. This is because he suspected culturism might not work. From the standpoint of the individual, the distancing of self from corporate values may be the preferred means of preserving and asserting self-identity.[102] This is closely related to the observation by Stephen Lukes, discussed in Chapter 2, that attempts to exercise the third dimension of power (in practice, hegemony) can never be more than 'partially' effective.[103] As Tourish et al. emphasised, 'the imprisonment of US POWs in Korea clearly does not exactly parallel the context of most contemporary organisations', even though there are 'interesting overlaps between these contexts'.[104] This is an important point that has been made by several authors. Culture 'is not a variable that can be created, discovered or destroyed by the whims of management' but 'some are in a better position than others to attempt to intentionally influence aspects of it'.[105]

97 Tourish, Collinson, and Barker, 'Manufacturing Conformity'.
98 James R. Barker, 'Tightening the Iron Cage: Concertive Control in Self-Managing Teams'. *Administrative Science Quarterly* 38, no. 3 (1993): 408–37.
99 Milgram, *Obedience to Authority*.
100 E.H. Schein, I. Schneier, and C.H. Barker, *Coercive Persuasion: A Socio-Psychological Analysis of the 'Brainwashing' of American Civilian Prisoners by the Chinese Communists* (New York: Norton, 1961).
101 Tourish, Collinson, and Barker, 'Manufacturing Conformity'.
102 Willmott, 'Strength Is Ignorance', 537.
103 Steven Lukes, *Power: A Radical View*, 2nd ed. (London: Palgrave, 2005).
104 Tourish, Collinson, and Barker, 'Manufacturing Conformity', 372–3.
105 V. Lynn Meek, 'Organisational Culture: Origins and Weaknesses'. *Organisational Studies* 9, no. 4 (1988): 453–73.

The other reason culturism fails is the contradictions it creates. For example, Peter Waring spoke of the 'paradox of prerogative' when management recognised the need for increased participation, but was unwilling to modify the practice and perception of managerial prerogative by providing employees with greater autonomy.[106] Ogbonna observed how the 'smile' campaign at a UK supermarket, 'Capro', contradicted both the old 'pile it high, sell it cheap' culture and the more recent increase in number of difficult customers they had to deal with, leading to their jobs becoming more demanding, and the strategy of tight supervision of employees. As one manager said, 'we are able to detect when a check out operator is not smiling or even when she is putting on a false smile … we call her into a room and have a chat with her'.[107] 'At the very best', concluded Ogbonna, 'many attempts to change culture are only successful at the overt, behavioural level'.[108] That is, managers may get employees to change their behaviour but not the way they think about the organisation. Then there is the example of the coffee giant Starbucks, which as part of its culturist efforts referred to its employees as 'partners', but then announced store closures, job losses and cuts to sick leave and other employee ('partner') benefits.[109]

You see this doublespeak up close. I spoke to someone who worked at an organisation in which management had decided to close down a workplace interstate, and expand the Brisbane workplace. But workers in Brisbane still felt insecure about their jobs. At a meeting, management held out an olive branch (and a written offer) saying 'we want to win your trust back'. The workers then looked at the offer that management had documented, and indicated their disagreement. The response from management was described as 'you're either in the bus, or under the bus'. So the rhetoric of 'trust' did not last very long.[110]

---

106 Peter Waring, 'The Paradox of Prerogative in Participative Organisations: The Manipulation of Corporate Culture?'. Paper presented at Current Research in Industrial Relations, Proceedings of the 12th AIRAANZ Conference, Wellington, February 1998, 423–30.

107 Emmanuel Ogbonna, 'Organisation Culture and Human Resource Management: Dilemmas and Contradictions'. In *Reassessing Human Resource Management*, ed. P. Blyton and P. Turnbull (London: Sage, 1992): 74–96.

108 Ogbonna, 'Organisation Culture', 90.

109 David Emerson, 'Starbucks Axes 61 Stores and 685 Jobs'. *Sydney Morning Herald*, 29 July 2008; Robert Booth and Patrick Strudwick, 'Starbucks to Slash Paid Lunch Breaks and Sick Leave'. *The Guardian*, 4 December 2012.

110 Personal communication.

All this raises an interesting ethical question: it is not just whether culturism ever can or does lead to better organisational performance that is at issue; also at issue is whether it is right for organisations to try to determine what employees think, not just how they behave, and to recruit, train and discipline employees on that basis.

Employees' ability to resist culturism depends on exposure to other influences, inside and outside the workplace, even before they enter the workforce. Surveillance technologies may enable organisations to exercise greater control on ideas discussed within the workplace by their employees. It also enables them to better (albeit imperfectly) manage ideas outside the workplace, in society as a whole. Some organisations seek to discipline, or even sack, employees who express dissenting views on social media.[111] It is one reason why the maintenance of the employment relationship is central: organisations can have very little power over the culture or behaviour of their workers if their workers are genuinely independent contractors. The employment relationship helps maintain control of workers—not just control over what employees do but, at least in the aspirations of some managers, control over their 'mindset' and helping them manage 'what they think'.[112] Not all large organisations seek cultural control and, as we will see in the next chapter, even for those that do not run culturist agendas, the employment relationship is important for other aspects of control. However, culturism makes the employment relationship all that more important where culture is in management's sights.

So, exposure to competing ideas outside the workplace matters because of the limits it places on culturism. But that exposure is, itself, facing challenges. The decline of newspapers and other traditional mass media encourages governments to ease anticoncentration laws and allow media firms to agglomerate, reducing diversity in views through those mechanisms, and promotes business models that focus on pandering to limited world views at the expense of balanced journalism.[113] The rise of the internet as a source of news in principle increases diversity, but there is evidence that people are increasingly participating in 'echo chambers', encouraged particularly by social media, that reinforce their own views

111 Joe Myers, 'Swearing on Social Media Really Could Cost You Your Job'. World Economic Forum, 24 April 2017.

112 Willmott, 'Strength Is Ignorance', 516.

113 The most renowned media organisation adopting that strategy is News Corporation. Jane Mayer, 'The Making of the Fox News White House'. *New Yorker*, 11 March 2019, www.newyorker.com/magazine/2019/03/11/the-making-of-the-fox-news-white-house.

and perversely reduce the diversity of views most people are exposed to.[114] Those resisting management efforts may become more fixed in their views, but less able to penetrate the media experience of those accepting of a corporate orthodoxy. Indeed, social media can be used to harass those who express dissenting views.[115]

Overall, the effects of technology can go either way. Uncontested, the most likely pathway is towards increasing the appearance of high-trust approaches at work but hiding the proliferation of low-trust approaches, especially when corporate norms are violated. Other pressures, though, may alter that. Mae could have gone either way in *The Circle*, as the contradictory endings of the book and the movie showed. So, what is necessary to effectively contest the direction of culturism and management strategy? Part of it is about the choices made by critical actors—not just the Maes of this world, but also regulators, policy-makers and civil society. That last player leads us to the other part of what makes a difference: the degree of collective organisation that, when it comes to the future of work, is the collective organisation of labour. That is something we will look at in Chapter 7. But first, in Chapter 6, we see how trends in management strategy and structure are affecting the employment relationship itself.

114 Michela Del Vicario et al., 'The Spreading of Misinformation Online'. *Proceedings of the National Academy of Sciences* 113, no. 3 (2016): 554–59.

115 Joshua A. Cuevas, 'A New Reality? The Far Right's Use of Cyberharassment against Academics'. American Association of University Professors, 17 January 2018.

6

Flexibility, the 'gig economy' and the employment relationship

Take a moment to imagine the future world of work. It could be a world in which trucks and other vehicles drive themselves. A world in which all your shopping is without human interaction, either done online or by you walking into an unstaffed shop. A world in which queries you have about anything, from legal or financial to technical or customer service matters, are answered not by a person but by a bot that sounds, maybe even looks, perfectly human. A world in which energy is generated on the roofs of houses and shared in communities, ugly transmission towers having long ago been torn down. A world in which robots provide assistance to the aged, the disabled, the young. A world in which giant workplaces like mines (though not coal mines, there will not be many of them) or factories or construction sites are fully automated and remotely controlled from some air-conditioned office in Sydney, or Dallas, or Mumbai. A world in which we will all be freelancers, pursuing the next contract like the Uber driver pursues the next ride. Maybe.

If this libertarian vision of a world of freelancers frees us from the drudgery of employment, it is also a nightmare for those who worry about equity and security in the future. In another corner sit those (often also from conservative political camps) who reassure us that nothing really is changing, and it will all work out in the end. Who to believe?

In this chapter I look at the interaction of matters we discussed in the preceding two chapters; that is, I look at trends in *work* in light of changing management structures and strategies. I look in particular at management and risk, including how management has responded to risk, and other factors including cost pressures and the pressure for accountability. This chapter considers the forms of flexibility that are sought by employers, their origins and their effects on employees, for example through their impact on security and insecurity. It examines 'precaritisation' of work through the push for flexibility. A common feature of precaritisation is the growth of nonstandard employment, including through casualisation and independent contracting, in which workers become self-employed and take on the risks of the self-employed. Yet claims that casualisation and self-employment have not increased are often made to dispute widespread perceptions that insecurity at work is increasing.[1] How can these things be reconciled? That is one of the matters this chapter will investigate. As will be seen, the best way to start to reconcile these facts is to understand two simple things about how large corporations work these days: (a) they want to minimise the costs and risks they face, and avoid accountability when things go wrong; and (b) they also need to maintain control over workers to ensure the end product has the features, including quality, that they want—and, to date, the best way to do that has been through the employment relationship.

In this chapter we also consider what aspects of digital change are affecting, and likely to affect, work and workplace relations. We investigate whether we are moving to a world of freelancers or the 'gig economy' (sometimes referred to as 'Uberisation'). We test whether digital platforms are fundamentally changing or destroying the employment relationship. We do this through the lens of 'not there' employment—the attempts by core capital to centralise profits and minimise costs, risks and accountability (through such devices as contracting out, franchising and the use of digital platforms), and the surprising resilience of the employment relationship. So we consider the reasons, in the logic of capitalism, for employment's resilience, and what this means for risk and insecurity.

---

1 Mark Wooden, 'Factcheck: Has the Level of Casual Employment in Australia Stayed Steady for the Past 18 Years?'. *The Conversation*, 23 March 2016, theconversation.com/factcheck-has-the-level-of-casual-employment-in-australia-stayed-steady-for-the-past-18-years-56212; Robert Sobyra, 'Australian Jobs Aren't Becoming Less Secure'. *The Conversation*, 17 July 2018, theconversation.com/australian-jobs-arent-becoming-less-secure-99739.

Management, uncertainty and flexibility

Writing in Europe in 1987, Wolfgang Streeck captured the mood that prevailed at the time, and to varying degrees since, in his article 'The Management of Uncertainty and the Uncertainties of Management'. Streeck emphasised how management faced the problem of finding ways of dealing with 'an unprecedented degree of economic uncertainty deriving from a need for continuous rapid adjustment to a market environment that appears to have become permanently more turbulent than in the past'.[2] He argued that the key concept for management had become 'flexibility', which he defined as 'a general capacity of enterprises to reorganise in close response to fluctuations in their environment'.[3] He identified both external (numerical) and internal (functional and temporal) flexibility (discussed below) and consequently two ways firms could seek to achieve organisational flexibility—through a 'return to contract' (what we call external flexibility) or 'extension of status' (internal flexibility). However, said Streeck, the 'management of uncertainty' remained incomplete due to the profound 'uncertainties of management' in this new regime as they faced other parties (especially trade unions) while they pushed for greater decentralisation in industrial relations. In doing this, Streeck explained the rising significance of flexibility for employers—it was a means by which management could minimise *risk*.

Management and risk

Risk is a consistent theme through management, and indeed the corporation can be seen as a device for limiting risk, in the interests of capital. In particular, the corporate form enables owners of capital to collectively undertake gambles (or risks) that have the potential to generate substantial returns while limiting the amount of liability that the owners of capital face if the activity goes pear-shaped. In the era since the end of the 1970s, several important changes in risk have taken place. As noted by Streeck, higher volatility in product markets has increased uncertainty for management.[4] Financialisation, discussed in Chapter 2, has substantially shortened the period in which the 'return' from risks is

2 Wolfgang Streeck, 'The Uncertainties of Management and the Management of Uncertainty'. *Work, Employment and Society* 1, no. 2 (1987): 281–308.
3 Ibid., 290.
4 Ibid.

meant to be retrieved (though there are some opposing forces as well, as we shall see in Chapter 9). Consequently, there have been efforts by capital to improve the rates of return associated with risk, by affecting both sides of the risk equation; that is, through transferring risk (uncertainty) from capital to labour, and increasing capital's share of returns (altering the share of income growth going to labour and profits). The last has been achieved both through changes in employment practices of corporations and through lobbying of the state to introduce regulatory changes that either transfer risk or increase capital's share of returns.

There are several ways in which risk-shifting has occurred. Researchers Mike Rafferty and Serena Yu identified changes in the world of work (the nature of work performed, the nature of demand for and supply of labour, the structure of jobs, the nature of bargaining, and pay and conditions); changes in working lives beyond the workplace (the way risk is experienced across a lifetime and how it connects with the world of work); and changes in the relationships between workers (the way workers experience and understand their lives, especially their shared experience of risk both at work and elsewhere).[5] Here, I centre attention on that key element focused on by Streeck: the management of uncertainty and its link to flexibility, though I start with some other issues surrounding risk.

Risk, randomness and the illusion of understanding

Cognitive psychologist Daniel Kahneman, whose work influenced the development of behavioural economics, had a lot to say about the way we think, a little to say about management and not much to say directly about work. But what he says in several areas (summarised in his book, *Thinking, Fast and Slow*) has implications for work and the role of management within it.[6] Of particular relevance here is the illusion of understanding.

Talking about risk or uncertainty is another way of saying that we cannot be certain that a particular event will happen, only that it has a (commonly imprecise) probability that can be attached to it. All sorts of random events influence this probability. But we love to think that we

5 Mike Rafferty and Serena Yu, *Shifting Risk: Work and Working Life in Australia*. A report for the Australian Council of Trade Unions (Sydney: Workplace Research Centre, University of Sydney, September 2010).

6 Daniel Kahneman, *Thinking, Fast and Slow* (New York: Farrar, Straus and Giroux, 2011).

are in control. So we will often ascribe agency for something that actually happened due to random variation. We grab the illusion of understanding that event. Naturally, we will take the credit if things go right and blame others if things go wrong. So, often the fault is not simply in failing to give enough recognition to others when things go right, or failing to accept blame ourselves when things go wrong; it is in failing to recognise that many of the good or bad things that happen are simply a result of chance events—what some would call good or bad 'luck' (perhaps as if 'luck' was somehow a characteristic that ascribed to people). Hence managers will often be seen to be good (or bad) depending on whether random events led to outcomes that (perhaps temporarily) looked good or bad. It creates an illusion of control for the CEOs themselves, and certainly for those observing them, such that 'when a particular executive fails, or is embroiled in a scandal, there is a quick defence that it is the individual who is at fault for not living up to the moral status of the position they hold'.[7]

It also means that you get to hear and see lots of heroic case studies, where management in seemingly difficult situations overcomes the odds to create a brilliant successful product through its own skill (or, alternatively, turns a good situation bad by making some unlucky errors). Kahneman gives the example of the story of Google, oft trumpeted as a major success of great owners and managers, when in fact a whole series of chance events happened to go their way.[8] These heroic tales overflow the bookshelves in airports. Some even get into university courses. We love to read case studies because they tell a coherent, plausible story from which we too can learn how to overcome the odds and succeed.

The trouble is, we do not get to see the studies of how other managers faced similar choices, made similar decisions and yet ended face-down, or for whom little changed. 'Stories of success and failure consistently exaggerate the impact of leadership style and management practices on firm outcomes.'[9] So firms with revered CEOs, who are granted prestigious press awards, subsequently experience falls in share price and

7 Peter Bloom and Carl Rhodes, *CEO Society: The Corporate Takeover of Everyday Life* (London: Zed, 2018), 49.

8 Kahneman, *Thinking, Fast and Slow*, Chapter 9.

9 Ibid., Chapter 19, citing Philip Rosenzweig, 'The Halo Effect and the Challenge of Management Inquiry: A Dialog between Phil Rosenzweig and Paul Olk'. *Journal of Management Inquiry* 19 (2010): 48–54.

operating performance.[10] This is because previous results (that led to their veneration) were simply unrepresentatively good and were followed by a 'reversion to the mean'. Often 'overcoming the odds' is, as the term 'odds' implies, simply a matter of probabilities: someone had to get lucky, and it's the ones who got lucky that we want to hear and learn from and idolise. If you read a case study of a successful firm or person, ask yourself: 'How different might things have been if one or two random events had gone another way?'.

Sometimes it is just these random events that will determine which particular cases get highlighted in public discourse; but sometimes they are chosen because somebody wants to push a particular policy barrow. While it is often said that there are lies, damned lies and statistics,[11] case studies are especially handy for those who wish to do this, as information can be selectively included or excluded when it is presented to an audience, and verifiability can be difficult. So, for example, an Australian employer lobby group in a widely publicised 1989 report made much of how the case studies it reported demonstrated both a 25 per cent productivity gap between Australia and the USA resulting from industrial relations regulations and the need for major industrial relations reform.[12] Details of the cases were sparse[13] and subsequent developments invalidated the claims. Two decades after most of the demanded reforms had been implemented, the 25 per cent 'productivity gap' remained.[14] Yet the commissioning organisation experienced the 'illusion of understanding' to such an extent that they had come to believe their own rhetoric. The same organisation also commissioned independent academic researchers to undertake case studies of 'excellence' in 30 organisations, only to

10 Kahneman, *Thinking, Fast and Slow*, Chapter 24, citing Ulrike Malmendier and Geoffrey Tate, 'Superstar CEOs'. *Quarterly Journal of Economics* 24 (2009): 1593–638.

11 This phrase was attributed, apparently incorrectly, to Disraeli by Mark Twain. For more information on the problem referred to, however, see Darrell Huff, *How to Lie with Statistics* (New York: W.W. Norton & Company, 1954).

12 Business Council of Australia, *Enterprise-Based Bargaining Units: A Better Way of Working*. Part 1 (Melbourne: BCA, 1989); Business Council of Australia, 'The Report That Will Change the Way We Work'. *Business Council Bulletin* 59 (1989): 38–39.

13 Stephen J. Frenkel and David Peetz, 'Enterprise Bargaining: The BCA's Report on Industrial Relations Reform'. *Journal of Industrial Relations* 32, no. 1 (1990): 69–99.

14 David Peetz, 'Does Industrial Relations Policy Affect Productivity?'. *Australian Bulletin of Labour* 38, no. 4 (2012): 268–92.

surprisingly find that their premise (that individual contracting was superior to collective bargaining) was wrong, as the academics found that 'both union and non-union workplaces were excellent'.[15]

Lobbyists have learnt not to leave the commissioning of reports, on issues on which they want to push a policy proposal, to chance. They now typically commission consultancy firms (who will do exactly what is asked of them) rather than independent researchers for that purpose, or 'think-tanks' established to promote the view for which the group, from which the commissioning organisation comes, wants support.[16]

This is not to say that case studies have no value. They are used a lot in studies of work. But readers should always be wary of agendas, of overgeneralising, and of attributing agency in place of either luck or selection bias in the cases or the data.

Related to the illusion of understanding are several other aspects of human perception. One is the illusion of hindsight—we think we were better at predicting things than we actually were, plus we 'believe that we understand the past, which implies that the future should be knowable, but in fact we understand the past less than we believe we do'.[17] The other is a tendency to 'overconfidence' in our perceptual and decision-making abilities (hence the willingness of people, as mentioned, to believe their own rhetoric).

Put these things together and management can be overly optimistic about how it is perceived by employees—in some cases wildly so, especially where countervailing employee voice mechanisms are limited. An example of this occurred after the *Employment Contracts Act 1991* (ECA) was introduced

15 Daryl Hull and Vivienne Read, *Simply the Best: Workplaces in Australia*. Working Paper 88 (Sydney: ACIRRT, University of Sydney, December 2003), 8. See also David Peetz, 'Hollow Shells: The Alleged Link between Individual Contracting and Productivity'. *Journal of Australian Political Economy* 56 (2005): 32–55.

16 On consultants, see Ross Gittins, 'Dark Art of Econometrics'. *Sydney Morning Herald*, 27 August 2007; Peter Martin, 'Is Tony Abbott's "Cop on the Beat" Worth $6 Billion?'. *Sydney Morning Herald*, 28 August 2013; Michael West, 'Ignore Page Count, Just Note Number on the Front'. *Sydney Morning Herald*, 8 March 2014. One organisation concerned later gained notoriety for suppressing results of a survey it had undertaken of its members that undermined its own position on reducing company tax: Laura Tingle and Phillip Coorey, 'Secret BCA Survey Does Not Back Tax Cuts Going to Jobs, Wage Rises'. *Australian Financial Review*, 26 March 2018, www.afr.com/news/secret-bca-survey-does-not-back-tax-cuts-going-to-jobs-wage-rises-20180326-h0xzm7#ixzz5BJxim97U. On think-tanks, see A. Salas-Porras and G. Murray, eds, *Think Tanks and Global Politics: Key Spaces in the Structure of Power* (Singapore: Palgrave Macmillan, 2017).

17 Kahneman, *Thinking, Fast and Slow*, 201–2.

in New Zealand. A survey of employees showed that 12 per cent of employees reported an increase in their trust of management, and 30 per cent reported a decline, with no differences between employees in firms with and without new individual contracts. But a contemporaneous survey of employers found that, in firms without new contracts, 23 per cent thought employee trust of management had increased (only 4 per cent conceded a fall), while in firms with new (mostly individual) contracts 42 per cent claimed an increase in employee trust of management, and only 6 per cent a fall.[18] Overconfidence, or management self-delusion, therefore was both common and strongest in firms where managers thought that individual contracts had brought employees closer to management (when the reality was often the reverse). Formal voice mechanisms were weakened (the ECA debilitated unions) and many managers believed, somewhat self-servingly, that individual contracts were a better form of voice.

Just as managers have an illusion of control, so they also seek to maintain or increase control. It does not feel good to be not in control, and it is not good to be seen as not in control. So it takes a lot of belief by managers and supervisors in the benefits of employee participation in decision-making, or in any social justice considerations, for them to follow a high-trust or a collectivist strategy. Alternatively, it takes strong employee organisation to force management to do those things. No doubt, in the future, there will be some employers following such paths, but if power shifts further from employees then managers will be less likely to pursue paths that employees seek.

Managers as employees

Finally, it is worth pausing to remember that managers are also employees, and sometimes they are subjected to the same contradictions and pressures as lower-level employees.[19] A study of managers in call centres found their ability to manage was undermined by role conflicts, micromanagement and lack of development or strategic direction, and their coping strategies

18 David Peetz et al., 'Workplace Bargaining in New Zealand: Radical Change at Work'. In *Workplace Bargaining in the International Context*, ed. David Peetz, Alison Preston, and Jim Docherty. Workplace Bargaining Research Project (Canberra: Department of Industrial Relations and Australian Government Publishing Service, 1993), 290–93.

19 Keith Townsend and Sue Hutchinson, 'Line Managers in Industrial Relations: Where Are We Now and Where to Next?'. *Journal of Industrial Relations* 59, no. 2 (2017): 139–52.

were a mixture of embracing and resisting.[20] So they experience, in sometimes quite specific ways, a number of the issues facing employees that are discussed elsewhere in this book; for example, issues regarding culture, gender, emotional labour, work intensity and ethics. At times in later chapters we use examples from managers to highlight certain aspects of those issues. How much, and in what ways, they experience those issues is often a function of how close to, or distant from, the top of the organisation they are—and therefore how much power they possess. Management is stressful work, especially for those who, as individuals, are troubled by the conflict between financial considerations and human considerations.

Flexibility explored

One person's flexibility is another person's uncertainty—just as one person's stability is another person's rigidity. The underlying questions, according to Richard Hyman, that we ultimately need to consider with flexibility are: who gains and who loses; and whose interests are promoted and whose interests are neglected.[21]

For Hyman, flexibility is 'more a rhetorical slogan than … an analytical instrument'.[22] The language of flexibility is value laden: flexibility is invariably portrayed as a 'good thing'. If someone is deemed not flexible, then they are portrayed as rigid—a 'bad thing'.[23] Economists and others frequently tell us that labour market flexibility is a good thing.

But we could, of course, give the term 'flexibility' the opposite connotation. For instance, we could say flexible = uncertain = a bad thing; and that rigid - stable = a good thing. In this interpretation, flexibility would be characterised as a social 'bad' as opposed to a social 'good'. As you can see, we need to separate out the prescriptive ('we should be flexible') component of the term flexibility from the analytical component (e.g. numerical vs functional).

20 Maeve Houlihan, 'Managing to Manage? Stories from the Call Centre Floor'. *Journal of European Industrial Training* 25, no. 2 (2001): 208–20.

21 Michele Salvati, 'A Long Cycle in Industrial Relations'. *Labour* 3, no. 1 (1989): 42–72.

22 Richard Hyman, *The Political Economy of Industrial Relations* (London: Macmillan, 1989).

23 Salvati, 'Long Cycle'.

This rise of the idea that 'flexibility' *by* employees was a desirable thing coincided with the opening up of market forces and the movement of neoclassical economic ideas ('market liberalism') to ascendancy in policy debates and decisions. The 'Great Recession' (as Americans described it) or 'global financial crisis' (as Australians called it) showed that many of the key propositions behind the neo-liberal model can no longer be assumed to be true.[24] For example, the highly 'flexible' US labour market generated worse increases in unemployment during the financial crisis than were generated by the less flexible European labour market, even though Europe suffered a larger fall in GDP.[25] Since then, austerity programs implemented in Europe, but not the USA, have prevented Europe from making the recovery in unemployment that was subsequently seen in the USA. In economic terms, demand, not flexibility, has driven the course of unemployment.

First, though, let us differentiate between flexibility *for* workers and flexibility *by* workers. Flexibility for workers occurs when companies change work practices or working time to better suit worker needs. Allowing workers to take time off to attend school concerts, enabling job sharing, permanent part-time work, '48/52' arrangements—these are all examples of employers being flexible *for* workers. Research shows these things are mostly effective in enabling better work–life balance, and are often aimed at increasing job satisfaction, attraction or retention of valuable employees.[26]

But when employers or politicians complain about a lack of flexibility, they usually mean flexibility *by* workers. Here researchers distinguish between two types of flexibility by workers. They are *functional* and *numerical* flexibility.

Forms of labour flexibility by employees

Functional flexibility is the employer's ability to deploy employees between activities and tasks to match changing workloads, production methods or technology. It is often loosely associated with multiskilling and the expansion of worker autonomy. *Numerical flexibility* is the employer's

24 John Quiggin, *Zombie Economics* (New Jersey: Princeton University Press, 2010).

25 David Peetz, Stephane Le Queux, and Ann Frost, 'The Global Financial Crisis and Employment Relations'. In *The Future of Employment Relations: New Paradigms, New Approaches*, ed. Adrian Wilkinson and Keith Townsend (Basingstoke: Palgrave Macmillan, 2011), 193–214.

26 Natalie Skinner and Janine Chapman, 'Work–Life Balance and Family Friendly Policies'. *Evidence Base* 4 (2013); Jason Hess, 'Ignore Flexible Working at Your Peril'. *Real Business* 5 February 2014, realbusiness.co.uk/ignore-flexible-working-at-your-peril/.

capacity to adjust labour inputs to fluctuations in output. Numerical flexibility in turn can be broken down into three forms. *External numerical flexibility* refers to nonstandard forms of employment—the ability to adjust the level of labour inputs, for example through use of casual labour, part-time workers, subcontracting, labour hire or fixed contract workers. *Internal numerical flexibility* (or temporal flexibility) refers to the ability to adjust the quantity and timing of work without engaging additional labour. '*Financial*' or *wage flexibility* refers to the ability to adjust wages up or downwards in line with output or market circumstances, through mechanisms such as piece rates, gain-sharing, productivity bonuses, incentive pay schemes or pay cuts.[27]

Different types of flexibility are often associated with different management styles. For example, numerical flexibility tends to be associated with low-trust styles. It may be linked to individualism (in that contracting and casualisation make it harder for unions to organise, and sometimes this is a purpose of casualisation or contracting out). On the other hand, some aspects of numerical flexibility (in particular, profit-sharing or productivity-related pay) *may* go hand in hand with employee participation mechanisms that in turn require high trust (though it may not always be provided). Indeed, it appears that contingent pay schemes only really work effectively when they are associated with employee ability to influence work, which, when profit-sharing or productivity-related pay are involved, means employee participation in decision making.[28] However, profit-pay and participation do not necessarily coexist. In short, it's complicated.

By contrast, functional flexibility tends to be disproportionately linked to higher trust approaches (you want employees to stay in the firm as they are trained in multiple skills and tasks, and this requires the building of some trust). It may be linked to collectivism in that internal labour markets (ILMs), often tied to functional flexibility, are also more favourable to unionism, and may force management to recognise collective

27 Karen Legge, *Human Resource Management: Rhetorics and Realities.* Management, Work & Organisations Series (Basingstoke, England: Macmillan Business, 1995).

28 John R. Cable and Felix R. Fitzroy, 'Co-operation and Productivity: Some Evidence from West German Experience'. *Journal of Economic Analysis and Workers Management* 14, no. 2 (1980): 163–80; Douglas Kruse, *Employee Ownership and Employee Attitudes: Two Case Studies* (Norwood Editions: Pennsylvania, 1984); Bjørne Grimsrud and Torunn Kvinge, 'Productivity Puzzles—Should Employee Participation Be an Issue?'. *Nordic Journal of Political Economy* 32, no. 2 (2006): 139–67; General Accounting Office, *Employee Stock Ownership Plans: Little Evidence of Effects on Corporate Performance* (Washington DC: GAO, March 1987).

organisations. And it might be linked to structured management, in that rules and procedures also tend to be linked to ILMs and their greater use of training. But the case should not be overstated: smaller firms may seek functional flexibility because they do not have enough staff for detailed specialisation, but they may also be too small to offer ILMs with strong career prospects. So these can be seen as theoretical tendencies rather than corollaries.

Functional flexibility

Functional flexibility denotes the ability of employees to move flexibly between different job tasks and assignments. While it appears that many employees are demonstrating functional flexibility in other work, Karen Legge's case-study evidence suggested that, in firms that sought to focus on functional flexibility, the degree of flexibility achieved was 'more modest than celebratory accounts of multiskilled teamworking or craft-based flexible specialisation might imply'.[29] Changes reportedly rarely involved radical skill enhancement. One study examined attempts at introducing full functional flexibility—basically everybody can do everything—at a Pirelli greenfield site. These attempts were eventually abandoned because of the importance of specialist knowledge that was lost with full functional flexibility; the importance of commitment that was associated with 'ownership' of a particular area; the cost and availability of training; and the problems of skill retention being weak if new skills were not constantly practised.[30]

A British study of collective agreements to achieve functional flexibility also detected problems. While most agreements contained promises of job security, they 'almost always implied a reduction in the workforce, if not through redundancies then by so-called natural wastage' resulting from anticipated rises in productivity.[31] According to Legge, the objective was 'increased managerial control over the deployment of labour and consequent labour intensification, with [quality of working life] outcomes secondary if not incidental'.[32]

29 Legge, *Human Resource Management*, 162; Tony Elger, 'Task Flexibility and Intensification of Labour in UK Manufacturing in the 1980s'. In *Farewell to Flexibility*, ed. Anna Pollert (Oxford: Basil Blackwell, 1991).

30 J. Clark, 'Full Flexibility and Self-Supervision in an Automated Factory'. In *Human Resource Management and Technical Change*, ed. J. Clark (London: Sage, 1993).

31 Income Data Services, *Flexible Working*. Study 407 (London: IDS, April 1988); Anna Pollert, 'The Flexible Firm: Fixation or Fact?'. *Work, Employment and Society* 2, no. 3 (1988): 281–316.

32 Legge, *Human Resource Management*, 169.

Numerical flexibility

External numerical flexibility is concerned with the ease of increasing or reducing the number of employees. Broadly speaking, there are two ways in which this can be achieved: by making it easy to hire or fire 'core' or 'permanent workers'; or by making it easy to have people working on 'peripheral' contracts—as casual employees, labour hire workers or dependent contractors.

One of the changes in employment relations from the mid-1980s was the restructuring of employment associated with the growth of nonstandard or atypical forms of employment, such as contract, part-time, casual, agency, homeworking, trainees and self-employment. Although it is common to include part-time in this list of nonstandard employment, this is not analytically very helpful, as part-time work can be permanent and is sometimes (not always) driven by the supply side (workers wanting part-time employment). The main exception—that is, the main instance where part-time noncasual work is precarious—is where underemployment is experienced.[33] So we focus most on contract, casual, agency, homeworking, trainees and *dependent* self-employment (i.e. where the worker has the appearance of being self-employed but is actually dependent upon one organisation to provide him or her with work). *Casual employment* is a term used in Australia to describe employment contracts in which the contract lasts only for the period of the current shift, though in practice employees are usually expected to stay for weeks, months or sometimes even years. In most other countries, *temporary employment* is a term used to describe employees whose period of engagement is not ongoing. Time series data are not easy to obtain, and most Australian studies rely on data about people with no access to paid holiday or sick leave (as most casuals lack such access). Most Australian casuals have no access to protection against unfair dismissal, redundancy pay or long-service leave. The closest analogy in the UK is 'zero hours contracts' (you have a 'job' but no guarantee that you will work in any particular week) while the OECD usually uses 'temporary employment' as its indicator of precarity in employment and includes Australian casual

33 Between 2010–11 and 2016–17, the number of hours sought, but not worked, by underemployed people in Australia grew by 31 per cent, five times the total growth in hours worked. See Australian Bureau of Statistics, 'Labour Account Australia, Quarterly Experimental Estimates', September 2017. Canberra 6150.0.55.003.

employment in that measure. There has not been much change in the past decade in the overall proportion of Australian employees who have access to holiday and sick leave.

Labour hire (where the worker is not a direct employee of the company for whom s/he is working) is another form of casual employment, and the growth of labour hire is part of the reason for the relative growth of *full-time* casual employment.[34] Employees paid by labour hire agencies are in uncertain 'triangular' relationships with the labour hire firm and the firm for whom they are doing work. Labour hire workers appear to have inferior occupational health and safety outcomes[35] and to lack protection from unfair dismissal and redundancy.

In *dependent contractor* relationships, the worker is not even an employee, even though they are mostly only working for one organisation (that in other circumstances would be called an 'employer'). The term 'independent contractors' is sometimes used in popular discourse to refer to both the above group and those who are genuinely independent and have many clients or customers.

Whereas external numerical flexibility allows the employer to change the number of *workers* they have at a point in time, internal numerical flexibility (or temporal flexibility) allows them to change when and for how many *hours* those employees work. Casual employment does both. Part-time employment contracts may (or may not) also allow the employer to vary hours per employee.

Another aspect of internal numerical flexibility is the capacity of employers to get more hours out of workers when needed, through *paid or unpaid overtime*. Over much of the last century, premiums or 'penalty rates' for working nights or weekends, and in particular premiums for overtime, reduced the incentive on employers to make existing employees work for extra hours (rather than take on additional workers). In the last quarter

34 If we take the liberty of labelling people without leave as 'casuals', then the number of 'casual' full-timers grew in Australia by 38 per cent between 2009 and 2017. So-called 'permanent' full-timers (that is, those with annual leave) grew by just 10 per cent. On the other hand, some organisations have found their reliance on part-time casuals has been counterproductive, as it meant workers had no commitment and were unreliable. So some large retailers now use 'permanent' part-timers rather than casuals. So-called 'casual' part-timers grew by just 13 per cent between 2009 and 2016. 'Permanent' part-timers grew by 36 per cent. See Australian Bureau of Statistics, 'Characteristics of Employment'. Canberra 6333.0.

35 E. Underhill, 'Changing Work and OHS: The Challenge of Labour Hire Employment'. Paper presented at the New Economies: New Industrial Relations conference, Noosa, February 2004, 544–51.

century, there has been a breakdown of the standard working-time model. A diminishing proportion of workers are employed for a standard 38 to 40 hours per week. A large proportion of the workforce are working either shorter hours (in part-time jobs) or longer hours.[36]

So, while part of internal flexibility concerns the number of hours people work, another part, one that employer organisations are putting more emphasis on, is about getting people to work when it best suits the employer—including on nights or weekends. Hence wage premiums for unsocial hours—that is, for working nights or weekends (referred to in Australia as 'penalty rates' and in New Zealand as 'penal rates')—are being challenged. These were established a long time ago, both as an effort to get people to work unsocial hours (i.e. to increase labour supply at those times) and to compensate people for the inconvenience of working those hours (part of what neoclassical economists would call a 'compensating wage differential'). Sundays have (in recent centuries) been associated with religious observance in some countries, and so the decline of religion has been used by some employers to argue that Sunday wage premiums are outdated, though the concept of a rest day has a much stronger lineage.[37]

Although it is argued by some that the '24/7' economy renders shift premiums obsolete, a counter is that it is still essential that people have time away from work on nights and weekends. In developed countries this is even more important now that two adults in a household are typically working, as otherwise the opportunities for a couple to spend time together would be very limited. Evidence indicates that people working at nights or weekends are more likely than others to be dissatisfied with the balance between their personal and family lives, and to report a deterioration in how well they get on with people at home. The partners of those working weekends are more likely than the partners of people who do not work weekends to want their spouses to get a different job and to complain about the way their social life is affected by their spouse's work responsibilities.[38]

---

36 For example, Australian Bureau of Statistics, 'Working Time Arrangements, Australia', November 2012. Canberra 6342.0.

37 David Peetz, Scott Bruynius, and Georgina Murray, 'Choice and the Impact of Changes to Sunday Premiums in the Australian Retail and Hospitality Industries'. *Journal of Industrial Relations* (2019), doi.org/10.1177/0022185618814578.

38 David Peetz et al., 'Quality and Quantity in Work–Home Conflict: Nature and Direction of Effects of Work on Employees' Personal Relationships and Partners'. *Australian Bulletin of Labour* 37, no. 2 (2011): 138–63.

To the extent that flexibility is associated with uncertainty, it is numerical flexibility that is at issue. The growth of numerical flexibility since the mid-1980s has been seen as signifying the growth of 'precaritisation'; that is, the creation of precarious jobs. People in casual jobs, including labour hire, fixed-term employees and dependent contractors, can be seen as in particularly precarious jobs. So too, however, may be a number of people in 'permanent' jobs, as they can still be made redundant or otherwise dismissed—especially in the context of the emergence of 'not there' employment, discussed below. Guy Standing coined a term, 'the precariat', to encompass what he considered to be a new and dangerous social class, evident globally, experiencing ongoing precarity in work and open to political extremism. It evokes, but does not mean the same as, Marx's 'lumpenproletariat', described as a dispossessed group at the bottom of society, including 'vagabonds … knife grinders, tinkers [and] beggars' who lacked class consciousness.[39] Precarity, however, affects more than just a particular class of people or the 'low skilled'—the precarity of casual ('sessional' or 'adjunct') university teachers, often with PhDs, is illustrative of this.[40]

That growth in casualisation since the 1980s should not be seen as the emergence of a new phenomenon. It is better understood as the reemergence of an old phenomenon, reflecting a reversal of the gains workers had achieved in much of the preceding part of the twentieth century. In Australia, for example, casual employment was a dominant feature of working-class employment in the 1870s and 1880s. This reflected the high seasonality of rural and downstream employment, the unpredictability of demand in manufacturing, and employers' ability to pass the costs of these things to employees (while maintaining an ILM for more trusted or important employees and relatives).[41]

39 Karl Marx, *The Eighteenth Brumaire of Louis Bonaparte* (London: The Electric Book Company, 1852; repr., 1998), 78. See also Robert L. Bussard, 'The "Dangerous Class" of Marx and Engels: The Rise of the Idea of the Lumpenproletariat'. *History of European Ideas* 8, no. 6 (2012): 675–92.

40 For example, Robyn May, David Peetz, and Glenda Strachan, 'The Casual Academic Workforce and Labour Market Segmentation in Australia'. *Labour and Industry* 23, no. 3 (2013): 258–75.

41 Jenny Lee and Charles Fahey, 'A Boom for Whom? Some Developments in the Australian Labour Market, 1870–1891'. *Labour History—A Journal of Labour and Social History* 50 (1986): 1–27.

Is risk about job insecurity?

We need to recognise that transferring risk need not be the same thing as making *jobs* insecure. Campbell and Burgess, in a significant review article, refer to precariousness as manifested not only in employment insecurity (including underemployment) but also in earnings insecurity and working-time insecurity (i.e. unpredictability of shifts).[42] Risk can simply be about making the *livelihoods* of workers insecure. If, in relative terms, wages are lowered, and workers are juggling which bill they can afford to not pay in which week, then people's livelihoods are precarious in a way that is not captured by data on the probability of unemployment or the rate of casualisation. Wages growth has slowed in many countries including Australia,[43] and 'in a majority of countries across the world wage growth in recent decades has lagged behind the growth of labour productivity'.[44] Over the past three decades, median real wages in the USA have barely improved,[45] and there an unexpected ill-health event can send even an insured family into penury.[46]

In economics, risk is typically correlated with returns (high risk implies high returns). In recent decades, large firms have shifted the risk component of that equation onto labour, but protected the returns for themselves (and so the labour share of national income has generally declined).[47] So risk transference has been an asymmetrical process that, in order to maintain returns to capital, has imposed greater precarity of livelihoods onto parts of labour than would otherwise occur, at a time when *average* incomes in society have been increasing.

42 Iain Campbell and John Burgess, 'Patchy Progress? Two Decades of Research on Precariousness and Precarious Work in Australia'. *Labour & Industry* 28, no. 1 (2018): 48–67.

43 Andrew Stewart, Jim Stanford, and Tess Hardy, eds, *The Wages Crisis in Australia: What It Is and What to Do About It* (Adelaide: University of Adelaide Press, 2018); Joe Isaac, 'Why Are Australian Wages Lagging and What Can Be Done About It?'. *Australian Economic Review* 51, no. 2 (2018): 175–90.

44 International Labour Office, *Global Wage Report 2016/17* (Geneva: ILO, 2016), xvi.

45 Drew Desilver, 'For Most U.S. Workers, Real Wages Have Barely Budged in Decades'. Fact Tank, Pew Research Center, 7 August 2018, www.pewresearch.org/fact-tank/2018/08/07/for-most-us-workers-real-wages-have-barely-budged-for-decades/.

46 Kimberley Amadeo, 'Medical Bankruptcy and the Economy'. The Balance (financial advisers), 3 February 2019, www.thebalance.com/medical-bankruptcy-statistics-4154729.

47 Jim Stanford, 'The Declining Labour Share in Australia: Definition, Measurement, and International Comparisons'. *Journal of Australian Political Economy* 81 (2018): 11–32; Loukas Karabarbounis and Brent Neiman, 'The Global Decline of the Labor Share'. *Quarterly Journal of Economics* 129, no. 1 (2013): 61–103; David Autor et al., 'Concentrating on the Fall of the Labor Share'. *American Economic Review* 107, no. 5 (2017): 180–85.

The flexible firm

As firm strategy changed again in the 1980s, one model that emerged to explain the new behaviours of corporations was the 'flexible firm' model. This model was principally developed by John Atkinson in the UK.[48] In the flexible firm model, employers seek an optimal balance between functional and numerical flexibility through segmenting the labour force into two groups: the core and periphery groups. The *core* of full-time employees enjoys job security, career development, high wages and are multiskilled. They occupy the primary ILM within the firm. The core group is the principal source of functional flexibility. The *periphery* is the source of numerical flexibility. So, by contrast to core employees, the periphery has job insecurity, poor career options, lower wages and low multiskilling.

The occupation of the employees who might comprise these groups is to some extent influenced by the adoption and uses of technology. For example, blue collar workers might be part of the stable core if the tasks they do require the use of the employee's discretion and judgment (e.g. in small batch production). From earlier, we could expect the core to be associated with high-trust management styles, perhaps structured management, perhaps collectivist approaches. By contrast the periphery would be associated with low-trust styles, more likely individualism, and possibly less structure. That in turn implies management may have different management styles for dealing with different parts of the workforce—something that, as we have seen, indeed happens.

There have been a number of criticisms of the flexible firm model.[49] Some relate to the ways in which employees are categorised. Precarity is not restricted to the group Atkinson describes as the periphery. Legge claims that the flexible firm model suffers from confusion as to whether it is a prescriptive model—considering 'what should be'—or a descriptive model, considering 'what is'.[50] At times, it appears to do both. Yet, if it is prescriptive it shows little evidence of being a conscious strategy.

48 John Atkinson, 'Manpower Strategies for Flexible Organisations'. *Personnel Management* (1984): 28–31; John Atkinson, *Flexibility, Uncertainty and Manpower Management*. IMS Report No. 89 (Brighton, UK: Institute for Manpower Studies, 1985). You may find out more about this model by reading Pollert, 'The Flexible Firm: Fixation or Fact?'. A graphical representation of the model is there at p. 284.

49 See the studies cited in Legge, *Human Resource Management*.

50 Ibid., 154.

Company survey data in the UK suggested that moves to greater numerical flexibility were mainly piecemeal, opportunistic and ad hoc rather than a result of strategic intent.[51] In Australia, casualisation appeared higher in workplaces with 'unstructured' rather than 'structured' management.[52] Internationally, however, 'one place where the core–periphery model undoubtedly has been strategically enacted is in the public services'.[53] If, on the other hand, it is meant as a descriptive model, Legge asks how does it improve on preexisting models of labour market segmentation? In essence, segmentation theorists argue that 'labour markets are characterised by noncompeting groups, and economic, social and political forces combine to differentiate the rewards of comparable groups of workers'.[54]

My concerns are several. The model treats part-time workers as part of the periphery, which is only true for some (mostly those underemployed or on temporary or casual contracts). It fails to explain why, in the face of all this flexibility, the employment relationship persists. It gives inadequate consideration to employer strategy towards employees and what determines that strategy—in particular, the importance for firms of avoiding accountability—and so has limited predictive value. In that sense, it privileges 'flexibility' above all other elements—hardly surprising as that is the focus of so much rhetoric from employers and policy-makers. But why doesn't everyone just use independent contractors? To be fair, though, it is a theoretical model that emerged in the 1980s, so it is hardly surprising that modifications should be required.

'Not there' employment

Even if moves to the flexible firm model were initially piecemeal, ad hoc and opportunistic, its appearance in the literature signalled pressure for some fundamental changes to the way firms organise. More than just reduce risk and cost, however, firms have also sought to achieve 'distancing' through what can be called 'not there' employment—a method of corporate organisation whereby firms can avoid accountability for misbehaviour by affiliates or subsidiaries by denying responsibility: 'We're not there!'. The term 'not there' employment is deliberately ironic: of course workers

51 Ibid., 160.

52 Ron Callus et al., *Industrial Relations at Work: The Australian Workplace Industrial Relations Survey* (Canberra: AGPS, 1991).

53 Legge, *Human Resource Management*, 161.

54 Peter Brosnan, David Rea, and Moira Wilson, 'Labour Market Segmentation and the State: The New Zealand Experience'. *Cambridge Journal of Economics* 19, no. 5 (1995): 667–96.

are experiencing the capitalist employment relationship, so in that sense it is very much 'there'; but it is also a device by which large corporations can say *we* are not there. So it is not necessarily *employment* that is 'not there', it is the *lead corporation*. At least, that is how it is meant to be in the eye of the intended beholder.

As a model of firm behaviour, it has some similarities to the 'flexible firm' model, but focuses less on forms of 'flexibility' and more on capital, accountability and transaction costs. 'Not there' employment facilitates a higher rate of noncompliance with labour laws. It is thus more akin to the process of 'fissuring' that has often been used to describe modern workplaces.[55] The terms 'fractured' and 'fragmented' have also been used.[56] And yet, the employment relationship persists. Many corporations are seeking to make greater use of 'flexible' labour, and engage in 'not there' employment to minimise costs and risk and to avoid responsibility for some of the labour costs they would otherwise incur and possible breaches of the law. They typically contract to others who in turn hire employees (or who subcontract to others, who in turn hire employees). So part of their workforce is 'flexibly' deployed. But they also retain an ILM for their 'core' employees. This bit, then, is what Atkinson referred to as the 'flexible firm' model in the 1980s. The details have changed a bit since then, but the central idea—many firms simultaneously operating an ILM-based core and a periphery participating in an external labour market—remains true.

So 'not there' employment is the process by which centres of capital (we might call these 'lead firms' or 'core capital') fragment what would otherwise be corporate structures in ways that maintain high control, minimise labour costs and risk, maximise centralised profits and minimise accountability for externalities. Thus, 'not there' employment is the key feature of an emerging 'not there' capitalism, in which the concentration of capital within product markets grows.[57]

55 David Weil, *The Fissured Workplace: Why Work Became So Bad for So Many and What Can Be Done to Improve It* (Cambridge: Harvard University Press, 2014).

56 Tony Dundon, 'The Fracturing of Work and Employment Relations'. *Labour and Industry* 29, no. 1 (2019): 6–18.

57 Andrew Leigh and Adam Triggs, 'A Few Big Firms'. *The Monthly*, 17 May 2017; John Van Reenen, 'Research: The Rise of Superstar Firms Has Been Better for Investors Than for Employees'. *Harvard Business Review*, 11 May 2017; Data Team, 'Corporate Concentration'. *Economist*, 24 May 2016; Autor et al., 'Concentrating on the Fall of the Labor Share'.

More precisely, the key methods of 'not there' employment are: control is retained by a central entity (e.g. the 'lead firms' in supply chains); production is undertaken within smaller entities (the 'dependent firms'—we might call them 'peripheral capital'), which are formally separated from the lead firms; core and dependent firms are linked by contract; and labour is ostensibly and directly controlled by the peripheral capital in dependent firms. That labour may be classed as 'employees' or as 'contractors', according to the context. Fundamentally, though, the employment relationship—hence 'not there' *employment*—persists, despite all the fissuring pressures.

The manifestations of this phenomenon vary between sectors and industries. In the public sector, the urge to minimise accountability is manifested as privatisation, or contractual relationships (such as 'public–private partnerships') made opaque through contracts that are 'commercial in confidence'. In the private sector, variations between industries may occur according to the nature of the product in that industry, the degree of competition, the share of costs represented by labour costs, the geographic scale of production, the nature of labour and labour organisation including exposure to secondary labour markets, occupational norms and the ideology and strategy of employers, among other factors. If there is one major difference with the casualised employment of the late nineteenth century that we saw, it is this: whereas at that time much peripheral labour was directly hired by the responsible employer,[58] under 'not there' employment a growing part of the responsibility for hiring peripheral labour rests with dependent firms or peripheral capital.

What determines the activities that are done 'in-house' and those that are 'not there'—undertaken in franchises, contractor firms or some other form of peripheral capital? Transaction cost economics, a form of institutional economics associated with writers such as Coase and Williamson, suggests that the transaction costs (including supervision costs) of having work done determine whether it is done in-house or by 'the market'.[59] This, correctly, puts the emphasis on control. As Gramsci said, 'discipline and a good state of production is only possible if there exists at least a minimum of

58 Lee and Fahey, 'Boom for Whom?'.

59 Ronald Coase, 'The Nature of the Firm'. *Economica* 4 (1937): 386–405; Ronald Coase, 'New Institutional Economics'. *American Economic Review* 88, no. 2 (1998): 72–74; Oliver E. Williamson, *Markets and Hierarchies: Analysis and Antitrust Implications* (New York: Free Press, 1975); Oliver E. Williamson, *Institutions of Capitalism* (New York: Free Press, 1985).

constitutionality, a minimum of consent on the part of the workforce'.[60] An aspect of this is being able to deliver, cheaply, products or services that might otherwise be considered too expensive: getting a product to a customer in time, or having a service available at an abnormal time.[61] In addition, the desire to minimise risk and to avoid accountability (to minimise the *appearance* of control) are also factors in deciding whether to internalise or externalise particular aspects of production. In effect, each corporation makes an assessment of whether the combination of these factors—cost, control, risk and accountability—makes internal or external production more attractive. Some of these things lend themselves to calculation more than others. Cost is the simplest thing to express as dollars while, at the other extreme, the benefits or disadvantages of minimising accountability may be very difficult to express as dollars, and so judgements about that (expressed as 'sticking to our core business') may be taken at a higher level in the organisation.

The employment relationship and the future

The rise of the 'gig economy', discussed in more detail below, has raised a debate about whether the employment relationship has a future at all. Yet despite all the predictions of the 'death of employment' (including a 2008 book by that title),[62] it has not happened and most likely will not happen.

The meme that the employment relationship is dying may be seen in a few ideas, not just the emergence of 'not there' employment. The first is the idea that, instead of the employment relationship, we are witnessing the rise of 'freelancing' or the 'gig economy' as workers become self-employed and contractors instead of employees. Second is the idea that workers will not want to stay with organisations any more—they want not one career, but lots of careers, even 'boundary-less careers' or 'portfolio careers'. The third one is the idea that firm size is decreasing, and large firms are no longer as important as they used to be.

60 Antonio Gramsci, *La Construzione Del Partito Comunista 1923–1926* (Turin: Einaudi, 1971), 6. Translated and cited in Anne Showstack Sassoon, ed., *Approaches to Gramsci* (London: Writers and Readers Publishing Cooperative Society, 1982), 103.

61 The extent to which consumer demands for timely delivery influence outsourcing in Australian road transport is presently being investigated by Kaylee Boccalatte.

62 Ken Phillips, *Independence and the Death of Employment* (Ballan, Vic.: Connor Court Publishing, 2008).

These ideas are clearly interrelated. They are also mostly either exaggerated or plain wrong. I address them in reverse order.

First, evidence shows that firm size is not decreasing.[63] Nor is workplace size declining structurally. Such measures vary with the state of the business cycle (a more prosperous economy means bigger businesses, on average), but there is not a clear long-term trend.

Second, while the employer demand for increased 'flexibility' is genuinely 'a thing', self-employment, by contrast, is not growing. Table 6.1, using OECD data, shows self-employment declining between 2000 and 2014 in 26 countries for which data were available, and increasing in only 11. Across those 37 countries, the unweighted average rate of self-employment fell by 2.2 percentage points over the period. Across the OECD (a smaller grouping), the weighted average rate of self-employment fell by 1.9 percentage points between 2000 and 2011. The death of employment is an international myth without international substance.

The mythology of the 'portfolio' career, as if workers like to be shunted from industry to industry over their lifetime, hides the likelihood that workers are more insecure than before. Some, of course, may prefer changes of career, but for others career changes are a euphemism that is forced upon them by the impermanency of work.

Table 6.1: Percentage change in self-employment, 37 countries, 2000–14

	Self-employment share		
	2000	2014	Change, 2000–2014
Turkey	51.4	34 .0	–17.4
Korea	36.8	26.8	–10.1
Greece	42.0	35.4	–6.5
Portugal	26.1	19.9	–6.3
Poland	27.4	21.4	–6.0
Iceland	18	12.5	–5.4
New Zealand	20.6	15.3	–5.4
Japan	16.6	11.5*	–5.1

63 See, for example, Stefan Hajkowicz et al., *Tomorrow's Digitally Enabled Workforce: Megatrends and Scenarios for Jobs and Employment in Australia over the Coming Twenty Years* (Brisbane: CSIRO, 2016), 41, Figures 14 & 15. The figures show declining shares of small business, even though the accompanying text suggests the opposite.

	Self-employment share		
	2000	2014	Change, 2000–2014
Brazil	37.1#	32.3	–4.8
Hungary	15.2	11.0	–4.2
Chile	29.8	25.9	–4.0
Mexico	36	32.1	–3.9
Italy	28.5	24.9	–3.5
Australia	13.5	10.2	–3.3
Switzerland	13.2	10.0	–3.2
Russia	10.1	7.2	–2.9
Spain	20.2	17.7	–2.5
Canada	10.6	8.8	–1.9
Israel	14.2	12.5	–1.7
Ireland	18.8	17.4	–1.4
Belgium	15.8	14.6	–1.2
Luxembourg	7.4	6.2	–1.2
USA	7.4	6.5	–1.0
Norway	7.4	7.2	–0.2
Columbia	51.8#	51.8	–0.1
Denmark	9.1	9.0*	–0.1
Germany	11.0	11.0	0.0
Sweden	10.3	10.3	0.0
Austria	13.3	13.3	0.1
Estonia	8.8	9.1	0.4
Finland	13.7	14.1	0.4
France	9.3	9.7*	0.4
Slovenia	16.1	18.6	2.5
Great Britain	12.8	15.4	2.6
Czech Republic	15.2	18.1	2.9
Netherlands	11.2	15.9*	4.7
Slovakia	8	15.4	7.4
Unweighted average (all)	19.3	17.1	–2.2
OECD average	17.7	15.8**	–1.9

Notes: * 2013 ** 2011 # 2001

Source: OECD database accessed 23 August 2016. The 3-digit country codes can be found at www.iban.com/country-codes.

Globally, only about half of all employed people are employees. That's mostly because, in developing countries, a lot of work is in the 'informal' sector outside the scope of employment regulation. In sub-Saharan Africa and South Asia, only about one in five employed people are employees earning a wage or salary. This is nothing new. As countries become more industrialised, the informal sector declines and the use of the employment model grows, as capitalism organises production through employees and the need for control of workers grows.

So there is another paradox: the rise of new models like Uber, with its use of contract labour rather than employees, exists side by side with the continuing importance of employment. That paradox is explained by two things: the resistance of employees to greater insecurity; and the ongoing efficiency of employment as a means to control worker behaviour, alongside the ongoing urge of capital to cut costs.

The first of these has already been discussed. The second warrants elaboration. The employment contract is open-ended, and it is impossible to put into it every aspect of what an employee must do. That problem is multiplied many times over when you move from an employment contract to a contract for service.

Contracting is a way of reducing costs and risk, increasing profits and avoiding accountability, but it is not effective for maintaining control, so firms may use a combination that involves contracting out to others (I call them 'mid contractors') that in turn often (not always) hire employees.

For most owners of capital, and for most CEOs, the corporation is the most efficient form of economic organisation and it most efficiently operates through employing people. This is fundamentally because the transaction costs in controlling workers through an employment relationship are lower than the transaction costs of alternatives, such as drawing up and implementing contracts with them as independent contractors. So, for example, a firm can more closely supervise employees than contractors, it can manage uncertainty better, it can minimise the risk of opportunistic behaviour, and it need not waste time and money renegotiating contracts with them when they turn up for work each day. In *The Circle*, Mae is an employee, even though her job (the equivalent of an Instagram 'influencer' of the 2010s) is in effect held by the self-employed at present; she is an employee of The Circle because that is how best the company can exercise control over her.

Even when firms contract out part of their operations, the people who end up doing the work are often still employees, because that is the most efficient way for a firm to run its business. For example, when a mining company gets what are known in the industry as 'contractors' in to work in a mine, they are usually employees of a contracting firm, that supplies just the workers (a 'labour hire' firm) or both workers and equipment. They work on the mine site, but are employees—hired on a casual basis and at much lower cost to the mines.

Through global value chains, an organisation can control a very large number of workers, while having very few as employees within its own organisations. The rest may be employees in contracting forms. In 2013, over 700,000 people were part of Apple's global value chain, but only 80,000 of them were employed directly by Apple itself.[64]

Another, growing, example is franchises: a large organisation like 7-Eleven or McDonald's may contract out business to many franchisees, but they in turn hire employees to work in the stores. Franchising is a way by which the owners of capital (at the top or peak of the hierarchy) contract out to 'franchisees' who run the outlets (fast food, retail, etc.) rather than the large firms running the outlets themselves. But most of the people who work in the outlets are employees—of the franchisees, rather than the capital at the top of the hierarchy.

The franchisors still control the product, but franchisees have responsibility for employment. The franchisees are also small businesses, and so less likely to comply with labour regulations than large firms.[65] Hence the franchisors gain the financial benefit from franchisees' low-cost way of operating. This model cuts costs and transfers risk down the chain—

64 Direct employment estimate from Bloomberg, quoted in Ricarda McFalls, *The Impact of Procurement Practices in the Electronics Sector on Labour Rights and Temporary and Other Forms of Employment*, (Geneva: International Labour Office, Working Paper WP313, 2016). Global value chain data implied from a statement by Tim Cook, Apple CEO, on a 2014 BBC *Panorama* program quoted in Thomas Clarke and Martijn Boersma, 'The Governance of Global Value Chains: Unresolved Human Rights, Environmental and Ethical Dilemmas in the Apple Supply Chain'. *Journal of Business Ethics* 143 (2017): 111–31.

65 Weil, *The Fissured Workplace*. Haroon Bhorat, Ravi Kanbur and Natasha Mayet, 'Estimating the Causal Effect of Enforcement on Minimum Wage Compliance: The Case of South Africa'. *Review of Development Economics* 16, no. 4 (2012): 608–23; Tim H. Gindling and Katherine Terrell, 'Minimum Wages, Globalization, and Poverty in Honduras'. *World Development* 38, no. 6 (2010): 908–18; Eric Strobl and Frank Walsh, 'Minimum Wages and Compliance: The Case of Trinidad and Tobago'. *Economic Development and Cultural Change* 51, no. 2 (2003): 427–50; Jeremy Buultjens, 'Labour Market Deregulation: Does Small Business Care?'. *International Journal of Employment Studies* 2, no. 1 (1994): 132–57.

which means jobs, or at least personal finances, are more insecure, and the opportunities for underpayment of workers (discussed in Chapter 10) are increased. Franchising has been growing in importance, and employment in franchisees as a share of total employment has likewise grown.[66]

Many organisations have sought to adopt the Uber platform model. I discuss that shortly. Others firms have tried to turn employees into faux 'independent contractors' (such as at Kemalex, in Australia, a few years ago) to avoid paying leave, superannuation and workers' compensation. Workers and unions have resisted this 'sham contracting'.[67] Most employees do not actually want to be contractors. Like employers, they prefer the stability of the employment relationship.

Meanwhile, a lot of the people who end up as the 'mid contractors' are probably people who would otherwise have been small-business owners or self-employed anyway. Circumstances differ between industries. For example, people who love trucks might buy one. They will then become owner-drivers—and sit at the bottom of the road transport industry supply chain. In the textiles, clothing and footwear industries, workers were forced to be contractors ('homeworkers') and as recently as a decade ago worked in Australia for pay averaging as little as $6 per hour with some receiving half that or less.[68]

That has been the pattern in those industries for a long time. Most new manifestations of 'not there' employment take one of two forms. In most industries new forms of 'not there' employment continue to ultimately rely on employees. In some, though—mostly associated with the 'platform economy'—core capital contracts to people, many of whom would have been self-employed anyway or, like many Uber drivers, have a 'main' job as an employee.[69] The sources of worker insecurity vary between industries, and a lot of variation between industries and periods

66 Lorelle Frazer, Scott Weaven, and Anthony Grace, *Franchising Australia 2014* (Brisbane: Griffith University, 2014).

67 Anthony O'Donnell, 'Reality Bites for Bosses of Nothing'. *Age*, 29 September 2005, www.theage.com.au/news/business/reality-bites-for-bosses-of-nothing/2005/09/28/1127804547436.html.

68 Mindy Thorpe, 'Outworkers'. In *Pay Equity in Queensland*, ed. David Peetz and Rosemary Hunter (Brisbane: Centre for Research on Employment and Work and Socio Legal Research Centre, Report to Department of Employment, Training and Industrial Relations, Queensland Government Submission, Pay Equity Inquiry, Queensland Industrial Relations Commission, No. B1568 of 2000), 99–114; Emer Diviney and Serena Lillywhite, *Ethical Threads: Corporate Social Responsibility in the Australian Garment Industry* (Melbourne: Brotherhood of St Laurence, 2007), 4.

69 Justin Fox, 'Your Uber Driver Probably Has Another Job'. *Bloomberg*, 20 February 2016, www.bloomberg.com/view/articles/2016-02-20/your-uber-driver-probably-has-another-job.

can be hidden by national aggregates. Franchising has grown in retailing; labour hire in mining; outsourcing in the public sector; second jobs in manufacturing; spinoffs in communications; casualisation in education and training; and global supply chains send jobs internationally to low-paid, often dangerous workplaces in a number of industries.

Even 'casual' or 'permanent' employment status (as proxied by access to paid leave) can be an inadequate indicator of worker insecurity. Employees at the bottom of the chain in many of these industries might have access to annual leave and sick leave. Offering leave is better for attracting labour and might be cheaper than paying the casual loading. There is also no need to hire someone on a casual contract if you can make them redundant when the work dries up—if, for example, you lose your contract with the main firm. If your firm can go bankrupt, then you often will not even have to pay redundancy benefits.

Other sources of worker insecurity might arise from weaknesses in the operation of labour-market institutions. In Australia, for example, firms have discovered they can terminate collective agreements, or get a handful of workers to sign new agreements that then apply to everyone, as a means of cutting pay and conditions.[70] Some firms put employees onto contrived arrangements that make them out to be contractors, often illegally.[71] The growing insecurity of workers, including through underemployment, and the concentration of economic power help explain why wage growth has been stagnating. Indeed, with wage growth low across most developed countries, that successful 'war on wages' may be the biggest single sign of worker insecurity.[72]

70 Josh Butler, 'Streets Look to Cut Workers Pay and Ice-Cream Fans Are Furious'. *Huffington Post*, 29 August 2017, www.huffingtonpost.com.au/2017/08/29/streets-look-to-cut-workers-pay-and-ice-cream-fans-are-furious_a_23187395/; Emma Field, 'Hundreds Rally in Gippsland at Longest Industrial Dispute in 40 Years'. *ABC News Online*, Australian Broadcasting Corporation, 28 June 2018, www.abc.net.au/news/2018-06-28/esso-protest-marks-12-months-with-union-gathering-at-longford/9918668.

71 'Factory Workers Strike over Contract Plan'. *The Age*, 3 May 2005, www.theage.com.au/national/factory-workers-strike-over-contract-plan-20050503-ge0344.html; Australian Government, 'Unfair Contracts and Sham Contracts' (Department of Innovation, Industry and Science, 2018), www.business.gov.au/people/contractors/independent-contractors/unfair-contracts-and-sham-contracts.

72 Mike Seccombe, 'The Truth About Wage Stagnation'. *Saturday Paper*, 12 May 2018, www.thesaturdaypaper.com.au/news/economy/2018/05/12/the-truth-about-wage-stagnation/15260472006221; Anna Patty, 'War on Wages: Australians Are Working Harder and Going Backwards'. *Sydney Morning Herald*, 5 August 2018, www.smh.com.au/business/workplace/war-on-wages-australians-are-working-harder-and-going-backwards-20170803-gxoh9c.html.

The 'platform' or 'gig' economy

Technology is often seen as fundamentally changing workplace relations through the 'platform economy', the 'gig economy' or 'freelancing'. These terms are often used interchangeably, as if to indicate that the growth of the gig economy is synonymous with 'freelancing'. The term 'freelancing' is used very loosely and often in multiple ways, and so some large estimates of the freelancing workforce are made. For example, the Freelancers Union, a lobby group (not a trade union) in whose interest it is to maximise the number of 'freelancers', defined them as including employees who at any time in the previous year had held a fixed-term job or a second job as a contractor, and so it claimed that freelancers made up 34 per cent of the US workforce.[73] Using a different definition, Kitching estimated freelancers at just 6 per cent of the UK workforce.[74] 'Freelancer' is such a poorly defined concept that we do not use it in the remainder of this chapter.

To get a clearer understanding of the platform economy, also known as the gig economy, we turn to Valerio De Stefano:

> The gig-economy is usually understood to include chiefly two forms of work: 'crowdwork' and 'work on-demand via apps' … The first term is usually referred to [sic] working activities that imply completing a series of tasks through online platforms … 'Work on-demand via apps', instead, is a form of work in which the execution of traditional working activities such as transport, cleaning and running errands, but also forms of clerical work, is channelled through apps managed by firms that also intervene in setting minimum quality standards of service and in the selection and management of the workforce.[75]

73 Freelancers Union and Elance-oDesk, *Freelancing in America: A National Survey of the New Workforce* (2013).

74 John Kitching, *Exploring the UK Freelance Workforce in 2015* (London: Association of Independent Professionals and the Self-Employed, 2016); Kitching's data indicate that the estimate would more than double if a broader occupational definition of freelancers were used.

75 Valerio De Stefano, *The Rise of the 'Just-in-Time Workforce': On-Demand Work, Crowdwork and Labour Protection in the 'Gig-Economy'*. Conditions of Work and Employment Series No. 71 (Geneva: International Labour Office, 2016), 1.

Platforms involve many workers. Uber, for example, has a global workforce of around 160,000; its US competitor Lyft has 50,000. Amazon Mechanical Turk (AMT) mediates crowdwork for up to 500,000 people internationally and Crowdflower 10 times that number.[76]

Still, this is only a small portion of the overall workforce. In the UK, the estimates of platform economy work are fairly consistent, probably reflecting similarities in data methods. The UK Chartered Institute of Personnel and Development (CIPD), drawing on its own online survey of 5,000 adults in December 2016, estimated 4 per cent of adults had been 'gig workers' at some time in the previous 12 months.[77] An online survey for the UK Department for Business, Energy & Industrial Strategy (BEIS) estimated that 4.4 per cent *of the population* in Great Britain had worked in the gig economy in the preceding 12 months.[78] Of those, just slightly under one-third provided services this way at least once a week. That is, roughly 1 per cent of British workers regularly participated in the platform economy.

American estimates are more variable. An August 2016 online survey by the Pew Research Center of 4,500 adults in the US found only 8 per cent of adults had used digital work or task platforms in the previous year.[79] It appeared to pick up especially more crowdworkers than the UK surveys. A more indirect estimate, by J.P. Morgan based on money transfers, put the number much lower: a cumulative 0.9 per cent of US adults had ever participated in the gig economy according to it.[80] US economists Lawrence Katz and Alan Krueger, based on 2015 data from an official labour force survey, estimated only 0.5 per cent of US workers had identified customers through an online intermediary, and noted this was close to two other, independently derived estimates.[81]

76 Ibid.

77 Chartered Institute of Personnel and Development, *To Gig or Not to Gig? Stories from the Modern Economy* (London: CIPD, March 2017).

78 Katriina Lepanjuuri, Robert Wishart, and Peter Cornick, *The Characteristics of Those in the Gig Economy* (London: Department for Business, Energy & Industrial Strategy, 2018).

79 Aaron Smith, *Gig Work, Online Selling and Home Sharing* (Pew Research Center, 17 November 2016).

80 Diana Farrell and Fiona Greig, *The Online Platform Economy: Has Growth Peaked?* (New York: JPMorgan Chase Institute November 2016).

81 Lawrence F. Katz and Alan B. Krueger, *The Rise and Nature of Alternative Work Arrangements in the United States, 1995–2015*. NBER Working Paper No. 22667 (Washington DC: National Bureau of Economic Research, September 2016), www.nber.org/papers/w22667.

Another study (not aimed at estimating its penetration) was undertaken by the ILO in 2016 and involved surveying 1,800 workers in Crowdflower and AMT.

It is likely that online surveys, by their nature, will overestimate the incidence of 'platform economy' workers relying on online apps, potentially by quite a bit, but that alone does not account for the discrepancies between estimates. Question wording also matters. Another important factor in interpreting these estimates is time-related: at any single point in time, only a small number of people will be employed in the gig economy, but a much larger number of people will have worked in it at some time over the previous year to supplement otherwise low incomes, sometimes only once and with minimal effect. There may be international differences, but it seems likely that 1 per cent or less of the workforce is regularly part of the platform economy in developed countries, many others dip their toes into it and then take them out again, the numbers are likely growing, but they are presently exceeded by the numbers of contractors and comparable workers who do not rely on apps for their work.

Despite its limited size, the 'platform' economy is a major area where digital technology has allowed a new form of work organisation to develop. There are many stories, ranging from exciting to horrifying, about work in the gig economy.[82] Some of the key points about the 'gig' economy from the above research and another ILO study[83] are as follows.

The use of digital work or task platforms is more common among younger workers. In the Pew survey, 17 per cent of 18–29 year olds, compared to 10 per cent of 30–49 year olds and just 4 per cent of 50–64 year olds, had earned money through digital work or task platforms.[84]

82 For example, Chartered Institute of Personnel and Development, *To Gig*; Steven Hill, 'Good Riddance, Gig Economy: Uber, Ayn Rand and the Awesome Collapse of Silicon Valley's Dream of Destroying Your Job'. *Salon*, 28 March 2016, www.salon.com/2016/03/27/good_riddance_gig_economy_uber_ayn_rand_and_the_awesome_collapse_of_silicon_valleys_dream_of_destroying_your_job/; A.J. Wood et al., 'Good Gig, Bad Gig: Autonomy and Algorithmic Control in the Global Gig Economy'. *Work, Employment and Society* 33, no. 1 (2018): 56–75.

83 This was undertaken by the ILO in 2016 and involved surveying 1,800 workers in Crowdflower and AMT. Janine Berg, *Income Security in the on-Demand Economy: Findings and Policy Lessons from a Survey of Crowdworkers* (Geneva: Inclusive Labour Markets, Labour Relations and Working Conditions Branch, International Labour Office, 2016).

84 Smith, *Gig Work*.

The use of digital work or task platforms is more common among lower income earners. In the Pew survey, the proportions of adults who had earned money through digital work or task platforms were 10 per cent in households with annual income less than $30,000, compared to 8 per cent with income of $30,000–$75,000 and 4 per cent in households with incomes above $75,000.[85] The incidence was also higher among blacks (14 per cent) and Latinos (11 per cent) than whites (5 per cent), and lower among those who had college (university) qualifications (6 per cent) than those with lower qualifications (9 per cent).

'Gig economy' work provides essential income for a minority of participants. In the CIPD survey, only 25 per cent of 'gig' workers said it was their main job.[86] In the Pew survey, 29 per cent of platform workers said that the income they earned from it was essential for meeting basic household needs, while 27 per cent said it was 'important' and 42 per cent 'nice to have, but not essential'.[87] In the BEIS survey, only 14 per cent of gig workers earned half or more of their total income from gig work.[88]

Many gig-economy workers have other jobs. In the CIPD survey, 58 per cent of gig-economy workers with other jobs had permanent jobs (compared to 78 per cent in the population at large). Only a minority (20 per cent) were self-employed.[89] Another survey by the ILO confirmed that the otherwise self-employed were only a minority of 'gig' workers, and only a minority had been running a business before taking up 'gig' economy work.[90]

A majority of 'gig' workers are chronically underemployed. In the CIPD survey, only 26 per cent said that, overall, they got enough work on a regular basis in the gig economy.[91] In the ILO survey, the most common reason given, when respondents were asked why they were not doing more crowdwork (or non-crowdwork), was that there isn't enough work.[92]

85 Ibid.
86 Chartered Institute of Personnel and Development, *To Gig.*
87 Smith, *Gig Work.*
88 Lepanjuuri, Wishart, and Cornick, *Characteristics.*
89 Chartered Institute of Personnel and Development, *To Gig.*
90 Berg, *Income Security.*
91 Chartered Institute of Personnel and Development, *To Gig.*
92 Berg, *Income Security.*

Expressed as an hourly rate, pay in the gig economy is low and often below minimum wages. In the CIPD survey, median earnings for transport or delivery was £6 per hour, and for short-term jobs was £7 per hour, below the then living wage of £7.20 per hour and the minimum wage for 21–24 year olds of £6.95 per hour.[93] In the BIES survey, only 36 per cent of those who disclosed earnings received less than £7.50 per hour but 85 per cent of those who were involved in gig work from one to three times a week in the gig economy had earned less than £5,000 from their work in the preceding 12 months.[94] In the ILO survey, median pay for AMT workers was US$4.65 per hour, well below the minimum wage.[95] A separate analysis of 3.8 million tasks on AMT found that the median pay was closer to US$2 per hour, much less than requestors paid, due in part to time between tasks (e.g. time spent searching for tasks) and tasks 'returned' (not completed, perhaps because the requestor's description was inaccurate).[96] In Australia, Unions NSW calculated that rates received via Airtasker for data entry, cleaning and sales were between AU$3 and AU$9 below the relevant minimum award rates.[97] Hence the Twitter user named 'Fair Gig for all' tweeted on a regular basis about vacancies on Airtasker for jobs paying below the minimum wage.[98]

Although platform economy workers are doing it tough, they also seem surprisingly optimistic, perhaps reflecting an optimism bias identified by Kahneman,[99] related to 'adaptive preferences'.[100] In the CIPD survey, only 49 per cent of 'gig workers' (compared to 56 per cent of other workers) said they were 'living comfortably' or 'doing alright'. However, 46 per cent of platform workers (compared to 26 per cent of other workers) expected their economic situation to improve over the coming year. And while only 57 per cent of platform workers (compared to 67 per cent of other workers) were saving for retirement through a pension plan,

93 Chartered Institute of Personnel and Development, *To Gig.*

94 Lepanjuuri, Wishart, and Cornick, *Characteristics.*

95 Berg, *Income Security.*

96 Kotaro Hara, Abi Adams, Kristy Milland, Saiph Savage, Chris Callison-Burch and Jeffrey P. Bigham, 'A Data-Driven Analysis of Workers' Earnings on Amazon Mechanical Turk', paper presented to CHI 2018 conference, Montreal, 21–26 April 2018, arxiv.org/pdf/1712.05796.pdf.

97 Unions NSW, *Innovation or Exploitation: Busting the Airtasker Myth* (Sydney: Unions NSW, 2016).

98 twitter.com/FairGigForAll.

99 Kahneman, *Thinking, Fast and Slow.*

100 Steven Lukes, *Power: A Radical View*, 2nd ed. (London: Palgrave, 2005), 124.

fully 33 per cent of platform workers (compared to 21 per cent of other workers) were confident they could live comfortably when they stopped working.[101]

Platform economy workers did not think highly of their training opportunities. Nor did their thoughts readily turn to trade unions when asked to whom they would take complaints.[102] For some 'platform economy' workers, like Uber drivers or their equivalent in other industries, who have a main job elsewhere, their attachment to work may be low and their willingness to organise resistance to their conditions of employment may be low. But for those who are reliant on gig-economy earnings as their sole source of income, their responses to attempts to organise to improve conditions of employment may be quite different. There are many media reports of such workers taking collective action, sometimes strike action, in support of improvements in pay or conditions, and some instances where they have won treatment equivalent to that of employees.[103] The whole idea of them being independent contractors, not employees, has been challenged in several jurisdictions, sometimes successfully,[104] and sometimes not (e.g. in Australia).[105] Uber says it is not a transport

101 Chartered Institute of Personnel and Development, *To Gig*.

102 Ibid.

103 Caroline O'Donovan, 'Uber Rallies Drivers against Teamster Unionization Efforts with Podcasts and Pizza Parties'. *Buzzfeed News*, 10 March 2017; Kate Minter, 'Negotiating Labour Standards in the Gig Economy: Airtasker and Unions New South Wales'. *Economic and Labour Relations Review* 28, no. 3 (2017): 438–54; Anna Sansom, 'Bicycle Couriers Protest against Takeaway Food Service Deliveroo'. *France24*, 12 August 2017, www.france24.com/en/20170812-france-paris-protest-food-delivery-service-deliveroo-financial-insecurity-emmanuel-macron; Zachary Kilhoffer, Karolien Lenaerts, and Miroslav Beblavý, *The Platform Economy and Industrial Relations: Applying the Old Framework to the New Reality*. CEPS Report No. 2017/12 (Brussels: Centre for European Policy Studies, 2017); Rebecca Burns, 'The Sharing Economy's "First Strike": Uber Drivers Turn Off the App'. *In These Times*, 22 October 2014, inthesetimes.com/working/entry/17279/the_sharing_economy_first_strike_uber_drivers_turn_off_the_app; Alison Griswold, 'Uber Just Caved on a Big Policy Change after Its Drivers Threatened to Strike'. *Slate*, 12 September 2014, www.slate.com/blogs/moneybox/2014/09/12/uber_drivers_strike_they_protested_cheap_uberx_fares_uber_backed_down.html; Adam Carey, 'Uber Strike: Group Calls for Drivers to "Log Off" in One-Day Protest over Pay and Conditions'. *The Age*, 12 March 2017.

104 BBC, 'Bike Courier Wins "Gig" Economy Employment Rights Case'. *BBC News*, 7 January 2017; Jamie Grierson and Rob Davies, 'Pimlico Plumbers Loses Appeal against Self-employed Status'. *Guardian*, 11 February 2017; Gregor Gall, 'Is Uber Ruling the Beginning of the End for Bogus Self-Employment?'. *The Conversation*, 5 November 2016.

105 'Uber Employee Question Not Settled: Expert', *Workplace Express*, 9 February 2018, www.workplaceexpress.com.au/nl06_news_selected.php?act=2&stream=1&selkey=56469 (subscription required), referring to [2017] FWC 6610 (21 December 2017).

company, it is a technology company, acting as a client to drivers, but it is clearly in competition with transport companies and celebrates providing that competition.[106]

There have been reports of a new labour-hire app called 'Squaddle', described as the 'Uber of hospitality.' This app allows 'contractors' to bid for work at restaurants and bars to fill last-minute staffing gaps.[107] Many firms are trying this approach, and app developers see it as a way of making lots of money. Platform firms both supply and discipline low-paid blue-collar contractors, for use by warehouses or other corporations, much like the day labour of the past.[108] They may even pretend to represent the interests of those contractors by compulsorily enrolling them as members in associations in which they have no voting rights.[109] It is a model that has already spread to many industries and occupations and that will likely find its way into almost any area of work that lends itself to casual employment or contracting, including some where those modes of employment have not been used before—because it provides for a new mechanism of control that partially takes the place of the employment relationship in exercising control, especially through the 'rating' functionality. That said, many US firms following the Uber model—like Cherry (car washes), Prim (laundry), SnapGoods (gear rental), Rewinery (wine) and HomeJoy (home cleaning)—have failed. One author argues, 'they provide crummy jobs that most people only want to do as a very last resort. These platforms show their workforce no allegiance or loyalty, and they engender none in return'.[110]

---

106 Jenna Castle, 'UberX vs Taxi—Which Is Best?'. *Choice*, Australian Consumers Association, 14 August 2017, www.choice.com.au/transport/cars/general/articles/uberx-vs-taxi-which-one-is-best; Stephen Corby, 'Uber vs Taxi'. *CarsGuide*, 31 October 2017, www.carsguide.com.au/car-news/taxi-vs-uber-30943; Caspar, 'Sydneysiders Have Spoken—and They Choose Ridesharing!'. Uber Newsroom, Uber, 10 October 2015, www.uber.com/en-AU/newsroom/sydney-has-spoken/.

107 Charlie Lewis, 'What Does the Gig Economy Do to Workers' Rights?'. *Crikey*, 13 April 2017; Laura Gartry, '"Uber for Hospitality" App Hopes to Shake up on-Demand Job Market'. *ABC News*, Australian Broadcasting Corporation, 6 April 2017, www.abc.net.au/news/2017-04-06/uber-for-hospitality-app-connects-workers/8419530.

108 Venee Dubal, 'The Digitalisation of Day Labor as Gig Work', *OnLabor*, 7 May 2019, onlabor.org/the-digitalization-of-day-labor-as-gig-work/.

109 Ibid.

110 Hill, 'Good Riddance'.

In effect, there is a major labour supply problem that many of these firms have been unable to reconcile. Uber itself has never made a profit. Despite the low wages, and frequent law-breaking,[111] its prices are too low, and its financiers are waiting for a return on their investment. It might appear that it aims to drive competitors (taxis) out of business and grow its market share and prices over the long run. Yet, if it does that, other platform-based ride services (such as Lyft) would step in and out-compete it. Perhaps it is hoping to hold on until driverless cars are available, in which case it would no longer have to worry about payments to drivers, but unless it hires those cars from owners it would face huge capital costs that it has so far avoided. Its hopes likely extend beyond driverless cars.

The biggest challenge to the employment relationship is in the 'platform economy'. This is because virtual platforms provide a new, cheap way of control that may replace the need for the employment relationship. It is not only the availability of electronic control and surveillance that makes this possible. It is also that the rating systems in many platforms minimise the costs of monitoring quality. Not only does the platform reduce the need for an employment relationship, it also reduces the need for intermediate or peripheral capital to organise labour on behalf of core capital.

However, there are still limits to the use of cost cutting and of platform control. The gig economy will grow, but it will not overtake the employment relationship.

Conclusions

Flexibility is not a concept restricted to the gig economy and has been important in work for over three decades. The language of flexibility, we have seen, is value laden. The platform (or 'gig') economy is a major area where digital technology has allowed a new form of work organisation to develop. It is an area of heightened flexibility by labour, income insecurity, minimal employee control, and barriers to labour organisation.

111 Benjamin Edelman. 'Uber Can't Be Fixed — It's Time for Regulators to Shut It Down'. *Harvard Business Review*, 21 June 2017, hbr.org/2017/06/uber-cant-be-fixed-its-time-for-regulators-to-shut-it-down.

The emergence of a new phase of capitalism, featuring 'not there' employment, signals some major challenges to labour and to regulators. But it does not signal the demise of the employment relationship and its replacement by a horde of freelancers. This is because cores of capital want to minimise costs and accountability, but they do not wish to minimise control. Their share of product markets increases. The paradox of the rise of new 'gig economy' models like Uber, and the continuing importance of employment, is explained by the ongoing efficiency of employment as a means to control worker behaviour, alongside the ongoing urge of capital to cut costs. The employment contract is open-ended, and it is impossible to put into it every aspect of what an employee must do. Contracting is a way of reducing costs and risk, increasing profits and avoiding accountability, but it is not effective for maintaining control. The contradiction discussed here is at the heart of 'not there' employment and its resolution plays out differently in different industries, but in the end the employment relationship provides a form of control that no other contractual relationship can achieve. Even when critical activities are outsourced to peripheral capital, the labour used by peripheral capital is often (not always) kept under control through the employment relationship, because this enables peripheral capital to control labour (and to minimise labour turnover costs) in the way it needs, to meet its obligations to core capital. The platform economy reduces the need for peripheral capital as an intermediary between core capital and labour.

7

Worker voice and collectivism

Out of Google offices around the world, at 11.10 am on 1 November 2018, poured 20,000 workers. They were walking off the job, most directly about the way the company was seen as having protected three senior employees accused of sexual harassment, but if you looked deeper you also saw complaints about pay discrimination, lack of transparency, racism and the treatment of contract workers.[1] That protection, it gradually transpired, included providing two of the controversial executives with exit packages worth a total of US$135 million (approximately AU$200 million).[2] The walkout was astonishing to many because Google, one of the largest tech companies in the world, was also notably nonunion. 'Google Walkout for Real Change' does not call itself a union, but its activists behave as if it is.[3] Google, meanwhile, tried to suppress collective organisation within the corporation, much as many nonunion employers had done.[4] The dispute continues, and since then its organisers have

1 Shirin Ghaffary and Eric Johnson, 'After 20,000 Workers Walked out, Google Said It Got the Message. The Workers Disagree'. *Recode*, 21 November 2018, www.recode.net/2018/11/21/18105719/google-walkout-real-change-organizers-protest-discrimination-kara-swisher-recode-decode-podcast.

2 Daisuke Wakabayashi and Katie Benner, 'How Google Has Protected Its Elite Men'. *New York Times*, 25 October 2018; Bryan Menegus, 'Google Agreed to Pay Execs Accused of Sexual Harassment $135 Million'. *Gizmodo*, 11 March 2019, gizmodo.com/google-agreed-to-pay-execs-accused-of-sexual-harassment-1833214767.

3 Jon Evans, 'What If Google Unionized?'. *Techcrunch*, 4 November 2018, techcrunch.com/2018/11/04/what-if-google-unionized/.

4 Josh Eidelson, Hassan Kanu, and Mark Bergen, 'Google Urged the U.S. to Limit Protection for Activist Workers'. *Bloomberg*, 24 January 2019, www.bloomberg.com/news/articles/2019-01-24/google-urged-the-u-s-to-limit-protection-for-activist-workers.

provided support for worker actions in other tech firms.[5] It shows that even in the virulently antiunion climate of Silicon Valley[6] (the location for *The Circle*), employees want voice.

Voice refers to a range of ways through which workers can influence decisions that affect them. As we've seen in previous chapters, management of employees has tended to move in two seemingly contradictory directions: towards tighter managerial control, or towards greater responsibility on employees. This pattern is likely to continue into the future. In which direction individual managers move will depend on the industry of the firm, the technology available to management, and the strategic direction chosen by managers, sometimes in response to pressures from owners, sometimes driven by their own preferences or the possibilities that arise from technology. Efforts by management to tighten control lead to resistance from employees and generate conflict, and the tendency of technological changes to enhance that capacity for managerial control makes that resistance no less likely. So management tries to persuade employees that it is all in their interests, often via culturism (as discussed in Chapter 5), and sometimes by adopting 'high-trust' approaches centred on enhancing employees' 'voice' at work

If management does not want to give employees voice, employees will want voice anyway. Most employees seek more say at work, sometimes calling it 'participation in decision-making' or even 'workplace democracy',[7] while psychologists refer to 'job control'. The phrase you sometimes hear about the workplace—'leave your brains at the gate'—is used by workers to summarise the dismissive view many bosses have about the contribution employees can make, and about how much say workers have in what they do at work. Whatever some employers have done voluntarily about employee voice, there is little doubt that the underlying trend is towards less worker power in the workplace, as explained in Chapter 2 and shown by the decline in union membership,[8] and the growth of managerial surveillance and control discussed in Chapter 5. So I want to explore this concept of 'voice', including how employees can, do and will exercise it.

5 See twitter.com/GoogleWalkout.

6 Noam Scheiber, 'Google Workers Reject Silicon Valley Individualism in Walkout'. *New York Times*, 6 November 2018, www.nytimes.com/2018/11/06/business/google-employee-walkout-labor.html?smid=nytcore-ios-share.

7 Richard B. Freeman and Joel Rogers, *What Workers Want* (Ithaca: ILR Press, 1999).

8 Organisation for Economic Co-operation and Development, *Employment Outlook* (Paris: OECD, 2017).

Voice

Voice is a term with complex and 'uneven' meanings—that is, different people use it to describe different things.[9] At the simplest level, it can be divided into *formal voice*, which is often referred to as 'employee participation', and *informal voice*, which concerns the day-to-day behaviour of management—the extent to which managers have 'open door' practices, engage in behaviours such as a daily 'walk around' the factory or office floor, or otherwise obtain, welcome and pay attention to the views of ordinary employees. Informal voice is very much a function of *management style*, particularly regarding the high-trust/low-trust dimension, discussed in Chapter 5. Our focus in this chapter is on formal voice, though beware that formal voice mechanisms will be blunted or even rendered ineffective if they are undermined by informal practices that ignore employee views. That said, just because something is formalised does not make it participatory. Formalised 'information sharing' does not equate to employee participation. Employee voice can only be said to exist if it travels 'upwards'; that is, if management decisions are influenced by what those 'below' them are saying or demanding. As we saw in Chapter 5, sometimes firms will want to give the appearance of being participatory in order to disguise a high level of control over employees.

A common distinction is also made between *direct* participation (e.g. productivity improvement groups, management employee meetings, quality circles and semiautonomous work groups); and *representative* (or 'indirect') participation (e.g. joint consultative committees, works councils and employee board representatives).

The most important way of categorising voice, though, is the extent to which it is *management-constrained* (conditional) or *employee-controlled* (independent). The issue of constraint and control here refers not just to whose voice is heard but also to who makes the decisions about whether employee voices will continue to be heard. This dimension is therefore closely related to the implications of employee voice for *power*. 'Management-constrained' implies lower employee power; 'employee-controlled' implies the opposite.

9 Tony Dundon and Derek Rollison, *Employment Relations in Non-Union Firms* (London: Routledge, 2004).

A voice mechanism is management-constrained if it is conditional on management's acquiescence, and so management can ultimately terminate an arrangement for voice. Most forms of 'employee participation' that you may have heard of come under this category. These include almost all 'direct' and some 'indirect' or 'representative' forms of employee participation. A voice mechanism is employee-controlled if it is independent of management's intent, and so management cannot unilaterally terminate an arrangement for voice. Some representative forms of employee participation are employee-controlled. In developed countries, by far the most common form of employee-controlled participation is trade unionism. Sometimes, though, the term may refer to 'works councils' (a form of representative participation found in parts of Europe), the activation of which may depend on employees specifying they want to have it. As they may be pressured against this, there are proposals to make this (called *Mitbestimmung* in Germany) compulsory.[10] So the distinction, while useful, is not without caveats. In some developing countries nongovernment organisations (NGOs) are mechanisms by which employees might independently express their voice.

Employee participation is promoted by different people for different reasons. Some managers, and some policy-makers, encourage employee participation because of the perceived potential to *improve economic performance,* and there is quite a lot of evidence that it does this.[11] Usually, such arguments are made about conditional voice, and that is the main reason management allows it to occur. Independent voice probably has a weaker, perhaps more neutral impact on economic performance due to opposing influences.[12] On the one hand, workers' knowledge of their situation can make major contributions to improving efficiency, and workers committed to a union tend on average to be more committed to

10 Werner Nienhüser, 'Employees Want Democracy in the Workplace'. *Magazin Mitbestimmung*, Hans-Böckler-Stiftung, 2018, www.boeckler.de/66359.htm.

11 George Strauss, 'Workers' Participation in Management'. In *Employment Relations: The Psychology of Influence and Control at Work*, ed. Jean F. Hartley and Geoffrey M. Stevenson (Cambridge, MA: Blackwell, 1992), 291–311; Derek C. Jones and Jan Svejnar, 'The Economic Performance of Participatory and Self-Managed Firms: A Historical Perspective and a Review'. In *Participatory and Self-Managed Firms*, ed. Derek C. Jones and Jan Svejnar (Lexington, MA: DC Heath & Co, 1982), 3–16; Department of Employment and Industrial Relations, *Industrial Democracy and Employee Participation: A Policy Discussion Paper* (Canberra: Working Environment Branch, DEIR and AGPS, 1986); John R. Cable and Felix R. Fitzroy, 'Co-operation and Productivity: Some Evidence from West German Experience'. *Journal of Economic Analysis and Workers Management* 14, no. 2 (1980): 163–80.

12 Richard B. Freeman and James L. Medoff, *What Do Unions Do?* (New York: Basic Books, 1984); Richard B. Freeman, 'What Do Unions Do? The 2004 M-Brane Stringtwister Edition'. *Journal of Labor Research* 26, no. 4 (2005): 642–68.

the organisation.[13] On the other hand, employees may resist management overtures, and worker control that cannot be negated by management can give them an effective tool for resistance and restricting output.[14] The net effect appears to depend on circumstances.[15] It is not designed to enhance organisational performance, but if employees want to use it in part for that purpose (which many rationally would—workers typically want to preserve their jobs and improve the prospects of their organisation) it will likely have the effect of improving organisational performance, as management is rarely the source of all wisdom.

Sometimes the benefits for performance arising from increased employee participation derive from the greater reliance on supervision by peers rather than supervision through a hierarchical chain of command. This sounds quite exciting for employees, but there is a different, grim angle on this coming from Barker's study of a firm he called 'ISE Electronics'.[16] Here, there was a shift from hierarchical, bureaucratic control to self-managing teams. Barker noticed that employees felt more closely watched than when they were under bureaucratic control. He described 'concertive control' as something that grows out of a substantial consensus about values, high-level coordination, and a degree of self-management by members or workers in an organisation'. Barker considered that:

> contrary to the proponents of such systems, concertive control did not free workers from [Max] Weber's iron cage of rational control. Instead, the concertive system, as it became manifest in this case, appeared to draw the iron cage tighter and to constrain the organisation's members more powerfully.[17]

13 As discussed in Chapter 5, this phenomenon is called 'dual commitment'. See reference 80 in that chapter.

14 Bernard Elbaum and Frank Wilkinson, 'Industrial Relations and Uneven Development: A Comparative Study of the American and British Steel Industries'. *Cambridge Journal of Economics* 3, no. 3 (1979): 275–303.

15 Sandra E. Black and Lisa M. Lynch, 'How to Compete: The Impact of Workplace Practices and Information Technology on Productivity'. *The Review of Economics and Statistics* 83, no. 3 (2001): 434–45; Eileen Appelbaum, Jody Hoffer Gittell, and Carrie Leana, 'High-Performance Work Practices and Sustainable Economic Growth'. Memo to Obama Administration, Brandeis University, 20 March 2011.

16 James R. Barker, 'Tightening the Iron Cage: Concertive Control in Self-Managing Teams'. *Administrative Science Quarterly* 38, no. 3 (1993): 408–37.

17 Ibid. See also Max Weber, *The Protestant Ethic and the Spirit of Capitalism* (Routledge, repr. 2013).

Still, not all systems of self-managing teams may have this effect: if culture is fragmented, pressure for concertive control will be weak. Even if it is intended to act in that way, as we saw in Chapters 3 and 5, no system of control is total.

While Barker's was an American case study, there was also Australian survey evidence from the 1990s to support his interpretations. It suggested that not all changes at work were being 'forced' upon employees against their 'will'. While many employees were being made to work harder as a consequence of the growing exercise of managerial prerogative, others were working harder in the context of what might appear to be greater employee control over their own working lives. Even changes that gave employees greater control over their working time appear to be associated with increased work intensity. Thus it may ironically *reduce* rather than enhance the autonomy of employees.[18] Moves either to 'high performance' work systems or their opposite, Taylorism, were both associated with increased work intensity and stress—two paths to work intensification.[19] Adverse effects such as this could limit the gains from participation. We can think of management seeking to loosen *direct* control of employee work methods and hours as a means of tightening control of employee *outputs*. There is some indication of increasing use by corporations of management-constrained participation mechanisms.[20]

So while workers typically want more say, they are not necessarily better off in all respects if this is designed to benefit management. Another, Danish study found that, while participation enhanced the quality of the working environment, increasing direct participation without increasing collective (indirect) participation could have a negative effect on employee psychological wellbeing 'if participation is limited to operational issues pertaining to job performance, framed by a top-down involvement scheme and/or linked to productivity targets and performance control of employees'.[21]

18 David Peetz, Cameron Allan, and Michael O'Donnell, 'Are Australians Really Unhappier with Their Bosses Because They're Working Harder? Perspiration and Persuasion in Modern Work'. Paper presented at Rethinking Institutions for Work and Employment, Selected Papers from the XXXVIII Annual Canadian Industrial Relations Association Conference, Quebec, 26–28 May 2001.

19 Ibid.

20 Richard B. Freeman, Peter Boxall, and Peter Haynes, eds, *What Workers Say: Employee Voice in the Anglo-American World* (Ithaca NY: ILR Press, 2007).

21 Ole Busck, Herman Knudsen, and Jens Lind, 'Who Is in Control? The Effect of Employee Participation on the Quality of the Work Environment'. Paper presented at European congress of International Industrial Relations Association, Copenhagen, June 2010.

In many firms, management will give employees enough autonomy, and the illusion of control, to improve productivity until the point when employees decide to challenge managerial authority or decisions in some way. Then it becomes very clear that employees have to submit to managerial directives in the absence of any countervailing employee power. In many ways, that is what we saw with 'Servo' and Starbucks in Chapter 5: 'members', 'associates' and 'partners' may have all felt they had their say, until they were performance-managed out of their job or made redundant. As the Danish researchers discovered, direct without representative participation—that is, without some form of independent voice—may be damaging, as 'collective participation, found at the workplaces with a democratic governance system of management–employee relations, is very helpful in resisting or compensating for strenuous psychological demands'.[22]

So greater productivity, for the benefit of the organisation, is one rationale for employee participation. A second rationale is a *social justice* one—a rationale more commonly associated with left-leaning political parties. According to this view, voice is justified because it is a right of employees to be able to influence the decisions that affect their working lives. That is, if society is pluralist outside the workplace, why should it become dictatorial once you step inside the workplace? Industrial democracy, and even economic democracy, are seen as corollaries of political democracy.

Although this rationale is about people's rights, it is bolstered by evidence showing that employee participation in decision-making is good for people who exercise it. For example, before you conclude from the earlier material that giving employees greater say doesn't help them deal properly with the long-hours issue, consider this: one Australian employee study showed that, despite working harder, employees experiencing greater say—including on hours—showed other benefits in areas like job satisfaction, training opportunities, use of skills and receipt of a pay rise.[23] In another study, of mine and energy workers, those who had no say over their hours and shifts reported more short-term illnesses. The use of sleeping tablets was higher among workers who had no say in their hours. Those who wished to reduce hours and had no say over their hours

22 Ibid.

23 Peetz, Allan, and O'Donnell, 'Are Australians Really Unhappier'.

were three-quarters more likely to use anti-depressants.[24] So, greater say over hours was associated with better health outcomes, even in a long-hours industry. That study also showed that mining and energy workers who had no say over when they could take time off were considerably more likely to say that they were getting on worse with people at home: 11 per cent said that how well they 'got on with people at home' had gone down over the previous two years, versus 6.5 per cent for whom it had gone up.[25] In a broader study, the mining industry was ranked the second worst on the index measuring the degree of interference between work and family life. One reason may be the divergence between hours preferred and hours worked.[26]

The third rationale for employee participation relates exclusively to employee-controlled voice. Just as a corporation is a collective of capital (a collection of shareholders seeking to maximise their economic power by combining), so too a union is a collective of labour. Workers come together to form unions in order to increase their bargaining power. In the absence of this, most workers would have little or no bargaining power as individuals when negotiating with a corporation, a collective of capital, over employment. That is, as there are some issues on which the interests of workers and employers are in conflict, it is rational for employees to want to improve their bargaining power, and to do so in a way that is not controlled by management. Whether employers think that employee voice is a good idea is irrelevant to this rationale—though it also happens to be the case that many employers prefer dealing with unions as this reduces their transaction costs in employee relations (hence some employers have a 'collectivist' style, discussed in Chapter 5). Employee-controlled or independent voice is what the rest of this chapter concentrates upon, as it represents the main means by which employees can seek to alter the direction in which management wishes to take them.

24 David Peetz, Georgina Murray, and Olav Muurlink, *Work and Hours Amongst Mining and Energy Workers* (Brisbane: Centre for Work, Organisation and Wellbeing, Griffith University, 2012), 11–12.

25 Ibid.

26 Natalie Skinner and Barbara Pocock, *Work, Life & Workplace Culture: The Australian Work and Life Index 2008* (Adelaide: Centre for Work + Life, University of South Australia, 2008).

Independent voice: Trade unionism

As mentioned, independent or employee-controlled voice—collective voice—mostly takes the form of trade unionism, at least in developed countries. Still, as former US Secretary of Labor Thomas Perez said recently:

> There are many ways to give voice to workers. Unions are certainly one way. There are also a number of non-profits that are working with taxicab drivers and home health workers and fast food workers, nonprofits that are very agile, and they're really standing up for low-wage workers trying to give voice.[27]

These new institutions might include cooperatives, worker centres, 'fast food strikes' or even 'Turkopticon', which rates organisations soliciting workers through the gig platform Amazon Mechanical Turk.[28] That said, I focus here on unions.

Some writers have distinguished between two forms of unionism, which broadly speaking can be described as unionism mostly outside the workplace (sometimes called 'political unionism', 'arbitration unionism', 'labourism', or, in a particular form, 'service unionism') and unionism mostly focused within the workplace (sometimes called 'organising unionism'). The terms 'organising' and 'service' unionism emerged initially in the USA and spread to other Anglophone countries in the 1990s, having particular salience in Australia because the arbitration system, within which Australian unions developed, had discouraged the development of workplace unionism.[29]

Workplace unionism is very important for the sustainability of unionism. Although that statement may seem obvious, for long periods in the twentieth century activism at the workplace was not encouraged by unions, especially in some Anglophone countries, whether because of fear

27 Thomas Perez, 'Video: A Message from Former US Secretary of Labor Thomas Perez to the Next Generation Workforce'. Shaping the Future of Work (Cambridge, MA: MIT and EdX, 2017), courses.edx.org/courses/course-v1:MITx+15.662x_3+1T2017/courseware/d670b05d28d1497fb57422c10cbb6319/f7b6dd9e996e4ec9b9981566a69a16eb/?child=first (subscription required).

28 Thomas A. Kochan, 'Video: All Innovations Are Local'. Shaping the Future of Work (Cambridge, MA: MIT and EdX, 2017).

29 Malcolm Rimmer, 'Work Place Unionism'. In *Australian Unions: An Industrial Relations Perspective*, ed. William Ford and David Plowman (Melbourne: Macmillan, 1989), 122–44; David Peetz and Janis Bailey, 'Dancing Alone: The Australian Union Movement over Three Decades'. *Journal of Industrial Relations* 54, no. 4 (2012): 524–41.

of loss of central control or 'wildcat' strikes or, in the case of Australia and New Zealand, the logic of arbitration systems that privileged advocacy skills in front of tribunals ahead of organising skills.

From the 1990s, unionism was in decline in many countries, especially in Australia. Although some attributed this to the decline of manufacturing, 'blue collar' jobs or other industrial or occupational change,[30] empirically this explanation does not hold up except for a relatively short period (mostly in the 1980s).[31] For example, in Australia, manufacturing employment virtually halved, from around 14.5 per cent to 7.5 per cent, between 1990 and 2016. But union density in manufacturing was only 5 percentage points above the national average in 1990 anyway, so that change in its share of employment could only account for about a third of a percentage point of union decline, out of the 27 percentage point decline in union density over this period—union density across Australia fell from 41 per cent in 1990 to about 14 per cent in 2016. Indeed, union density *within* manufacturing fell from 46 per cent in 1990 to little over 12 per cent in 2016—greater than the decline across the nation, in fact.[32] Density declined within all industries and occupations, and structural effects associated with industry of employment were small. The decline of public sector employment had a more noticeable effect, but still only accounted for a minor portion of union decline. In other countries, composition change among industries or occupations after 1990 does

---

30 For example, 'union decline has broadly tracked the declining share of jobs held by blue-collar workers': Bradley Bowden, 'Three Charts On: The Changing Face of Australian Union Members'. *The Conversation*, 4 July 2017, theconversation.com/three-charts-on-the-changing-face-of-australian-union-members-80141.

31 In the UK, compositional change between 1983 and 1989 accounted for about 30 per cent of the decline in density. Francis Green, 'Recent Trends in British Trade Union Density: How Much of a Compositional Effect?'. *British Journal of Industrial Relations* 30, no. 3 (1992): 445–58. In Australia during the 1980s its contribution could have been up to a half. David Peetz, *Unions in a Contrary World: The Future of the Australian Trade Union Movement* (Cambridge: Cambridge University Press, 1998). Its contribution appeared considerably smaller in most other OECD countries: Jelle Visser, 'Trends in Trade Union Membership'. In *Employment Outlook* (Paris: Organisation for Economic Co-operation and Development, 1991), 97–134.

32 Australian Bureau of Statistics. 'Trade Union Members'. Canberra 6325.0; Australian Bureau of Statistics. 'Characteristics of Employment'. Canberra 6333.0.

little to explain declines in density.[33] All of this is nothing new: that the fastest growing sectors of employment have been hardest to unionise is 'a problem as old as the union movement'.[34]

Some workplaces that were previously unionised were deunionised. Union collapse at Australian workplaces in the 1990s occurred most commonly where unions had weak workplace organisation, where there was no delegate presence or where delegates were inactive or unions were not involved in workplace bargaining. Workplace delegates, therefore, played a vital role in preventing deunionisation. Workplaces with active unions were more likely to resist deunionisation.[35]

The response of unions in several (mostly Anglophone) countries to the crisis of the 1990s was to place increasing emphasis on the future of *workplace unionism*. This concept—or at least, 'organising'—re-emerged in the USA and Canada,[36] and led, in Australia, to the establishment of 'Organising Works', a centre (since renamed) run through the Australian Council of Trade Unions (ACTU) for training union activists. This became the model for the Organising Academy, established by the British Trades Union Congress. These agencies promoted the 'organising model' of unionism. At the core of this concept of 'organising' was the fermentation of workplace activism, through developing and providing support for workplace delegates. The idea was that members be empowered to solve problems themselves, as opposed to having paid union officials

33 Frank Walsh and Eric Strobl, 'Recent Trends in Trade Union Membership in Ireland'. *Economic and Social Review* 40, no. 1 (2009): 117–38; Claus Schnabel, 'Union Membership and Density: Some (Not So) Stylized Facts and Challenges'. *European Journal of Industrial Relations* 19, no. 3 (2013): 255–72.

34 R. Archer, 'Organising: An International Perspective'. In *Unions 2001*, ed. Evatt Foundation (Sydney: 1995).

35 Peetz, *Unions in a Contrary World.*

36 The word 're-emerged' is used because many argue that this is how unionism originally formed and, in North America, the 'organising' approach owed much to the work of Saul Alinsky who, in the 1930s, led the organising of a depressed Chicago 'slum'. Saul D. Alinsky, *Reveille for Radicals* (Chicago: University of Chicago Press, 1946); Saul D. Alinsky, *Rules for Radicals* (New York: Random House, 1971).

solve them on their behalf.[37] In practice, organising unions engaged in both 'organising' and 'servicing' activities (acting as agents in response to member queries), but they may have had dedicated functions within the union to deal with servicing requests ('member service centres'), leaving organisers to do organising work. A union approach that did not extend beyond the workplace would be crippled. The ability to refer beyond the workplace—and by reference to considerations beyond the workplace, to make demands upon management—is one of the characteristics distinguishing between management-constrained and employee-controlled forms of voice.

Recent patterns of union membership show interesting, in some cases seemingly contradictory, features. In most Anglophone countries, for example, employees have reported that they desired a cooperative relationship between the union and management at the workplace.[38] Not only did they see that the union needed to behave cooperatively; they also expected management to reciprocate by cooperating with the union to solve workplace problems. Detailed questioning revealed that, to workers, cooperation meant management sharing power and authority with unions, not some sort of sham whereby management leads and the union cooperates by following. Union members were more vigorous in demanding that management cooperate more with unions than that unions cooperate more with management,[39] and almost unanimously wanted unions to continue to vigorously defend their interests. Thus the meaning of 'cooperation' was quite complex, and a long way from 'acquiescence'. Union members were more likely to have taken part in industrial action where they saw unions as

37 Examples of studies or publications that related to organising include: Bradon Ellem, 'New Unionism in the Old Economy: Community and Collectivism in the Pilbara's Mining Towns'. *Journal of Industrial Relations* 45, no. 4 (2003): 423–41; Patricia Findlay and Alan McKinlay, 'Union Organising in "Big Blue's" Backyard'. *Industrial Relations Journal* 34, no. 1 (2003): 52–66; Christopher L. Erickson et al., 'Justice for Janitors in Los Angeles: Lessons from Three Rounds of Negotiations'. *British Journal of Industrial Relations* 40, no. 3 (September 2002): 543–67; David Peetz, *Brave New Workplace: How Individual Contracts Are Changing Our Jobs* (Sydney: Allen & Unwin, 2006), Chapter 7; Bob Carter and Rae Cooper, 'The Organizing Model and the Management of Change: A Comparative Study of Unions in Australia and Britain'. *Relations Industrielles* 57, no. 4 (Fall, 2002): 712–42; *Unions@Work* (Melbourne: ACTU, 1998); Kate Bronfenbrenner, Sheldon Friedman, Richard W. Hurd, and Rudolph A. Oswald, eds, *Organising to Win* (Ithaca NY: ILR Press, 1998).

38 This is another example of dual commitment, mentioned in an earlier footnote. For data, see Freeman, Boxall, and Haynes, *What Workers Say*. This includes the chapter David Peetz and Ann Frost, 'Employee Voice in the Anglo-American World: What Does It Mean for Unions?'. In *What Workers Say: Employee Voice in the Anglo-American World*, ed. Richard B. Freeman, Peter Boxall, and Peter Haynes (Ithaca NY: ILR Press, 2007).

39 In Australia, the numbers for these two last estimates were 82 per cent and 66 per cent, respectively.

having tried to cooperate with management.[40] It may seem paradoxical, but it meant members were more likely to get involved in union actions if they perceived the union as reflecting their own interests—as being 'democratic'. We will come back to this.

Union density among young workers has been very low. Yet research finds that generally young people are not opposed outright to unionism—this is not surprising, given the evident responsiveness of young voters to left-wing causes in elections in the USA and UK.[41] Young people tend, instead, to be simply unaware of what unionism is, partly because many of them do not have parents who are union members.[42] So there is a generational aspect to union membership. Where they have an opinion (which is not so often), young employees are as likely to *want* to belong to a union as older employees, but much less likely to actually belong, perhaps because they have less opportunity to join, and have lower awareness of workplace issues.[43] As the proportions of young workers who are socialised by unionised parents falls, however, ignorance of unions and workplace issues increases. Some unions use a range of strategies to allow young people to 'sample' unionism or 'activist' programs that target young members.[44] Researchers urge unions to explain unions' raison d'etre and their internal processes to young workers but also to 'allow young members to contribute to bringing about the kinds of changes they are calling for'.[45]

40 David Peetz, 'Workplace Cooperation, Conflict, Influence and Union Membership'. In *Contemporary Research on Unions: Theory, Membership, Organisation and Non-Standard Employment*, ed. G. Griffin, Monograph No. 8 (Melbourne: National Key Centre in Industrial Relations, 1996), 309–46.

41 Sarah Wildman, 'How Angry Young Voters Help Explain the Historic UK Election Upset'. *Vox*, 13 June 2017, www.vox.com/world/2017/6/13/15771640/bernie-corbyn-melenchon-uk-election-young-voters-youth-vote; Kei Kawashima-Ginsberg, Noorya Hayat, Abby Kiesa, and Felicia Sullivan, 'Donald Trump and Young Voters' (Medford, MA: Tufts University, Center for Information and Research on Civic Learning and Engagement, June 2016), civicyouth.org/wp-content/uploads/2016/06/Trump-and-Youth-Vote.pdf, 4.

42 Freeman, Boxall, and Haynes, *What Workers Say*.

43 Julian Teicher et al., 'Employee Voice in Australia'. In *What Workers Say: Employee Voice in the Anglo-American World*, ed. Richard B. Freeman, Peter Boxall, and Peter Haynes (Ithaca NY: ILR Press, 2007); David Peetz, Robin Price, and Janis Bailey, 'Ageing Australian Unions and the "Youth Problem"'. In *Young People and Trade Unions: A Global View*, ed. Lefteris Kretsos and Andrew Hodder (Palgrave Macmillan, 2015).

44 Janis Bailey et al., 'Daggy Shirts, Daggy Slogans? Marketing Unions to Young People'. *Journal of Industrial Relations* 52, no. 1 (2010): 43–60.

45 Mélanie Dufour-Poirier and Mélanie Laroche, 'Revitalising Young Workers' Union Participation: A Comparative Analysis of Two Organisations in Quebec (Canada)'. *Industrial Relations Journal* 45, no. 5–6 (2015): 418–33.

Union members tend to report high levels of satisfaction with their union.[46] Many nonmembers would be willing to join a union, given the opportunity, including approximately a third of all workers in nonunionised workplaces in several countries in one 2000s study,[47] probably rising to nearly half of US nonmembers by 2017.[48] These 'frustrated nonmembers' are typically on low incomes (often in the secondary labour market), in small workplaces or enterprises, or young. Those with more unmet workplace 'needs' are more likely to want unionism.[49]

Are unions doomed by the shift to individualism?

Some of the above considerations, such as the high satisfaction with unions among members, and stresses on wages and working conditions in recent years, might suggest there would be reasons why unions could grow. Yet the idea is often dismissed because of modern attitudes. One of the common suggestions made in talking about the future of work is that there will be no more unions because we will be working as freelancers and nobody will want unions any more as we will all want to be—and all will be—treated like individuals, with individualistic values and philosophies.[50] As seen in earlier chapters, we will not all be working as freelancers and will not all be treated like individuals at work. But what about our values? People have been saying for 30 years or more that we are becoming individualistic in our philosophies and that this will preclude collective behaviour in the future. Class is said to be losing its significance and individuals embedded in market relations, making their own choices, undergoing 'individuation', fashioning their own identities, isolated and egocentric.[51]

---

46 Freeman, Boxall, and Haynes, *What Workers Say*; Peetz, *Unions in a Contrary World*.

47 Freeman, Boxall, and Haynes, *What Workers Say*.

48 Thomas Kochan et al., 'Who Wants to Join a Union? A Growing Number of Americans'. *The Conversation*, 31 August 2018, theconversation.com/who-wants-to-join-a-union-a-growing-number-of-americans-102374.

49 Freeman, Boxall, and Haynes, *What Workers Say*.

50 Peter Frase, 'Delusions of the Tech Bro Intelligentsia'. *Jacobin*, 21 October 2013. www.jacobinmag.com/2013/10/delusions-of-the-tech-bro-intelligentsia/.

51 Ulrich Beck, *Risk Society: Towards a New Modernity* (London: Sage, 1992); Rainer Zoll, 'Failing to Modernize?'. *European Journal of Industrial Relations* 1, no. 1 (1995): 119–28; Ben Valkenburg, 'Individualization, Participation and Solidarity'. *European Journal of Industrial Relations* 1, no. 1 (1995): 129–44.

The numbers show otherwise. It is true that respondents can interpret survey questions in different ways in different geographic contexts, so standardised questions are not all that useful for telling you whether, say, Norway is less individualistic than the USA. But standardised questions asked in the same place at different times can give you a pretty good idea as to whether, and in which direction, beliefs in that place have changed. And generally speaking they show no net general drift towards individualism. If anything, the opposite is the case. For example, a question asking respondents, across up to two dozen countries, to choose between 'freedom' and 'equality' shows on average a leftward drift in more countries than not, over a series of periods from 1981–83 to 2008.[52] Several international studies have found majority support for government action to reduce inequality or for reducing the gap between the pay of chief executive officers and ordinary wages.[53] American public attitudes against wide differentials between the highest income earners and the rest appeared to harden from 1987 to 1999.[54] Despite massive changes in the occupational structure, patterns of class identification are very similar in the twenty-first century to what they were two to four decades earlier in Britain, Australia, the USA or Canada.[55] Consistently, opinion polls had shown around half the US workforce had identified as working or lower class from at least the early 1970s onwards.[56] Yet this was largely considered irrelevant by media commentators and politicians. Almost none used the term 'working class' in public discourse for years (preferring, if anything, 'middle class') until Donald Trump colonised the term in 2016.

---

52 A 'leftward drift' here refers to moves towards attitudes supportive of collective or redistributive action by labour or the state. IFO Institute for Economic Research, 'Database for Institutional Comparisons in Europe' (University of Munich, 2008).

53 GlobeScan/BBC World Service, 'Wide Dissatisfaction with Capitalism — Twenty Years after Fall of Berlin Wall' (London: BBC, 2009), 9 November; S. Kiatpongsan and M.I. Norton, 'How Much (More) Should CEOs Make? A Universal Desire for More Equal Pay'. *Perspectives on Psychological Science* 9, no. 6 (2014): 587–93; International Labour Office, *Economic Security for a Better World* (Geneva: Socio-Economic Security Programme, ILO, 2004).

54 Lars Osberg and Timothy Smeeding, '"Fair" Inequality? Attitudes toward Pay Differentials: The United States in Comparative Perspective'. *American Sociological Review* 71, no. 3 (2006): 450–73.

55 Mike Savage, 'Individuality and Class: The Rise and Fall of the Gentlemanly Social Contract in Britain'. In *Social Contracts under Stress: The Middle Classes of America, Europe, and Japan at the Turn of the Century*, ed. Olivier Zunz, Leonard James Schoppa, and Nobuhiro Hiwatari (New York: Russell Sage, 2002), 47–65; Chris Arnot, 'No Such Thing as a Classless Society'. *Guardian*, 7 October 2009, www.guardian.co.uk/society/2009/oct/07/class-influence-british-sense-identity; David Peetz, 'Are Individualistic Attitudes Killing Collectivism?'. *Transfer—European Review of Labour and Research* 16, no. 3 (2010): 383–98.

56 National Opinion Research Center, General Social Survey Data Explorer: Subjective Class Identification (Chicago: University of Chicago, 2019), gssdataexplorer.norc.org/variables/568/vshow.

Changes in attitudes do not explain the decline in union density in Australia or elsewhere among advanced industrialised nations. Rather, the reasons are principally institutional. Chief among them have been employer strategies that increasingly focus on achieving nonunion status, 'distancing' and cost minimisation. These have been assisted by government strategies, particularly in Anglophone countries, that have marginalised unions through legislation, privatisation and administrative action.[57] The greater use of 'not there' employment has made it harder for unions to organise, by fragmenting bargaining and placing workers into jobs where price competition makes wage claims difficult. Weak unionism and weak regulation in turn encourage 'not there' employment, because the cost gains are higher and the potential for underpayment greater where workers are relocated to an entity where they are unable to organise resistance. At the heart of these strategies by both employers and governments is the rise of market liberalism or 'neo-liberalism'. To varying degrees (particularly in Australia, where the legacy of the award system's effects on unions was pervasive) unions exacerbated this by having difficulty in adapting to these changing circumstances—what Pocock called 'institutional sclerosis'—in the face of neo-liberalism.[58] Unions found it hard to redirect resources internally, to enable them to demonstrate power in ways that ensured retention of members.

Unionism is what economists call an 'experience good', so for current or recent union members the public image of unions matters little in determining workers' decision to stay, compared to their own experiences. However, unions' public image is important in shaping the behaviour of people who have never belonged to one,[59] and recruitment may become more difficult in the future, as fewer people have experience of unions that influences their decision to join and fewer people have union parents. There is already evidence that 'never joining' has increased;[60] so unions' public image, including that developed by the firms for which people work, becomes more influential in choices about union membership.

57 Peetz, *Unions in a Contrary World.*

58 Barbara Pocock, 'Institutional Sclerosis: Prospects for Trade Union Transformation'. *Labour & Industry* 9, no. 1 (1998): 17–33.

59 Peetz, *Unions in a Contrary World.*

60 Alex Bryson and Rafael Gomez, *Why Have Workers Stopped Joining Unions?* (London: Centre for Economic Performance, London School of Economics and Political Science, November 2003).

Collective behaviour is unlikely to go away, even if people are unwilling or unable to join unions. Collective behaviour arises where a number of conditions are met.[61] The first is that others also share needs or grievances felt by individuals—that is, grievances are collective. The objective circumstances promoting collectivism—the existence of exploitation creating grievances—are set to continue. Nor is there any sign that the values enabling collectivism are in decline. Where people possess *values* that promote altruistic or mutually supportive behaviour, that reinforce trust among members of the group, or that emphasise the welfare of a group as a whole as opposed to that of successful individuals, then collective attitudes and the scope for collective behaviour will be strengthened. Where people share common social identities, they are likely to act together, but where they lack a sense of common identity or are divided they are unlikely to act together.[62] Where people possess beliefs of collective efficacy, that is, they sense agency and believe they have the power to achieve their goals through collective behaviour, they will be more likely to behave collectively,[63] as 'a collective of self-doubters is not easily forged into a collectively efficacious force'.[64]

Collective action also depends on potential participants having collective values—such as concern about inequality, solidarity or the belief that acting together is a 'good thing'. It also requires coordination, through connections or networks between members of the group; the existence of collective mobilisers (e.g. union delegates or leaders) who can mobilise collective cooperation; and democratic (collective) coordination (as opposed to autocratic or individual coordination) within the collective. How much all this translates to the exercise of collective power will also depend on the institutional and environmental responses to collective action (including the actions of the state, the behaviours of corporations and employers, and the condition of the labour market). There has been a major decline in collective labour institutions (trade unions) and in collective industrial conflict (measured by numbers of strikes or working days lost) over the past

61 Peetz, *Brave New Workplace.*

62 Caroline Kelly and Sara Breinlinger, 'Identity and Injustice: Exploring Women's Participation in Collective Action'. *Journal of Community & Applied Social Psychology* 5 (1995): 41–57; John E. Kelly, *Rethinking Industrial Relations: Mobilization, Collectivism, and Long Waves.* Routledge Studies in Employment Relations (London, New York: Routledge, 1998). John Kelly's book is one of the more important in understanding union mobilisation.

63 Albert Bandura, *Self-Efficacy: The Exercise of Control* (New York: W.H. Freeman & Company, 1997); John Kelly, 'British Trade Unionism 1979–89: Change, Continuity and Contradictions'. *Work, Employment and Society* special issue (1990): 29–60.

64 Bandura, *Self-Efficacy*, 480.

three decades. There is little evidence, however, that this is due to a decline in collective values, as these have changed little.[65] Rather, changes in the institutional framework, in particular the policies and actions of the state and employers, offer more persuasive explanations.

If people are prevented from acting collectively through unions, they will look for other means of doing so. Even if unions can no longer play the role of mobilisers, there is no reason to think that collective grievances will go away, or that common work identities will disappear.[66] Actions may be more disorganised, individualistic, self-destructive, even violent, but dissatisfaction and resistance are unlikely to go away.

Power and activism

Unions aim to achieve gains for their members by obtaining and exercising power in the workplace and elsewhere. Richard Hyman made one of the classical observations on union power.[67] He noted the significance for a union of the *power of* its members, its ability to advance their interests. But he also identified the importance of a union's *power over* its members, without which it would not have *power for* its members. In other words, a union can only exercise collective power on behalf of its members 'if, and to the extent that, it can mobilise disciplined collective action on the part of its members'.[68] It needs to be able to promote solidarity among and enforce discipline within its membership.

This also relates back to one of the oldest issues that have faced collectives of any type, since people came together to form villages and societies, tradesmen came together to form guilds and workers came together to form trade unions: the problem of the 'free rider'. In biology and economics this is termed the problem of the 'cheat'—someone who obtains the benefits of membership of a group without contributing towards the

65 Peetz, *Brave New Workplace*; David Peetz, 'Are Collective Identity and Action Being Squashed by Individualism?'. In *Work and Identity: Contemporary Perspectives on Workplace Diversity*, ed. Shalene Werth and Charlotte Brownlow (New York: Palgrave, 2018).

66 Peetz, 'Squashed by Individualism?'.

67 *Industrial Relations: A Marxist Introduction* (London: Macmillan, 1975).

68 Ibid., 65.

costs.[69] For trade unions, free riders dilute the bargaining strength of the group, reducing the impact of any collective action on an employer and the power resources available to union members. Free riding appears to have recently increased in Australia and some other countries, due not to changing values but to institutional developments.[70]

Some of the major research on union renewal has been among Canadian academics. From there, Lévesque and Murray point out, the 'key factors currently challenging union power clearly cut across the different national institutional arrangements in which unions are embedded'. Levesque and Murray identified four key 'power resources' for unions:

1. internal solidarity (sufficiently cohesive identities to pursue their goals; and 'deliberative vitality'—the participation of members in the life of their union);
2. network embeddedness (the degree to which unions are linked to their own and other union organisations, community groups, social movements or other types of actors);
3. narrative resources (the range of values, shared understandings, stories and ideologies that aggregate identities and interests, translate and inform motives and create a sense of efficacy)[71] that frame understandings and union actions;
4. infrastructural resources (material, human, processes, policies and programs).[72]

69 The issue of free riding, in nature, ancient societies and modern collectives, is discussed in Chapter 2 of Peetz, *Brave New Workplace*, and more extensively by other authors; for example, John Stewart, *Evolution's Arrow: The Direction of Evolution and the Future of Humanity* (Canberra: Chapman Press, 2000).

70 For instance, union density has, in Australia, declined by more than collective bargaining coverage, as it is convenient for many employers to continue to negotiate with a union than go through the upheaval from shifting to non-union negotiation. David Peetz and Serena Yu, *Explaining Recent Trends in Collective Bargaining*. Research Report 4/2017 (Melbourne: Fair Work Commission, February 2017). Changes in union density also appear greater than changes in union density in Sweden, Slovenia and Switzerland, but the trends appear in the other direction in the UK, USA and Germany.

71 Albert Bandura, 'Exercise of Personal and Collective Efficacy in Changing Societies'. In *Self-Efficacy in Changing Societies*, ed. Albert Bandura (Cambridge: Cambridge University Press, 1995): 1–45; Bandura, *Self-Efficacy: The Exercise of Control.*

72 Christian Lévesque and Gregor Murray, 'Understanding Union Power: Resources and Capabilities for Renewing Union Capacity'. *Transfer—European Review of Labour and Research* 16, no. 3 (2010): 333–50.

However, as Levesque and Murray point out, resources alone are not enough—unions must be capable of using them as the context changes. For example, intensified competition and globalisation have weakened pattern bargaining (lodging of similar claims with the other side across a number of bargaining sites). They have also weakened union links to political processes so that 'external solidarity resources derived from previous patterns of network embeddedness are not providing the leverage on which past patterns of union action relied'.[73] This increases the importance of the workplace, while highlighting unions' need to develop new ways of organising beyond the workplace and articulating back to it including through developing new forms of networks. One illustration is the increasing (though still limited) use by unions of social media[74] and online actions.[75] As 'understanding … union resources and capabilities is critical to an understanding of efforts to enhance union power', Lévesque and Murray identified four key strategic *capabilities* required for union power. These were unions' abilities to put forward an agenda ('framing'); intermediate between contending interests to foster collaborative action and activate networks; reflect on, build, anticipate and act upon change, and spread these lessons throughout the organisation ('learning'); and articulate actions over time (short term versus long term) and space (including the multiple levels at which unions act).

How does the future of unions look in relation to these issues? One of the major weaknesses of progressive groups has been their inadequate framing of political debate and union rhetoric about inequality.[76] Framing is a major challenge when the media are replete with stories—some beat-ups, some fictional and some based on grim facts—about poor union governance, misbehaviour or corruption. Years of observing unions suggest to me that, while many individuals are great learners, the organisations themselves often are not, despite many years passing since Pocock had remarked on this problem not long after the start of unions'

---

73 Ibid., 345.

74 Alex White, *Social Media for Unions* (Melbourne: Aleithia Media and Communications, 2010), alexwhite.org/2010/12/social-media-for-unions/.

75 LabourStart, *Labourstart Australia* (2014), www.labourstart.org/2013/country.php?country=Australia&langcode=en.

76 Anat Shenker-Osorio, *Don't Buy It: The Trouble with Talking Nonsense about the Economy* (New York: Public Affairs, 2012). In Australia, this is despite the successful 'Your Rights at Work' campaign that led to the defeat of the Howard government—a campaign framed in terms of 'rights'. Kathie Muir, *Worth Fighting For: Inside the Your Rights at Work Campaign* (Sydney: UNSW Press, 2008). The Your Rights at Work campaign also failed, despite lofty ideals, to *deeply* engage community groups and build strong linkages with them. Peetz and Bailey, 'Dancing Alone'.

reform process.[77] On articulation, a critical link is that between the paid and unpaid levels of the union—between the office and the workplace. Effective union mobilisation requires power and capabilities on many levels. But perhaps the first of these, the foundation, is the workplace, and that is worth some special focus here.

Building workplace organisation and democratisation

Workplace power for unions requires workplace activism. Workplace activism requires effective delegates, as the collapse of Australian unionism in the 1990s showed.[78] Activism also requires delegates with a sense of efficacy, as confidence and self-belief are a strong predictor of activism, even stronger than self-assessed skill levels.[79] Workplace power requires support by the union office, particularly organisers, for workplace delegates.[80] While unions are more than just a form of workplace social capital,[81] workplace power requires delegates have access to networks, internal and external to the workplace, formalised or informal, that provide support, information and ideas. And it requires that delegates, and members, have a sense that they can and do influence what the union itself does. Democracy within unions is a precondition for success. It is not just a question of a union's power for its members depending in part on power over its members:[82] in a world without wage arbitration, workers cannot have power in the workplace if they do not have power in the union.[83]

Some of the implications, of what unions need to do to value and empower delegates, are obvious but not always easy. The research shows that activism is severely hampered unless workplace delegates are trained. Setting aside resources for education promotes learning within and by organisations. Training enhances not only the skills but also the confidence of delegates for engaging in activism, and for spreading the load to others with different

77 Pocock, 'Institutional Sclerosis'.

78 Peetz, *Unions in a Contrary World*.

79 David Peetz, Carol Webb, and Meredith Jones, 'Activism Amongst Workplace Union Delegates'. *International Journal of Employment Studies* 10, no. 2 (2002): 83–108.

80 David Peetz and Barbara Pocock, 'An Analysis of Workplace Representatives, Union Power and Democracy in Australia'. *British Journal of Industrial Relations* 47, no. 4 (2009): 623–52.

81 Paul Jarley, 'Unions as Social Capital: Renewal through a Return to the Logic of Mutual Aid?'. *Labor Studies Journal* 29, no. 4 (2005): 1–26.

82 Hyman, *Industrial Relations*, 65.

83 Peetz and Pocock, 'Workplace Representatives'.

but complementary capabilities or interests.[84] The research also shows that formal training of delegates is almost wasted if resources are not also put into the follow-up of training, to imprint the lessons. The formal and the informal are two very important sides of the training coin.[85] Devoting resources to training is expensive but not necessarily controversial; the structural changes needed to ensure it is followed up and complemented can be both. The provision and facilitation of *opportunities* for networking is as important for developing supportive networks for delegate networks as is the provision of training itself.[86]

To be capable and motivated, delegates require both training and meaning from the union. By 'meaning' I refer to a sense of what the union stands for, through an articulation of union values through the union organisation.[87] It also is about a sense of real say in the decisions that affect delegates and members, both direct participation in decision-making (influencing the day-to-day decisions about work as a member and delegate) and indirect participation (influencing the decisions of the union itself).

Democratisation, in this context, is not just about having elected structures. Generally and on average, elected structures are good. However they do not have much impact if people are elected to positions unopposed, along factional lines. At times, certain forms of elected positions (such as elected organisers in some unions) can retard reform processes within unions and maintain the status quo. Union democracy is a contested and paradoxical concept. Democratisation is more about how much ability members and delegates have, to shape what the union does. It is about how a union functions, and how open it is to members' preferences and their diversity. The correlates of perceived democracy within unions suggest it is closely related to a willingness of the union to embrace and respond to broad constituencies, both inside and outside, such as those representing women's interests.[88]

84 Peetz, Webb, and Jones, 'Activism'; Peetz and Pocock, 'Workplace Representatives'.

85 David Peetz and Michael Alexander, 'A Synthesis of Research on Training of Union Delegates'. *Industrial Relations Journal* 44, no. 4 (2013): 425–42.

86 David Peetz et al., 'The Meaning and Making of Union Delegate Networks'. *Economic and Labour Relations Review* 26, no. 4 (2015): 596–613.

87 Christian Levesque and Gregor Murray, 'Local Versus Global: Activating Local Union Power in the Global Economy'. *Labor Studies Journal* 27, no. 3 (2002): 39–65; Lévesque and Murray, 'Understanding Union Power'.

88 David Peetz and Barbara Pocock, 'Community Activists, Coalitions and Unionism'. In *Trade Unions in the Community: Values, Issues, Shared Interests and Alliances*, ed. D. Buttigieg, et al. (Adelaide: Heidelberg Press, 2007).

So, are unions becoming more workplace-focused? The evidence of the past two decades suggests that in several countries the answer is 'yes'. Are they becoming more democratic? That is much harder to assess. Their formal structures appear to be changing to make it harder for individuals to unilaterally control or 'run off with' resources, but 'professionalisation' may also reduce directly elected positions. One-off surveys in Australia have tended to suggest that members and organisers felt that, at the time of the survey, their 'say' in decision-making was increasing,[89] but there are not enough of these to demonstrate a trend. One could tentatively answer with 'probably' but 'not quickly enough'.

Unionism in the platform economy

The changing nature of work is often seen as creating major difficulties for unions. There is no doubt that casualisation and the shift from the public to the private sector damages unions, because union density is lower among casual and temporary workers and, compared to the public sector, among private sector workers. That said, empirically, these structural changes account for only a minority of the decline in union density in countries like Australia, and most of that happened in the 1980s.[90] The issue is not so much a change in the composition of the workforce but a change in management (and government) strategies, involving more aggressive approaches towards trade unions and worker organisation as a means of minimising costs, transferring risk and regaining control, including through restructuring of capital, fragmentation through use of contractors, outsourcing, franchises, labour hire and spinoffs. These all create problems for union organisation: a union that undertakes industrial action in a contractor firm and interrupts supply, or that succeeds in obtaining higher wages for its members in that contractor firm, may find the employer of its members cut off from work and its members out of a job, regardless of whether they have 'permanent' or 'temporary' employment contracts. Others might decide not to risk it.

89 David Peetz and Barbara Pocock, 'Organising and Delegates: An Overview'. Association of Industrial Relations Academics of Australia and New Zealand conference, Sydney, February 2005; Peetz and Pocock, 'Workplace Representatives'; David Peetz, Chris Houghton, and Barbara Pocock, 'Organisers' Roles Transformed? Australian Union Organizers and Changing Union Strategy'. *Journal of Industrial Relations* 49, no. 2 (2005): 151–66; ibid.

90 Peetz, *Unions in a Contrary World*; David Peetz, 'Trend Analysis of Union Membership'. *Australian Journal of Labour Economics* 8, no. 1 (2005): 1–24.

That said, these new forms of capitalist organisation are not invulnerable. Kim Moody refers to the 'new terrain of class conflict' that arises from tightly integrated production and logistics systems, with companies that are 'bigger, more capital-intensive, and more economically rational'. It provides, he says, opportunities for unions to 'take advantage of the vulnerable points in just-in-time logistics and production to bring some of these new giants to heel'.[91] This harks back to an idea that has been around for a long time: workers have more power when they are strategically located, meaning they are located at points in the production process that are vulnerable to disruption. The JIT system increases the number of vulnerable points in the production process.

One of the biggest challenges facing unions in the future is the development of the 'platform economy', discussed in Chapter 6. People doing such work have the classic characteristics of casual employees—fragmented, lacking commitment to the organisation and hence to any union, often not highly engaged with their work—or more commonly contractors, who do not even have an 'employer' and so lack the protections, such as they exist, of employment law (though this depends on the specific legal context). In addition, those working for one firm may still be geographically separated from each other, perhaps by thousands of kilometres, perhaps in different time zones, and having no face-to-face contact with their fellow workers. So they may be classed as 'self-employed'. In Australia, the likelihood of union membership among 'casual' employees is just a quarter of what it is among 'permanent' employees, and among the self-employed (owner-managers of enterprises without employees) it is just one-eleventh.[92] So 'platform economy' or 'gig' workers appear very difficult for unions to organise. Yet, as we saw in Chapter 6, they are also highly susceptible to exploitation, with many (but not all) being paid below the equivalent of relevant minimum wage rates.

The result has been some seemingly spontaneous resistance by gig workers to their situation, alongside some rather innovative efforts by unions to engage with them. Among the efforts by unions to engage, the Austrian union vida set up a works council for food delivery cyclists working for Foodora (predominantly in Vienna), with the ultimate aim of establishing

91 Quoted in Chris Brooks and Kim Moody, 'Labor's New Sources of Leverage'. *Labor Notes*, 12 August 2016, www.labornotes.org/MoodyInterview.

92 Australian Bureau of Statistics, 'Characteristics of Employment'.

a collective agreement for all bicycle delivery services.[93] Unions New South Wales (a peak union body in an Australian state) in 2017 negotiated 'agreed minimum standards' for engagements negotiated through Airtasker in that state.[94] A Swedish union negotiated an *industry*-wide collective agreement that covers workers in Bzzt, an Uber-style organisation using electric taxis.[95] In the USA, the Service Employees Industrial Union had largely negotiated an agreement with Airbnb about unionisation of and pay rates for housekeepers, until it withdrew in the face of severe criticism from members and other unions.[96] A newly established union of Uber drivers in France organised a strike and road blockades, leading to the intervention of the state and negotiations over a minimum wage for Uber drivers.[97] Germany's IG Metall established the 'FairCrowdWork' platform, enabled self-employed crowdworkers to join the union, negotiated agreements with eight platforms to respect the minimum wage, and promoted the 'Frankfurt Declaration on Platform-Based Work' that also involved large unions from Austria, Denmark, Sweden and the USA.[98] Britain's GMB union backed cases run by drivers or riders against several gig firms, arguing (successfully) that they had been misclassified as self-employed rather than employees.[99] It also negotiated an agreement with Hermès providing couriers the option of 'self-employed plus' status, which included union representation, minimum wage guarantees and paid recreation leave.[100]

93 vida, 'Betriebsrat Für Fahrradzustelldienst Foodora'. vida (Austrian transport and service union), 2017, www.vida.at/cms/S03/S03_0.a/1342577497037/home/artikel/betriebsrat-fuer-fahrradzustelldienst-foodora.
94 Kate Minter, 'Negotiating Labour Standards in the Gig Economy: Airtasker and Unions New South Wales'. *Economic and Labour Relations Review* 28, no. 3 (2017): 438–54.
95 Hannah Johnston and Chris Land-Kazlauskas, *Organizing on-Demand: Representation, Voice, and Collective Bargaining in the Gig Economy*. Conditions of Work and Employment Series No. 94 (Geneva: Inclusive Labour Markets, Labour Relations and Working Conditions Branch, International Labour Office, 2018).
96 Sam Levin, 'Airbnb's Controversial Deal with Labor Union Falls Apart after Intense Backlash'. *Guardian*, 22 April 2016.
97 Zachary Kilhoffer, Karolien Lenaerts, and Miroslav Beblavý, *The Platform Economy and Industrial Relations: Applying the Old Framework to the New Reality*. CEPS Report No. 2017/12 (Brussels: Centre for European Policy Studies, 2017).
98 Ibid.
99 Ibid; Robert Booth, 'Addison Lee Wrongly Classed Drivers as Self-Employed, Tribunal Rules'. *Guardian*, 26 December 2017.
100 Sarah O'Connor, 'Gig Economy Agreements Promise a Brighter Future for Trade Unions'. *Financial Times*, 26 February 2019.

Indeed, in a number of jurisdictions, attempts by platform companies to define workers as self-employed have been challenged in courts and at times overturned, with tribunals or courts in parts of the USA, UK and Brazil ruling that various groups of platform workers are employees, not self-employed. Foodora went into administration (a weak form of bankruptcy) in Australia after a regulator argued to a tribunal that its workers were underpaid by being classified as contractors.[101]

And then there have been the spontaneous efforts of seemingly unorganised gig workers to organise 'strikes' or other forms of what would normally be seen as industrial action, including Deliveroo workers in France, Uber drivers in California and New York, and Uber Eats workers in Britain.[102] Some workers do these things without any structure. Sometimes they set up their own forms of worker collective, be they to organise production through cooperatives[103] or power through association.[104] In a book of essays about platform worker cooperatives, the editors point to the imbalance of power between any cooperative and the huge private firms in the markets: the latter 'aren't coming to dominate just because of a good idea and a charismatic founder; they grow out of supportive ecosystems, including investors, lawyers, sympathetic governments and tech schools'.[105] Despite some lower overheads (no extracted surplus), cooperatives struggle against the ability of large capitalist entities to consume competition.

---

101 BBC, 'Bike Courier Wins "Gig" Economy Employment Rights Case'. *BBC News*, 7 January 2017; Matt Hamilton, 'Judge Finds NYC Uber Drivers to Be Employees; Upstate Impact Debated'. *Timesunion*, 12 September 2016, www.timesunion.com/allwcm/article/Judge-finds-NYC-Uber-drivers-to-be-employees-11220139.php; Jamie Grierson and Rob Davies, 'Pimlico Plumbers Loses Appeal against Self-employed Status'. *Guardian*, 11 February 2017; David Marin-Guzman, 'Foodora Enters Voluntary Administration'. *Australian Financial Review*, 17 August 2018. More details are in Chapter 10.

102 Anna Sansom, 'Bicycle Couriers Protest against Takeaway Food Service Deliveroo'. *France24*, 12 August 2017, www.france24.com/en/20170812-france-paris-protest-food-delivery-service-deliveroo-financial-insecurity-emmanuel-macron; Rebecca Burns, 'The Sharing Economy's "First Strike": Uber Drivers Turn Off the App'. *In These Times*, 22 October 2014, inthesetimes.com/working/entry/17279/the_sharing_economy_first_strike_uber_drivers_turn_off_the_app; Alison Griswold, 'Uber Just Caved on a Big Policy Change after Its Drivers Threatened to Strike'. *Slate*, 12 September 2014, www.slate.com/blogs/moneybox/2014/09/12/uber_drivers_strike_they_protested_cheap_uberx_fares_uber_backed_down.html; Sarah Butler, 'Uber Eats Drivers Plan Protest against Cuts in Pay Rate Per Delivery'. *Guardian*, 26 August 2016, www.theguardian.com/technology/2016/aug/25/ubereats-drivers-plan-protest-cuts-pay-rate-per-delivery-london-uber.

103 Sarah Kaine, Danielle Logue, and Emmanuel Josserand, 'The "Uberisation" of Work Is Driving People to Co-operatives'. *The Conversation*, 28 September 2016.

104 Many of the alternatives are discussed in Johnston and Land-Kazlauskas, *Organizing on-Demand*.

105 Trebor Scholz and Nathan Schneider, *Ours to Hack and to Own: The Rise of Platform Cooperativism, a New Vision for the Future of Work and a Fairer Internet* (New York: OR Books, 2017).

The most effective form of collective response appears to be when platform workers work with, form, or become part of, a union, and work with others with experience in building collective power.

For many unions, this is new territory that they are venturing into; but for some, it has been the nature of the work that they have always been organising. Unions representing workers in the film, video and theatrical industries have been organising gig workers—that is, those engaged in single musical performances or shows—for decades. In Hollywood, for example, unions representing independent contractors have long negotiated with the centres of capital—movie producers and firms—to guarantee minimum pay and benefits, and those unions reinforce the values, sense of efficacy and collective identity of those workers.[106] In Canada, entertainment unions have made use of cultural policy to promote adequate labour standards and employment rights.[107]

Technological changes that make it easier for employers to *dis*organise workers into fragmented units can also be used by unions. For example, Facebook technology has been used by some unions, such as United Voice in Australia, not only to organise their own members (indeed, many unions have a social media presence) but also to mobilise nonmembers around particular issues or interest groups, such as underpayment of workers in the hospitality industry. That said, few union delegates across Australian unions in the mid-2010s made substantial use of Facebook or Twitter for union matters.[108]

In the USA, Walmart has been one of the most determined and successful employers at keeping unions out, even closing stores after they unionised,[109] so a new organisation, 'OUR Walmart' ('Organisation United for Respect at Walmart'), was established by the United Food

106 W. Harry Fortuna, 'The Gig Economy Is a Disaster for Workers. Hollywood's Unions Can Help Them Learn to Fight Back'. *Quartz,* 1 September 2017, qz.com/1052310/hollywood-unions-offer-the-perfect-model-for-the-beaten-down-workers-of-todays-gig-economy/.

107 Amanda Coles, 'Unintended Consequences: Examining the Impact of Tax Credit Programmes on Work in the Canadian Independent Film and Television Production Sector'. *Canadian Journal of Communication* 31, no. 3 (2010): 519–40.

108 Peetz et al., 'The Meaning and Making of Union Delegate Networks'.

109 Rhéal Séguin, 'Ex-Wal-Mart Workers Win Battle'. *Globe and Mail,* 17 September 2005; Benedict Sheehy, 'Corporations and Social Costs: The Wal-Mart Case Study'. *University of Pittsburgh Journal of Law and Commerce* 24 (2004): 1–39; Michael P. Vandenbergh, 'The New Wal-Mart Effect: The Role of Private Contracting in Global Governance'. *UCLA Law Review* 54 (2007): 913–70; Paul Weinberg, 'Closure of First Unionised Wal-Mart Sends Chilling Signal'. Inter Press Service News Agency, 15 April 2005.

and Commercial Workers Union to support and, at times, mobilise workers, first through Facebook and then through a customised app ('WorkIt') that Walmart warned its employees ('associates') not to download.[110] The campaigning by OUR Walmart, through organising in workplaces from outside workplaces, led to public demonstrations and to Walmart raising wages to over $10 per hour and some victories for pregnant workers, though OUR Walmart continued to campaign for much more.[111] By mid-2017, the app had seen cumulative totals of over 150,000 Walmart employees from 3,100 stores engaged in discussions, with 50,000 per week seeing messages from OUR Walmart and 40,000 in private groups linked to the organisation. When Walmart employees use the app to ask questions, they may be answered by an AI bot (if the question is simple), by fellow members of online communities, or by volunteers or union employees if very complicated. Membership costs $5 per month. Although Walmart infiltrates and monitors the WorkIt community, and pressures employees not to participate, the structure appears to have been resilient.[112] The WorkIt approach has been spreading to other countries, including Australia.[113]

These new forms of union responses to new work organisation or technology often involve quite different repertoires of action to traditional unionism: perhaps less reliance on militancy and industrial action, more reliance on new methods of communication and campaigning. They may also sometimes use less hierarchical organisational structures, with OUR Walmart, for example, having more of a network form than a traditional union structure. Rather than seeing these techniques as taking the place of conventional union methods, it is more appropriate to interpret them as supplementing these methods—as ways of developing collective (rather than individual) grievances, building collective values and identities,

110 Eduardo Munoz, 'Walmart Warns Workers Not to Use App Helping Them Understand Company's Labor Rules'. *RT*, 17 November 2016, www.rt.com/usa/367062-walmart-worker-app-workit/; Andy Kroll, 'Walmart Workers Get Organized—Just Don't Say the U-Word'. *Mother Jones*, March/April 2016, www.motherjones.com/politics/2013/02/our-walmart-black-friday-union/.

111 Sean McElwee and Amy Traub, 'Don't Believe the Wal-Mart Hype: Here's Proof It Still Isn't Paying Its Workers Enough'. *Salon*, 19 September 2015, www.salon.com/2015/09/19/dont_believe_the_wal_mart_hype_heres_proof_it_still_isnt_paying_its_workers_enough/; Mike Hall, 'Our Walmart Wins Some Victories for Pregnant Workers'. *People's World*, 10 April 2014, www.peoplesworld.org/article/our-walmart-wins-some-victories-for-pregnant-workers/.

112 Discussion with and talk by Dan Schlademan, Co-Director of Organisation United for Respect, Sydney, 26 June 2017.

113 David Marin-Guzman, 'How "Young Tech Dudes" Are Decentralising Unions with Blockchain, AI'. *Australian Financial Review*, 28 December 2017. Ignore the blockchain in this article, focus on the AI.

and perhaps critically developing a sense of collective efficacy. Building networks that facilitate collective action are also essential purposes of such techniques, while the unions themselves become collective mobilisers and, through flatter structures, promote democratic coordination.

As this book shows, though, the platform economy and new technologies at the workplace are not really the main game in the future of work. The main game is more about who has power. After all, Walmart is not a tech firm, the platform economy is still quite small, but there have been huge changes in union density, public policy and financialisation over recent decades. American activists Sarita Gupta, Stephen Lerner and Joseph McCartin dismiss concerns about technology and instead urge unions to find 'new ways of organizing and bargaining' in a world characterised by 'fissuring', financialisation, austerity, concentrated power, widening inequality and unwillingness by the state to act for workers.[114] They suggest 'bargaining for the common good', in which unionised (or even nonunion) workers take action that 'advance[s] the shared goals of workers and their allies'—that is, other community groups. They suggest organising against large, core companies to challenge not just their treatment of workers but also monopolisation. And they suggest targeting banks and private equity, in part to attempt to 'regulate from below' and to engage with external groups affected by finance capital. The emphasis is on extending unions' focus outside the employment relationship to broader social and economic issues, working with the rest of civil society.[115] This is perhaps the most promising but probably the most difficult thing for unions to do. Working with community groups was an unfulfilled aim of Australian unions' otherwise successful 2007 'Your Rights @ Work' campaign.[116] It is slow: unions often have a tactical rather than strategic focus and want to play a dominant role in an alliance, disengaging other groups.[117] It faces legal barriers that other forms of union cooperation do not: competition law in many countries, constraining or prohibiting collective action

114 Sarita Gupta, Stephen Lerner, and Joseph A. McCartin, 'It's Not the "Future of Work," It's the Future of Workers That's in Doubt'. *American Prospect*, 31 August 2018, prospect.org/article/its-not-future-work-its-future-workers-doubt.

115 Ibid.

116 Kathie Muir and David Peetz, 'Not Dead Yet: The Australian Union Movement and the Defeat of a Government'. *Social Movement Studies* 9, no. 2 (2010): 215–28.

117 Amanda Tattersall, *Power in Coalition: Strategies for Strong Unions and Social Change* (Ithaca NY: Cornell University Press, 2010); Jane Holgate, 'The Sydney Alliance: A Broad-Based Community Organising Potential for Trade Union Transformation?'. *Economic and Industrial Democracy* 39, no. 3 (2015).

outside of labour law, is not just a challenge to organising workers classed as 'self-employed' or 'contractors', it is a challenge to all 'bargaining for the common good'.[118]

In the end, it is the taking of collective action that damages the profitability of capital and forces capital to concede workers' demands. It can also force the state to concede. Sometimes this is achieved through causing reputational harm to corporations or the state—examples include some international campaigns around multinational codes of conduct (discussed in Chapter 9) as well as, in Australia, the 'Destroy the Joint' campaign, and union campaigns against attempts by some firms to substantially reduce wages through the use of contractors (Carlton United Breweries) or terminating agreements (Streets).[119] More often, damage is achieved through the withdrawal of labour. The failure of previous attempts to organise Walmart workers in the face of strong and sophisticated employer opposition suggested that the old methods were not working there. The methods of leverage used by OUR Walmart—damaging the reputation of the firm through street demonstrations and other public actions—point to how threatening profits will always be the ultimate means by which workers achieve gains relative to capital, no matter what the mode of production is.

In extending from tackling the corporations that hire workers to 'bargaining for the common good', unions may also find the state actively mobilises against labour in ways that it does not always do when labour just takes on those corporations. The state, though, responds to very different incentives to corporations. Maximising votes and legitimacy are not the same as maximising profits, and the political strategy for achieving concessions from the state need not be the same as that for achieving concessions from capital.

---

118 Johnston and Land-Kazlauskas, *Organizing on-Demand.*

119 AAP, 'Union Launches Streets Ice-Cream Boycott for Australian Summer'. *Guardian*, 30 October 2017, www.theguardian.com/australia-news/2017/oct/30/union-launches-streets-ice-cream-boycott-for-australian-summer; Jane Caro, ed., *Destroying the Joint: Why Women Have to Change the World* (Brisbane: University of Queensland Press, 2013).

Conclusion

While some corporations may encourage their workers to conditionally exercise 'voice', and may increasingly do this in future to facilitate productivity or even disguise other, pervasive methods of control, it is only through independent voice mechanisms—mostly trade unions—that workers can guarantee they have some control at work. These employee-controlled mechanisms have been in decline for several decades, not because of changing attitudes by employees, but because of the institutional changes that neo-liberalism has encouraged.

There is no single solution that applies universally, but common to success is a focus on the workplace, albeit with strong articulation outside the workplace, and an emphasis on democracy. Some unions are successfully adapting to the fragmentation created by modern management strategies by adopting new techniques that promote collective recognition of grievances, efficacy, identity, values and networks. Strength in these will be key to the success of collective mobilisation in future.

If the voice of workers—that is, the collective power of labour—does not increase, in the face of the growth of other centres of power in society, it is unlikely that the outcomes for workers from developments in the future of work will be good. This is a critical aspect of the 'sliding doors' situation that society faces. We saw in Chapter 1 how significant unions are for reducing inequality in incomes, wealth and power in society. So the choices that unions make will have a crucial impact on workers and on society, as will the choices made by policy-makers that affect the ability of unions, and other collective forms of labour, to organise.

8

Women and segmentation

In 1888, a group of women, mostly teenagers, were working in London factories, making matchsticks. The pay was low and employment conditions were poor. The work was dangerous, exposure to phosphorous often leading to disfigurement and an early, painful death. Workers' pay was docked for seemingly arbitrary reasons. One day, after yet another worker was visibly victimised, the women had had enough. The women went on strike, refusing to return to work until things changed. They won, and the impact on labour relations across society was profound. Others followed suit in striking, from coal miners to female garment workers, even in the US. Conditions improved. British union membership trebled over the next 30 years.[1]

A century plus later, much has changed, but some things remain the same. Working conditions, particularly regarding occupation health and safety, have improved. Women remain militant. Gender-based pay discrimination has persisted through most societies; in some (like Australia) it was institutionalised through legally binding decisions or enactments until explicit discrimination was technically abandoned in the

1 Most of the strikers were at a Bryant and May factory, though this company is unrelated to the modern-day firm of the same name. A.J. Arnold, *'Ex Luce Lucellum'? Innovation, Class Interests and Economic Returns in the Nineteenth Century Match Trade*. Paper No. 04/06 (Exeter: University of Exeter, 2004), business-school.exeter.ac.uk/documents/papers/accounting/2004/0406.pdf; Ali Alkhatib, Michael S. Bernstein, and Margaret Levi, 'Examining Crowd Work and Gig Work through the Historical Lens of Piecework'. Paper presented at CHI'17—*Proceedings of the 2017 CHI Conference on Human Factors in Computing Systems*, Denver, CO, 6–11 May 2017): 4599–4616; Catherine Best (Kelsey), 'Meet the Matchstick Women—the Hidden Victims of the Industrial Revolution'. *The Conversation*, 8 March 2018, theconversation.com/meet-the-matchstick-women-the-hidden-victims-of-the-industrial-revolution-87453.

1970s.[2] The gap between men's and women's pay—the 'gender pay gap'—has reduced but it endures in most countries.[3] The term 'gender gap' may also refer to situations in which women receive poorer working conditions than men or may have inferior experiences such as being harassed more commonly at work than men. Thus the 'gender gap' is an indicator of disadvantage experienced by women at work.[4]

In this chapter we focus on the issues of gender and related segmentation at work. It starts with a discussion of the broad institutional factors shaping how gender and work interact: the domestic sphere, its link to social values and norms, regulation through the state and unions and the role of organisational policies and practices. The situations of and problems faced by women are quite different in female-dominated and male-dominated work, so the largest part of this chapter gives attention to the specific circumstances of women in female-dominated and male-dominated work. In doing that, we also look to the future: are female-dominated jobs under threat, or is the greater threat from what is happening to women in male-dominated jobs? The chapter includes brief discussion of some of the other issues facing women no matter whether they are in a 'men's job' or a 'women's job'.

With the title 'Women and segmentation', the focus is very much on gender as a source of disadvantage, rather than on other factors that may create disadvantage in the labour market, such as age (being young, or old), disability, race or ethnicity. Some factors involved in labour market disadvantage (such as labour market segmentation and regulation distance) have general application across many forms of disadvantage. Others (such as the role of the domestic sphere) are specific to understanding disadvantage associated with gender. Importantly, no matter whether a female worker is in a 'men's job' or a 'women's job', her situation is also made more difficult if she also possesses one of these other sources of disadvantage. Researching

2 Suzanne Franzway, 'The Changing Sexual Politics of Gender Regulation by Unions'. In *Women, Labor Segmentation and Regulation: Varieties of Gender Gaps*, ed. David Peetz and Georgina Murray (New York: Palgrave Macmillan, 2017), 61–78.

3 For example, Alison C. Preston, 'Female Earnings in Australia: An Analysis of 1991 Census Data'. *Australian Bulletin of Labour* 26, no. 1 (2000): 38–58; Phyllis Tharenou, 'The Work of Feminists Is Not Yet Done: The Gender Pay Gap—a Stubborn Anachronism'. *Sex Roles* 68, no. 3–4 (2013): 198–206; Rebecca Cassells et al., 'The Impact of a Sustained Gender Wage Gap on the Australian Economy'. Report to the Office for Women, Department of Families, Community Services, Housing and Indigenous Affairs (Canberra: NATSEM, University of Canberra, November 2009).

4 David Peetz and Georgina Murray, *Women, Labor Segmentation and Regulation.*

this is what is referred to as studying 'intersectionality'.[5] One of those forms of intersectionality, and the one that is discussed in the latter part of this chapter, is the intersection of gender and migrant status. It could be persuasively argued there are other, more important ones, such as the intersection of gender and 'race'.[6] In the USA, for example, 'race' is the principal cleavage in the labour market, and the factor most closely linked to class and disadvantage. Its role is explicitly tied to the history of slavery.[7] In Europe, however, 'race' is almost a taboo term in many circles, and in several countries the collection of racial statistics is illegal,[8] probably a tie to the history of war. More research and academic discourse there focuses on the related themes of ethnicity, migrants and migration. There is not sufficient space here to do justice to either issue, but the issues discussed later in this chapter are more akin to those relevant in Europe (and among the Hispanic population of North America).

Institutions and gender at work

How gender interacts with work is influenced by a number of institutions. These include domestic labour; social values and norms; and the state—including the regulatory and legal framework and the behaviour of the state as employer and provider of social infrastructure and services such as childcare.

Domestic labour and the workplace

The domestic sphere is a central factor in gender segmentation of the labour force—perhaps, ultimately, the driving force for the durability of gender inequality. Men were traditionally available for working long hours,

5 Kimberlé Williams Crenshaw, 'Demarginalizing the Intersection of Race and Sex: A Black Feminist Critique of Antidiscrimination Doctrine, Feminist Theory and Antiracist Politics'. *University of Chicago Legal Forum* 1989, no. 1 (1989): 139–67.

6 'Race' is in quotation marks because of strong genetic evidence there is no biological concept of race, it is entirely a social construct. See *Race: The Power of an Illusion* (California Newsreel in association with the Independent Television Service, 2003), summarized at www.youtube.com/watch?v=Y8MS6zubIaQ or read the transcript at newsreel.org/transcripts/race.htm. See also Audrey Smedley, 'The History of the Idea of Race … And Why It Matters'. Paper presented at Race, Human Variation and Disease: Consensus and Frontiers conference, Warrenton, VA, 14–17 March 2007.

7 Kevin B. Anderson, 'Marx's Intertwining of Race and Class During the Civil War in the U.S.'. *Journal of Classical Sociology* 17, no. 1 (2017): 24–36; Smedley, 'History of Idea of Race'.

8 Karina Piser, 'Breaking France's Race Taboo'. *Nation*, 10 August 2018. www.thenation.com/article/breaking-frances-race-taboo/.

only because someone was at home doing all the things that needed to be done to get men to work and to produce the next generation of workers. It is a variant on this model that is depicted in Atwood's *The Handmaid's Tale*. This traditional 'breadwinner' model of domestic organisation has declined as more women enter the labour force and participate in paid labour, a phenomenon that has been gathering pace since the 1960s.

The tasks allocated within the domestic sphere are largely replicated in the market sphere. For example, as women have entered the workforce, and activities that were previously undertaken within the household now have to be organised through the market, those paid occupations previously done in the household tend to be undertaken in the market by women. Tasks that are done seemingly for free in the home are generally perceived to be of low value in the formal economy and, as we see later, receive low pay and status.[9]

Social values and norms

The role of women in domestic labour shapes and is in turn shaped by social values and norms that prioritised roles of women as homemakers. Attitudes towards working women vary considerably between societies. Depending on the strength and scope of 'conservative' views about women's roles, in some societies women may, as a result of such values, be barred from particular occupations or industries, prevented from working at all if they are married, or paid substantially less than men who are doing exactly the same work. In fact, *all* of those things happened in several countries until at least the 1960s or 1970s, and in some countries they still do—not just in Atwood's Gilead.[10]

Social values and norms are not created from thin air, of course. They reflect the reinforcement of ideas (to serve the interests of powerful groups) through socialisation and the contestation of ideas. Socialisation may occur within the home; within the primary and secondary education systems; through the mass media; through religious institutions; and within the workplace. The contestation of ideas may occur as objective circumstances raise doubt about the validity of dominant values (e.g. the idea never really

9 Damian Grimshaw and Jill Rubery, *Undervaluing Women's Work*. EOC Working Paper Series (Manchester: Equal Opportunities Commission and European Work and Employment Research Centre, University of Manchester 2007).

10 To see a realistic cinematic depiction of those things in a contemporary society outside the industrialised world, see the 2012 Saudi movie *Wadjda*.

seemed fair to most single women that they should be paid less than single men); as social movements (such as the feminist movement) challenge the interests of powerful groups; through alternative institutions and media; and even in tertiary education (e.g. racism is negatively correlated with education levels).

As we saw in previous chapters, dominant groups may seek to maintain and exercise their power by attempting to shape the values and preferences of those in the dominated group, sometimes using members of the dominated group (as in *The Handmaid's Tale*'s Aunts). Yet, as we also saw, the control so exercised is almost always only partial, and sometimes eventually collapses. Values such as fairness (or even self-preservation) can directly confront existing cultural practices and eventually overturn them. The women in *The Handmaid's Tale* attempted (often successfully) to flee Gilead for Canada, and eventually (though we are not told precisely how) Gilead collapsed.

There is another aspect of norms and behaviour we must consider. A fundamental difference between men and women is their experience of violence, best summarised by Margaret Atwood's observation, long after writing *The Handmaid's Tale*, that men are 'afraid women will laugh at them' while women are 'afraid of being killed'.[11] The implicit *threat* of violence, even if never actualised, can help suppress the wage demands of any group,[12] including women. Violence does not only occur in the domestic setting, of course. It is also potentially relevant at work. One important aspect of many women's experience at work is harassment, which might be sexual or simply sex-based (i.e. arising from the fact that the offender's coworker is a woman).[13] Gender-based harassment is one way in which the threat or actuality of violence is manifested at work, and so prohibitions on sexual harassment, as implemented through judge-based law in the USA, have been shown to increase female labour

11 Margaret Atwood, *Curious Pursuits* (London: Hachette Digital, Little Brown Book Group, 2009). This line was also uttered by one of the characters in the second TV series of *The Handmaid's Tale*.

12 Peter Bachrach and Morton S. Baratz, *Power and Poverty: Theory and Practice* (New York: Oxford University Press, 1970).

13 One recent example, by no means the most extreme, concerned the ANZ Bank. Andrew Robertson, 'ANZ Controversy: Stricter Penalties May Be Needed to Improve Bank Culture'. *The Drum* (Australian Broadcasting Corporation, 2016), 22 January, www.abc.net.au/news/2016-01-22/robertson-penalties-may-be-needed-to-improve-bank-culture/7106804.

force participation and relative female incomes.[14] The less strict are prohibitions on any form of violence, including harassment, the more likely that harassment of women will be higher and their relative incomes will be lower.

Some organisations have 'employee action plans' that provide counselling or assistance to employees who have experienced domestic violence, and a growing number of collective agreements in Australia contain domestic violence clauses, enabling people to access leave in such situations. It is only used by a small proportion of workers but, for those who do, it is extremely important.[15]

Regulation

A key factor influencing the situation of women at work is the roles played by regulation and by the state. There are three aspects of what the state does that have a critical impact on women's situation.

The law and regulatory framework

Just as attitudes vary hugely between societies, so too does the legal framework: from Scandinavia (where parental leave available on birth of a child can only be fully used if it is shared between fathers and mothers) to Pakistan (in parts of which girls are unable to even attend school, let alone gain skilled employment). Within a country, legislation on such matters as sex discrimination and equal employment opportunity, the rules of industrial tribunals[16] and decisions of courts[17] can have major impacts on what happens in the workplace.

14 Daniel L. Chen and Jasmin Sethi, *Insiders and Outsiders: Does Forbidding Sexual Harassment Exacerbate Gender Inequality?* John M. Olin Centre for Law, Economics and Business (Cambridge, MA: Harvard Law School, 2011), www.law.harvard.edu/programs/olin_center/Prizes/2008.pdf.

15 There is a range of research in this area; for example, Suzanne Franzway, C. Zufferey, and D. Chung, 'Domestic Violence and Women's Employment'. Paper presented at the Our Work, Our Lives National Conference on Women and Industrial Relations, Adelaide, 21 September 2007; Sylvia Walby, Jude Towers, and Brian Francis, 'Mainstreaming Domestic and Gender-Based Violence into Sociology and the Criminology of Violence'. *Sociological Review* 62, no. S2 (2014): 187–214; Jeff Hearn, 'The Organization(s) of Violence: Men, Gender Relations, Organizations and Violences'. *Human Relations* 47, no. 6 (1994): 731–54. Data on the incidence of domestic violence in Australia were published by the ABS (Australian Bureau of Statistics, 'Recorded Crime—Victims, Australia, 2014'. Canberra 4510.0; Australian Bureau of Statistics, 'Recorded Crime—Offenders, Australia, 2014–15'. Canberra 4519.0.

16 Such as those shaping the restructuring of Australian awards in the 1980s.

17 For example, a 1980s judicial finding that BHP had discriminated against women in its 'last-on-first-off' firing practices.

The state as employer

Legislation is not the only way by which the state affects the workplace. The state is itself a large employer, and its practices can be models for private sector employers, particularly large ones. For example, equal opportunity requirements on Australian public service employers have been more detailed and demanding than those affecting private sector employers. Entitlements (such as annual leave or maternity leave) may be put in place first in public sector organisations and then spread through comparison pressures to larger private sector employers.

State infrastructure and services

The state affects the workplace through the allocation of resources in the budget. As just one example, the availability of affordable childcare, in appropriate locations, is a key factor enabling women to participate in the labour force and influencing the number of hours they work. The availability, generosity and conditions for parental leave are another. In Sweden, for example, part of the parental leave entitlement in effect must be taken by the father, so male involvement in child rearing (or 'childcare') is much higher.

Thus the state regulates by setting rules and procedures that shape the framework, but also by example (as employer) and by the allocation of public resources. The state matters when its behaviour reflects something different to what would otherwise have come about as a result of the operation of existing social values and norms held by people in power and operating in a market. So if the state passes laws that just formalise what everybody would have done anyway, it will make no difference. In *The Handmaid's Tale*, the state created regulations that were out of step with many people's views. In that story, as with most regulatory paradigm shifts, attitudes evolved to adjust to and in many cases accept the new norms embodied in the regulation, though many continued to resist. But if laws preclude discriminatory behaviour when *some* employers would otherwise behave in a discriminatory manner, then regulation will make a difference to the gender gap at work.

Trade unions and women

The state is not the only regulatory institution. Unions also perform that function. Unions regulate work by negotiating collective agreements with employers that shape the pay and conditions of workers. They constrain the freedom of management to exercise its prerogative to manage workers in whatever way they see fit. They also put pressure on the state (governments, courts and tribunals) to establish or improve minimum wages or minimum conditions of employment in a number of areas.

As with the state, if unions just reflect the values of people with power, they make no positive difference to gender at work. For example, up until the 1960s, trade unions paid little attention to women,[18] and indeed supported unequal wages for men and women, institutionalising the discriminatory norms of the time. That is, their position reflected the dominance of the 'family needs' or 'male breadwinner' notion in wage fixing and union ideology. Unions primarily concerned themselves with organising and representing male members. Unions as a regulatory institution reinforced the lower pay of women compared to men and essentially did nothing to alter the situation of women.

Around the 1960s—under the rising influence of the women's movement—union policy changed. They tended to support equal pay and thus union rules and agreements reduced the ability of managers to pay men and women differently. Still, women were, and remain, underrepresented in unions at all levels, and underrepresentation is most severe in the senior levels of unions.[19] Women are also underrepresented among union delegates. However, underrepresentation of women in union officialdom and delegate structures has been easing.[20] A number of researchers have referred to the poor performance of unions in serving their female members and the lack of interest by male-dominated unions in women.[21]

18 For example, Franzway, 'Changing Sexual Politics by Unions'.

19 Ibid.; Geraldine Healy and Gill Kirton, 'Women, Power and Trade Union Government in the UK'. *British Journal of Industrial Relations* 38, no. 3 (2000): 343–60; Barbara Pocock, 'Women Count: Women in South Australian Trade Unions' (Adelaide: Centre for Labour Studies, University of Adelaide, 1992).

20 For example, Barbara Pocock, 'Gender and Activism in Australian Unions'. *Journal of Industrial Relations* 37, no. 3 (1995): 377–400; Jane Parker and Julie Douglas, 'Can Women's Structures Help New Zealand and UK Trade Unions' Revival?'. *Journal of Industrial Relations* 52(4) (2010): 439–58; Rae Cooper, 'The Gender Gap in Union Leadership in Australia: A Qualitative Study'. *Journal of Industrial Relations* 54, no. 2 (2012): 131–46.

21 For example, Franzway, 'Changing Sexual Politics by Unions'; Des Storer and Kay Hargreaves, 'Migrant Women in Industry'. In *Social Policy and Problems of the Workforce*, ed. Steven Staats (Melbourne: Australian Council of Trade Unions, 1976), 39–104.

Yet union density has been slightly higher among females than males in several countries (such as Sweden, the UK, New Zealand and Australia) for several years now.[22] Women are disproportionately employed in the public sector, which has higher union density than the private sector, and now this more than offsets the downward effect on women's overall density arising from the concentration of women in particular occupations and in casual or temporary employment.[23] The evidence generally suggests that, when they are in similar situations in the labour market, females and males are now equally likely to join unions.[24] Women appear to have more to gain from union membership than men, as those with weaker labour market positions often (though not always) have more to gain from unionisation. That is another way of saying the gender gap in pay or conditions is lower for unionised workers.[25] Unionisation appears positively linked to gender equity: countries with higher rates of union density tend to have higher ratios of female to male earned income and higher scores on the United Nations Gender Development Index.[26]

Regulation distance

Not all workers are equally affected by regulation. Those on low wages are more likely to be affected by minimum wage laws than other workers, and those minimum wage laws apply equally to men and women (but there are more women than men in low-wage jobs affected by minimum wages). Those in larger and unionised workplaces are much more likely to be covered by a collective agreement. Those in senior management positions are less likely to be affected by any wage regulation by unions or the state. Lower-level employees, especially those without union membership, are

---

22 Australian Bureau of Statistics, 'Employee Earnings, Benefits and Trade Union Membership, Australia'. Canberra 6310.0; Australian Bureau of Statistics, 'Characteristics of Employment'. Canberra 6333.0.

23 David Peetz, 'Trend Analysis of Union Membership'. *Australian Journal of Labour Economics* 8, no. 1 (2005): 1–24.

24 For example, Paul F.M. Grimes, 'The Determinants of Trade Union Membership: Evidence from Two Australian Surveys' (Research School of Social Sciences, The Australian National University, 1994).

25 For example, David G. Blanchflower, 'Changes over Time in Union Relative Wage Effects in Great Britain and the United States'. In *The History and Practice of Economics: Essays in Honor of Bernard Corry and Maurice Preston*, ed. Sami Daniel, Philip Arestis, and John Grahl (Edward Elgar, 1999); Andrew Jackson and Grant Schellenberg, *Unions, Collective Bargaining and Labour Market Outcomes for Canadian Working Women: Past Gains and Future Challenges*. Research Report 11 (Canadian Labour Congress, 1999).

26 Data from International Labour Organization, *Statistics of Trade Union Membership* (Geneva: ILO Bureau of Statistics, 2006); United Nations, 'Human Development Report 2004: Statistics' (UN, 2005).

less likely to be aware of their rights under antidiscrimination or equal opportunity legislation. The greater the practical 'distance' of employees from regulation, by definition, the less affected their situation will be by it. Low 'regulation distance' implies rules or behaviours are in place that will reduce the gender wage gap, provided that the content of the regulation is itself more favourable for women than the norms of those in positions of power that they override.[27] However, the outcome will depend on the interaction with labour market segmentation, the focus of the later part of this chapter.

Organisational policies and practices

How gender interacts with work is also influenced *within* the workplace, by organisational policies and practices, and by interactions with trade unions in the workplace. Two organisations within the same industry and region may sometimes have quite different gender patterns of employment and pay, depending on the characteristics of the organisation and its management.

For example, whether gender segmentation (more about that shortly) is eased or exacerbated in the workplace depends on such matters as: policies and practices for handling harassment; mechanisms to ensure that policies and procedures are 'gender neutral'; whether individual managers endorse and propagate such values; whether there are systems in place to ensure that equity issues are taken into account in employment relations practices; the ability of organisations to ensure that 'discretionary' decision-making is gender neutral (e.g. the provision of 'market loadings' in salaries); the level of transparency in pay (a female supervisor testified that she only discovered she was being paid less than her male subordinates when the company went bankrupt and the pay details emerged in court);[28] and the existence, content and quality of training of line managers, and how it is followed up.

As you can infer from the above, policy is one thing, practice may be another, and the values and behaviour of individual managers are often critical within a particular work area. Policies will constrain behaviour

27 Peetz and Murray, *Varieties of Gender Gaps*.
28 Lisa M. Maatz, 'The Awful Truth Behind the Gender Pay Gap'. *ForbesWoman*, 7 April 2014.

but they can rarely cover every possible aspect of behaviour, and so organisational culture becomes as important as the formal rules—though of course culture is itself influenced by the rules and policies in place.

The intertwining of policy and culture was highlighted in *The Handmaid's Tale*, where harassment and discrimination were so institutionalised that a specific practice of rape was ritualised. This may seem such a fictional world as to be irrelevant, but in many male-dominated institutions (such as the military) analogous behaviours were accepted,[29] sometimes as part of initiation ('hazing') ceremonies. There is a long history of rape being used by military forces as a weapon of war.[30] The cultural embeddedness of sexist or violent practices is why more enlightened military leaders have encountered great resistance to banning them.[31]

Norms of negotiation within organisations

The experiences of women in any workplace will be influenced by the form wage negotiation takes, as this has a particular impact on women. A number of studies indicate that women tend to be overrepresented in occupations and industries with relatively weak bargaining power.[32] In collective bargaining situations, women generally have similar power and militancy to men. But in individualised employment relations, where women are expected to 'negotiate' their pay and conditions, they are especially disadvantaged.

Studies have shown that women and men negotiate differently, particularly in relation to money, meaning that—if negotiations take place at all—women are likely to undersell themselves, relative to men, in individual contract negotiations (or, more accurately, men are more

29 ABC News, 'Family Says Cadet Raped, Told to "Suck It Up"'. *ABC News*, 7 April 2011, www.abc.net.au/news/2011-04-07/family-says-cadet-raped-told-to-suck-it-up/2626738?site=news; Simon Santow, 'Defence Lobby Returns Fire over Cadet Sex Claims'. *ABC News*, 17 April 2011, www.abc.net.au/news/2011-04-07/defence-lobby-returns-fire-over-cadet-sex-claims/2624172?site=news.

30 Susan. A. Brownmiller, *Against Our Will: Men, Women, and Rape* (New York: Simon & Schuster, 1975).

31 Anne Summers, 'The Education of David Morrison'. *Anne Summers Reports* 11 (2015): 22–34; David Wroe, 'Defence Boss Blasts "Stalking Horse" Critics of Australian of the Year David Morrison'. *Sydney Morning Herald*, 24 February 2016, www.smh.com.au/politics/federal/defence-boss-blasts-stalking-horse-critics-of-australian-of-the-year-david-morrison-20160224-gn2swe.html.

32 See, for example, Glenda Strachan and John Burgess, 'Employment Restructuring, Enterprise Bargaining and Employment Conditions for Women Workers'. Paper presented at the Current Research in Industrial Relations conference, AIRAANZ, Brisbane, 1997, 321–29.

likely to exaggerate their abilities).[33] An implication claimed by one writer is that 'manifestations of hubris—often masked as charisma or charm—are commonly mistaken for leadership potential, and that these occur much more frequently in men than in women'; in other words, a disproportionate number of incompetent men become managers.[34] That said, it is questionable how much, if any, of the blame for a gender gap should be placed at the feet of women's agency, as much of this behavioural difference is likely a structural effect, arising from socialisation processes, not just before the workplace but within and outside it. The media, for example, focus on female CEOs' gender, family and personal life when writing stories about them, but not when writing about male CEOs.[35] Their colleagues do likewise and look for an 'ideal manager' who is free of encumbrances, able to adopt masculinist, warlike rhetoric and make the 'hard decisions'.[36]

A related concept is that of 'unconscious bias', whereby decision-makers favour characteristics associated with males rather than females and in negotiations will favour a male over a similarly qualified female without realising they are doing so. Organisational responses to this have included ensuring that women are represented on all selection panels (or even on panels in conferences, where people often network and attain recognition), and providing training on recognising and offsetting unconscious bias to managers. The latter is controversial in some instances: one critic wonders how managers can detect something of which they are not conscious,[37] though it probably helps promote good practice in other instances. Often the bigger problem is that women are not appearing as candidates for

33 David Peetz, 'Collateral Damage: Women and the Workchoices Battlefield'. *Hecate* 33, no. 1 (2007): 61–80; Linda Babcock and Sara Laschever, *Women Don't Ask: Negotiation and the Gender Divide* (Princeton, NJ: Princeton University Press, 2003); Lisa A. Barron, 'Ask and You Shall Receive? Gender Differences in Negotiators' Beliefs and Requests for a Higher Salary'. *Human Relations* 56, no. 6 (2003): 635–62; Rosabeth Kanter, *Men and Women of the Corporation* (New York: Basic Books, 1977); Muriel Niederle and Lise Vesterlund, *Do Women Shy Away from Competition? Do Men Compete Too Much?* NBER Working Paper No. 11474 (Cambridge, MA: National Bureau of Economic Research, July 2005).

34 Tomas Chamorro-Premuzic, 'Why Do So Many Incompetent Men Become Leaders?'. *Harvard Business Review blog* (22 August 2013).

35 Rockefeller Foundation and Global Strategy Group, *CEOs & Gender: A Media Analysis* (New York: Rockefeller Foundation, 26 October 2016), www.rockefellerfoundation.org/report/infographic-media-influence-perceive-women-leadership/.

36 David Peetz, Georgina Murray, and Mahan Poorhosseinzadeh, 'Why Do Women at the Top of Organizations Do Worse?'. In *Women, Labor Segmentation and Regulation: Varieties of Gender Gaps*, ed. David Peetz and Georgina Murray (New York: Palgrave Macmillan, 2017).

37 Mike Noon, 'Pointless Diversity Training: Unconscious Bias, New Racism and Agency'. *Work, Employment and Society* 32, no. 1 (2018): 198–209.

consideration by selection panels anyway, and responses to that often require examining the structural issues behind this. 'Unconscious bias' seems, however, to go further than favouring characteristics associated with men. Women who demonstrate some 'male' characteristics, such as assertiveness—even hubris—appear to be penalised for the same things men are rewarded for.[38] The social construction of charisma appears highly gendered, not only helping incompetent men to become leaders, even CEOs, but also keeping women away from those positions.[39]

Labour market segmentation

Labour market segmentation is also critical to understanding the situation of women. Institutions and markets interact to produce the phenomenon of labour market segmentation. It is well recognised that there are 'female-dominated' and 'male-dominated' jobs, and the extent to which jobs can be characterised as 'male' or 'female' (or 'Turkish', 'Vietnamese', etc.) is what people are talking about when they refer to labour segmentation. Through labour market segmentation, labour markets are effectively divided into groups with different bargaining power and status, enabling workers with similar productivity to be paid differently according to their place in the labour market hierarchy.[40]

Labour market segmentation divides male and female jobs; it also segments employees from non–English speaking backgrounds, intermittently unemployed people, Indigenous Australians and people with disabilities. For certain jobs, employers prefer to hire from the less advantaged segments of the labour force, because the lack of choice means that workers there are prepared to work for less and to accept worse conditions. In segmented labour markets, skills associated with marginal groups are given less value than those associated with more powerful groups of employees.[41]

38 Julie E. Phelan and Laurie A. Rudman, 'Prejudice toward Female Leaders: Backlash Effects and Women's Impression Management Dilemma'. *Social and Personality Psychology Compass* 4, no. 10 (2010): 807–20.

39 On the role of charisma in selecting CEOs, see Peter Bloom and Carl Rhodes, *CEO Society: The Corporate Takeover of Everyday Life* (London: Zed, 2018).

40 Peter Brosnan, 'Labour Markets and Social Deprivation'. *Labour and Industry* 7, no. 2 (1996): 3–34.

41 Ibid.

There are several sources of gender segmentation of labour markets,[42] several of which have been indicated already. Some jobs are socially defined as 'women's jobs'. There is male resistance to female employment in 'men's jobs'. Women's jobs are seen as possessing less skill content than men's jobs. Women may experience difficulties balancing paid work and domestic work. Employers may discriminate against women in terms of hiring, pay and promotion, for example due to a belief that women would be likely to leave a job to have children. In addition, a high rate of casualisation of part-time work means a lack of career paths for many women. In the USA, labour segmentation has been declining, though at a diminishing rate, since the 1970s (i.e. segmentation reduced quite a bit in the 1970s, but very little over the 2000s).[43] Segmentation also appears to have declined a little in Australia, and current forecasts suggest it will also decline in the future.[44] The pattern in most industrialised countries is that the female share of total employment has risen over the past two decades, leading to a growth in the female employment share in most industries and occupations, regardless of whether they were male- or female-dominated; the exceptions are mainly in some male-dominated industries or occupations, for example computing in many industrialised countries.[45]

The forms gender gaps take and the ways in which they are created is influenced by what labour market segments you are looking at (is it male-dominated, female-dominated or mixed?) and the extent of 'regulation distance' (is work in this industry heavily or lightly regulated, or unregulated?).[46] For example, where work is female-dominated, the main issue affecting pay is undervaluation, which results from either longstanding norms (where regulation distance is high) or the incorporation of norms into formal rules such as statutes, awards and agreements (where regulation distance is low). Where work is male-dominated, individual

42 Margaret Power, 'Woman's Work Is Never Done—by Men: A Socio-Economic Model of Sex Typing in Occupations'. *Journal of Industrial Relations* 17, no. 3 (September 1975): 225–39.

43 Francine D. Blau, Peter Brummund, and Albert Yung-Hsu Liu, *Trends in Occupational Segregation by Gender 1970–2009: Adjusting for the Impact of Changes in the Occupational Coding System*. IZA Discussion Paper No. 6490 (Bonn: Forschungsinstitut zur Zukunft der Arbeit, 2012).

44 David Peetz and Georgina Murray, 'Women's Employment, Segregation and Skills in the Future of Work'. *Labour and Industry* 29, no. 1 (2019): 132–48.

45 Bernard Keane, 'The Looming Crisis for Women in Oz Tech'. *Crikey*, 16 March 2016; Bernard Keane, 'What's Driving Women out of Tech Industries?'. *Crikey*, 17 March 2016; Bernard Keane, 'Rape Fears and Harassment, but Bright Spots for Women in Tech, Too'. *Crikey*, 18 March 2016.

46 David Peetz, 'Regulation Distance, Labour Segmentation & Gender Gaps'. *Cambridge Journal of Economics* 39, no. 2 (2015): 345–62.

women may be disadvantaged by pay discrimination (where regulation distance is high) or by career barriers or sex-based harassment (where regulation distance is low).[47]

The experiences of women in female-dominated work, and in male-dominated work, show two quite different aspects of the problems of gender at work. That is what we look at in the rest of this section. Of course, as we have already seen, women also face issues in workplaces where they are neither tokens nor the 'dominant' group. So labour segmentation does not explain everything about women's situation at work, but it still plays an important role.

Women in female-dominated work

'Female-dominated work' might refer to an industry (what the *employer* makes or does) or an occupation (what the *employee* does in their job) where female employees predominate. Examples of female-dominated industries include residential care services, social assistance services, library services and private households employing staff. On the other hand, some examples of female-dominated occupations include aged-care workers, childcare workers, librarians, primary school teachers, nurses, dental assistants, laundry workers, receptionists and hairdressers.

A common feature of many female-dominated jobs is *undervaluation.* At the heart of undervaluation of women's wages are gender-based notions of skill. Segmented 'men's' and 'women's' jobs involve different skills and attributes. Women's jobs are likely to involve personal and social relationships—common in service-industry jobs. There is a tendency to downgrade the skills of these jobs because they are associated with 'female' skills: gender differences in skill content of jobs appear to have been considerably less than gender differences in pay.[48] This relates to some aspects of emotional labour, discussed below. This undervaluation of female skill is particularly evident where the job is part-time—often reflecting the perception that part-time work is not a 'real' job.

47 Peetz and Murray, *Varieties of Gender Gaps.*

48 Sara Horrell, Jill Rubery, and Brendan Burchell, 'Unequal Jobs or Unequal Pay?'. Social Change and Economic Life Initiative Working Paper No. 6 (Oxford: Economic and Social Research Council, January 1989).

On average, women's wages are lower than men's wages.[49] Research indicates that women experience lower earnings quite early in their career. Women tend to have lower returns for education and training (but see later). Still, the gender wage gap cannot be explained by women's interruptions to labour force participation due to child rearing.[50] While the gap between men's and women's earnings is partly due to factors such as the higher proportion of women working part-time, the lower level of overtime earnings among women and the underrepresentation of women in higher paid (e.g. managerial) occupations, part of it is also due to the undervaluation of skills associated with 'women's work'. The skills associated with women's work may be undervalued not only by employers, unions and male employees but also by women themselves.

A number of female-dominated jobs are characterised not only by low wages but also by poor working conditions. This is especially the case where gender and other forms of disadvantage intersect, as we shall see later. In addition, anything that widens the distribution of income overall will tend to widen income inequality between men and women. This may offset the effects of other actions aimed at reducing gender pay gaps.[51]

Emotional labour and emotion work

Many female-dominated jobs have links back to the domestic sphere. Many of those require emotional labour, as do many female-dominated jobs that do not relate to the domestic sphere. Emotional labour is expended when an employee must manage and at times modify their own emotions (i.e. to induce or suppress their own feelings), while considering and quite often attempting to manage the emotions of the customer or client. This concept derives much from the path-breaking work of Arlie Hochschild and subsequently Sue Bolton.[52]

---

49 See footnote 3 in this chapter. But note that many of those studies control for occupation and/or industry. This means that they may understate the genuine gender pay gap, as controlling for industry and occupation removes much of that part of the gap that is due to labour market segregation, and instead mainly measures the impact of direct discrimination between men and women doing the similar work for different rates of pay.

50 Russell Rimmer and Sheila Rimmer, *More Brilliant Careers* (Canberra: AGPS, 1994).

51 Gillian Whitehouse, 'Recent Trends in Pay Equity: Beyond the Aggregate Statistics', *Journal of Industrial Relations* 43, no. 1 (2001): 66–75.

52 Arlie Hochschild, *The Managed Heart* (Berkeley and Los Angeles: University of California Press, 1983); Sharon C. Bolton and Carol Boyd, 'Trolley Dolly or Skilled Emotion Manager? Moving on from Hochschild's Managed Heart'. *Work, Employment & Society* 17, no. 2 (2003): 289–308.

In earlier chapters two divergent trends in the management of employees were discussed: increased reliance on supervision and tight management of employees; and increased reliance on the discretion of employees. These affect several different modes of work: rule-driven work, which increasingly includes work driven by mathematical algorithms; emotion work; and creative work.

The technological changes discussed earlier provide some examples of the tendency towards the first (rule-driven work).[53] Perhaps technological changes will also place greater value on workers with the capacity to undertake the second (emotion work) and the third (creative work). While rule-driven work features the tightening of direct managerial supervision, and creative work features the contrasting widening of employee discretion (a loosening of direct managerial supervision), emotion work often faces increased demands through a combination of both rules and discretion (e.g. for airline stewards, care workers or call-centre operators).

Emotional labour is typically exerted by women because of their common situation in 'caring' occupations. Such occupations are often not afforded the same status as those with male-defined 'skills'. Sometimes the ability to undertake emotional labour is defined not as a 'skill' but as an 'attribute', for which rewards are often not forthcoming. Yet it may require training and be performed in difficult circumstances.[54]

Some authors (including Hochschild) draw a distinction between 'emotional labour' and 'emotion work'. Emotion work 'requires one to induce or suppress feelings in order to sustain the outward countenance that produces the proper state of mind in others'.[55] Both emotional labour and emotion work involve an attempt to invoke a particular emotional reaction in another person. The difference is that emotional labour means you are trying to get a particular emotional response in a customer or client, while in emotion work that could be anyone, including your coworkers. So, one way of looking at the distinction between the two is to see emotional labour as demanded by the employer, while emotion work

53 See also Cathy O'Neill, *Weapons of Math Destruction: How Big Data Increases Inequality and Threatens Democracy* (New York: Crown Publishing Group, 2016).

54 Mike Noon and Paul Blyton, *The Realities of Work: Experiencing Work and Employment in Contemporary Society* (Basingstoke: Palgrave Macmillan, 2002).

55 Hochschild, *Managed Heart*, 7.

is what is necessary to get by in one's job, including through interactions with customers, supervisors and perhaps staff. By this schema, emotional labour is a subset of emotion work.

The use of emotion work is particularly common among women with chronic illness. Emotion work can be a consequence of the stigma and stress that women with chronic illness suffer. One of the main issues they have to consider is whether or not to disclose their illness. To decide not to disclose their illness means that these women need to constantly be aware of their appearance or symptoms to limit the suggestion that something is not quite right. Of course, for some this is not an issue if their illness is visible (in which case it is often labelled a 'disability').[56] The issue of disclosure can also have implications for power in the workplace.[57] Other 'equity groups' face similar challenges; for instance, people who have suffered from mental illness.

Rules and discretion

So how is it that, as I said above, emotion work is often linked to increased demands through a combination of both rules and discretion? On the one hand, organisations may seek to put in place rules about the emotions that staff must display, from Capro's smile campaign mentioned in Chapter 5 to the requirements on airline staff, waiters or care workers. On the other hand, organisations cannot directly control and quantify how staff express or internalise emotions; they can try, but this is even more difficult than trying to control the effort that workers put into their jobs. Employee discretion determines how and how much emotion work is expressed.

Moreover, rules often produce outcomes that require employees to come up with ways of managing the emotions of clients. One of the repeated funny scenes in *Little Britain* concerns a travel agent who invariably responds 'computer says "no"' after customers try to make a booking, and the humour lies partly in the agent's steadfast unwillingness to emote in any way. For a deadly serious contrast, watch Ken Loach's *I, Daniel Blake*, and the UK scenes in the shopfronts of the public agency responsible for social security and employment, where the rules under which staff work

56 Shalene Werth, 'Stigma, Stress and Emotional Labour: Experiences of Women with Chronic Illness at Work'. Paper presented at 25th AIRAANZ Conference, Auckland, February 2011. Yes, it's worth reading Werth.

57 Shalene Werth, David Peetz, and Kaye Broadbent, 'Issues of Power and Disclosure for Women with Chronic Illness in Their Places of Work'. In *Work and Identity: Contemporary Perspectives on Workplace Diversity*, ed. Shalene Werth and Charlotte Brownlow (New York: Palgrave, 2018).

require them to impose penalties and hardship on low-income earners on benefits. They also have to manage the emotions of those clients to avoid distress, despair or even violence. The staff appear heartless but they are engaging in emotional labour. Some staff try to find a workaround for their clients, some internalise the values of the system, some just try to survive. It would be similar for Centrelink staff in Australia, trying to deal with the repercussions of the thousands of false invoices issued under what became known as 'Robo-debt'.[58]

Ironically, even as computers and algorithms increasingly take the role of humans as decision makers,[59] there is no let-up in the importance of emotional labour, and the growing importance of 'service' work makes emotional labour even more central. It is not easy to measure emotional content, but it is easy to measure other aspects of the work of emotional labourers, and it will become easier with technological change. Employers can (and do) count how long a call-centre worker takes on a break, or how many clients a care worker sees in a defined period. But this may be counter to the stated function of the organisation and the norms of the employees. The latter may resist, as in a study of Norwegian health and social services occupations, where researchers found that employees rejected some of the standards of their employers, who in turn had standardised 'neo-Taylorist' service agreements with public agencies. Employees provided additional services in accordance with their own standards. Employees 'misbehaved', obstructing management control of their work and its attempts to increase efficiency.[60] These conflicts are likely to become more common as micromeasurement spreads.

Future employment of women and female-dominated work

Discussion of the future of work has focused a lot on the type of jobs that new technology will create or destroy and, to a lesser extent, the nature of employment or contracting relationships related to the growth of platform technologies. Little consideration has been given to how gender fits into this (aside from occasional consideration of the gender aspects of the types

58 Mike Steketee, 'Government by Algorithm'. *Inside Story*, 5 April 2018; Doug Dingwall, 'Centrelink Accused of Intimidating Clients with AFP Letters'. *Australian Financial Review*, 4 August 2017; Terry Carney, 'The New Digital Future for Welfare: Debts without Legal Proofs or Moral Authority?'. *UNSW Law Journal Forum* 41, no. 1 (2018): 1–16.

59 O'Neill, *Weapons of Math Destruction*.

60 Jörg W. Kirchhoff and Jan C. Karlsson, 'Expansion of Output: Organizational Misbehaviour in Public Enterprises'. *Economic and Industrial Democracy* 34, no. 1 (2013): 107–22.

of jobs that will be created or destroyed), nor to the long-term effects of changing technology on the digital–biological interface, and how this affects gender and work.

One way of looking at it is to ask: who will be better suited by the jobs of the future—men or women? The correct answer is 'there will be no difference' in that both sexes can do just about all jobs equally well, but, to the extent that there are socially constructed 'men's jobs' and 'women's jobs', it is important to investigate whether 'men's jobs' or 'women's jobs' will grow more rapidly. One way to examine this is to look at the jobs that are forecast to grow and decline over the next decade (the type of issue examined in Chapter 4), and whether 'men's jobs' or 'women's jobs' are forecast to grow by more. Using occupational projections by the US Bureau of Labor Statistics for the decade 2016–2026,[61] and separate data on the percentage of female employment in occupations, it appears projected US employment growth will be slightly higher in 'women's jobs' than in 'men's jobs'.[62] Likewise, if the female proportion of employment in each occupation remained unchanged, and the employment in each industry grew (or shrank) as projected, female employment as a proportion of total employment would grow slightly. This should not be a surprise. As mentioned in Chapter 4, some of the biggest employment growth is likely to be in care-related jobs, like aides and carers and health professionals, which have higher rates of female employment than many manual jobs.

A second approach is to ask: will men's jobs or women's jobs be more affected by technological change? That is, will 'women's jobs' be replaced more or less readily than 'men's jobs'? Using as a starting point the work of Frey and Osborne (F&O) of the *relative* susceptibility to automation of different types of jobs, especially 'male' versus 'female' jobs,[63] and considering the gender composition of occupational employment, it appears that the gender differences in automation effects are not big, and if anything men's jobs are slightly more likely to be automated than women's jobs.[64] Jobs held by women appear slightly less likely than jobs

61 Bureau of Labor Statistics, Table 1.7 Occupational projections, 2016–26, and worker characteristics, 2016 (Numbers in thousands), www.bls.gov/emp/ind-occ-matrix/occupation.xlsx; and Table 11, Employed persons by detailed occupation, sex, race, and Hispanic or Latino ethnicity, www.bls.gov/cps/cpsaat11.htm.

62 Peetz and Murray, 'Women's Employment'.

63 Carl Benedikt Frey and Michael A. Osborne, *The Future of Employment: How Susceptible Are Jobs to Computerisation?* (Oxford: Department of Engineering Science, University of Oxford, 2013).

64 Peetz and Murray, 'Women's Employment'.

held by men to be replaced by technology. This was most likely because many female jobs (especially those in 'large' occupations) have a high 'caring' element.

This was consistent with an attitudinal study by University of Sydney researchers, who surveyed 2,000 Australians and found that, overall, women were more optimistic than men about automation and their jobs. Men were over 10 percentage points more likely than women to be somewhat or very concerned about potentially losing their job because of machines or computer programs replacing human workers, about losing their job due to their industry shrinking, or about losing it because of being unable to keep up with the technical skills required. Yet only two in five women currently working felt they could access free or affordable training, equipping them for better jobs. For the authors, addressing existing gendered inequities in employment were important issues for the future.[65]

Women in male-dominated work

The jobs in male-dominated occupations are not undervalued in the way that jobs in female-dominated occupations are. But the workplace experiences of women in male-dominated work are often problematic for other reasons.

One of the path-breaking studies on women in male-dominated work was undertaken in the 1970s by Rosabeth Moss Kanter.[66] She identified issues associated with women's vulnerability when they are 'tokens within a skewed group'. A 'token' group is a group that represents less than 15 per cent of a workforce and is overwhelmingly outnumbered by a 'dominant' group. Although Kanter wrote about women as a token group, she pointed out that related issues arise for token groups along other dimensions—for example, 'racial' minorities within a workplace. She studied the experience of female salespeople in a workplace dominated by men, and identified a series of problems including:

- high visibility, leading to high pressures on performance;
- polarisation (differences between 'tokens' and 'dominants' are exaggerated), which leads dominants to heighten the group boundaries between themselves and the token group;

65 Marian Baird et al., *Women and the Future of Work* (Sydney: Australian Women's Working Futures project, University of Sydney Business School, 2018).

66 Rosabeth Moss Kanter, 'Some Effects of Proportions on Group Life: Skewed Sex Ratios and Responses to Token Women'. *American Journal of Sociology* 82, no. 5 (1977): 695–990.

- assimilation of women into 'traditional' female roles (e.g. female salespeople ending up always making the tea), which leads to 'role entrapment'.

Emerging out of her work was the concept of 'critical mass'; that is, women (or other minorities) needed to represent more than 15 per cent of a work group in order to be able to have any effect. (The term 'critical mass' actually developed in the political science literature in response to Kanter's work, though she did not use the term herself.)[67] Subsequent writers have spoken of the insufficiency of 'critical mass' as a criterion for change and point to the importance of critical *actors* and critical *acts*.[68]

Eveline and Booth looked exactly at that issue: at women working in the traditional male preserve of mining, and the sexual politics of employing women in precious-gem mining in Western Australia, including how women mobilised against systemic male dominance.[69] The company sought to hire women at this new mine in the 1980s, in part for public relations reasons in the context of new antidiscrimination laws, and in part because women workers, it was thought, would 'civilise' the men. This was quite an important consideration in a fly-in fly-out (FIFO) operation, in which workers would be flown in from Perth and stay for two weeks at a time in company camps, as the company had no intention of establishing a township to service the mine. Moreover, it wanted to recruit 'greenfields' (untrained or 'cleanskin') recruits as operators—a practice identified in Chapter 5 as being associated with culturism—and used psychological and attitudinal testing to choose employees. It wanted a workforce that would not be inclined towards unionism (though, as we saw earlier, women are not really less union-oriented than men).

Eventually, despite all public relations efforts, female employment at the mine fell. When the mining company won a second award for its achievements in promoting equal employment opportunity, three women

67 Drude Dahlerup, 'The Story of the Theory of Critical Mass'. *Gender and Politics* 2, no. 4 (2006): 511–22; Sarah Childs and Mona Lena Krook, 'Should Feminists Give up on Critical Mass? A Contingent Yes'. *Gender and Politics* 2, no. 4 (2006): 522–30.

68 Childs and Krook, 'Should Feminists'; S. Grey, 'Does Size Matter? Critical Mass in New Zealand's Women MPs'. *Parliamentary Affairs* 55, no. 1 (2002): 19–29; Karen Beckwith, 'Numbers and Newness: The Descriptive and Substantive Representation of Women'. *Canadian Journal of Political Science* 44, no. 2 (2007): 27–49; Karen Beckwith and Kimberly Cowell-Meyers, 'Sheer Numbers: Critical Representation Thresholds and Women's Political Representation'. *Perspectives on Politics* 5, no. 3 (2007): 553–65.

69 Joan Eveline and Michael Booth, 'Gender and Sexuality in Discourses of Managerial Control: The Case of Women Miners'. *Gender, Work and Organisation* 9, no. 5 (2002): 556–78.

allegedly left in disgust, including at the way in which the company had failed to replace women who had left. The women at Emsite were sometimes denied information about dangers on the job and were subjected to 'practical jokes' and pornographic 'pin-ups', and some felt continually 'on trial' or began organising resistance. Since then, many things have changed but many things have also not, if a study of women working in the Queensland coal mines two decades later is anything to go by.[70] This harassment of and discrimination against women is not just a blue-collar phenomenon. We see it reported among economists and CEOs, very prestigious white-collar occupations.[71]

Discrimination and harassment are not restricted to male-dominated work (which, after all, only accounts for a minority of working women). The key distinction is that in any workplace, women might be subjected to harassment or discrimination by *individual* coworkers or bosses, whereas in workplaces where women are a token group,[72] negative attitudes and harassment may take a more *collective* form, reflecting the male-dominated *culture* of the workplace, especially if implicitly sanctioned by management.[73] In 'mixed' gender occupations, males are not numerically large enough to sustain a dominant culture of collective sex-based harassment, especially as norms opposed to sex-based harassment have become much more widespread in recent years. There, sex-based harassment seems more likely both to be individual and to be 'called out'. Indeed, many other aspects of male culture are also likely to be weakened, such as male-focused notions about 'ideal' workers.

Emotion work in male-dominated occupations?

Male-dominated occupations have not been considered a domain for emotion work. But this is not necessarily a fair depiction. For example, in the miners' studies just referred to, women often engaged in 'presentational emotion management'[74] to appear mainstream. That is,

70 Georgina Murray and David Peetz, *Women of the Coal Rushes* (Sydney: UNSW Press, 2010), Chapter 6.

71 Justin Wolfers, 'Even Famous Female Economists Get No Respect'. *New York Times*, 11 November 2015; Alice H. Wu, 'Gender Stereotyping in Academia: Evidence from Economics Job Market Rumors Forum'. SSRN, August 2017, pdfs.semanticscholar.org/5eb3/f36b34a9d6379a4de6923ceed99a9bc22a77.pdf?_ga=2.156327803.1957153287.1567424486-1023833107.1567424486; Ben Casselman and Jim Tankersley, 'Women in Economics Report Rampant Sexual Assault and Bias'. *New York Times*, 18 March 2019;. Peetz, Murray, and Poorhosseinzadeh, 'Women at the Top'.

72 Kanter, 'Some Effects of Proportions'.

73 Peetz, 'Regulation Distance'.

74 The term was defined in Bolton and Boyd, 'Trolley Dolly', 291.

they often engaged in emotion work.[75] Assuming the language and norms of 'the boys' may be a strategy commonly used by the women, a form of 'assimilation' into male culture—a different use of the word to that by Kanter.[76] For some women, this emotion work may be 'deep acting';[77] that is, the women's emotional state adapts to match that of the men in their work environment. For others it may be 'surface acting', when the employee's internal feelings and the external portrayal of feelings are not consistent. Putting a 'brave face' on things may be a form of emotion work used to deal with harassment. In such a situation, surface acting can be more stressful for women than deep acting. The presentational emotion work performed by many women in male-dominated occupations is aimed, explicitly or implicitly, at precluding gender-based discrimination or harassment in those situations. If you fit in, you are less likely to be a target, the reasoning goes.

The biggest problems for many women at work—certainly the problems causing the most emotional distress—relate to discrimination and harassment, which, as mentioned, are not restricted to male-dominated work. Women devise multiple strategies to deal with these, many of which involve some form of emotion work.

The gap at the top

In Chapter 2 we looked at power, resource dependency and labour market power. The women with the greatest labour market power are those with the greatest command over resources; that is, they are those in senior managerial and senior executive positions. Yet here is an interesting paradox: gender inequality in pay appears to increase as women move higher up the ladder.[78] The relative power disadvantage experienced by women vis-à-vis men appears worst for those women at the top end of the labour market—those with the greatest power. This is the 'powerful women's paradox'.

75 Georgina Murray, David Peetz, and Olav Muurlink, 'Structuring Gender Relations among Coal Mine Workers'. In *Women at Work: Labor Segmentation and Regulation*, ed. D. Peetz and G. Murray (New York: Palgrave Macmillan, 2017), 119–36.

76 Kanter, 'Some Effects of Proportions'.

77 Hochschild, *Managed Heart.*

78 See, for example, Association of Professional Engineers, Scientists and Managers Australia, *Women in the Professions Survey Report 2007* (Melbourne: APESMA, 2007); Peetz, Murray, and Poorhosseinzadeh, 'Women at the Top'.

At senior levels of companies, the Australian Government's Equal Opportunity in the Workplace Agency (EOWA) census of large firms found that, in 2010, women held only 8 per cent of executive key-manager positions among the top 200 companies on the Australian stock exchange (the ASX200), as did 12 per cent in the UK, 14 per cent in the USA, 17 per cent in Canada and 19 per cent in South Africa. Only 38 per cent of ASX200 companies had at least one female executive manager, as did 61 per cent of UK, 68 per cent of Canadian, 71 per cent of US and 77 per cent of South African firms. Women held 8 per cent of Australian board directorships, as did 9 per cent of New Zealand, 9 per cent of UK, 14 per cent of Canadian, 15 per cent of US and 17 per cent of South African firms.[79] Earlier, in relation to remuneration, the EOWA had found that in 2008 the overall median pay for Australian senior women was 58 per cent of the overall median pay for men; female chief financial officers and chief operating officers earned half the wage of their male equivalents; and in CEO positions women earned two-thirds the salary of their male counterparts.[80]

What explains this 'powerful women's paradox'?[81] One feature in the determination of senior-level pay is the greater discretion over pay at more senior levels and the greater importance of individual negotiation at those levels than below. In the absence of meaningful regulation over pay at that level (i.e. in the context of high 'regulation distance'), the issue in this male-dominated group is not so much gender differences in individual negotiation styles (discussed earlier) as gendered norms about what makes for an 'ideal manager' and the critical role those norms play in determining who is allowed to become a senior manager and how much they will be paid.[82]

It is possible, but not certain, that this is changing. Whether this might be due to highly paid women's awareness of and willingness to use antidiscrimination law, their ability to use the media, the innate newsworthiness of high-profile actions or something else is unclear, and

79 Equal Opportunity for Women in the Workplace Agency, *2010 Australian Census of Women in Leadership* (Sydney: EOWA, 2010).

80 Equal Opportunity for Women in the Workplace Agency, *Gender Income Distribution of Top Earners in ASX200 Companies: 2006 EOWA Census of Women in Leadership* (Sydney: EOWA, 2008).

81 David Peetz and Georgina Murray, 'The "Powerful Women Paradox": Why Women at the Top Still Miss Out'. In *Macht Und Employment Relations. Festschrift Für Werner Nienhüser*, ed. H. Hossfeld and R. Ortlieb (Mering, Bayern: Rainer Hampp Verlag, 2013), 181–86.

82 Peetz, Murray, and Poorhosseinzadeh, 'Women at the Top'.

the barriers remain substantial. Little wonder that most women think that self-driving cars will be a normal mode of transportation before women will make up half of the CEOs at Fortune 500 companies.[83]

The future employment of women and male-dominated work

I earlier pointed out that the overall prospects for women's employment were relatively positive, in that female-dominated jobs appeared less likely to be automated than male-dominated jobs. Perhaps the bigger issue for women is what role they will have in the key jobs of the future that will be most influential, when many of those jobs are male-dominated.

Men dominate in managerial jobs. They dominate in jobs related to engineering, computing and ICT (information and communication technology).[84] In most industries and occupations in most developed countries the female share of employment has risen over the past two decades. Rising female labour-force participation rates mean that female employment has grown faster than male employment. Yet in computing and IT, the reverse has happened. In most developed countries (the data in Table 8.1 relate to Europe), the female share of IT occupations has fallen. In Australia, the female share in computer system design and services virtually halved between 1985 and 2015, a remarkable shift.

Internationally, this is an employment area that is not welcoming of women. Recent scandals such as 'gamergate' and mistreatment or sexual harassment in some high-tech companies focused attention on the poor situation of women in this cluster.[85] The 'Google Walkout' was prompted

83 Rockefeller Foundation and Global Strategy Group, *Women in Leadership: Why It Matters* (New York: Rockefeller Foundation, 12 May 2016), www.rockefellerfoundation.org/report/infographic-media-influence-perceive-women-leadership/.

84 For engineering, see M. Teresa Cardador and Brianna Caza, 'The Subtle Stressors Making Women Want to Leave Engineering'. *Harvard Business Review*, 23 November 2018, hbr.org/2018/11/the-subtle-stressors-making-women-want-to-leave-engineering?utm_source=twitter&utm_medium=social&utm_campaign=hbr.

85 Eliana Dockterman, 'What Is #Gamergate and Why Are Women Being Threatened About Video Games?'. *Time*, 16 October 2014, time.com/3510381/gamergate-faq/; John Naughton, 'Want to Succeed in Tech? Try Not to Be a Woman …' *Guardian*, 11 June 2017; Sam Levin, 'Accused of Underpaying Women, Google Says It's Too Expensive to Get Wage Data'. *Guardian*, 27 May 2017; Valentina Zarya, 'Female Programmers Make Nearly 30% Less Than Their Male Counterparts'. *Fortune.com*, 16 November 2016; Sarah Kessler, 'Tech's Big Gender Diversity Push, One Year In'. *Fast Company*, 2015, www.fastcompany.com/3052877/techs-big-gender-diversity-push-one-year-in; Keane, 'Looming Crisis'; Keane, 'What's Driving Women'; Keane, 'Rape Fears and Harassment'. See also footnotes 1 and 2 in Chapter 7.

by the handling of sexual harassment by that company.[86] This was once a female-dominated occupation—the women who did almost all the computational work to get men into space, highlighted in the movie *Hidden Figures*, were called *computers*. This flipped to a seriously male-dominated occupation as its prestige and pay increased and senior men erected hegemonic barriers to women entering at any levels.[87] Now, male-dominated groups still operate with norms that privilege males and male behaviour at the expense of females. High regulation distance[88] has minimised any constraints.

Table 8.1: Share of females in employment, employed ICT specialists, 2005 and 2015, European countries

	Female employment share in ICT specialists (%)		
	2005	2015	Change
Iceland	22.5	22.6	0.1
Netherlands	14	13	–1.0
Switzerland	15.8	14.6	–1.2
Belgium	16.3	15.1	–1.2
Finland	24	22.4	–1.6
Portugal	17.1	15.3	–1.8
France	18.4	16.6	–1.8
Italy	15.7	13.8	–1.9
Spain	19.3	17.4	–1.9
Norway	19.2	17	–2.2
Sweden	21.2	18.9	–2.3
Bulgaria	30.4	27.7	–2.7
Denmark	21.4	18.5	–2.9
Germany	19.6	16.3	–3.3
Croatia	21.2	16.5	–4.7
Cyprus	22.8	17.1	–5.7
Austria	20.6	14.2	–6.4

86 Daisuke Wakabayashi and Katie Benner, 'How Google Has Protected Its Elite Men'. *New York Times*, 25 October 2018; Bryan Menegus, 'Google Agreed to Pay Execs Accused of Sexual Harassment $135 Million'. *Gizmodo*, 11 March 2019, gizmodo.com/google-agreed-to-pay-execs-accused-of-sexual-harassment-1833214767.

87 Marie Hicks, *Programmed Inequality: How Britain Discarded Women Technologists and Lost Its Edge in Computing* (Cambridge, MA: MIT Press, 2017); Nathan Ensmenger, *The Computer Boys Take Over: Computers, Programmers, and the Politics of Technical Expertise* (Cambridge, MA: MIT Press, 2010).

88 Peetz and Murray, *Varieties of Gender Gaps*.

	Female employment share in ICT specialists (%)		
	2005	2015	Change
United Kingdom	22.9	16.2	–6.7
Romania	34.9	27.2	–7.7
Ireland	29.8	18.6	–11.2
Greece	25.3	13.2	–12.1
Luxembourg	24.9	12.6	–12.3
Lithuania	32.5	20.1	–12.4
Slovenia	30.4	16	–14.4
Poland	32.8	13.5	–19.3
Czech Republic	29.3	9.9	–19.4
Slovakia	32.4	11.4	–21.0
Latvia	46.2	24.7	–21.5
Hungary	37.8	11.9	–25.9
Estonia	48.7	20.3	–28.4
EU (28)	22.2	16.1	–6.1

Source: Eurostat ec.europa.eu/eurostat/data/database

Only when their gender is masked online are the high capabilities of female coders acknowledged.[89] But the mask of anonymity online for commenters makes women the target of a disproportionately high amount of online abuse,[90] often perpetrated by 'well-organised international syndicates' of online 'trolls'.[91] So it is little wonder that women now avoid working in IT.

89 Josh Terrell, Andrew Kofink, Justin Middleton, Clarissa Rainear, Emerson Murphy-Hill, Chris Parnin, and Jon Stallings, 'Gender Bias in Open Source: Pull Request Acceptance of Women Versus Men'. *Peer Journal of Computer Science* 3, no.1 (May 2017).

90 Becky Gardiner, Mahana Mansfield, Ian Anderson, Josh Holder, Daan Louter and Monica Ulmanu, 'The Dark Side of Guardian Comments'. *The Guardian*, April 12, 2016, www.theguardian.com/technology/2016/apr/12/the-dark-side-of-guardian-comments.

91 Ginger Gorman, 'Internet Trolls Are Not Who I Thought—They're Even Scarier'. *ABC News*, 1 February 2019, www.abc.net.au/news/2019-02-02/internet-trolls-arent-who-i-thought-ginger-gorman-troll-hunting/10767690.

Segmentation and intersections between ethnicity and gender

The concept of 'intersectionality theory', within sociology, recognises diverse identities and therefore diverse interests of 'membership groups' (e.g. women, young workers, ethnic minorities). Intersectionality is a term coined in the 1980s to explain the interacting effects of disadvantage.[92] The core idea is that disadvantage is not just 'additive' but 'multiplicative'. Economists call this an 'interaction effect'. Psychologists call this a 'moderator'. But intersectionality theory has a very specific focus on forms of disadvantage.

When examining the intersection between ethnicity and gender at workplaces, the key differences are between those who do and do not fluently speak the dominant language in the host society—within Anglophone countries, between migrants from non–English speaking background (NESB) and other employees. This represents the boundary along which segmentation is established.

An example of intersectionality is that NESB women migrants face barriers by virtue of gender, race/ethnicity and related issues such as dress or first language, and family responsibilities. The net impact may be that even skilled women migrants may become unemployed or underemployed, when compared to the general population.

To look more at the special circumstances of migrant women, we must first mention some general issues concerning ethnicity. Many stories of exploitation through underpayment of workers (e.g. in agriculture, in franchises) concern migrant workers. The most commonly exploited have been migrants on temporary work visas.[93] For example, in Australia it was reported that franchisees in the 7-Eleven chain deliberately chose a particular type of temporary migrant to facilitate exploitation.[94] Three particular sources of disadvantage (low power for employees) in some of these recent cases have been language issues, reluctance to report breaches

92 Crenshaw, 'Demarginalizing the Intersection'.

93 Stephen Clibborn, 'Why Undocumented Immigrant Workers Should Have Workplace Rights'. *Economic and Labour Relations Review* 28, no. 3 (2015): 465–73.

94 See Chapter 10.

due to employer threats to deport by informing immigration authorities, and lack of knowledge of the industrial relations system. There is more about migrants and disadvantage in enforcing their rights in Chapter 10.

Although migrants may receive higher pay, on average, than other employees, this is because they have, on average, considerably higher skills. Indeed, they are disadvantaged in terms of the pay appropriate for their level of skill and experience, probably in part because of a higher probability of experiencing unemployment, problems in locally recognising overseas qualifications, discrimination, and intra-household decisions taken in the context of the above.[95] While temporary migrants may be concentrated in hospitality and agriculture, longer-term NESB migrants had historically been concentrated in manufacturing,[96] which is now in long-term decline in most industrialised countries and many newly industrialising ones.[97] This creates some particular issues regarding handling structural adjustment in the economy.

NESB migrants have overall been no less supportive of unionism than other workers. While ethnic differences can be used by employers to divide employees and dampen unionism, ethnicity can also be used by unions to mobilise worker support around common interests. Unions can

---

95 Thorsten Stromback, *The Earnings of Migrants in Australia*. Conference Paper No. 46 (Canberra: Bureau of Labour Market Research, 1984); Christina Ho and Caroline Alcorso, 'Migrants and Employment: Challenging the Success Story'. *Journal of Sociology* 40, no. 3 (2004): 237–59; Prem J. Thapa, 'On the Risk of Unemployment: A Comparative Assessment of the Labour Market Success of Migrants in Australia'. *Australian Journal of Labour Economics* 7, no. 2 (2004): 199–229; Sue Ressia, 'Starting from Scratch: Skilled Dual Career Migrant Couples and Their Search for Employment in South East Queensland'. *International Journal of Employment Studies* 18, no. 1 (2010): 63–88; Yvonne Riaño and Nadia Baghdadi, 'Understanding the Labour Market Participation of Skilled Immigrant Women in Switzerland: The Interplay of Class, Ethnicity, and Gender'. *International Migration and Integration* 8, no. 2 (2007): 163–83; John Rynderman and Catherine Flynn, '"We Didn't Bring the Treasure of Pharaoh": Skilled Migrants' Experiences of Employment Seeking and Settling in Australia'. *International Social Work* 59, no. 2 (2016): 266–83.

96 *The Industrial Relations of Migrant Employment* (Canberra: Bureau of Immigration and Population Research/AGPS, 1993).

97 For OECD countries, see Organisation for Economic Co-operation and Development, *Chapter 1. Knowledge Economies: Trends and Features*. OECD Science, Technology and Industry Scoreboard 2015 (Paris: OECD, 2015). For declines between the 2000s and 2010s in manufacturing's share in economies such as Argentina, Brazil, Chile, Korea, Taiwan, Hong Kong, Singapore and South Africa, see International Labour Organization, 'Employment by Sex and Economic Activity (Thousands)' (ILOSTAT, ILO, 2019), www.ilo.org/ilostat/faces/oracle/webcenter/portalapp/pagehierarchy/Page27.jspx.

also create notions of common interest that straddle ethnic divisions.[98] That said, some key problems for migrants in collective bargaining relate to consultation and communication.[99]

Turning to migrant women, there has been high segmentation of NESB women, their being overrepresented in blue-collar occupations and with lower access to external and in-house training.[100] In relation to pay, female NESB migrants appear more disadvantaged than male migrants.[101] Other key issues for NESB women have included occupational health and safety, harassment, traditional narrow job structures (especially in the textiles clothing and footwear (TCF) industry) leading to major barriers to career opportunities, and outwork.[102]

Recalling the concept of labour flexibility (Chapter 6), the starkest example of disadvantage facing migrant women comes in the form of clothing outworkers.[103] Migrant women have been disproportionately represented in the 'outworker' sector of TCF, where pay and conditions are among the

---

98 Santina Bertone and Gerry Griffin, *Immigrant Workers and Their Unions* (Canberra: AGPS, 1992); also Jock Collins, *Migrant Hands in a Distant Land: Australia's Post-War Immigration* (Sydney: Pluto, 1988); Constance Lever-Tracy and Michael Quinlan, *A Divided Working Class* (New York: RKP, 1988); Callus and Knox, *The Industrial Relations of Migrant Employment.*

99 EMD Workforce Development, *Migrants and Workplace Bargaining: Australian Case Studies.* Industrial Relations Research Series No. 11, Workplace Bargaining Research Project (Canberra: Department of Industrial Relations, AGPS, 1994); Department of Industrial Relations, *Enterprise Bargaining in Australia: 1994 Annual Report* (Canberra: AGPS, 1995); Department of Industrial Relations, *Enterprise Bargaining in Australia: 1995 Annual Report* (Canberra: AGPS, 1996); Santina Bertone, *Enterprise Bargaining and Employees from a Non-English Speaking Background.* Report to DIR for 1994 Enterprise Bargaining Report (Canberra: Department of Industrial Relations, 1995); Caroline Alcorso, *The Effects of Enterprise Bargaining on Employees from NESB.* Report to DIR for 1995 Enterprise Bargaining Report (Canberra: Department of Industrial Relations, 1996).

100 Caroline Alcorso and Graham Harrison, *Blue Collar and Beyond: The Experiences of Non-English Speaking Background Women in the Australian Labour Force* (Canberra: Commonwealth State Council on Non-English Speaking Background Women's Issues, Office of Women's Affairs/AGPS, 1993).

101 Stromback, *The Earnings of Migrants in Australia*; Jawad Syed and Peter A. Murray, 'Combating the English Language Deficit: The Labour Market Experiences of Migrant Women in Australia'. *Human Resource Management Journal* 19, no. 4 (2009): 413–32; Uzi Rebhun, 'A Double Disadvantage? Immigration, Gender, and Employment Status in Israel'. *European Journal of Population,* 24, no. 1 (2008): 8–113.

102 Alcorso and Harrison, *Blue Collar and Beyond*; see also D. Storer and K. Hargreaves, 'Migrant Women in Industry'. In *Social Policy and Problems of the Workforce, Vol. 1*, ed. S. Staats (Melbourne: Social Welfare Unit, Australian Council of Trade Unions, 1976), 39–104.

103 Mindy Thorpe, 'Outworkers'. In *Pay Equity in Queensland*, ed. David Peetz and Rosemary Hunter (Brisbane: Centre for Research on Employment and Work and Socio Legal Research Centre, Report to Department of Employment, Training and Industrial Relations, Queensland Government Submission, Pay Equity Inquiry, Queensland Industrial Relations Commission, No. B1568, 2000), 99–114; see also Annie Delaney, 'A Comparison of Australian and Indian Women Garment and Footwear Homeworkers'. In *Women, Labor Segmentation and Regulation: Varieties of Gender Gaps*, ed. David Peetz and Georgina Murray (New York: Palgrave Macmillan, 2017), 193–210.

worst, if not absolutely the worst, in labour markets in many industrialised countries. They represent a classic 'periphery' workforce comprising people who are typically classed not as employees but as contractors. Their situation has been so stark that, at times, special regulatory arrangements have been put in place to cover these outworkers.[104] Disadvantage is not restricted to industrialised countries. Women in the Indian footwear industry seem 'invisibilised' out of the sight of protective regulation or unionism.[105]

Gender and ethnicity also intersect for women in dual-career migrant couples. Sue Ressia found that couples negotiated between each other in order to decide who would pursue their chosen career ahead of the other. The difficulties for women migrants in leaving the home and entering the workforce were shown in several cases where women's decisions were based on perceived family needs. Migrant families encountered financial difficulties and problems in managing childcare. There were migrant women who set aside careers for which they were well qualified, either to take lower-status jobs or leave the labour force, as a result of their husbands' perceived career needs, problems with recognition of overseas qualifications, or problems with childcare.[106] So even though the worst examples of people being exploited through the intersection of gender and ethnicity occur in female-dominated occupations (the TCF industries), the problems of the intersectionality of gender and ethnicity are not restricted to female-dominated occupations. Issues such as setting aside careers to take lower-status jobs or leave the labour force can affect migrant women in many fields, including even some well-paid professions dominated by men.

If large-scale labour migrations were a major feature of the globe through the twentieth century, the pressure for such migrations is likely to be even greater through the remainder of the twenty-first century. Globalisation increases awareness of life outside the village, and the relative circumstances of the lowest income earners globally have deteriorated, even if, for those in the middle, there has been a major improvement. More importantly, climate change (which will be discussed more in the next chapter) will create large populations of tens or hundreds of millions, whose housing

104 Igor Nossar et al., 'Protective Legal Regulation for Home-Based Workers in Australian Textile, Clothing and Footwear Supply Chains'. *Journal of Industrial Relations* 57, no. 4 (2015): 585–603.
105 Delaney, 'Australian and Indian'.
106 Ressia, 'Starting from Scratch'.

becomes uninhabitable due to droughts, extreme temperatures or wildfires or rising sea levels.[107] The first three causes might, in certain circumstances, be temporary but the last, in this context, is very permanent. Climate change disproportionally affects poor rural populations, who have the least resources to leave their home but will be the most needy if they do.[108] The stronger is resistance to action to deal with climate change, the greater will be the size of displaced populations. The effects of large-scale refugee migrations on recipient countries are controversial and beyond the scope of this book, but the issues include what impact will this have on economic activity (possibly up?), wages, especially of the low-skilled (possibly down?), and the introduction of labour-saving technology (possibly slowing it?). One likely effect could be to intensify the segmentation of labour within recipient societies, with migrant women still most disadvantaged, and put pressure on regulators and interest groups seeking to maintain equity and fair pay and conditions for all.

Conclusion

Today's matchstick girls are found across societies. Women have enthusiastically participated in marches to boost carer's wages in New Zealand, to protest President Trump in the USA, or to support a living wage in a number of countries. They have demonstrated and struck as nurses, as apparel workers, as teachers, as electronics assemblers and even as building and construction workers. Working conditions are less oppressive for women than they were 130 years ago, but there still is, and will be, a lot for women to talk about, protest about and strike about. *Plus ça change, plus c'est la même chose.*

Gender is a major fracture line in workplaces. It separates occupations and industries from each other, and defines the different ways in which people will experience work. The domestic sphere is a central factor in gender segmentation of the labour force. Social norms and values play a critical role not only in shaping the domestic sphere but also in influencing laws that affect the gendered nature of work. Just as attitudes

107 The New York Times Editorial, *Climate Refugees: How Global Change Is Displacing Millions* (New York: New York Times, 2017). This book (a collection of NYT stories) opens with the sentence: 'There will be 50 million of them by 2050—or 200 million, depending on which expert you ask.'
108 Etienne Piguet, Antoine Pécoud, and Paul de Guchteneire, 'Migration and Climate Change: An Overview'. *Refugee Survey Quarterly* 33, no. 3 (2011): 1–23.

vary hugely between societies, so too does the legal framework. Regulation distance interacts with labour segmentation to create different forms of disadvantage for women and migrants in different occupations and industries. The experiences of women in female-dominated work, and in male-dominated work, show two quite different aspects of the problems of gender at work. A common feature of many female-dominated jobs is undervaluation of women's wages arising from gender-based notions of skill. Undervaluation is especially severe for women in female-dominated migrant work. The jobs in male-dominated occupations are not undervalued in the way that female-dominated occupations are. But the workplace experiences of women in male-dominated work are often characterised by problems such as visibility, polarisation and, potentially, assimilation of women into 'traditional' female roles.

While the experiences of women in 'token' or male-dominated work have specific problems attached, they also face issues in work where they are neither tokens nor the 'dominant' group. Discrimination and harassment are not restricted to male-dominated work. In any workplace, women might be subjected to harassment or discrimination by *individual* coworkers or bosses; whereas in workplaces where women are a token group, negative attitudes and harassment may take a more *collective* form, reflecting the male-dominated *culture* of the workplace, especially if implicitly sanctioned by management.

The relative power disadvantage experienced by women vis-à-vis men appears to worsen as women rise up the labour market and further away from regulation and as they get further from adolescence and more disadvantaged by the lingering effects of the household division of labour. Male hubris, often disguised as charisma, enables some men to be greatly overrewarded, especially at senior levels in organisations. Unionisation appears positively linked to gender equity and women appear no less inclined towards unionism than men.

Gender and ethnicity intersect to produce heightened disadvantage, both through what happens in the workplace (locating migrant women in some of the worst, lowest paid jobs) and in the domestic sphere (where decisions about women's labour force advancement will be heavily constrained by sometimes traditional family considerations). The prospect for future large-scale climate-related migrations is unlikely to ease this disadvantage.

Women appear less likely than men to be adversely affected by automation and AI. Yet women are a declining minority in ICT, where behavioural and attitudinal norms in this male-dominated sector force many women out, prevent others from entering an industry characterised by harassment (including by anonymous trolls) and undervaluation of women's work (unless anonymity makes gender invisible). It seems that, as the status of the industry and occupation have changed, men have sought to 'control' it and make it valued 'men's' work. Meanwhile women have been discouraged from entering it by a misogynistic culture created by men. The toxic phosphorus of matchsticks has been replaced by the poison of online harassment and discrimination.

While the future of work might give slight advantage to women, it is likely to still be men making the key decisions that shape what work looks like. So the key challenges for women are not about 'Who gets replaced by machines?' but about 'Who has power as machines increase the scope for capital accumulation?' That is, the gender problem in future employment is not addressed by changing the technology of production, but by changing the power relations in production. This is going to be a site of contestation for a long time. But no one can be complacent: the world Margaret Atwood constructed in *The Handmaid's Tale* reminds us of the fragility of women's gains, when they have not colonised the sources of power. It is not just in postrevolutionary Iran that women experience major setbacks. As I write this, the USA is contemplating reconsidering *Roe v Wade*[109] and many states either are preparing, or already have in place, legislation that would restrict women's rights if that decision of almost half a century ago were overturned.[110] Such reversals remain possible for decades to come.

---

109 *Roe v Wade* 410 U.S. 113 (1973), the major case establishing women's right to an abortion, by considering constitutional validity of laws that criminalised or restricted access to abortions.
110 Julia Jacobs and Matt Stevens, 'With Abortion in Spotlight, States Seek to Pass New Laws'. *New York Times*, 8 February 2019, www.nytimes.com/2019/02/08/us/abortion-laws.html.

9

Sustainability, ethics and work

It is October 2004. Over 2,000 mostly unionised forestry workers from across Tasmania, Australia, have travelled to Launceston to welcome and cheer a political announcement. Some 250 trucks are parked on the edge of the small city. Wearing blue overalls and bright yellow safety gear, workers crowd into a large hall. Others overflow into a nearby park. The announcement they cheer is one made by a conservative prime minister, who is promising to allow timber companies to cut down trees that environmentalists want to save, saving jobs in the forestry industry instead. The unionists wave signs and banners criticising, as lies, the policies of the Labor Party, a party that had been established by the unions a century earlier.[1] At the election weeks later, the government will be returned.

Fast forward 13 years, to the other side of the world. A 'people's climate march' is underway in a number of American cities. The rallies protest government policies dismantling environmental protections and moratoriums on coal leases on public land. Central to organising the marches have been a number of unions. One union had issued a press release warning that 'Working families disproportionately experience high pollution levels by being exposed to environmental hazards both at home and at work'.[2]

1 Annie Guest, 'CFMEU Approves of Howard's Forest Policy'. *PM*, Australian Broadcasting Corporation, 6 October 2004.

2 Larry Rubin, 'Unions Are All in for People's Climate March, April 29'. *People's World*, 10 April 2017, www.peoplesworld.org/article/unions-are-all-in-for-peoples-climate-march-april-29/.

The contrast with the Tasmanian union's action of 2004 could hardly be starker. The Tasmanian unions' actions in prioritising jobs over the environment had been quite characteristic of unions in such times and earlier. By the time of the American marches, demonstrations about climate with heavy union involvement could also be seen in Canada, Australia and across Europe as unions called for a 'just transition' to a low-emission society.[3] By no means has it been a universal transformation across the union movement. In 2019, a key committee of the American peak union body, the AFL-CIO, lobbied against the 'Green New Deal' proposed for debate in the US House of Representatives.[4] Still, there has been a remarkable change in the perspectives key players held about the relationship between jobs and the environment, and about the sustainability and indeed the ethics of previously longstanding practices.

This chapter investigates the meanings of sustainability and ethics. In part, it considers one of the 'mega-drivers of change' in the world of work: climate change. However, the issues of ethics and sustainability go beyond this. This chapter brings together many of the issues we have discussed, under the broad banner of ethics and sustainability. We start with definitions of the concepts, and consider the ways in which the two concepts are related. We then identify several of the ethical issues that are raised by matters we have discussed previously. We look at sustainability issues at the micro, societal and systemic levels. We discuss barriers to sustainability. We consider the nature of the matters that would be addressed by firms and employees adopting sustainable approaches to employment relations within the workplace. We also discuss matters relating to corporate social responsibility (CSR). In doing this we ask, among other things: what are the future effects of climate change on work and productivity? What are the future demands for sustainability and responses to climate change? How are they affecting, and how will they affect, employees?

3 Martin Lukacs, '"Historic" Toronto Climate March Calls for New Economic Vision'. *Guardian*, 7 July 2015, www.theguardian.com/environment/true-north/2015/jul/06/historic-toronto-climate-march-calls-for-new-economic-vision; Ben Doherty and Shalailah Medhora, 'Climate Change Protests across Australia—Tens of Thousands March'. *Guardian*, 29 November 2015, www.theguardian.com/environment/2015/nov/29/climate-change-marches-australia-sydney-canberra-perth-weekend-of-protest; European Trade Union Congress, *ETUC Declaration on the Paris Agreement on Climate Change* (Brussels: ETUC, 15 January 2016), www.etuc.org/en/document/etuc-declaration-paris-agreement-climate-change.

4 Colby Itkowitz, Dino Grandoni, and Jeff Stein, 'AFL-CIO Criticizes Green New Deal, Calling It "Not Achievable or Realistic"'. *Washington Post*, 12 March 2019.

Definitions, timeframes and externalities

Sustainability

Sustainability, it was said, is 'economic development that meets the needs of the present generation without compromising the ability of future generations to meet their own needs'.[5] This definition originated with the United Nations World Commission on Environment and Development (known as the Brundtland Commission) and was later refined by the 1992 UN Commission on Environment and Development.[6] As a definition it is obviously broad, concerning economies as a whole, but the concept of sustainability also relates to individual businesses and can be seen as extending beyond solely environmental considerations. So another way of looking at sustainability of individual activities is to adjust this definition slightly, to indicate it refers to *economic activity that meets present needs without compromising the ability to meet future needs.*

In this context, we also need to remember a point made by Frances Flanagan: 'the process of "sustaining" requires human labour. It means more than simply saying "no" to damaging acts of consumption; it also means saying "yes" to … activities that are positively necessary'.[7] In other words, we should not just ask whether a particular activity is compatible with sustainability, but also what other activities are needed to make for a sustainable society. In the end, the societal-level definition of the Brundtland Commission is the most relevant.

Timeframes and externalities in sustainability

Fundamentally there are two key conflicts that affect questions of sustainability. They relate to timeframes and externalities of actions.

The first is the competition between two logics: that of *short-termism* versus that of *long-termism*. Sustainability requires that actions be undertaken with a focus on the long term, not just the short term. This is fairly self-evident: if actions are undertaken with net short-term benefits to the parties but net long-term costs, then those actions cannot be sustained.

5 Gro Harlem Brundtland, *Our Common Future: The World Commission on Environment and Development* (Oxford: Oxford University Press, 1987).

6 William R. Blackburn, *The Sustainability Handbook: The Complete Management Guide to Achieving Social, Economic and Environmental Responsibility* (Washington DC: Earthscan, 2007).

7 Frances Flanagan, 'Climate Change and the New Work Order'. *Inside Story*, 28 February 2019, insidestory.org.au/climate-change-and-the-new-work-order/.

But there is more to it than this. The second aspect is the extent to which costs and benefits are *internalised* or *externalised.* Sustainability requires that the costs of transactions be internalised to the parties—that is, the party creating a cost bears the cost, not making someone else incur it—and that the benefits to each party exceed the costs. If this does not occur, and instead some component of costs is externalised (passed onto another, third, party), then overproduction (at least, overproduction of costs) will occur. In response, those external parties who are bearing the externalised costs (the third parties) will eventually seek to reimpose costs onto the transacting parties, making the original arrangement unsustained. Depending on the issue there may ultimately be the potential for systemic collapse.

Not all externalities are negative. Sometimes there may be positive externalities (benefits) from private transactions. For example, if there are societal benefits of higher education—in the form of say greater mutual understanding and social cohesion—then the total benefits may exceed the private benefits, and a positive externality has arisen. If this is the case, then some public subsidy may be warranted (though this is not the only rationale for public subsidy). Our interest for this chapter, however, is in the externalising of costs.

Ethics and sustainability

Ethics means different things to different people. A dictionary will say it is 'of or pertaining to morality' and 'the moral principles by which a person [or group] is guided', while 'moral' in turn refers to matters 'pertaining to the *distinction between right and wrong*'.[8] Clearly, different people will have different views as to what is right and what is wrong, and most people will find ways to define their own actions as constituting 'right'. Still, that does not downplay the importance of identifying ethical considerations in work and organisations.

Liberal market economists often define ethics out of existence by taking the outcome of any free market as ethical and any deviation from that as, by comparison, unethical. It justifies the status quo, or at least

8 Compact Oxford English Dictionary, 1991, 534, 1114, emphasis added, cited in Joanne B. Ciulla, 'Ethics and Leadership Effectiveness'. In *The Nature of Leadership*, ed. John. Antonakis, Anna T. Cianciolo, and Robert J. Sternberg (Thousand Oaks, CA: Sage, 2004).

neo-liberalism. Yet, by most readings, many of the consequences of neo-liberalism[9] (such as poverty and environmental degradation) are unethical. Conscious choices are to be made about what is right and what is wrong.

There is probably no ethical framework that everybody will agree upon, because of differences in interests (rich people will have a different view of what is 'right' from poor people) and personality (authoritarians will have a different view of what is 'right' from people with more 'open' personalities).[10] If you have read this far in the book, however, you probably agree that an ethical society is one that is sustainable and that has some fair distribution of income and opportunity.

While sustainability may not immediately be conceived of as an ethical issue, and these concepts are not the same, a few thoughts will show strong ties.

For one thing, it is simple to argue that it is *unethical behaviour* to impose costs upon a third party that does not benefit (by an amount greater than the costs) from the action concerned. For example, a truck operator who, presumably to save costs, dumped a truckload of asbestos in a street outside childcare centres in an inner city suburb in Sydney[11]—internalising the financial benefits from clearing the rubbish away from a building site, but externalising the substantial costs almost wholly onto the residents and schoolchildren of that suburb—was acting unethically by any standards.

Similarly, focusing on the short term rather than the long term has major implications for intergenerational equity. For example, depleting or polluting a resource, making it unable to be used by future generations, is ethically dubious, especially as it is unlikely that future generations will be compensated for this. In other words, unsustainable behaviour is unethical.

9 See, for example, Chapter 2.

10 Openness is a term from the psychological literature, and the scale of 'openness', part of the 'five factor model' that has dominated personality research, is a measure of the degree to which a person leans towards or away from authoritarian characteristics. Andrew J. Cooper, Luke D. Smillie, and Philip J. Corr, 'A Confirmatory Factor Analysis of the Mini-IPIP Five-Factor Model Personality Scale'. *Personality and Individual Differences* 48, no. 5 (2010): 688–91; Stephen A. Woods and Sarah E. Hampson, 'Measuring the Big Five with Single Items Using a Bipolar Response Scale'. *European Journal of Personality* 19 (2005): 373–90.

11 Leesha McKenny, '"Absolute Disgrace": Asbestos Dumped Outside Childcare Centres'. *Sydney Morning Herald*, 19 March 2013.

The second aspect of the link between ethics and sustainability is that ongoing relations between parties depend upon trust between the parties, which in turn requires a perception by each party that the other will behave ethically towards them. If employees feel that they can no longer trust management to behave ethically, or management believes that the employees' negotiators cannot be trusted, then it is much more difficult to negotiate an agreement between the two sides, and much more difficult to sustain an ongoing relationship. Resistance, and subsequent overt and covert conflict, are much more likely to occur.[12]

In other words, unethical behaviour is usually unsustainable. Usually—but not always. In the extremes, it need not be the case. Paying workers the highest wages may be ethical but, in terms of surviving market competition, not economically sustainable. Insisting that all economic activities involving carbon emissions immediately halt may be sustainable but not ethical, at least in the eyes of the current generation of workers who could feel it unethical that they suddenly lose their jobs. But such extremes are rare; for example, few proposals for addressing climate change involve immediate halts to carbon emissions—and the push for zero net emissions of carbon by 2050 does not require such immediate halts. (As long ago as 2013 the Australian Energy Market Operator found it would be feasible to operate the Australian energy market with 100 per cent renewable energy.)[13] So ethics and sustainability usually overlap a lot, but they are not the same thing.

Hence, one of the well-used definitions of the principles of sustainability performance by corporations has, as the first of nine items, 'ethics'.[14] Another refers to employment practices that promote personal and professional employee development, diversity and empowerment.

In Chapter 4 we saw how ethical issues have arisen and been handled in relation to artificial intelligence. That chapter highlighted both the importance of ethical considerations and the problems of leaving ethical matters to be resolved voluntarily through consideration by individuals:

12 This argument was first made by Keshena de Silva in 2014.

13 Tristan Edis, '100% Renewables Is Feasible: AEMO'. *The Australian* (Climate Spectator), 29 April 2013, www.theaustralian.com.au/business/business-spectator/100-renewables-is-feasible-aemo/news-story/4a4df3b317ea8bcb6b594926977d1f0c.

14 Marc J. Epstein and Marie-Josée Roy, 'Improving Sustainability Performance: Specifying, Implementing and Measuring Key Principles'. *Journal of General Management* 29, no. 1 (2003): 15–31, cited in Marc J. Epstein, *Making Sustainability Work: Best Practices in Managing and Measuring Corporate Social, Environmental and Economic Impacts* (Sheffield: Greenleaf, 2008).

there is an important role for regulation as well. It is not just about AI, however. Ethical issues extend into almost all aspects of current and future work canvassed in this book, even if their ethical implications have been only implied, but not necessarily considered explicitly, in these chapters. For example:

- When management adopts a 'low-trust' or 'high-trust' approach towards employees, is either approach ethically superior to the other?
- Is it ethically appropriate for firms to seek to individualise employment-relations practices when some or many employees would prefer to belong to a trade union?
- Is it ethically correct to seek to impose a monoculture upon employees within an organisation—or should diversity in views and behaviours be permitted or even encouraged?
- Is it ethically correct to make employees behave in ways that go against their personal beliefs, in order to maximise the profits of the corporation?
- What are the ethical dimensions of the use of power? Is it right for a corporation to use its bargaining power against employees? Is it right for employees to combine together into a union and threaten to—or even actually—withdraw their labour from the corporation?
- Is it right that women are paid, on average, less than men, even when hours and qualifications are taken into account? Is it right, or wrong, to seek to change this?
- Is it right that discrimination or even harassment may occur on the basis of gender, ethnicity, disability, chronic illness, age or other matters?
- Is it right that technological change might result in some workers losing their jobs, even if society as a whole has higher living standards? What would constitute fair treatment of them?
- Is it right that nonunion members can free ride on the benefits obtained by unionists? Alternatively, would it be right for nonunionists to be forced to join a union in workplaces where the majority of employees are unionists? How, ethically, can such contradictions be resolved?[15]

---

15 Examples of efforts to deal with this conundrum are at David Peetz, 'Co-operative Values, Institutions and Free Riding in Australia: Can It Learn from Canada?'. *Relations industrielles/Industrial Relations* 60, no. 4 (2005): 709–36; and Mark Harcourt et al., 'How a Default Union Membership Could Help Reduce Income Inequality'. *The Conversation*, 21 January 2019, theconversation.com/how-a-default-union-membership-could-help-reduce-income-inequality-110021.

- Is it right that democracy often stops when you walk inside the workplace gate? Should employees have a say and, if so, how much of a say in the running of their workplace? Should it be their decision as to whether they resist collectively against managerial decisions they do not like?
- Is it right that employees have to engage in emotional labour? Should they be made to engage in surface acting, 'pretending' certain emotions? Should they be made to in effect change their emotions through deep acting? If so, should they be compensated and, if so, by how much?
- Is it right if employees can be hired and fired 'at will'?
- Is it right to differentiate in pay between different workers according to some 'objective' measure of performance? Or according to some 'subjective' measure of performance?
- How much allowance should employers ethically make for the personal needs of employees? How much allowance should employees make for the profit needs of their employer?

Those are just *some* of the ethical issues we have encountered here. Some of them are matters on which there would probably be little disagreement between readers. For example, few would say that it is acceptable to discriminate in pay on the grounds of gender or to allow harassment at work. Some are matters on which Ethics Committees (which all universities have) would have very clear views (e.g. on the matter of making employees behave in ways that go against their personal beliefs). For example, it is clear that no modern university would give its imprimatur to the Milgram experiments of the 1960s,[16] as they would be considered deeply unethical. Yet as recently as 2010 a French documentary team recreated a related scenario, *Le jeu de la mort* (or 'The Game of Death'), in which TV contestants thought they were applying electric shocks to other contestants, and audience members cheered them on.[17] So, ethical standards vary hugely between universities and the mass media. It is no wonder that a globally popular 'reality' TV show based on 24-hour surveillance of contestants was named *Big Brother*, evoking the alleged evil mastermind in *Nineteen Eighty-Four*.[18] Perhaps that repeated implicit messaging in turn conditioned the seemingly muted response to

16 Stanley Milgram, *Obedience to Authority* (New York: Harper & Row, 1974).

17 Telegraph, 'French Contestants Torture Each Other on TV Game of Death'. *Telegraph* (UK), 17 March 2010 2010.

18 George Orwell, *Nineteen Eighty-Four: A Novel* (Harmondsworth: Penguin, 1949; repr., 1976).

revelations about mass electronic surveillance by the US National Security Agency. If so, it would illustrate something we saw in Chapter 5, that the extent of ethical responsiveness to dissenting ideas is in part a function of exposure to content in the media.

Some other ethical questions raised above, however, are likely to generate more explicit disagreement—for example, positions on performance pay, employee participation or trade unionism. Some of this may be based simply on whether people sympathise with employees or management, or in particular whether their work location directs their sympathies towards one or the other. People's moral frameworks tend to adjust to suit the circumstances in which they find themselves, otherwise they may experience cognitive dissonance.[19] That is, people often have beliefs that are convenient for their situation.

So, many of the above are significant in their own right as ethical issues. But ethical considerations may also affect the success of workplace relations, for example in shaping productivity and sustainable performance. A sense of fairness in the distribution of benefits or power is critical to work.

Forms of sustainability

There are several different forms of sustainability—in effect, sustainability at different levels within social systems. We consider each of these.

Microlevel sustainability: Employees and firms

In workplace relations, the microlevel is normally the level most focused on. The issues here are manyfold. A simple example is that of personal health. Earlier we saw the growth of rotating 12-hour shifts and of drive-in drive-out and fly-in fly-out working arrangements in the mining industry. The Australian Coal and Energy Survey (ACES) indicated the presence of long hours, work–life balance problems and the transfer of the burden of housework onto mineworkers' partners (i.e. costs were being externalised to the partner). That survey additionally showed short-term illnesses were higher among workers who reported no say in their working hours and had a desire to work fewer hours, as well as among those who felt unsafe for various reasons including working night shifts, those who slept badly,

19 Leon Festinger, *A Theory of Cognitive Dissonance* (Stanford, CA: Stanford University Press, 1957).

and those who were dissatisfied with how much free time they had. There were also indications of psychological illness among those who reported no say in their working hours and had a desire to work fewer hours, and among partners who reported that their mineworker spouses were too tired or emotionally exhausted from work.[20]

This tells us that, in examining sustainability at this and other levels, one thing we should consider is the extent to which the costs and benefits are internalised or externalised. Are the benefits of the transaction (the selling of mineral products) being shared principally between the firm and the customer, while the costs are disproportionately imposed on employees? If employees are experiencing adverse health effects, and firms are not engaged in the investment necessary to prevent these adverse health effects, then some of the costs are being externalised to employees. The history of the mining industry is full of examples where inadequate investment in OHS meant that employees paid with their lives—the ultimate form of cost externalisation. We saw this in three successive mine disasters in the central Queensland town of Moura, in 1976, 1984 and 1995, in which 36 people were killed.[21] We saw it more recently in a coal mine explosion, in which 301 miners were killed, in Turkey—a country where each year one in 10 workers in mining and quarrying have an 'occupational accident'.[22] The death toll from coal mining in China is even worse, resulting in the closure of many mines in recent years.[23]

Another recent and tragic example of this approach in a different industry was the collapse in April 2013 of a building containing garment factories (the Rana Plaza) in Bangladesh, leading to the death of 1,127 workers. Eighty per cent of Bangladeshi garment workers are female. The costs of cheap clothing were externalised onto employees, who were ordered to work that day on threat of dismissal (and, in some cases, beatings), despite

20 David Peetz, Georgina Murray, and Olav Muurlink, *Work and Hours Amongst Mining and Energy Workers* (Brisbane: Centre for Work, Organisation and Wellbeing, Griffith University, 2012).
21 Georgina Murray and David Peetz, *Women of the Coal Rushes* (Sydney: UNSW Press, 2010), Chapter 3.
22 Mustafa Sönmez, 'Mining: The Sector with Low Added Value, High Loss of Life'. *Hurriyet Daily News*, 26 May 2014, www.hurriyetdailynews.com/mining-the-sector-with-low-added-value-high-loss-of-life.aspx?PageID=238&NID=66933&NewsCatID=347.
23 Wang Ming-Xiao et al., 'Analysis of National Coal-Mining Accident Data in China, 2001–2008'. *Public Health Reports* 126, no. 2 (2011): 270–75; Reuters, 'China to Speed up Closing Small-Scale Coal Mines to Improve Safety'. Reuters, 12 June 2017.

cracks having previously appeared in the building walls.[24] The benefits were gained by the factory owners and managers, and corporations and customers in the West (possibly including you). Two weeks later, under considerable pressure, the government agreed to let employees establish a trade union without the employer's permission.[25] This may not sound like much of an accomplishment, but previously workers were not permitted to form a trade union without approval of management, and union activists had been beaten and tortured. We return to this incident later on.

A colleague of mine who often travels to Bangladesh says he was very worried about what would happen if a significant earth tremor hit Dhaka. Hundreds of earlier deaths in Bangladesh have been caused by workers being locked behind closed doors in factories that caught fire. One unionist I spoke to told me of a woman who had jumped from a burning factory building, not to save her life (she did not expect to live) but to save her body, so that her family would be able to identify, and bury, her. Astonishingly, she survived. After that fire, labour activists faced the grim task of searching through the wreckage—for labels and receipts, which they found—as otherwise the clothing chains would deny they had ever made use of this building, in a classic case of 'not there' employment.

A high-profile employer in the Third World is Foxconn, with huge factories in China, producing parts for smartphones (probably including the one in your purse or pocket). It plays a key part in the 'not there' employment supply chains of several large phone companies that enable Apple to directly employ barely a tenth of the workers in its supply chain. Foxconn has been characterised by strict management, low wages, worker discontent, explosions and numerous suicides.[26] There are continuing questions as to whether employment conditions in Apple's supply chain are at all improving, and whether factories are being robotised anyway

24 Human Rights Watch, '"Whoever Raises Their Head Suffers the Most": Workers' Rights in Bangladesh's Garment Factories'. Human Rights Watch, www.hrw.org/report/2015/04/22/whoever-raises-their-head-suffers-most/workers-rights-bangladeshs-garment.

25 Jason Burke, 'Bangladesh Eases Trade Union Laws after Factory Building Collapse'. *Guardian*, 13 May 2013, www.guardian.co.uk/world/2013/may/13/bangladesh-trade-union-laws.

26 Mark Anner, 'Corporate Social Responsibility and Freedom of Association Rights: The Precarious Quest for Legitimacy and Control in Global Supply Chains'. *Politics and Society* 40, no. 4 (2012): 609–44; Charles Duhigg and David Barboza, 'In China, Human Costs Are Built into an Ipad'. *New York Times*, 25 January 2012.

and thousands of workers sacked.[27] These questions are asked alongside debates in several countries over the tax paid by large corporations such as Apple.[28] These all raise some interesting ethical issues.

Microlevel costs are not only felt by employees. As suggested, it is not sustainable for employees to continue working in situations that damage their personal lives or physical or psychological health, or maybe that of their partners. As a result, employees resist, and firms will face high labour turnover costs where working arrangements are not sustainable. The Australian mining industry, where firms face unusually high labour turnover despite very high wages, is an example of this individualised resistance to unsustainable employment practices.[29]

Sustainability at the firm level requires other things: for example, the firm must be capable of making a profit, and there must be a 'fair' distribution of benefits. On the former, it is interesting to note that a recent Harvard Business School study indicated that firms that explicitly focused on 'short termism' faced greater risks and financial problems than companies that focused on creating long-term value. Short-termism was measured by researchers' analysing the content of transcripts of company conference calls, and the risks included a higher cost of capital and a lower return on assets. They were also more likely to report very small positive earnings, and to violate loan covenants. One reason was that their investors also adopted like-minded approaches, which led to higher stock-price volatility.[30]

27 Duncan Jefferies, 'Is Apple Cleaning up Its Act on Labour Rights?'. *Guardian*, 5 March 2014, www.theguardian.com/sustainable-business/apple-act-on-labour-right; Jane Wakefield, 'Foxconn Replaces 60,000 Factory Workers with Robots'. *BBC News*, 25 May 2016, www.bbc.com/news/technology-36376966. Thomas Clarke and Martijn Boersma, The Governance of Global Value Chains: Unresolved Human Rights, Environmental and Ethical Dilemmas in the Apple Supply Chain. *Journal of Business Ethics* 143 (2017): 111–31.

28 Lee Sheppard, 'How Does Apple Avoid Taxes?'. *Forbes*, 28 May 2013, www.forbes.com/sites/leesheppard/2013/05/28/how-does-apple-avoid-taxes/; Simon Santow, 'Google, Apple and Microsoft Deny Tax Avoidance at Senate Inquiry, Labor Says Australians Don't Accept Their Practices Are "Genuine"'. *ABC News Online*, Australian Broadcasting Corporation, 8 April 2015, www.abc.net.au/news/2015-04-08/google-apple-microsoft-deny-tax-avoidance-senate-inquiry/6379024; Michael West, 'Multinationals' Brazen Tax Avoidance'. *Saturday Paper*, 13–19 May 2017.

29 David Peetz and Georgina Murray, '"You Get Really Old, Really Quick": Involuntary Long Hours in the Mining Industry'. *Journal of Industrial Relations* 53, no. 1 (2011): 13–29.

30 Harvard Business School, 'How a Short-Term Strategy Can Backfire'. Strategy + Business, Harvard Business School, 2012, www.strategy-business.com/article/re00191?pg=all, citing Francois Brochet, Maria Loumioti, and George Serafeim, *Short-Termism, Investor Clientele, and Firm Risk*. Harvard Business School Accounting & Management Unit Working Paper No. 12-072 (Cambridge, MA: Harvard Business School, 2012), papers.ssrn.com/sol3/papers.cfm?abstract_id=1999484.

So, short-term focus in profits is inconsistent with long-term growth. Mind you, executive pay schemes that emphasise short-term incentives—and there are many[31]—help drive this behaviour.

It is also plausible (indeed likely) that short-termism among company boards is driven by short-termism among investors—that is, within important parts of finance capital. Regardless of whose short-termism drove the behaviour, it seems that, in the long run, short-termism undermines sustainable profitability.

Societal-level sustainability

Ethical income distributions affect economic sustainability at the societal level. In cross-national analysis, researchers from the International Monetary Fund (an institution long known for its strong support for liberal market policies) in recent years have commented that 'more inequality seems to spell less sustained growth'.[32] They found that reductions in inequality were more important than any other factor (e.g. trade openness or external debt, the latter being of minimal importance) in explaining the duration (i.e. the sustainability) of growth periods.

Aspects of workplace policy also affect sustainability at that level. Incentive schemes in the financial sector were a significant element in the global financial crisis, because of their distorting effect on behaviour.[33] The use of incentive schemes for managers was identified as a reason why the economic performance in Iceland experienced unsustainable procyclical extremes of boom and bust before and during the global financial crisis.[34] This should not surprise us. Incentive schemes in Australia drove a raft of financial misbehaviour so bad that a conservative government was forced to hold a royal commission that disclosed widespread deceit and

---

31 Ann Tenbrunsel and Jordan Thomas, *The Street, the Bull and the Crisis: A Survey of the US & UK Financial Services Industry* (New York: The University of Notre Dame and Labaton Sucharow LLP, May 2015), www.secwhistlebloweradvocate.com/pdf/Labaton-2015-Survey-report_12.pdf; see also Johnson interviewed in Andrew Robertson, 'ASIC Is Waving a Big Stick at Directors'. *The Business* (Australian Broadcasting Corporation, 2016), 15 April, www.abc.net.au/news/2016-04-15/asic-is-waving-a-big-stick-at-directors/7331522, at 4'23" (link expired).

32 Andrew G. Berg and Jonathan D. Ostry, 'Equality and Efficiency: Is There a Trade-Off between the Two or Do They Go Hand in Hand?'. *Finance and Development* 48, no. 3 (2011): 12–15.

33 David Peetz, Stephane Le Queux, and Ann Frost, 'The Global Financial Crisis and Employment Relations'. In *The Future of Employment Relations: New Paradigms, New Approaches*, ed. Adrian Wilkinson and Keith Townsend (Basingstoke: Palgrave Macmillan, 2011), 193–214.

34 Robert H. Wade and Silla Sigurgeirsdottir, 'Iceland's Rise, Fall, Stabilisation and Beyond'. *Cambridge Journal of Economics* 36 (2012): 127–44.

exploitation of customers and of barely functioning regulators.[35] While incentive payments are often accepted as a matter of faith, particularly in market liberal economics, as promoting good behaviour, in practice they often produce counterproductive results in a wide range of areas including, for example, occupational health and safety.[36]

Systemic sustainability

The biggest and most important level at which sustainability can be considered is the systemic level—the system (often referred to as the global ecosystem) within which society and economy exist. In earlier times we thought about how the actions of firms, in dumping pollution into the environment, were engaged in classic externalising of costs onto local ecosystems and communities. In *The Handmaid's Tale*, there is frequent reference to the 'Colonies', unidentified distant toxic dumps with labour camps to which noncompliant women were sent. Since that was written, concern has grown to cover the impact of rising carbon dioxide emissions upon the global environment and global society. It is not just people in former colonies who are threatened by the toxicity of those emissions to the planet.

The peer-reviewed evidence overwhelmingly shows that growing carbon dioxide emissions are leading to dangerously rising sea levels and severe consequences for ecosystems, forestry, agriculture, energy consumption, water resources and human mortality unless major changes occur in economic behaviour.[37] If anything, the situation is worse than previously

---

35 Royal Commission into Misconduct in the Banking Superannuation and Financial Services Industry, *Final Report* (Canberra: Australian Government, February 2019).

36 Andrew Hopkins and Sarah Maslen, *Risky Rewards: How Company Bonuses Affect Safety* (Farnham, UK: Ashgate, 2015), 28. They cite Richard E. Fairfax (Deputy Assistant Secretary), 'Employer Safety Incentive and Disincentive Policies and Practices'. Occupational Safety and Health Administration, Memorandum for Regional Administrators, Whistleblower Program Administrators (Washington DC: US Department of Labor, 2012), 12 March. See also Michael Quinlan, Philip Bohle, and Felicity Lamm, *Managing Occupational Health and Safety: A Multidisciplinary Approach* (Palgrave Macmillan, 2010).

37 M. Diesendorf, 'Climate Change and the Economy'. In *Readings in Political Economy: Economics as a Social Science*, ed. George Arygous and Frank Stilwell (Melbourne: Pluto Press, 2010), 15–18; Derek S. Arndt, Molly O. Baringer, and Michael R. Johnson, 'State of the Climate in 2009'. *Bulletin of the American Meteorological Society* 91, no. 7 (2010): S1–S224; Intergovernmental Panel on Climate Change, 'Summary for Policymakers'. In *Global Warming of 1.5°C*. An IPCC Special Report on the impacts of global warming of 1.5°C above pre-industrial levels and related global greenhouse gas emission pathways, in the context of strengthening the global response to the threat of climate change, sustainable development, and efforts to eradicate poverty, edited by V. Masson-Delmotte et al. (Geneva: World Meteorological Organization, 2018).

thought, because scientists appear to have a 'bias towards underestimation' of the effects of climate change on sea levels, the polar caps and methane emissions from thawing permafrost and lakes.[38] What seemed like alarmist predictions at the time turned out to be overly cautious.

Apart from the above implications for the societies in which corporations trade, there are also more direct implications for employment relations. For example, as labour productivity is reduced during periods of high humidity, research published in *Nature Climate Change* indicates that labour productivity will be damaged in many countries as a result of climate change.[39] The impact on productivity, for people not experiencing the increasingly expensive benefits of air-conditioning, will be quite substantial, especially for people in warmer or mid-latitude climates. This is one of many indicators that it is much cheaper to deal with climate change now than to wait until some date in the future.

It is largely in response to these global threats, and to other related concerns, that corporate literature and rhetoric increasingly refers to sustainable development, to the need for a 'green firm' responding to the 'sustainability imperative', and to a 'triple bottom line' encompassing social, environmental and financial matters.[40]

Barriers to sustainability

Why isn't more happening? The fundamental barrier to sustainability is the logic of the economic system. Liberal market economist Milton Friedman claimed that the firm has no social responsibilities other than

38 Katharine Hayhoe and Robert E. Kopp, 'What Surprises Lurk within the Climate System?'. *Environmental Research Letters* 11, no. 12 (2016): 1–3; Martin Wik et al., 'Biased Sampling of Methane Release from Northern Lakes: A Problem for Extrapolation'. *Geophysical Research Letters* 43, no. 3 (2016): 1256–62; Chris Hope and Kevin Schaefer, 'Economic Impacts of Carbon Dioxide and Methane Released from Thawing Permafrost'. *Nature Climate Change* 6 (2016): 56–9.

39 Charis Palmer and Sunanda Creagh, 'Climate Change Linked to Declines in Labour Productivity'. *The Conversation*, 25 February 2013, theconversation.com/climate-change-linked-to-declines-in-labour-productivity-12407, citing John P. Dunne, Ronald J. Stouffer, and Jasmin G. John, 'Reductions in Labour Capacity from Heat Stress under Climate Warming'. *Nature Climate Change* 3 (2013): 563–6.

40 Dallas M. Cowan et al., 'A Cross-Sectoral Analysis of Reported Corporate Environmental and Sustainability Practices'. *Regulatory Toxicology and Pharmacology* 58, no. 3 (2010): 524–38; David A. Lubin and Daniel C. Esty, 'The Big Idea: The Sustainability Imperative'. *Harvard Business Review*, May 2010, 42–50, hbr.org/2010/05/the-sustainability-imperative; Daniel C. Esty and Andrew Winstone, *Green to Gold: How Smart Companies Use Environmental Strategy to Innovate, Create Value and Build Competitive Advantage* (New Haven: Yale University Press, 2006).

to itself: 'the social responsibility of business is to increase its profits'.[41] As Joel Bakan argued in *The Corporation*, corporate decision-makers must always:

> act in the best interests of the corporation, and hence its owners. The law forbids any other motivation for their actions, whether to assist workers, improve the environment or help consumers save money … As corporate officials … they have no legal authority to pursue such goals as ends in themselves—only as means to serve the corporation's own interests, which generally means to maximise the wealth of its shareholders.[42]

Both writers, posed at opposite ends of the political spectrum, echo Marx's view that the actions of a capitalist do not 'depend on the good or ill will of the individual', because 'competition brings out the inherent laws of capitalist production' as if they were 'external coercive laws having power over every individual capitalist'.[43] Bakan, as a lawyer, focuses on the situation regarding formal legal obligations, which may vary between jurisdictions, and maximising profit need not be seen as always acting in the best interests of shareholders. As a comment on the logic of capital, however, his remarks have considerable validity. In *The Corporation*, Bakan seeks to point to numerous examples, from the failure of Enron to the privatisation of water in Bolivia, where corporations, in pursuing a single, profit-maximising objective, have shown callous unconcern for the feelings of others, incapacity to maintain existing relationships, reckless disregard for the safety of others, deceitfulness, incapacity to experience guilt and failure to conform to social norms regarding lawful behaviour. He argues that, if the corporation were a natural person, these attributes would (on a standard World Health Organization personality checklist) lead to that person being diagnosed as a 'psychopath'. This is a very different image to that of the utopian free market in which buyers and sellers, individually pursuing self-interest, collectively produce the best possible outcome. But it does better to explain why, around three decades after the Bhopal disaster in India, Dow Chemical, the owner of the corporation whose factory exploded and killed over 10,000 people with hundreds of thousands harmed, still declined to clean up the area contaminated by the

41 Milton Friedman, 'The Social Responsibility of Business Is to Increase Its Profits'. *New York Times Magazine*, 13 September 1970.

42 Joel Bakan, *The Corporation: The Pathological Pursuit of Profit and Power* (London: Constable & Robertson, 2004).

43 Karl Marx, *Capital, Volume 1* (London: The Electric Book Company, 1887; repr., 1998), 389.

explosion.[44] For all we know, the vast majority of shareholders in Dow may believe this to be a tragic situation, but the corporation does not behave as if it does.[45] Thus the corporation is to Bakan 'an externalising machine',[46] something that is inherently incompatible with sustainability.

Added to this, since the 1980s, have been the effects of financialisation, which 'transforms the functioning of economic systems at both the macro and micro levels'.[47] Ownership of large corporations has shifted from families and individuals to finance capital.[48] Finance capital is more mobile and the costs of entry and exit are lower than for family capitalists. This has implications for workplace relations, more so when there are alternative opportunities for finance capital to make high profits via 'accumulation by dispossession'.[49] Economic blogger Peter Dorman recently commented:

> One consequence of a longer-term orientation is an incentive for greater investment, and an important venue for this investment is the enterprise's workforce. A high-investment personnel strategy is one in which more resources are devoted to cultivating human capital and worker attachment to the firm. The latter is fostered through internal labor markets, rent-sharing and a more favorable, or at least less resistant, attitude toward worker voice … Financialization is linked to inequality and greater precariousness of work because there is little incentive to expend resources in the present to capture the return to investments in the workforce that materialize (uncertainly) well into the future.[50]

44 Amnesty International, *28 Years Later, Women in Bhopal Still Waiting for Justice* (New York: 3 December 2012), www.amnestyusa.org/news/news-item/28-years-later-women-in-bhopal-still-waiting-for-justice.

45 David Peetz, *Brave New Workplace: How Individual Contracts Are Changing Our Jobs* (Sydney: Allen & Unwin, 2006).

46 Bakan, *Corporation*, Chapter 3.

47 Thomas I. Palley, 'Financialization: What It Is and Why It Matters'. Working Paper No. 525 (Annandale-on-Hudson, NY: Levy Economics Institute, 2007), papers.ssrn.com/sol3/papers.cfm?abstract_id=1077923.

48 David Peetz and Georgina Murray, 'The Financialisation of Global Corporate Ownership'. In *Financial Elites and Transnational Business: Who Rules the World?*, ed. Georgina Murray and John Scott (Cheltenham: Edward Elgar, 2012).

49 Discussed in Chapter 2. See David Harvey, 'The "New" Imperialism: Accumulation by Dispossession', Socialist Register 40 (2004): 63–87; David Harvey, The New Imperialism (Oxford: Oxford University Press, 2003).

50 Peter Dorman, 'Financialization and the Incredible Shrinking Time Horizon'. Econospeak, 2013, econospeak.blogspot.com.au/2013/05/financialization-and-incredible.html.

This also has implications for global sustainability. The climate crisis should be seen in the context of conflicting capitalist visions; between, on the one hand, those focusing on short-term profit, increasingly associated with the 'financialisation' of modern economies, and, on the other hand, those focusing on long-term considerations, accounting for sustainability.[51]

There are other barriers to global sustainability of course. Lobbyists, using the same tactics (and partly the same personnel) that tobacco companies used to confuse or discredit the science on smoking,[52] along with some major media corporations and a spread of blog sites, give the impression that there is debate within the scientific community on the existence of anthropogenic global warming. In fact, over 97 per cent of climate scientists recognise the reality of human-made climate change.[53] Studies have used a variety of methodologies to come to similar conclusions about the climate. Yet the muddying of the water has affected public opinion and severely restricted governments' willingness to take action. Among the broader public, understanding is hampered by people's unfamiliarity with the studies, frequent exposure to counter-ideas from those with an interest in continuing carbon emissions, and the cognitive dissonance that leads people to often reject evidence that runs counter to their own theories and ideologies and to welcome evidence that supports their belief systems. In the case of climate change, where the evidence is overwhelming, the selective use of evidence and failure to take account of the totality of the evidence is known as 'cherry-picking'. As one mistruth is exposed, another rises to take its place. (It was common, for example, for climate

---

51 David Peetz and Georgina Murray, *Global Wellbeing and Climate-Interested Investors' Motives*. Working Paper (Brisbane: Centre for Work, Organisation and Wellbeing, Griffith University, 2013), www.griffith.edu.au/__data/assets/pdf_file/0012/569559/Global-wellbeing-and-investors-motives-Peetz,-Murray.pdf.

52 Naomi Oreskes and Erik Conway, *Merchants of Doubt: How a Handful of Scientists Obscured the Truth on Issues from Tobacco Smoke to Global Warming* (London: Bloomsbury, 2010).

53 John Cook et al., 'Quantifying the Consensus on Anthropogenic Global Warming in the Scientific Literature'. *Environmental Research Letters* 8, no. 2 (2013), iopscience.iop.org/article/10.1088/1748-9326/8/2/024024/pdf; see also Kyle Hill, 'The Overwhelming Odds of Climate Change'. *Scientific American: Blogs* (20 May 2013), blogs.scientificamerican.com/overthinking-it/2013/05/20/the-overwhelming-odds-of-climate-change/; James Powell, 'The State of Climate Science: A Thorough Review of the Scientific Literature on Global Warming' (Science Progress, Center for American Progress, 2012), scienceprogress.org/2012/11/27479/.

denialists to argue that the world has been cooling since 1998.[54] Now the nine hottest years in recorded history have been since 2004,[55] so this myth has been put away, and others created to take its place.)[56]

There is, however, an important difference between achieving consensus on action on global sustainability and action on sustainability in employment relations. In the long run, it is not in the interests of capital—even finance capital—to create an uninhabitable planet. So in essence the conflict is one between those parts of capital and the state with a short-term perspective, and those with a long-term perspective ('patient capital'). The former are, in effect, extracting value from the latter. On this matter, the interests of labour are not in conflict with those of the latter group.

On employment relations, though, the conflict of interest between labour and capital—over how the benefits will be distributed—is fundamental and in some ways irreconcilable. Yet at the same time, as we know, there are also core overlaps in interest—each needs the other to survive. So achieving sustainability in employment relations will always be a form of compromise, and one in which the parameters will likely never be fully resolved.

Corporate social responsibility

A concept closely related to questions of ethics and sustainability is that of 'corporate social responsibility' (CSR). It is an idea that prompted Friedman's riposte mentioned above, that the only social responsibility a corporation has is to its profits. There are a wide range of definitions and concepts behind this label, making a single definition controversial but 'at the heart of many of the differing definitions of CSR is a commitment from companies to produce some sort of social or environmental benefit,

54 Michael Mann, *The Hockey Stick and the Climate Wars: Dispatches from the Front Lines* (New York: Columbia University Press, 2012).

55 Climate Central, 'The 10 Hottest Global Years on Record', *Climate Central*, 6 February 2019, www.climatecentral.org/gallery/graphics/the-10-hottest-global-years-on-record.

56 Skeptical Science, 'Global Warming and Climate Change Myths', *Skeptical Science*, 2019, skepticalscience.com/argument.php.

which goes beyond merely the basic compliance with the law'.[57] Citing Blowfield and Frynas,[58] Burchell refers to three key aspects of this 'umbrella' approach, being that corporations have responsibilities:

- for their impact on society and the natural environment, beyond compliance with the law;
- for behaviour of those with whom they deal (e.g. within supply chains);
- to manage their relations to wider society, either to add value to the business or to society.

The proposition that corporations would engage in CSR activities for reasons other than adding value to the business runs counter to the idea that profit maximisation is the sole purpose of the corporation (seen as embedded in the law in some countries, and in the writings of Friedman and Bakan). There are two possible ways for observers and policy-makers to reconcile these perspectives.

The first is to believe that the form of corporate behaviour varies according to their institutional environment and that these differ between nation states. There is a literature based around the notion of 'varieties of capitalism',[59] which distinguishes between 'liberal market economies' (LMEs) such as the USA and UK and 'coordinated market economies' (CMEs) such as those in Scandinavian countries, Germany and Japan. In addition, patterns of corporate ownership appear to differ between these 'varieties'. For example, in many large German companies the largest, dominant shareholdings are by individuals, families or other small groupings, whereas in the USA the largest shareholdings are by banks and other forms of finance capital.[60] Thus financialisation is much more important, to date, in the USA than in Germany. Financialisation in turn emphasises maximisation of short-term returns. It encourages profit as the sole criterion for corporate behaviour and promotes short-termism. Inequality is higher in the USA: American firms on average are less sympathetic to employee interests and unions than European-based

57 Jon Burchell, 'Just What Should Business Be Responsible For? Understanding the Concept of CSR'. In *The Corporate Social Responsibility Reader*, ed. Jon Burchell (Oxford: Routledge, 2008).

58 Michael Blowfield and Jedrzej George Frynas, 'Setting New Agendas: Critical Perspectives on Corporate Social Responsibility in the Developing World'. *International Affairs* 81, no. 3 (2005): 499–513.

59 Peter A. Hall and David W. Soskice, *Varieties of Capitalism: The Institutional Foundations of Comparative Advantage* (Oxford: Oxford University Press, 2001).

60 David Peetz, Georgina Murray, and Werner Nienhüser, 'The New Structuring of Corporate Ownership'. *Globalizations* 10, no. 5 (2013): 711–30.

firms (union density in the USA is among the lowest in the OECD), and European firms tend to show greater willingness to adopt sustainability principles in relation to the environment.[61] So, perhaps the Bakan/Friedman perspective is more about LMEs than CMEs. Perhaps.

The alternative response is to believe that the profit-maximising objective is not just a result of any nation's particular corporate laws but is fundamental to the nature of the corporation as a collective of capital. That is, the logic of capitalism means that capitalists behave this way as if the law made them do so.[62] If this is the case, then as firms seek to maximise profit the only way to ensure that firms engage in socially responsible behaviour is to change the legal/institutional framework to make it mandatory. If there are differences between how corporations behave in LMEs and CMEs, it is because the laws force them to behave differently. In the short term, a CEO or senior manager of a corporation, acting individually or as a group, may exercise agency and be able to pursue some CSR objectives; but in the long run this runs up against the financialised logic of capital and is only sustainable if the law requires them to act this way.

Companies engaged in CSR will typically produce voluntary reports on their CSR activities. Most large corporations will do this, for the public relations benefits. Some may have deeper, more genuine engagements. These reports take many formats, but the Netherlands-based Global Reporting Initiative (GRI) provides a common framework. One recent critique argued that 'sustainability reporting does not currently meet the needs of stakeholders interested in the labour practices performance of Australian companies'.[63]

Finance and industry associations

The United Nations (UN) became directly involved in attempting to promote CSR, and several years ago helped set up, through seed funding, the UN Principles for Responsible Investment (PRI). This was a UN-backed (but member-financed) 'network of international investors' and other corporations willing to agree to six key principles on environmental,

---

61 Asset Owners Disclosure Project, *AODP Global Climate 500 Asset Owners Index 2017* (Sydney: AODP, 2017), aodproject.net/wp-content/uploads/2017/04/AODP-GLOBAL-INDEX-REPORT-2017_FINAL_VIEW.pdf.

62 Marx, *Capital, Volume 1*, 389.

63 Banarra Consulting, *2010 Labour Practices in Sustainability Reporting—a Review* (Sydney: Report for the Construction, Forestry, Mining and Energy Union, Mining and Energy Division, 2010).

social and governance (ESG) issues. It aimed 'to help investors integrate the consideration [of ESG] issues into investment decision-making and ownership practices, and thereby improve long-term returns to beneficiaries'.[64] Based in London, it promoted 'evidence that ESG issues can be material to performance of portfolios, particularly over the long term'. It had 1,484 signatories who were either investors or asset managers in May 2017, plus 223 'professional service partner' signatories.

There are several other privately established institutions designed to promote investment more specifically in climate-friendly activities. It appears that, even in a financialising world, climate-interested (long-term focused) investors are able to successfully pressure large transnational corporations to adopt at least some carbon-friendly actions,[65] so it is possible that pressure on corporations to engage in CSR behaviours may arise not only from workers and NGOs but also from elements of finance capital focused on longer-term issues (i.e. 'patient' capital).

On the other hand, industry associations may act in the opposite direction. Data drawn from Influence Map (a UK-based nonprofit organisation) suggest major discrepancies between the positions of target corporations, and of industry or trade associations representing them.[66] This is also evident within specific industries, such as oil.[67] Perhaps this is because the associations' behaviour becomes responsive to and dominated by the target corporations with the most to lose from responding to the climate crisis; or they take on an ideological role within capital; or the behaviour of the industry or trade associations is a better reflection of the genuine interests and preferences of target corporations (whose public statements might not be taken at face value). There are major benefits for

64 United Nations Principles for Responsible Investment, 'FAQs' (UNPRI, 2013), www.unpri.org/about-pri/faqs/ (site discontinued).

65 David Peetz and Georgina Murray, 'Financialization of Corporate Ownership and Implications for the Potential for Climate Action'. In *Institutional Investors' Power to Change Corporate Behavior: International Perspectives, Critical Studies on Corporate Responsibility, Governance and Sustainability*, ed. Suzanne Young and Stephen Gates (Bingley, UK: Emerald, 2013), 99–125.

66 David Peetz et al., *Corporations, Their Associations, and Climate Action* (Canberra: Association of Industrial Relations Academics of Australia and New Zealand/SSRN, 2017), papers.ssrn.com/sol3/cf_dev/AbsByAuth.cfm?per_id=589529.

67 Ibid.; Elysse Morgan, 'Woodside Boss Peter Coleman Calls for Australia to Introduce a Carbon Price'. *ABC News*, 13 November 2018, www.abc.net.au/news/2018-11-14/woodside-ceo-peter-coleman-argues-for-carbon-price/10494026.

corporations in 'distancing' accountability[68]—it is the same philosophy behind the 'not there' employment model. Interesting comparisons can also be drawn with employer associations in industrial relations.[69]

Pressures from finance capital are more likely to relate to climate sustainability issues than to labour issues, as the latter still tend to throw up questions about the conflict of interest between labour and capital, whereas the long-term survival of the planet is in the interests of both. That said, managers of workers' pension funds[70] have been criticised for themselves adopting too short-term a focus.[71] Yet short-term financial returns in one year typically do not correlate with returns the next year anyway.[72] To the extent that pension funds represent the interests of (retired or retiring) workers, a sustained longer-term focus by them may have implications for corporate labour relations behaviour as well. Others argue that workers' pension funds should not concern themselves with these issues, and indeed that worker involvement in pension fund boards reduces returns to members. However, evidence indicates institutionalised workers' pressure probably increases financial returns, most likely because it reduces opportunities for rent-seeking behaviour by financiers involved in pension funds.[73]

Indeed, it is possible that the 'tide is turning'. A recent report by the Asset Owners Disclosure Project (AODP) described 'a fundamental power shift … from short-termers to long-termers'.[74] That the financial industry has been slow, even reluctant, to fund the Adani Carmichael mine in central

68 David Peetz, 'Why Establish Non-Representative Organisations? Rethinking the Role, Form and Target of Think Tanks'. In *Think Tanks: Key Spaces in the Global Structure of Power*, ed. Alejandra Salas-Porras and Georgina Murray (New York: Palgrave Macmillan, 2017).

69 Peetz et al., *Corporations, Their Associations, and Climate Action.*

70 The equivalent in Australia is superannuation funds.

71 Trades Union Congress, *Investment Chains: Addressing Corporate and Investor Short-Termism* (London: TUC, 2006).

72 Daniel Kahneman, 'The Surety of Fools (Don't Blink! The Hazards of Confidence)'. *New York Times*, 19 October 2011, MM30; Christopher B. Philips, 'The Case for Indexing'. Vanguard Research (Valley Forge, PA: The Vanguard Group, 2011), personal.vanguard.com/pdf/icrpi.pdf; Richard E. Ferri, *The Power of Passive Investing* (Hoboken, NJ: Wiley, 2010).

73 David Peetz, *The Relationship between Collective Representation and National Pension Fund Outcomes* (Melbourne: Industry Super, January 2019).

74 Asset Owners Disclosure Project, *Active Ownership* (Sydney: AODP, 2017), aodproject.net/active-ownership/.

Queensland is possibly one example of that phenomenon.[75] It also seems from anecdotal discussions that the interest of Australian superannuation funds in these issues is increasing,[76] but there is still a long way to go before workers' pension funds give primacy to the long-term sustainability of the planet on which all economic activity occurs.

There are several potential reasons for this shift, besides the changing economics of renewable technology, the worsening climate outlook and shifting policies in countries like China and India. New tools are being developed to enable investors to quantify the impact of climate on their investments. In financial circles, the more things can be counted, the more they count. Pension funds need to invest over long periods of time, and so are now forced to invest with climate change in mind. They cannot afford to have 'stranded assets' on their books. There is a rational reason, within the logic of finance capital, for this rethinking.

Reinsurers—essentially large firms that provide insurance for insurance companies—face the same issue. They need to minimise exposure to extreme weather events, which are increasingly influenced by climate change. Indeed one, Munich Re, funded the early climate change research.[77] Some worry that, after 2050, extreme weather events could become so abrupt and severe as to be 'uninsurable'.[78] Fund managers are creating financial products to enable investment in climate change adaptation. And some investors are taking more control over their investments, rather than leaving them in the hands of fund managers, so they can give appropriate priority to climate issues.[79]

75 David Peetz and Georgina Murray, 'The Government Is Swimming against the Tide on Westpac's Adani Decision'. *The Conversation*, 3 May 2017, theconversation.com/the-government-is-swimming-against-the-tide-on-westpacs-adani-decision-76950. At time of writing, the proposed project had been reduced to less than half the announced size and was to be 'self-financed' (as still no financial institution would support it), if it ever goes ahead. John Quiggin, 'Adani's Rail Line Cut Shows Project Is on Life Support but Still a Threat to Climate'. *Guardian*, 15 September 2018, www.theguardian.com/environment/commentisfree/2018/sep/16/adanis-rail-line-cut-shows-project-is-on-life-support-but-still-a-threat-to-climate.

76 From discussions with the author.

77 Jeffrey Ball, 'Who Will Pay for Climate Change?'. *New Republic*, 3 November 2015, newrepublic.com/article/123212/who-will-pay-climate-change.

78 Ibid.; Jason Murphy, 'Climate Change Could Make the World "Uninsurable"'. *Crikey*, 14 March 2019, www.crikey.com.au/2019/03/14/climate-change-could-make-the-world-uninsurable/.

79 Asset Owners Disclosure Project, *Active Ownership*; Georgina Murray and David Peetz, 'Financial Markets, Climate Change, and Paradoxes of Coordination and Intervention'. *Perspectives on Global Development and Technology* 15, no. 5 (2016): 455–79; Celine Herweijer, N. Patmore, and R. Muir-Wood, 'Catastrophe Risk Models as a New Tool to Investigate the Financial Risks Associated with Climate Change Impacts and Cost-Benefits of Adaptation'. *IOP Conference Series: Earth and Environmental Science* 6 (2009), doi.org/10.1088/1755-1307/6/9/392021; Glenn W. Laper, 'Lombard Odier Launches Climate Bond Fund with AIM'. *NordSIP* (Nordic Sustainable Investment Platform), 6 March 2017, nordsip.com/2017/03/06/lombard-odier-launches-climate-bond-fund-with-aim/.

This is not to say that financiers around the world are responding uniformly to climate issues. Nor has finance uniformly abandoned short-termism. 'Climate-interested investors' currently account for no more than a third of the ownership of the world's very large corporations, and quite a bit less than that using stricter definitions.[80] However, as renewable energy becomes cheaper, inexorably widening the gap with the cost of carbon-fuelled energy, and the externalities of the latter become priced into costs faced by producers, financiers will increasingly behave *as if* they cared about sustainability. Whether that is enough for the planet is, however, another matter—without widespread carbon pricing, it is almost certainly not.

Workers, sustainability and a 'just transition'

Some environmental groups seek negative economic growth to resolve the conflict between the economy and the environment. Yet this is a politically and probably a socially impossible approach: there is no currently known economic system in which negative growth would lead to anything but higher unemployment. Negative growth could not be achieved by a reduction in labour productivity, as the logic of technological change is to increase labour productivity. The only possible route to lower productivity would be substantial reductions in hourly wages, so that capital-intensive technology is discarded in favour of less productive, labour-intensive technology. Such large wage cuts or job losses—that is, a recession—would be unacceptable to trade unions and to voters. They would likely also lead to a right-wing backlash, potentially violent, targeting migrants or other minorities for taking some of the few jobs that remain, and dismantling the prospects of sustained action on climate change. Nor would negative financial returns be accepted by finance capital.

An alternative to wage cuts or job losses would be major cuts in working hours while hourly wages were kept stable. This, too, would lead to major reductions in weekly incomes and hence major resistance. Moreover, while the idea that we could reduce working hours to share the burden may be noble, it fails to account for how the capitalist economy works. As we saw in Chapter 3, reduced working hours did not happen following the expected wave of technological change after the 1970s, counter to predictions from

80 Peetz and Murray, 'Financialization of Corporate Ownership'.

that decade.[81] Perhaps over the very long term a social compromise can be reached in which slower or negative growth is accepted in return for cuts in working hours and weekly incomes, and for the regulated imposition of a maximum number of working hours for all people—perhaps with state-guaranteed minimum incomes and state-enforced maximum incomes. There is debate about moving from a 'linear' to a 'circular economy', in which there is a lower level of activity and resources are not ultimately wasted but systematically reused.[82] However, we are a long way from that point and the planet does not have enough time to wait.

In the meantime, can a compromise be found between environmental and labour interests—between the planet and jobs? If carbon emissions are not to be minimised through a reduction in gross domestic product, then it requires a very large reduction in *carbon intensity* (the amount of carbon emissions used in producing a unit of GDP). Recycling, enforced by regulation (not just individual voluntary decisions) is a step towards that, but just a small one.

Large changes in relative prices are central to achieving a major change in carbon intensity. Some of these have already happened: the price of solar panels, at US$101.65 per watt in 1975, was just US$0.61 in 2015; so annual global installations of solar capacity rose from 2 MW in 1975 to 64,892 MW in 2015.[83] Wind energy prices have also fallen, while battery storage has recently moved from a theoretical nicety to economic viability, with a large 2017 battery installation in South Australia rendering irrelevant most of the debate about the intermittency of renewable electricity.[84] Favourable shifts in prices have been assisted by technological developments that have responded to well-known needs, but not all new technologies are helpful: because of the electricity used in complex calculations across multiple high-end computers, the trade in Bitcoin, a speculative cryptocurrency reliant on blockchain technology, consumes approximately as much energy as Ireland.[85]

81 See Chapter 3.

82 Teresa Domenech, 'Explainer: What Is a Circular Economy?'. *The Conversation*, 25 July 2014, theconversation.com/explainer-what-is-a-circular-economy-29666.

83 Michael Graham Richard, 'This Striking Chart Shows Why Solar Power Will Take over the World'. *Treehugger*, 15 April 2015, www.treehugger.com/renewable-energy/striking-chart-showing-solar-power-will-take-over-world.html.

84 Kyree Leary, 'Elon Musk's Huge Battery in South Australia Made $1 Million in Profit in Just a Few Days'. *Science Alert*, 25 January 2018, www.sciencealert.com/south-australia-tesla-battery-earns-million-neoen-company.

85 The Economist, 'Why Bitcoin Uses So Much Energy'. *The Economist*, 9 July 2018, www.economist.com/the-economist-explains/2018/07/09/why-bitcoin-uses-so-much-energy.

While changes in market prices make new coal-fired power plants economically unviable, we cannot expect the market to solve the climate crisis. After all, the failure of the market over two centuries to incorporate externalities into resource pricing caused the crisis in the first place. A high carbon price—some have suggested over US$100 per tonne[86]—will also be needed to drive a redirection of economic activity to low-emission behaviour. Perhaps ideally, a scientifically informed estimate would be made of what level of carbon the environment can absorb, and the market would then set a price for that quantity. This was the theory behind an emissions trading scheme ('cap and trade'), which operates in a number of jurisdictions, though various exemptions or special arrangements can undermine the policy logic.

Government intervention need not be restricted to the pricing of externalities. Most governments seek to actively subsidise certain forms of renewable energy or recycling. Although, in terms of economic theory, a pure model of emissions trading would render such subsidies unnecessary, in practice emissions trading has been far from pure and carbon pricing would be well supplemented by such interventions anyway. Carbon pricing leads to higher consumer prices, including of electricity, but the Australian Government's attempts to offset these higher prices through fiscal compensation reaped little in the way of political benefits. Polls suggested that voters preferred the revenue raised by carbon pricing be used to subsidise renewable energy anyway,[87] and supported action to address climate change.[88] It seems that the best way of dealing with political opposition to carbon pricing is not to offer compensation but to address the core issues, gaining the support of unions, many workers and parts of capital.

In practice, setting a carbon price may be administratively cleaner than setting a quantity. In discussions with climate-interested investors within finance capital, carbon pricing seems more of a focus for action than the tradability of emissions. While both carbon pricing and emissions trading are unambiguously liberal market solutions to a clear market failure,

86 In an interview with the author.

87 Matthew J. Kotchen, Zachary M. Turk, and Anthony A. Leiserowitz, 'Public Willingness to Pay for a US Carbon Tax and Preferences for Spending the Revenue'. *Environmental Research Letters* 12, no. 9 (2017), iopscience.iop.org/article/10.1088/1748-9326/aa822a/pdf.

88 David Peetz and Georgina Murray, 'Class, Attitudes and Climate Change'. In *Public Opinion, Campaign Politics and Media Audiences: New Perspectives on Australian Politics*, ed. Bridget Griffen-Foley and Sean R. Scalmer (Melbourne: Melbourne University Press, 2017).

probably the strongest opposition has come from those associated with the party of capital in the most neo-liberal industrialised economy in the world (the USA), illustrating the limits of market liberal ideals amidst the reality of neo-liberal policy regimes.

As mentioned, major changes in economic structures can lead to major problems of structural unemployment, and hence a need for substantial structural adjustment[89] programs, enabling retraining, creation of new jobs, subsidisation of new technologies and income maintenance for displaced workers. An adjustment program and subsidies could be financed at least in part through carbon price revenue—though it is not clear whether that would be enough.

As hinted at the beginning of this chapter, one of the important work-related features of this area is the changing role of trade unions. Once focused almost exclusively within nation-state borders, as a locale for influencing their ability to regulate workplace behaviour, they are increasingly turning to transnational action. They are doing this through such mechanisms as negotiating codes of conduct, in an effort to regulate workplace behaviour in multiple locations, as what happens in one workplace may ultimately affect those on the other side of the globe. (Employers being able to reduce costs by cutting corners on safety in Third World countries makes it harder for unions to organise, or even maintain employment, in factories elsewhere.) There is more on codes of conduct in Chapter 10.

Union roles on environmental sustainability are also changing. Whereas once they could be relied on to 'defend jobs' regardless of environmental implications, an increasingly sophisticated approach to environmental and climate change issues is becoming apparent, in some but not all unions, including some where this would be quite unexpected—probably a result of increasing awareness of long-term implications for their membership.[90] In the end, though, it is the nature of trade unions that environmental and climate issues will be secondary to matters regarding the direct employment relationship. Where unions have had a dominant role in labour supply (such as at the time of Sydney's 'Green Bans' in the

89 The meaning of 'structural adjustment' here is totally different to that used by the IMF.

90 Ray Markey, Joseph McIvor, and Chris F. Wright, *Climate Change and the Australian Workplace: Final Report for the Australian Department of Industry on State of Knowledge on Climate Change, Work and Employment* (Sydney: Macquarie University, 2014).

1970s),[91] placing the environment first has not been at the significant expense of employment. It is harder when unions lack such power over labour supply. It is especially hard since, as discussed in Chapter 4, the composition of future labour demand—the jobs of the future—is hard to predict.

Most of the focus of trade union action in recent years has been not in opposing action on climate change but in achieving a 'just transition'. The term means different things to different participants, but typically involves some combination of improvements for workers and communities, at the same time as the issue of climate change is addressed.[92] So a representative set of elements in a just transition is environmental remediation, energy 'democracy', 'green' jobs, worker retraining, revitalisation or diversification of energy sources for local communities, and community agency. As the climate warms, heat stress becomes a more important occupational health and safety issue for union action, and plays an increasingly important role in building standards.

Just transition is not a concept that is easy to attain. For example, wages in 'green' jobs (jobs in renewable energy industries or in sectors of the manufacturing or service sectors where production assists in the reduction of greenhouse gases) are typically lower than in coal. This is the case even if renewables are installed where coal extraction or burning was previously located. More commonly, though, green jobs are in different locations to the old coal jobs, so in the absence of effective state intervention there are not enough jobs for those displaced as the market moves from high-emissions to renewable energy production. Nor is it inherently the case that they will be 'good' jobs.[93]

Unions in different countries think of just transition in different ways. The issues vary between developed and developing countries. A just transition for German coal unions, seeking to move their members into green jobs as carbon-emitting technology is phased out, may be seen as injustice by worker representatives in developing countries who supply raw materials

91 Meredith Burgmann and Verity Burgmann, *Green Bans* (Sydney: UNSW Press, 1998); Greg Mallory, *Uncharted Waters: Social Responsibility in Australian Trade Unions* (Brisbane: Boolarong Press, 2005).
92 An example is ACTRAV Bureau for Workers' Activities, *Just Transition Towards Environmentally Sustainable Economies and Societies for All* (Geneva: International Labour Organization, ILO ACTRAV Policy Brief, 2018).
93 Helen Masterman-Smith, 'Green Collaring a Capital Crisis?'. *Labour and Industry* 20, no. 3 (2010): 317–30.

or components to old works. In many nations, particularly but not exclusively in the developing world, worker representative organisations may be ill-equipped to deal with just transition issues, whether because they are too poorly organised, too locally focused or ignored by national governments. Other civil society groups may be prominent in promoting low-carbon development but with possibly quite different perspectives.

So the concept of 'just transition' raises a number of questions identified by researchers.[94] What policy mechanisms are needed to make retraining for fossil fuel workers and green jobs a viable reality? Is it possible for communities to have more control over economic redevelopment planning without transferring financial responsibility away from corporations? How can the urgency of decarbonisation be balanced with the long-term goal of democratising the grid? What about communities that are not agitated to advocate for themselves amid energy transitions? Bigger than these, however, are some fundamental questions about resolving the contradiction between the need for employment and the need for a move to zero-emission economic activity, discussed above. And there is the big political question, about how to garner the political constituency necessary to respond to the issue. This seems to relate in some way to making use of the potential for common interests between unions, many environmental groups and parts of industrial and finance capital.

Conclusions

Two key conflicts on the capital side affect questions of sustainability: the competition between the two logics of short-termism or long-termism; and the extent to which costs and benefits are internalised or externalised. On the labour side, there is a conflict between the needs for employment and for a sustainability built on production methods with low carbon intensity, and there are contradictions in building consensus for a just transition.

Many aspects of work have ethical dimensions, and ethics have implications for workplace relations, organisational commitment and turnover. What *should* we do about climate change? What *can* we do?

94 For example, at the International Sociological Association's world congress in Toronto, July 2018.

In analysing issues of ethics and sustainability, we need to take account of the role of regulation in bringing about sustainable and ethical behaviour, and how effective corporate social responsibility really is or can be. We saw a bit of that in the last part of Chapter 4, and for more on that we will turn to Chapter 10. Some changes are inevitable including, centrally, changes in prices that will make some old industries uneconomic and new ones prosper. Still, sustainability, particularly environmental sustainability, is the area where some of the biggest choices are to be made, and where the difference between making the right choice and the wrong choice is literally a matter of life and death for many. And regulation is not just about the critical matter of pricing: it goes to issues like the uses permitted for water, for rural land, for native forests and for urban space; the types of mines or other carbon-relevant economic activities that are enabled; the levels, locations and types of pollution that are allowed and the fees that society charges to permit such pollution; and obligations on producers, retailers and consumers for recycling, waste, obsolescence and reparability.

While the toxic wastelands used for labour camps depicted in *The Handmaid's Tale* may not seem such a likely scenario, the general point it draws is valid: those without power will most suffer the consequences of environmental degradation, and those with high power will avoid them. The elite will have the resources to maintain their *relative* standard of living, whether it be through building walls, new communities or private armies. For most workers, though, the prospects of climate change are serious and negative. We looked in general at the downwards transfer of risk in Chapter 6. The exposure of the world's poor to the dangers of climate change, while the rich seek to insulate themselves from it, would be the starkest and most serious manifestation of the transfer of risk, without commensurate returns, from an elite within capital to a mass of labour.

In the meantime, we can also expect some major changes in the world of work. There are obvious ones like the loss of jobs in coal mines, oil wells, coal-fired power plants, manufacture and distribution of petrol cars and the like; and the growth of jobs in the manufacture, construction or maintenance of wind turbines, solar panels, electric cars, public transit and seawalls. Other changes will affect how work is done. Energy systems may become more decentralised and possibly less controlled by large corporations. Ways will need to be found: to undertake work, particularly outdoor work, in a hotter climate; to produce food (predominantly vegetable-based rather than animal-based) from less arable lands and from oceans with declining fish stocks and growing numbers of jellyfish;[95] and to accommodate, often in industrialised nations, untold numbers of climate refugees from countries that have not been a major source of migrants until now. Those migration flows might produce the biggest unpredictable impact of climate change on work.

95 Lisa-Ann Gerschwin, *Stung! On Jellyfish Blooms and the Future of the Ocean* (Chicago: University of Chicago Press, 2013).

10

Regulation and the futures of work

In the movie *Sliding Doors*, the life of the main character changes radically according to which of the two seemingly innocuous scenarios takes place at the beginning: either she gets onto the train before the carriage doors close behind her, or they close in time to prevent her boarding. A seemingly random event shapes how the rest of her life plays out. And it is true that much of what eventually happens to us—more than we like to imagine—is shaped by random events outside our control.[1] But it would be false to think that *everything* is outside our control. Although the sliding doors in that movie were outside the control of the protagonist, much of what happens in the future is not. It is much more like the scene in *The Circle*, where Mae has the opportunity to reveal and confront the true nature of the organisation, and consciously chooses not to, than that at the beginning of *Sliding Doors*. Critical junctures[2] shape futures, and these are a result of conscious decisions by one or more parties.

As the world has become more complex and 'globalised', private and public policy-makers have felt more like events are outside their control. Public policy has always had a problem of translating ideas into practice,

1 Daniel Kahneman, *Thinking, Fast and Slow* (New York: Farrar, Straus and Giroux, 2011). See also Chapter 5 of this book.

2 Ruth Berins Collier and J. David Collier, *Shaping the Political Arena: Critical Junctures, the Labour Movement and Regional Dynamics in Latin America* (Princeton NJ: Princeton University Press, 1991).

and many fine aims have been frustrated in implementation.[3] But now the problems are intensified by the seeming power of the market, and the reconstruction of transnational capital, in neo-liberal times. Regulation has appeared increasingly difficult—to some, hopeless. Some have sought innovative approaches by new means of regulation, either public or private. Others have had to deal with the difficulty of implementing regulations that presently exist.

In this chapter we look at regulatory responses to changes in the world of work, particularly those arising from the shift towards 'not there' employment discussed in Chapter 6. 'Not there' employment has several effects.

One is that it redefines the formal protections applying to workers. Some workers end up excluded from the formal protection of labour law because they are no longer defined as employees—typically as contractors. Other workers end up still covered by labour law but working under the terms of an agreement with or policies administered by a different organisation—typically as 'labour hire' (the term used in Australia) or 'temporary agency' workers (the term used in Europe where, if sent to another EU country, they are 'posted' workers). This almost never means better conditions and usually means inferior conditions.

A second effect is that, within the host country of capital, 'not there' employment encourages noncompliance with laws on minimum pay and conditions, because it puts responsibility for employment onto that part of capital which is least knowledgeable about those laws and which is most tempted, or encouraged, by the logic of cost-minimising market competition to circumvent those laws anyway.

A third effect is that 'not there' employment encourages both noncompliance with and exclusion from labour law protections by use of global supply chains, where much of the work is undertaken in developing countries by entities that are technically and often practically separate from the organisation at the top of the capital chain.

3 Jeffrey L. Pressman and Aaron Wildavsky, *Implementation: How Great Expectations in Washington Are Dashed in Oakland; or Why It's Amazing That Federal Programs Work at All, This Being a Saga of the Economic Development Administration as Told by Two Sympathetic Observers Who Seek to Build Morals on a Foundation of Ruined Hopes* (Berkeley: University of California Press, 1973).

Some of the effects mentioned above interact with changes in technology. For example, the emergence of platform-based 'gig' work is naturally dependent on the development of relevant platform technology. In turn, it enables a particular form of 'not there' employment that allows a shift in worker status from employee to purported independent contractor, because of the particular form of control that platform technology allows. On a larger scale, the emergence of global supply chains has already been facilitated by technological developments that have enabled rapid transportation, almost instantaneous communication, efficient record-keeping and hence coordination on a global scale.

So in this chapter we look at the above aspects as case studies of the challenges facing regulation in the future of work, and of the policy choices to be made. We examine the challenges posed by future types of work, including through the gig economy. We investigate the problem of noncompliance (sometimes referred to as 'wages theft'), the factors that promote it and the changing methods used in enforcement. And we peer into the maintenance of labour standards in global value chains or global production networks. Before that, we contextualise it by considering the purpose of regulation, the different forms of regulation by the state (such as the laws of employment and work, the welfare state, trade agreements and international law), which leads into discussion of innovation in regulation (e.g. through international codes of conduct applied to transnational firms) and the potential of and limitations on those innovations, drawing on the example of the response to the Rana Plaza collapse in Bangladesh. How can and will parties respond to increasing pressures for codes of conduct and corporate social responsibility? While technology has posed challenges for regulation, we will also make brief mention of some of the technologies that will assist in regulation.

Purpose and forms of regulation

The aim of regulation, put crudely, is to bring about outcomes different to those that would occur in its absence. In effect, this means outcomes different to those that would be delivered by a market.

It would be noble to say that this was in order to create outcomes that alleviated inequality in opportunities and power and improved the lot of the vulnerable. In practice, much regulation is for a different purpose: frequently, to strengthen or entrench the position of those in power.

Those with the most resources have the greatest capacity to influence government, and the wealthy and large corporations have the greatest financial resources. In *The Circle*, the corporation used its power ruthlessly to ensure that no regulation adversely affected it. A body of literature in the Marxist tradition argues that it is inevitable that the state will act in the interests of capital, either because the state is dominated by members of the ruling class or people with close ties to it, or because the structure of economic power ensures that, in the end, the state will act for capital.[4] Divisions within the ruling class complicate but do not in themselves refute this interpretation.[5] Many instances can be cited of the state acting to serve interests of the wealthy and large corporations with great financial resources.[6]

However, workers and other groups outside the ruling class also mobilise and put pressure on the state to act in *their* interests. If the pressure is strong enough, particularly if those in the state feel their legitimacy and claim to power is threatened, the state responds by making concessions. So it is that improvements in workers' conditions—ranging from reductions in the working week, improved leave or higher minimum wages—are achieved. Indeed, we theorised in Chapter 8 that one factor (not the only one) that may reduce gender gaps is the proximity of an occupation to regulation, as regulation reduced the capacity for the norms of those with power to determine the distribution of power and rewards.[7] Policy-makers in the state vary in their ideological perspectives and orientations,

4 Nicos Poulantzas, *State, Power, and Socialism*. Translated by Patrick Camiller (London: Verso, 1980); Ralph Miliband, *The State in Capitalist Society* (New York: Basic, 1969); Nicos Poulantzas and Ralph Miliband, 'The Problem of the Capitalist State'. In *Ideology in Social Science: Readings in Critical Social Theory*, ed. R. Blackburn (New York: Pantheon Books), 238–62.

5 For example, conflicts between mining and non-mining capital, between financial and industrial capital, or between national and transnational capital. See references in previous footnote plus William Carroll, 'The Corporate Elite and the Transformation of Finance Capital: A View from Canada'. *Sociological Review* 56, no. s1 (2008): 44–63; William Carroll, *The Making of a Transnational Capitalist Class* (London: Zed Books, 2010); Richard Deeg and Iain Hardie, 'What Is Patient Capital and Who Supplies It?'. *Socio-Economic Review* 14, no. 4 (2016): 627–45; Georgina Murray, *Capitalist Networks and Social Power in Australia and New Zealand* (Aldershot: Ashgate, 2006); Jean Philippe Sapinski, 'Climate Capitalism and the Global Corporate Elite Network'. *Environmental Sociology* 1, no. 4 (2015): 268–79.

6 For example, Thomas Stratmann, 'The Market for Congressional Votes: Is Timing of Contributions Everything?'. *Journal of Law and Economics*. 41, no. 1 (1998): 85–114; Allan Holmes et al., *Did Billionaires Pay Off Republicans for Passing the Trump Tax Bill?* (Washington DC: Centre for Public Integrity, 7 February 2019), publicintegrity.org/business/taxes/trumps-tax-cuts/did-billionaires-pay-off-republicans-for-passing-the-trump-tax-bill/.

7 David Peetz and Georgina Murray, *Women, Labor Segmentation and Regulation: Varieties of Gender Gaps* (New York: Palgrave Macmillan, 2017).

and some enter that arena specifically to advance the interests of those they see as underprivileged, though in most developed countries most are constrained in what they can do by political possibilities.

One problem facing policy-makers, especially politicians, from both left and right is that it may sometimes undermine their legitimacy (especially with voters or commentators linked to the other side) if others see them as being driven by ideological or interest-driven objectives. So policies will often be advanced in terms of the purported benefit they produce for the greater, public good—often by claims of boosts to productivity growth, which provide the potential for increases in living standards (a potential that, of course, is not always realised).[8] So the true purpose of policies will often be obfuscated.

This chapter, however, does not focus on the prevarications of politicians. Rather, it looks at some specific aspects of the regulation of work that, in particular, attempt to use regulation to overcome some of the problems identified in earlier chapters. That is the purpose of the type of regulation of interest here.

Regulation takes a number of forms. The obvious way in which work is affected by regulation is through employment law or labour law. Employment law may focus on collective issues: what happens when an employer plans to or takes action to retrench or otherwise dismiss a group of employees; what collective rights to information do employees have; what happens when employees have a collective grievance; when they want to strike and when they do strike; when an employer takes industrial action, and so on. Employment law may also focus on individual issues: what happens when an individual is dismissed, what happens when discrimination against a particular employee has occurred, and so on. Over recent decades, this 'individual' employment law has generally expanded in developed countries, but (on average) little has happened to expand collective employment law, and in some countries collective employment law has been in retreat.[9] That said, there is little empirical reason to believe that, in the developed world outside Australia, there has been any

8 David Peetz, 'Does Industrial Relations Policy Affect Productivity?'. *Australian Bulletin of Labour* 38, no. 4 (2012): 268–92.

9 Alan Bogg and Tonia Novitz, 'Links between Individual Employment Law and Collective Labour Law: Their Implications for Migrant Workers'. In *Migrants at Work: Immigration and Vulnerability in Labour Law*, ed. Cathryn Costello and Mark Freedland (Oxford: Oxford Scholarship Online, 2014).

reduction in the right to strike available to employees.[10] If anything, most shifts have been in the opposite direction (mainly through improvements in the rights of Easter European workers), though the most common pattern is of stability in the broad nature of the law on the right to strike. However, a number of governments, in Anglophone countries especially, have passed laws that make it easier for employers to bypass unions and have undertaken administrative action to weaken unions.[11]

State regulation affecting work is not restricted to employment or labour law. Welfare or social security law affects work, by influencing the incentives on people to enter the labour force, find work, return to work after pregnancy, work longer or shorter hours and in some cases to undertake industrial action. The provision of social services affects the availability of people to undertake work (e.g. through availability of childcare). Indeed, as we saw in the opening chapters, the range of liberal market regulations that affect the operation of product and financial markets without any obvious relationship to labour markets can nonetheless have a major impact on work. These latter areas—those associated with product and financial markets—might have had a greater impact on work and workers than employment law itself.

International law, through conventions of the International Labour Organization, the United Nations, the World Trade Organization or other bodies, affects numerous aspects of work. Trade agreements may affect the capacity of nation-states to regulate employment, and the extent to which workers in one country are seen to be in competition with workers from another country.

Although regulation is something normally seen as being associated with the state, other actors may also seek to regulate work. As mentioned in Chapter 8, unions aim to regulate work through the making of collective agreements with employers, even if those agreements might not be formalised or have the full force of the law. Employers, especially larger ones, establish rules and procedures to make sure that managers

10 David Peetz, 'Industrial Action, the Right to Strike, Ballots and the Fair Work Act in International Context'. *Australian Journal of Labour Law* 29 (2016): 133–53, using data from Jelle Visser, 'Data Base on Institutional Characteristics of Trade Unions, Wage Setting, State Intervention and Social Pacts, 1960–2011 (ICTWSS), Version 4.0' (Amsterdam: Amsterdam Institute for Advanced Labour Studies, University of Amsterdam, 2013).

11 David Peetz, *Unions in a Contrary World: The Future of the Australian Trade Union Movement* (Cambridge: Cambridge University Press, 1998).

and supervisors do things in ways that are consistent with the aims of the employer. This is often referred to as 'internal regulation', and so the shift to 'deregulation' is often analysed as instead being a shift from external to internal regulation.[12] Governments may sometimes seek to encourage or 'incentivise' particular behaviours from employers, rather than passing laws requiring or prohibiting particular behaviours, and so this is sometimes referred to as 'soft' regulation, in contrast with the more traditional form of 'hard' regulation—that is, laws that require or prohibit something.[13]

The challenges arising from changes in corporate organisation, state regulation and work itself have made traditional employment law more difficult, including by challenging the traditional conception of employee or traditional forms of accountability in employment, and these have led to various attempts to find new ways of regulating in ways that affect work. They are the focus of the rest of this chapter.

New forms of work and workers

As discussed in earlier chapters, there has been a lot of recent controversy about the use of 'independent contractors' in place of employees, something potentially encouraged by the expansion of 'not there' employment.[14] 'Independent contractors' may be subject to protection through workplace health and safety legislation, for example in Australia and some other countries, but are not entitled to other employee benefits such as minimum wages or workers' compensation. There is considerable international evidence that workplace health and safety outcomes are poorer for contractors than for employees.[15] Indeed, a related effect arises

12 For example, John Buchanan and Ron Callus, 'Efficiency and Equity at Work: The Need for Labour Market Regulation in Australia'. *Journal of Industrial Relations* 35, no. 4 (1993): 515–37.

13 Keith Sisson and Paul Marginson, *'Soft Regulation'—Travesty of the Real Thing or New Dimension?* ESRC 'One Europe or Several' Programme, Working Paper 32/01 (Brighton: University of Sussex, Sussex European Institute, 2001).

14 Some of the material in this section first appeared in David Peetz, *The Operation of the Queensland Workers' Compensation Scheme*. Report of the Second Five Yearly Review of the Scheme (Brisbane: Parliament of Queensland, June 2018).

15 Michael Quinlan, *The Effects of Non-Standard Forms of Employment on Worker Health and Safety*. Conditions of Work and Employment Series No. 67 (Geneva: International Labour Office, Inclusive Labour Markets, Labour Relations and Working Conditions Branch, December 2015).

with labour-hire workers: workplace health and safety outcomes are poorer for labour-hire workers—often referred to as 'temporary agency workers' in the literature—than for conventional employees.[16]

So questions arise as to whether particular people should be classed as employees rather than independent contractors under employment law, and therefore be treated as employees not only for workers' compensation purposes but also for purposes of minimum hourly wages and other entitlements under employment law. Criteria (or 'indicia') have been developed by tribunals, the courts and even the taxation authorities to determine whether workers are employees or independent contractors. When firms portray people who are clearly employees as independent contractors, and thereby withhold from them one or more of their employee entitlements (such as minimum hourly wages, leave or superannuation), they may be prosecuted for engaging in what is termed 'sham contracting' in Australia.

Often the indicia lead to ambiguous outcomes, at least in the eyes of lawyers, so cases contesting whether particular people are employees or independent contractors still end up before the tribunals or courts.

One recent development in case law occurred in the California Supreme Court. It broadened the meaning of 'employee' there, redefining the test used in determining whether a worker was an employee or independent contractor by replacing an assessment against various indicia with an 'ABC test'. Under the ABC test, a worker is assumed to be an employee unless the employer can prove *all* of three criteria:

1. The worker is free from direction and control in the performance of the service, both under the contract of hire and in fact;
2. The worker's services must be performed either:
   i. outside the usual course of the employer's business; or
   ii. outside all the employer's places of business (e.g. a firm engaging seamstresses to make clothing could not call them independent contractors);

16 Ibid.; Anthony Forsyth, *Victorian Inquiry into the Labour Hire Industry and Insecure Work: Final Report* (Melbourne: Industrial Relations Victoria, Department of Economic Development, Jobs, Transport & Resources, 2016).

3. The worker must be customarily engaged in an independently established trade, occupation, profession, or business of the same nature as the service being provided.[17]

The ABC test brings more workers under the definition of 'employee' than do most other indicia. It has the advantage of covering most groups of workers who would be thought as being under the 'employ' of a more powerful organisation. At time of writing, the ABC test applied in three US states for aspects of workers' compensation or unemployment insurance. However, law in these states does not normally set precedent in other countries. Still, an option available to policy-makers is to legislate the ABC test or some variant of it.[18] It would have the advantage of bringing within the scope of employment law a wider group of workers who could be seen to be vulnerable to exploitation by more powerful organisations, those engaging in 'not there' employment. Doing this might, however, reducing certainty for some other workers as to whether they are covered by employment law.

A related matter is the question of who is responsible for the welfare of labour-hire employees, who are in a 'triangular relationship' with the host employer and the labour-hire firm that is their employer at law. For example, in Québec, Canada, premiums for workers' compensation are the responsibility of whichever, out of the host employer or the labour-hire firm, is considered to have the greater control over the employee.[19] While ideal at a theoretical level, the practical impact is to lead to a substantial amount of litigation over who is responsible for premiums, and it becomes almost a case-by-case issue for determining who pays. It is

17 *Dynamex Operations West, Inc. v. Superior Court*, discussed in Michael S. Kun and Kevin D. Sullivan, 'California Supreme Court Adopts "ABC Test" for Independent Contractors'. Wage and Hour Defense Blog, Epstein Becker Green, 30 April 2018, www.wagehourblog.com/; Todd Lebowitz, 'California's Top Court Creates New Test for Independent Contractor vs. Employee, Re-Interprets 102-Year Old Definition'. Who Is My Employee?, Baker Hostetler LLP, 30 April 2018, whoismyemployee.com/.

18 The Dynamex decision formed the model for Bill AB5 in California. An example of a variant is that applied by Justice Bromberg in Australia, though this is probably less likely to see people defined as independent contractors, rather than employees, than the ABC text. *On Call Interpreters and Translators Agency Pty Ltd v Federal Commissioner of Taxation (No 3)* (2011) 214 FCR 82, discussed in Andrew Stewart et al., *Creighton & Stewart's Labour Law*, 5th ed. (Sydney: Federation Press, 2016). Other cases cited there were *FWO v. Quest South Perth Holdings Pty Ltd* (2015) 228 FCR 346, *Fenwick v. World of Maths* [2012] FMCA 131, *FWO v. Metro Northern Enterprises Pty Ltd* [2013] FCCA 216 and *Predl v. DMC Plastering Pty Ltd* [2014] FCCA 1066.

19 Katherine Lippel et al., 'Legal Protections Governing the Occupational Safety and Health and Workers' Compensation of Temporary Employment Agency Workers in Canada: Reflections on Regulatory Effectiveness'. *Policy and Practice in Health and Safety* 9, no. 2 (2011): 69–90.

hardly, then, a satisfactory solution. One option for other jurisdictions might be to have the premiums still paid by the labour hire firm but the experience rating (i.e. the discount or addition to premium liabilities, based on claims paid) of the host employer to also partially include the effects of injuries incurred by labour-hire workers while on the premises of or working for such a firm (i.e. the effects would be at least shared between the host employer and the labour-hire firm).

What about 'gig economy' workers? The issue of whether platform economy workers are employees or independent contractors has been tested in courts, tribunals and administrative bodies in a number of jurisdictions. The end result has been far from conclusive. On the one hand, a number of cases have led or could lead to some workers in platform industries being classed as employees. This includes several cases in the UK;[20] France;[21] one in New York City, USA;[22] a ruling in the European Court of Justice, which held that Uber was a transportation company, not a technology company, raising questions about whether its workers would be treated as employees;[23] and a case about Foodora in Australia—though the local offshoot went into voluntary administration, enabling the international firm to avoid its employment-related liabilities.[24]

20 Gregor Gall, 'Is Uber Ruling the Beginning of the End for Bogus Self-Employment?'. *The Conversation*, 5 November 2016; Robert Booth, 'UK Government Delays Possible Reforms to Gig Economy Practices'. Guardian, 6 December 2017; Natasha Bernal, 'Uber Heads for Supreme Court after Losing Appeal on Worker Rights'. *Telegraph*, 19 December 2018, www.telegraph.co.uk/technology/2018/12/19/uber-heads-supreme-court-losing-appeal-worker-rights/; BBC, 'Bike Courier Wins "Gig" Economy Employment Rights Case'. *BBC News*, 7 January 2017; Ben Chapman, 'Gig Economy Ruling: Couriers Carrying Blood for NHS Win Right to Collective Bargaining'. *Independent*, 1 March 2018, www.independent.co.uk/news/business/news/nhs-gig-economy-couriers-blood-transfusions-union-recognition-the-doctors-laboratory-a8235446.html; Robert Booth, 'Addison Lee Wrongly Classed Drivers as Self-Employed, Tribunal Rules'. *Guardian*, 26 December 2017; Jamie Grierson and Rob Davies, 'Pimlico Plumber Loses Appeal against Self-employed Status'. *Guardian*, 11 February 2017.

21 Laura Kayali, 'French Court: Uber and Drivers Tied by "Work Contract"'. *Politico*, 11 January 2019, www.politico.eu/article/french-court-uber-and-drivers-tied-by-work-contract/.

22 Matt Hamilton, 'Judge Finds NYC Uber Drivers to Be Employees; Upstate Impact Debated'. *Timesunion*, 12 September 2016, www.timesunion.com/allwcm/article/Judge-finds-NYC-Uber-drivers-to-be-employees-11220139.php.

23 Zeeshan Aleem, 'Europe's Top Court Just Said Uber Isn't a Tech Company—It's a Cab Company'. *Vox*, 20 December 2017, www.vox.com/world/2017/12/20/16800476/uber-eu-europe-taxi-regulation.

24 Workplace Express, 'FWO Drops Foodora Test Case'. *Workplace Express*, 3 September 2018, www.workplaceexpress.com.au/nl06_news_selected.php?act=2&nav=10&selkey=57119 (subscription required).

On the other hand, different cases have led, in effect, to their being classed as nonemployees. This included cases in the USA[25]—though one judge commented that Uber and Lyft 'present a novel form of business that did not exist at all ten years ago' and added, 'With time, these businesses may give rise to new conceptions of employment status'[26]—plus the UK[27] and Australia.[28] In one of the Australian cases, however, the tribunal observed it might be that notions about what was necessary for an employment relationship to be established 'are outmoded in some senses and are no longer reflective of our current economic circumstances'.[29] The comments coming out of some cases, and the variety of outcomes, suggest the law is far from settled and changes in statute law may yet be forthcoming.

Among mainstream employers, organisational control of employees' working time has become less important over recent decades than organisational control of the product employees generate for the employer. It is an aspect of the two paths towards increased hours or work intensity identified in earlier chapters: yes, one involves tighter direct control over employees' hours, but the other involves a loosening of direct control of hours and tasks and replacing it with internalisation of the need to work longer hours to 'get the job done'.[30] Yet control of working time remains one of the indicia used to determine whether someone is an employee or a contractor. The Philadelphia US District Court decision acknowledged that Uber could terminate a driver's access to the Uber app; deactivate a driver for cancelling trips, failing its background check policy, falling short of the minimum required 4.7-star driver rating, or soliciting payments outside of the Uber app; make deductions against a driver's

25 Lawrence J. Hanley, 'Inside Uber's Latest Move to Exploit Its Drivers and Hide Behind the Court'. *Huffington Post*, 6 April 2017.

26 *Razak v. Uber Technologies Inc.*, U.S. District Court for the Eastern District of Pennsylvania, Case No. 2:16-cv-00573, p. 25.

27 Sarah Butler, 'Deliveroo Wins Right Not to Give Riders Minimum Wage or Holiday Pay'. *Guardian*, 15 November 2017.

28 *Kaseris v. Rasier Pacific V.O.F* [2017] FWC 6610 (21 December 2017); *Pallage v. Rasier Pacific* [2018] FWC 2579 (11 May 2018); [2019] FWC 4807 (12 July 2019).

29 [2017] FWC 6610 (21 December 2017), at [66].

30 Mentioned in Chapters 3, 5 and 7 of this book. See Griffith Work Time Project, *Working Time Transformations and Effects* (Brisbane: Queensland Department of Industrial Relations, 2003); David Peetz et al., 'Race against Time: Extended Hours in Australia'. *Australian Bulletin of Labour* 29, no. 2 (2003): 126–42; David Peetz, Cameron Allan, and Michael O'Donnell, 'Are Australians Really Unhappier with Their Bosses Because They're Working Harder? Perspiration and Persuasion in Modern Work'. Paper presented at Rethinking Institutions for Work and Employment, Selected Papers from the XXXVIIIth Annual Canadian Industrial Relations Association Conference, Quebec, 26–28 May 2001.

earnings; and limit the number of consecutive hours that a driver may work. Yet against the more traditional indicia, Uber was not considered an employer and its drivers were independent contractors.[31]

Perhaps the best indication of who holds power in the relationship between Uber and its drivers lies in the pay the drivers receive. The rates of pay and conditions many 'gig economy' workers receive would be illegal were they treated as employees,[32] and for some at least the means by which they are classified as contractors rather than employees appears to have an element of contrivance about it. Thus, for example, Uber's declaration that it is not in the business of passenger transport, it is merely a technology company acting as a client to drivers,[33] appears to defy commonsense understandings of what Uber does—why would it be competing with taxi companies and testing driverless cars if it was not involved in transport?—and designed to enable a particular definition of its workers.[34]

There may also be flow-on effects that affect many other workers. If firms that provide substandard pay and conditions outcompete those providing standard pay and conditions, then the latter group will be forced to match the former or go out of business (leading to greater noncompliance with laws). If the latter go out of business, the former group would be able to raise prices as its market share increases. This appears to be the strategy of some platform firms—for example, Uber has never made a profit despite undercutting competitors,[35] but appears to anticipate profitability when it has achieved sufficient market share. (We'll come back, in Chapter 11, to what 'market' is relevant here.) The strategy of increasing market shares, to achieve dominance, appears to be gaining traction. Dominant firms now appear to embody a lower labour share in income than other firms. Increasing concentration in product markets within industries is associated with greater declines in the labour share in

31 *Razak v. Uber Technologies Inc.*, 27–8.

32 See Chapter 6.

33 Tom Brant, 'Uber to European Court: We're Not a Transportation Company'. *PCMag*, 29 November 2016, www.pcmag.com/news/349940/uber-to-european-court-were-not-a-transportation-company.

34 For example, Caspar, 'Sydneysiders Have Spoken—and They Choose Ridesharing!'. *Uber Newsroom*, Uber, 10 October 2015, www.uber.com/en-AU/newsroom/sydney-has-spoken/.

35 Ryan Felton, 'Uber Is Doomed'. *Jalopnik* (2017), 24 February, jalopnik.com/uber-is-doomed-1792634203; Andrew J. Hawkins, 'Uber Reportedly Lost $1.27 Billion in Just Six Months'. *The Verge*, 25 August 2016, www.theverge.com/2016/8/25/12647814/uber-loss-billion-2016-travis-kalanick-lyft.

those industries.[36] The implications of that for other firms' labour shares would be significant. Many people working for firms in those sectors could be low paid and vulnerable.

The distinction between workers who do 'crowdwork' and those who do 'work on-demand via apps' is important from both an analytical and policy perspective.[37] Most of the policy possibilities focus on extending coverage to those who do 'work on-demand via apps'. This includes platforms like Deliveroo, Foodora, Uber, Uber Eats and Airtasker. This is because of the greater difficulties in providing coverage for crowdwork, when much crowdwork is undertaken across borders internationally. For example, an American app may facilitate an Indian crowdworker performing work for a client organisation or individual in, say, the UK one hour and Spain the next. By contrast, for those platform workers doing work on-demand via apps, the worker and the client are located near each other, regardless of where the app is owned, and this occurs through multiple uses of the app. This commonality of location is crucial for the potential of regulation.

An example of what is possible in labour regulation, and the complexities of it, for 'gig economy' workers is in the area of workers' compensation. The development of the technologies that enable the development of platform work, and more importantly enable the platform intermediaries to command a portion of the payment to the worker, provide an opportunity for regulatory intervention. If payment can be deducted for the intermediary, it can also be deducted for other purposes. A platform that controls 'contractors' provides a more accessible mechanism for regulation of the work and conditions of 'contractors' (whether by the state or by unions) than would be the case if workers were fragmented through thousands of unrelated contracts.[38] That said, the treatment of gig economy workers in terms of other aspects of labour law (such as those relating to minimum wages) is more complex.

Various people have called for a set of protections, including in some cases a minimum wage, to apply to all workers predominantly dependent on one organisation for earnings, regardless of whether they are employees or contractors. The difficulty with a minimum wage rate is

36 David Autor et al., 'Concentrating on the Fall of the Labor Share'. *American Economic Review* 107, no. 5 (2017): 180–85.

37 Defined in Chapter 6 of this book.

38 Chris Burns, 'Can a New Nordic Online Portal Help Protect Digital Economy Workers?'. *Equal Times*, 13 July 2017, www.equaltimes.org/can-a-new-nordic-online-portal?lang=en#.XHiuPdhKhvd.

that payments for many contractors are based on completion of the task rather than the time it takes. New York City sought to deal with this issue for drivers for 'rideshare' firms (Uber, Lyft and the like) by using a standardised 'utilisation rate' to convert piece rates to hourly pay.[39] This was immediately challenged by Lyft, but not by Uber, probably because both saw the former would be disadvantaged in competition with the latter due to Lyft's lower utilisation rate. For Uber, removing competition may be more important here than obtaining the cheapest possible labour.

The lesson is that, if we are to apply minimum standards outside the employment relationship, we need to be creative as it may be difficult to draft a single, comprehensive law. One option for a national government might be to declare a national minimum wage—and that it applies to a wide range of workers, not just employees—but establish a tribunal to determine how it is to be implemented, in each sector, outside the traditional employment relationship. It would make determinations on application from interested parties who would lodge proposals on how implementation in their sector should occur. Implementation of a minimum wage on each section would not rely on new legislation being passed, just a new tribunal decision. Naturally, parties and tribunals would learn from the successful and failed experiences of other sectors and countries.

The same principle could be applied to other types of minimum standards, not just minimum hourly wages.

Noncompliance

An apparently growing issue for regulators of employment is the problem of noncompliance—referred to by Australian unions as 'wage theft' as it concerns money that rightfully belongs to the employees after they have worked the requisite hours. It has implications not just for those workers directly affected: if one group of workers can be paid well below the legal minimum, that opens opportunities for employers to apply pressure to other workers, using the implicit or explicit threat of replacing them with

39 Grace Dobush, 'Lyft Claims That NYC's New Driver Minimum Wage Makes It Even Harder to Compete with Uber'. *Fortune*, 31 January 2019, fortune.com/2019/01/31/lyft-uber-nyc-driver-minimum-wage-lawsuit/.

lower-paid workers. This section mainly focuses on Australian examples, but the observations about the factors facilitating underpayment have international application.[40]

There are many ways in which this specific type of exploitation can occur. Examples include being underpaid for regular hours; not receiving premiums for work at unsocial times on nights or weekends (penalty rates); unpaid working hours or overtime; unpaid trials or internships; failing to receive entitlements like pension contributions (superannuation); having illegal deductions made from pay for alleged poor performance or breakages; being sexually harassed; being unlawfully or unfairly dismissed; inadequate breaks; mistreatment or excessive control; or being exposed to danger. Only some are caught in published statistics.

One group often not defined as employees are interns. These are people—usually young—who work for an employer for a defined period of time without payment. Interns, like other people on 'work experience' or 'volunteers', would be unlikely to be categorised as employees by an ABC test or anything similar because of the absence of a beneficial contract (i.e. a contract that involves payment to the volunteer or intern). Internships and work experience have long been part of the educational experience and often formalised into the curricula of educational institutions. Volunteering has been around for as long as society. The group of concern here, though, is that affected by the newly emerging trend in labour markets: the growth of 'work experience' without pay in commercial organisations, as a way of gaining entry into the labour market for that particular industry. Sometimes interns are promised that there would be an educational or training component that does not eventuate, and they end up doing menial tasks; other times they end up doing work that more directly generates surplus for the organisation. Shorter-term arrangements might be referred to as 'trials'.

This is a relatively recent phenomenon, and reflects changes in labour markets as underemployment and credentialism have grown, especially among young workers. Such internships are seen as a way by which individuals can gain a competitive edge in the labour market. However, as corporations increasingly take advantage of the opportunity provided by free labour through such internships, and demand 'experience' in the

40 Some of the material in this section was originally published in David Peetz, 'Debt in Paradise: On the Ground with Wage Theft'. *Griffith Review* 61 (2018): 185–91.

industry as a prerequisite for entry-level paying jobs—as already occurs in some industries (e.g. broadcast and print media)[41]—the competitive edge largely disappears. The factor that was once a 'competitive edge' becomes a new (higher) standard—an example itself of credentialism.[42] There is reason to believe that 'a growing number of businesses are choosing to engage unpaid interns to perform work that might otherwise be done by paid employees'.[43] The legality of unpaid commercial internships is highly dubious.

Some groups of employees are disproportionately likely to be underpaid. Those most vulnerable are those most likely to be afraid or tolerant of mistreatment, and least likely to complain. They include workers with temporary migration visas, where the employer has the upper hand in making it not worthwhile to complain. People on a backpacker's visa in Australia, for example, need to work 88 days in their first year to be entitled to an extra year in Australia. Those days are certified by their employer. So underpaid workers are unlikely to complain to an authority. Many workers worry about losing their jobs if they complain.[44]

The outcomes affect others working in retail or hospitality, including students (for whom it is often their only source of income), sole parents or single-income earners working full-time.[45]

Some examples from Australia show how it works. One study that interviewed 21 international students in Melbourne cafes and restaurants found all were in casual jobs, all were underpaid and some did work for which they weren't paid at all.[46] Ashleigh Mounser, a student at the University of Wollongong, starting with a university chat room, compiled a list of 60 underpaying employers near that university. Many paid either $10 or $15 per hour, well below the legal minimum.[47] Newspaper

41 Andrew Stewart and Rosemary Owen, *Experience or Exploitation? The Nature, Prevalence and Regulation of Unpaid Work Experience, Internships and Trial Periods in Australia*. Report for the Fair Work Ombudsman (Adelaide: University of Adelaide, 2013), 245.

42 See Chapters 1 and 4.

43 Stewart and Owen, *Experience or Exploitation?*, 245.

44 Others may find alternative redress. See the film *88 Days*, made by a British backpacker in Australia who experienced this sort of treatment: www.88daysdocumentary.com/.

45 David Peetz, *The Impact of the Penalty Rates Decision on Australian and Victorian Workers in Retail and Hospitality Industries* (Melbourne: Department of Economic Development, Jobs Transport and Resources Commissioned Research Report, 2017).

46 Iain Campbell, Martina Boese, and Joo-Cheong Tham, 'Inhospitable Workplaces? International Students and Paid Work in Food Services'. *Australian Journal of Social Issues* 51, no. 3 (2016): 279–98.

47 Anna Patty, 'The Great Student Swindle'. *Sydney Morning Herald*, 9 December 2016.

stories contain repeated variations on this theme: a special investigation of underpayments of Vietnamese students and migrants, with some staff paid as little as $6 per hour;[48] an Indian family who were threatened with deportation after their 'sponsor' demanded $30,000 for the visa and insisted on free labour for over two years;[49] or 90 Korean backpackers underpaid thousands for work on a farm.[50] Underpayments became so common among restaurateurs that when one was caught the excuse was that underpayment is 'normal'.[51] Hence a tour operator told an online newsletter that unpaid work in exchange for accommodation, meals or experiences were not uncommon there, 'not because businesses up here are greedy capitalist pigs but because it's necessary to survive in this socialist Australian economy'.[52] Some businesses treat 'wage theft' as legitimate business practice in the face of tight competition. In January 2014, the chief executive of a major employer body was reported as saying that thousands of retailers and restaurants were paying workers in cash and reaching illegal private agreements about conditions, to avoid award minimums.[53] It was an attempt to persuade policy-makers to cut those award minimums. But it was also an admission of illegal behaviour by thousands of his constituents.

Migrant workers—especially temporary migrant workers—lack power. Language limitations mean that many do not know their rights, are not confident to enforce them, or find there are very few places where they are wanted. They work in industries where workers are easily replaced, where unfair dismissal is hard to prove and with few meaningful remedies, and collective organisation is difficult. An agent or employer with the same

48 Olivia Nguyen and Trinh Nguyen, 'Exclusive: Exploitation of Vietnamese Students Rampant among Melbourne Businesses'. SBS Vietnamese (Special Broadcasting Service), 20 April 2017, melbournetoday.net/exclusive-exploitation-of-vietnamese-students-rampant-among-melbourne-businesses/.

49 Adele Ferguson, 'Blackmail, Extortion and Slavery at a Restaurant near You'. *Sydney Morning Herald*, 25 March 2017.

50 Felicity Caldwell, 'Korean Backpackers Underpaid Thousands of Dollars on Qld Farm'. *Canberra Times*, 11 September 2016.

51 David Marin-Guzman, 'Popular Restaurant Chain Caught in Underpayments Scandal'. Workplace Insight (Thomson Reuters, 2016), 19 January.

52 Travel Today, 'Qld Tour Operator Hits Back at "Enemies"'. *Travel Weekly*, 6 January 2015, www.travelweekly.com.au/article/qld-tourism-operator-hits-back-at-enemies/.

53 John Lehman, 'Businesses Forced to Pay Workers in Cash and Strike Black Market Labour Deals to Survive Workplace Laws'. *Daily Telegraph*, 22 January 2014.

background ('co-ethnicity') may seem like their best opportunity, maybe the one person they can trust, someone who will make them an offer they cannot refuse. So a common theme in exploitation is co-ethnicity.[54]

Visa conditions give employers considerable power. In countries like Australia, international students can only work a certain number of hours per week, but with low wages this is often not enough. An employer can then threaten to disclose actual hours worked to immigration authorities. This not only affects migrant workers from non–English speaking backgrounds. It is not as if most of these temporary migrants do not know their rights. One online survey of temporary migrants showed a majority knew they were receiving less than the minimum wage.[55] More important was the power imbalance.

Franchisees of 7-Eleven—an Australian franchise that was the focus of some major media investigations—commonly hired international students, because of these visa restrictions. At times, they worked twice the allowed hours, and received half the award pay. The business model of the head firm made it almost inevitable that franchisees had to underpay staff, or they would go bust.[56] This is the logic of franchising in 'not there' employment. Similarly, oil company Caltex,[57] also the subject of a major investigation for underpayment of workers, was able to put the blame back onto franchisees: it set up a $20 million compensation scheme for workers, but four months later no worker had been paid out while 116 stores had been thrown out of the franchise. Allan Fels, formerly in charge of 7-Eleven's compensation scheme until that company found a better way to accommodate its corporate objectives, described Caltex's compensation fund as a 'public relations stunt'.[58]

---

54 Workplace Express, 'Ombudsman Cautions against Exploitation of Overseas Workers by Their Own'. *Workplace Express*, 7 February 2017; Selvaraj Velayutham, 'Precarious Experiences of Indians in Australia on 457 Temporary Work Visas'. *Economic and Labour Relations Review* 24, no. 3 (2013): 340–61; YaoTai Li, 'Constituting Coethnic Exploitation: The Economic and Cultural Meanings of Cash in Hand Jobs for Ethnic Chinese Migrants in Australia'. *Critical Sociology* 43 no. 6 (2017): 919–32.

55 Laurie Berg and Bassina Farbenblum, *Wage Theft in Australia: Findings of the National Temporary Migrant Work Survey* (Sydney: Migrant Worker Justice Initiative, 2017).

56 Adele Ferguson and Klaus Toft, '7-Eleven: The Price of Convenience'. *Four Corners*, ABC, 30 September 2015, www.abc.net.au/4corners/7-eleven-promo/6729716.

57 Until 2015, Chevron was a 50 per cent shareholder in Caltex.

58 Mario Christodoulou, 'Caltex Announces $20m Compensation Fund but Admits No Liability for Underpaid Workers'. *Sydney Morning Herald*, 1 May 2017; Adele Ferguson, 'Caltex Cleans up in Worker Compo "Hoax"'. *Newcastle Herald*, 16 September 2017.

And yet, for all the cases brought against employers, it remains a viable option for employers to underpay workers as part of their business model. It is rare for a prosecution to occur, when weighed against the number of underpayment cases that come to the inspectorate's attention. If an employer gets caught, but then provides back-pay, they normally escape prosecution; or they might be asked to commit to an 'enforceable undertaking' to back-pay staff. Some firms doing that have been simultaneously underpaying other workers.

The responses of policy-makers vary between jurisdictions, influenced by the choices and strategies of policy-makers and also the extensiveness of the legal safety net. Some issues apply across a number of jurisdictions, including the limited level of resources available to labour inspectorates in the context of public sector cutbacks, a tendency for inspectorates to focus on educating and cooperating with employers rather than prosecuting lawbreakers, except for the most recalcitrant, and the reluctance of policy-makers to change the provisions in temporary migration schemes to minimise the incentive to give or accept underpayment. Some other issues are more specific to jurisdictions. For example, in Australia some states have introduced legislation to license labour-hire operators, excluding from licenses those who have a record of underpaying employees. Federal 'vulnerable workers' legislation introduced in 2017 imposes some liability on franchisors for the behaviour of their franchisees, but there are loopholes if the franchisor did not 'know' that breaches were occurring.

A major problem in Australia is conflicting interests: the main labour inspectorate (the Fair Work Ombudsman) is also responsible for regulating unions and enforcing their compliance with industrial procedures. Its record of kid-glove treatment of corporate offenders is such that it would likely be better to abolish it and start again with a new, focused and untainted labour inspectorate. The problems of labour inspection are not unique to Australia. They cause concern in many countries. Many years ago, when I was doing a report on minimum wages in a developing country, the local labour inspectorate cheerfully took me to talk with an employer that they said was paying below the minimum wage. In some places, labour laws are seen as targets, not requirements. In many, labour inspectors develop a cosy relationship with the people they have to deal with, the employers, and whom they do not want to send out of business. If regulators took the same approach to product safety or chemicals there would be more employers in business and fewer live workers. A reason unions in Australia campaign with the rhetoric of 'wage theft' is to confront this idea that financial crimes against workers are not really crimes, not in the same league as financial crimes against others—or financial crimes *by* workers. It is why that hospitality employer body was happy to report that thousands of retailers and restaurants were acting illegally:[59] it was defining and defending the legitimate, if not necessarily legal, interests of capital.

Unions in many countries, including Australia, usually cannot take action against underpayment because the workers affected are not members. They also have less power in contemporary times, due to changes in labour and product markets, legislation and declining membership. Under earlier legislative regimes, unions could inspect workplace records to seek out underpayments, but that is no longer permitted in Australia. Another approach taken by unions has been to try to put pressure on the value chain (supply chain). In the textiles, clothing and footwear (TCF) industries, over two decades unions sought to persuade governments to treat outworkers (technically independent contractors) as employees. They achieved some success in this, with New South Wales the first to pass laws that in effect deemed TCF outworkers as employees.[60] In building cleaning, Australian unions sought to achieve supply-chain regulation by the state and by lead companies (initially building owners), most recently through the Cleaning Accounting Framework.[61] This built on David Weil's concept of 'strategic enforcement' in the face of limited resources and the fissuring of employment.[62] That same idea is evident in attempts by unions to achieve regulation of international supply chains, discussed in the next section.

59 Lehman, 'Businesses Forced'.

60 Igor Nossar et al., 'Protective Legal Regulation for Home-Based Workers in Australian Textile, Clothing and Footwear Supply Chains'. *Journal of Industrial Relations* 57, no. 4 (2015): 585–603; Igor Nossar, Richard Johnstone, and Michael Quinlan, 'Regulating Supply Chains to Address the Occupational Health and Safety Problems Associated with Precarious Employment: The Case of Home-Based Clothing Workers in Australia'. *Australian Journal of Labour Law* 17 (2004): 137–64.

61 Sarah Kaine, Emmanuel Josserand, and Martijn Boersma, 'How to Stop Businesses Stealing from Their Employees'. *The Conversation*, 8 September 2017.

62 David Weil, 'Creating a Strategic Enforcement Approach to Address Wage Theft: One Academic's Journey in Organizational Change'. *Journal of Industrial Relations* 60, no. 3 (2018): 437–60.

Codes of conduct and beyond

As we saw in earlier chapters, the growth of international trade has enabled corporations to externalised damage to the community while internalising profits.[63] In recent decades the externalising of harm has attracted substantial criticism and has led to the emergence of the corporate social responsibility (CSR) movement. The CSR movement pressures corporations to reject the pure form of the shareholder primacy model of corporate governance in favour of an approach that factors in the community's interests as well as profits. CSR pressure demands that transnational corporations (TNCs) ensure labour standards are upheld in their supply chains. Supply chains include procurement of raw materials, manufacturing, distribution, marketing and sales. Under this business model, use of separate, often unrelated legal entities reduces legal obligations and costs.[64] Sitting at the top of the supply chain are often retailers or large brand names. Suppliers—unrelated corporate entities—often in turn further outsource eventually to factories where workers are employed.[65] The cost savings and distancing benefits to lead corporations are substantial but they also affect the conditions of employment of workers, and resistance to this puts pressure on head corporations to demonstrate some CSR.

As part of the emergence of CSR, discussed in Chapter 9, recent years have seen the substantial growth in codes of conduct for corporations. These typically apply to large TNCs and encompass their supply chains, as many points on the supply chain are subcontracted rather than owned by TNCs, a common form of 'not there' employment. They usually relate

63 Joel Bakan, The Corporation: The Pathological Pursuit of Profit and Power (London: Constable & Robertson, 2004).

64 Paul Harpur, 'Labour Rights as Human Rights: Workers' Safety at Work in Australian-Based Supply Chains' (Queensland University of Technology, 2009), citing Lisa M. Fairfax, 'The Impact of Stakeholder Rhetoric on Corporate Norms'. *University of Iowa Journal of Corporation Law* 31 (2006): 675–8; Jedrzej Frynas, Scott Pegg, and J. George Frynas, eds, *Transnational Corporations and Human Rights* (New York: Palgrave Macmillan, 2003), 53–78; Benita Beamon, 'Measuring Supply Chain Performance'. *International Journal of Operations and Production Management* 19 (1999): 275–92; Richard Johnstone and Therese Wilson, 'Take Me to Your Employer: The Organizational Reach of Occupational Health and Safety Regulation'. *Australian Journal of Labour Law* 19 (2006): 3–26; Paul Harpur, 'Clothing Manufacturing Supply Chains, Contractual Layers and Hold Harmless Clauses: How OHS Duties Can Be Imposed over Retailers'. *Australian Journal of Labor Law* 21, no. 3 (2008): 316–39.

65 Nossar, Johnstone, and Quinlan, 'Regulating Supply Chains'; Paul Harpur, 'Regulating Multi-National Corporations through State-Based Laws: Problems with Enforcing Human Rights under the Alien Tort Statute'. *Australian International Law Journal* 13 (2006): 233–46.

to employment matters—though they can also cover environmental or other social issues. The codes may require that employees have certain rights (e.g. to organise) or require certain safety standards be enforced.

While in practice corporations are being pressured through the CSR movement to uphold human rights and general values, corporations are not legally bound to adhere to such standards.[66] Corporations are pressured to be seen to uphold such values arguably due to a threat to their corporate image and profits.[67]

Corporations may respond to CSR pressure by targeting those areas that give them the most kudos for the least cost. Walmart, for example, focuses on building up its reputation on environmental CSR and downplaying the significance of labour standards. Its drive for environmentally friendly practices extends to Walmart seeking to purchase its products from suppliers who are environmentally friendly. Walmart claims it 'helped' one of its suppliers adopt more environmentally friendly manufacturing practices.[68] Walmart links this focus on environmental concerns back to its drive for profits, claiming that caring for the environment makes 'good business sense'.[69] In relation to labour practices, Walmart has a far poorer record. It shows little sign of ensuring labour conditions in its supplier factories are protected[70] and actively suppresses its own employees' labour rights. Managers were told, 'you are our first line of defense against unionization'[71] and provided with a *Manager's Toolbox to Remaining Union Free*. There was a union-busting team of staff to fly into any Walmart outlet which attempted to unionise.[72] It appears Walmart was attempting to minimise the negative media attention of their violations of employees' labour rights through promoting their high ethical standards in relation to the environment and focusing upon their low consumer prices. This might succeed, as some researchers claimed customers only altered their

66 Harpur, 'Regulating Multi-Nationals'.

67 Michael K. Addo, 'Symposium: Human Rights Perspectives of Corporate Groups'. *Connecticut Law Review* 37 (2005): 667–89.

68 Wal-Mart, 'Home Page' (2008), Wal-Martstores.com/GlobalWMStoresWeb/navigate.do?catg=217 (site discontinued).

69 Ibid.

70 Charles Kernaghan et al., Making Barbie, Thomas & Friends, and Other Toys for Wal-Mart: The Xin Yi Factory in China (National Labor Committee (USA), 2007).

71 Wal-Mart Stores Inc., 'A Manager's Toolbox to Remaining Union Free' (unpublished company document, 1997).

72 Benedict Sheehy, 'Corporations and Social Costs: The Wal-Mart Case Study'. *University of Pittsburgh Journal of Law and Commerce* 24 (2004): 1–39.

purchasing practices if they felt unethical conduct may impact upon them.[73] The abuse of workers may not affect many customers, while environmental degradation affects the survival of the planet. This means customers may react negatively to environmental abuse, but may have a lesser reaction to labour abuses.

True, corporations have recognised that adverse publicity could hurt their profits.[74] In response to the media attention, some corporations have made a public show of improving working conditions in their supplier factories.[75] As the main motivator of corporations is negative publicity, most corporations engage in socially responsible conduct primarily as a marketing strategy.[76]

So a common criticism of codes of conduct is that they are often more show than substance, providing a public relations front for a company but without bringing about genuine change.[77] In response, pressure may be applied to TNCs to sign agreements to make their codes enforceable and in particular to expose them to independent audit (e.g. a factory visit by an agreed team of inspectors who are independent of the company, rather than appointed by it). These agreements typically are made where the net costs of signing up are less than the net costs to the firm of not signing up. This occurs when workers in the home (usually developed) country of the TNC have sufficient bargaining power and motivation to do this; or where the brand name of the company is sufficiently well known that it is susceptible to brand damage from campaigns waged against it.

73 Jeffrey Mercer, 'Corporate Social Responsibility and Its Importance to Consumers' (The Claremont Graduate University, 2003).

74 Adrian Barnes, 'Do They Have to Buy from Burma? A Pre-Emption Analysis of Local Anti-Sweatshop Procurement Laws'. *Columbia Law Review* 107 (2007): 426–56.

75 Ibid.; Wang Chuanli and Dong Gang, 'Social Responsibilities of Transnational Corporations'. *Frontiers of Law in China* 2, no. 3 (2007): 378–402.

76 Peter Jones, Daphne Comfort, and David Hillier, 'What's in Store? Retail Marketing and Corporate Social Responsibility'. *Marketing Intelligence & Planning* 25, no. 1 (2007): 17–30; Jack Yan, 'Corporate Responsibility and the Brands of Tomorrow'. *Brand Management* 10, no. 4–5 (2003): 290–302.

77 Naomi Klein, *No Logo: Taking Aim at the Brand Bullies* (New York: Picador, 2000); Duncan Pruett, *Looking for a Quick Fix: How Weak Social Auditing Is Keeping Workers in Sweatshops* (Amsterdam: Clean Clothes Campaign, 2005).

Unions in many industries thus establish global union federations and seek to negotiate 'international framework agreements' with TNCs.[78] Some activist campaigns are directed at large, developed-nation brand-name retailers who stock products made in Third World countries.

Action along these lines began to emerge in response to the Rana Plaza collapse in Bangladesh, through demands on retailers and label owners to sign a five-year commitment to conduct independent safety inspections of factories and pay up to $500,000 per year toward safety improvements.[79] The local and international unions were able to use the publicity arising from the building collapse to pressure the brand corporations. Many had initially denied any involvement with the factory, but activists were able to provide proof—labels and invoices—gathered from the rubble.

Eventually two competing models emerged there. The first was the Accord on Fire and Building Safety in Bangladesh, signed by 10 union federations and 163 garment manufacturing and retail corporations from 20 countries. It provided for independent inspections of factories, obligations to pay for safety repairs and renovations, and protections for the right to refuse dangerous work or to enter dangerous buildings. Importantly, there was legal enforceability of these rights in the home country of the brand corporation (i.e. if the brand corporation did not force its suppliers to take the above action, it in turn could be sued in its home country). The International Labour Organization (ILO) provided the independent chair of the governing body.[80]

The second model, in response to concerns by corporations like Walmart and Gap that they did not want to face the higher costs the Accord might imply, was the Alliance for Bangladesh Worker Safety, signed by 26 corporations (mostly from North America) but no unions, with corporate-controlled factory inspections, no guarantees of safety repairs or renovations, no guaranteed rights to refuse dangerous work or to enter

78 For example, Ruth Barton and Peter Fairbrother, 'The Local Is Now Global: Building a Union Coalition in the International Transport and Logistics Sector'. *Relations Industrielles* 64, no. 4 (2009): 685–703; Elizabeth Cotton and Rebecca Gumbrell-McCormick, 'Global Unions as Imperfect Multilateral Organizations: An International Relations Perspective'. *Economic and Industrial Democracy* 33, no. 4 (2012): 707–28.

79 Huff Post Business, 'Bangladesh Factory Safety Accord: At Least 14 Major North American Retailers Decline to Sign'. *Huffington Post*, 17 May 2013, www.huffingtonpost.com/2013/05/17/bangladesh-factory-safety-accord_n_3286430.html.

80 bangladeshaccord.org/; Clean Clothes Campaign, 'Comparison: The Accord on Fire and Building Safety in Bangladesh and the Gap/Walmart Scheme'. 4 July 2013, www.cleanclothes.org/resources/background/.

dangerous buildings, and no legal enforceability (other than the payment by manufacturers of fees to the Alliance.[81] The Alliance is therefore seen by labour activists as an attempt by corporations to give the appearance of action (its website claims it is the 'driving force for creating a safer garment industry for all factory workers') in a highly emotive area without actually doing anything.

The difference between the two approaches is critical. The Accord had around 50 staff, including engineers who undertook safety audits. Under the Accord, some 1,104 factory inspections were undertaken up to September 2014, finding a total of 80,000 safety breaches. Only two factories were closed, but all factories had at least one major safety problem. These had to be remedied. For example, if a worker activist showed an inspector around a factory and was sacked the next day for doing so, under the Accord he or she had to be reinstated or the brand corporation must sever its ties with that factory. Under the Alliance, by contrast, the factory owner would get a letter.[82] I imagine it would go into the round file.[83]

Many relevant Australian corporate groups are covered by the Accord (Cotton On Group, Forever New, Kmart, Pacific Brands, Pretty Girl Fashion Group, Speciality Fashions, Australia's Target and Woolworths), as are many international brands (including Esprit, H&M, Zara, C&A, Adidas, Loblaw, Tesco, Benetton and Mango). However, the Just Group (chaired by Solomon Lew, with CEO Mark McInnes, a controversial hire from David Jones,[84] and which owns the brands Just Jeans, Jay Jays, Jacqui E, Portmans, Dotti, Peter Alexander and Smiggle) joined Walmart and Gap's Alliance (along with companies like Macy's, US Target, The Warehouse, Costco, Canadian Tire and a number of North American employer associations).

81 Ibid.; www.bangladeshworkersafety.org/en.

82 Juliane Reinecke and Jimmy Donaghey, 'After Rana Plaza: Building Coalitional Power for Labour Rights between Unions and (Consumption-Based) Social Movement Organisations'. *Organization* 22, no. 5 (2015): 720–40.

83 The bin.

84 John Durie, 'David Jones CEO Mark McInnes Resigns after Sexual Harassment Complaint'. *The Australian*, 18 June 2010; Stephen Mayne, 'McInnes is back, but is Lew's blokey board ready for backlash?', *Crikey*, 25 March 2011, www.crikey.com.au/2011/03/25/mcinnes-is-back-but-is-lew%e2%80%99s-blokey-board-ready-for-the-backlash/.

Bangladeshi labour activists said, in effect, 'don't stop buying garments made in Bangladesh, but put pressure on the labels' to guarantee safety and working conditions. The extent to which this is successful depends on which of these two 'models' succeeds. The difficulty for consumers who have not read this book, and hence for this form of action, is knowing which code of conduct has substance and which is a facade.

The Accord and its successor led to restructuring of the Bangladeshi garment industry, with a number of city-based small manufacturers closing as production for the West is increasingly concentrated in larger factories on urban fringes. Ties with over 500 factories were terminated for non-compliance.[85] Still, much of the industry was not affected, as significant exports also went to China, which did not engage in such processes. That said, it is a model that might find salience in other countries (e.g. corporations that are willing to abide by good practice find it less costly to go through the Accord inspection processes than to have multiple audit teams from different organisations inspecting at different times, even if the former have legal enforceability).

What happens after the initial five-year Accord expired in 2018 will be important but is, at time of writing, uncertain. Bodies like Human Rights Watch and other activists and unions wanted the Accord to stay in place; the government and especially local employers wanted it terminated or at least replaced by something with less independence. There was support from overseas to maintain the Accord. The matter was to be heard by the Bangladesh Supreme Court in mid-2019,[86] with much concern focused on the need to build local institutions to enable effective labour regulation in light of what some saw as the '"shocking unreadiness" by Bangladeshi regulators to oversee the ready-made garment industry'.[87] There was no such problem for Walmart and Gap's Alliance. The public relations crisis having passed, as always planned, the Alliance ceased to exist in December 2018.[88]

85 BDApparel News Desk, 'Bangladesh's Factories Must Never Become Death Traps Again: HRW'. *BDApparel News*, 5 February 2019, www.bdapparelnews.com/Bangladeshs-factories-must-never-become-death-traps-again-HRW/270.

86 Ibid.

87 UNI global union, 'Six Years after Rana Plaza: Remembering What was Lost and Protecting the Progress That Has Been Made'. *News*, 24 April 2019, www.uniglobalunion.org/news/six-years-after-rana-plaza-remembering-what-was-lost-and-protecting-progress-has-been-made.

88 'The Alliance for Bangladesh Worker Safety has ceased operations as planned on December 31, 2018. All email directed to the Alliance will not be received.' www.bangladeshworkersafety.org/.

Alternative grievance mechanisms

A different approach that has been taken to international regulation of TNCs is the grievance mechanisms established through the Organisation for Economic Co-operation and Development (OECD) guidelines on TNCs. These enable interested parties (including individual unions or global union federations) to raise complaints with 'national contact points' (usually a bureaucrat in a government department) in home countries of the TNCs. These differ from codes of conduct in an important respect: rather than the question of engagement being up to the company, they are up to the national government of the country in which the company is domiciled, and a company can be dragged into the process even where it does not wish to be, if the government is determined to participate.[89] Not all countries participate with equal enthusiasm, and in the USA, for example, it appears that if a TNC does not wish to participate then the home government does not push it. Analysis by Ford and Gillan suggests that roughly three-fifths of complaints get accepted as being able to be heard, and of those about half produce positive outcomes for the complainant.[90] While the process has many problems, its existence shows that there are multiple avenues available for those seeking to regulate the labour activities of transnational capital.

Conclusions

The state still has a key role to play in creating and enforcing the rights associated with workplace citizenship, the rights applying under codes of conduct, and the management of social and systemic sustainability via such issues as the redistribution of income, wealth and power, the pricing of externalities such as carbon and the way in which financial regulation affects the focus on short- and long-term rates of return.

Yet regulation is increasingly difficult as the effects of globalisation spread and render nation-states less powerful, and as neo-liberalism renders the state less willing to intervene anyway. Developments in technology provide additional challenges.

89 Michelle Ford and Michael Gillan, 'The OECD Guidelines as a Supranational Mechanism of Labor Conflict Resolution'. Paper presented at *Conflict and its Resolution in the Changing World of Work: A Conference and Special Issue Honoring David B. Lipsky* (DigitalCommons@ILR, 2017).
90 Ibid.

This chapter shows three ways in which parties have responded, and can respond, to changes in the economic environment and labour market that provide regulatory challenges.

On the first issue (the definition of workers), it appears that changes in the labour market, including those driven by new technology and the growing emphasis on 'not there' employment, have run ahead of both statutory law and judge-made law. The judiciary tries to respond but appears at times to be waiting for legislators to catch up. There are opportunities for legislators to do that, by expanding the reach of employment law and (perhaps in different ways) of particular aspects of labour law (such as in workers' compensation). This includes revisiting the definition of a 'worker' or at least the possibility of some minimum standards applying to all employees, and thinking innovatively about how such aims might be achieved. A good approach seems to be to establish general minimums at law, while leaving it to specialised bodies to determine the detail in areas where employment status is not demonstrable.

On the second issue (noncompliance), inspectorate compliance action appears increasingly inadequate, and hampered in Australia and elsewhere by inadequate resources and/or conflicting responsibilities for the inspectorate. Unions, largely now locked out of active labour inspection in Australia, have sought to achieve supply-chain regulation through pressuring the state and corporations.

On the third issue (international value chains), states are reluctant to act for fear of losing investment, but unions use leverage where they can to force accountable regulation across the value chain, under the auspices of the lead company that heads the value chain. In this context, we need to take account of the role of regulation in bringing about sustainable and ethical behaviour. There are genuine doubts about the efficacy of 'internal' regulation by corporations, due to the nature of the logic of the corporation (typically profit-maximisation). Some campaigns (such as those promoting codes of conduct) seek to affect or shape internal regulation and even the internal logic of corporations. Some researchers see this as a new form of regulation that may supplant state regulation in an era where the state is in retreat. But there is considerable evidence that it matters a great deal whether any internal codes of conduct are ultimately enforceable. If they remain within the control of the corporation, with no external enforceability under law, then there is genuine doubt as to their longevity—their sustainability. An example is the differences between the 'Accord' and the now defunct 'Alliance' on Bangladesh worker safety, the former imposing legal rights and obligations and being the subject of continuing contestation between capital, labour and the state, while the latter was a classic example of something ephemeral established as public relations crisis management. To the extent that it succeeds in undermining the imposition of legal rights and obligations, public relations crisis management threatens workers' lives.

All of these are about different, but related, aspects of labour regulation. Labour regulators are finding it increasingly difficult to respond to the critical issues in today's labour markets. But as discussed in early chapters, labour regulation is not the only aspect of regulation that affects labour. There are broader questions about other types of regulation, of society and the economy that are also highly relevant to labour. And there are major issues about how the regulatory environment responds to climate change and what this means for the future of work. We looked at some of that in Chapter 9, and we turn to broader issues of responding to the world outside the workplace in the final chapter.

11

In conclusion—on realities and futures outside the workplace

This book began with two *Sliding Doors* scenarios for the future—one not quite utopian, one not quite dystopian.[1] Through the rest of this book, we have seen what the realities of work presently look like, and how the choices that we make will determine which futures of work we end up with.

The present realities and choices

The present realities of work can be summarised like this: shaped by over three decades of financialisation and the broadly neo-liberal policy frameworks that have accompanied, facilitated and been encouraged by financialisation, employers and workers have been increasingly operating in an environment that is driven more by financial considerations and less by the personal preferences, benevolent or otherwise, of wealthy families or individual industrialists.[2] It is the logic of money, not the emotions of moguls, that have increasingly determined what happens. (Moguls are not dead—witness News Corporation's Rupert Murdoch[3]—but, as sole owners of large corporations, they are less common these days.)[4]

1 See Chapter 1 of this book.

2 Chapter 2.

3 Jane Mayer, 'The Making of the Fox News White House'. *New Yorker*, 11 March 2019, www.newyorker.com/magazine/2019/03/11/the-making-of-the-fox-news-white-house.

4 G. Murray and D. Peetz, 'The Financialisation of Global Corporate Ownership'. In *Financial Elites and Transnational Business: Who Rules the World?*, ed. G. Murray and J. Scott (Cheltenham: Edward Elgar, 2012).

The phenomenon of globalisation has also accompanied these changes, and it makes a difference, but it is often given attribution for things that are not of its doing. Blame those South Americans or Asians for taking your jobs? No, it's really the beancounters who did it—if you can blame any individuals at all. One of the great things about the developments of the last three decades, at least from the point of view of those who benefit, is that so much of what happens can be said to be inevitable. 'Sorry you lost your job, but that's economics.' Or that's the market. Or that's globalisation. Or that's just the way it is. More flexibility and more uncertainty are inevitable, we are told.[5] This depersonalisation of accountability takes power away from individual workers and it makes them feel that even organising collectively no longer gives them the power they used to have. Over three decades of financialisation and neo-liberalism have seen union density decline in most countries, sometimes quite dramatically, even though attitudes are quite stable, and people still want unions, on average, as much as they used to.[6]

So with developments in the economy and society seemingly taking an inevitable turn, we also look to the effects of technology with a sense of inevitability. Artificial intelligence is coming, cloud computing is coming, 3D printing and big data and new biotechnologies are coming, and they will have 'these' effects (whatever 'these' are) and nothing can be done about it, as it is all inevitable.[7]

Agency and variability

Yet despite the greater influence of 'the market', individuals still have agency, and quite a lot of it. Managers who run companies or units within companies do so with a wide range of styles and strategies.[8] They do this partly because no one has really worked out what the magic formula is (though many people make a lot of money telling you what that formula is), partly because they find themselves in different industries or circumstances that promote particular styles, and partly because managers really are individuals with individual differences and psychological urges that vary in their intensity. Some want their employees to prosper, some want to be able to exercise control, or at least to demonstrate control.

5 Chapter 6.
6 Chapters 2 and 7.
7 Chapter 4.
8 Chapter 5.

Some like rules and procedures, some don't. Some have their favourites and dislikes, some act without fear or favour. Some believe their workers have rights to organise or act collectively or to act on their own beliefs, some don't and seek to exercise cultural control over their workforce. Some read widely, some don't. Some are influenced by the ideas of their peers in other firms or other units or employer organisations, some are not. Most want to advance in the organisation (otherwise, why would they become managers?) and so they will adopt the ideals of profit maximisation and seek to curry favour with their superiors or the shareholders' representatives, but they still have quite diverse views, and operationalise them in diverse ways, on how to maximise that profit and gain support from their superiors.

Even finance capitalists vary in their preferences and behaviour. Some look to the short term, some to the long term. Some genuinely are concerned for the planet, some couldn't care less. They vary hugely in their tolerance or welcoming of risk. Always, their behaviour is constrained by what *looks* to them like a good or a bad investment, so they all believe in market solutions ahead of collective action, but they may behave quite differently in similar situations because of those individual differences.[9]

Likewise, workers as well as officials in worker organisations have agency and differ greatly in their choices, preferences and actions. Therefore workers and worker organisations vary substantially across space and time in how they respond to particular situations.[10]

So it may be fair to say that, one day, someone somewhere will invent X, where X is some new technology that has certain capabilities. But predicting what will happen *after* X is invented is another matter altogether, because it depends on who owns X; the actions of managers, capitalists, financiers, workers, worker organisations and governments after X is invented; and the structures that have been put in place up until the time when X was invented. All those predictions from the 1970s that new technology would reduce working hours and create a leisure society were off-beam because they failed to take accurate account of the social and economic context in which technological change was occurring.[11]

9 Chapter 9.
10 Chapter 7.
11 Chapter 3.

Current directions

What, then, does the immediate future hold? At present, under the influence of financialisation and neo-liberal policy frameworks, industrial capital is reorganising as core firms seek to minimise costs, risks and, importantly, accountability, by outsourcing, spinning off subsidiaries, setting up franchises, or using contracting firms, labour hire or contract workers themselves—in other words, 'not there' employment.[12] Again, a great advantage is that accountability is depersonalised: you no longer lose your conditions, or your job, or your hand, because of some action or inaction by a well-known global firm. You lose them because 'that's what we have to do in order to survive in the modern marketplace'. It boils down to simple economics. Large firms take up, on average, a growing share of activity in product markets, but with less responsibility.

Yet this process of fragmentation, precaritisation and risk-shifting has limits, and frequently reaches them, because in order to maintain control over their products firms need to maintain control over labour. Managers seek ways to exercise control of labour, sometimes helped by developments in technology. In the end, though, the employment relationship is critical to maintaining managerial control over labour. Without the employment relationship, capital cannot seek to exercise cultural control over workers. Even when large firms use outsourcing, spinoffs, labour hire or franchises to avoid accountability, in the end the workers in those firms are usually hired as employees, because that's the only way even peripheral capital can maintain the necessary control over labour. The causes of the limits to the spread of market relations into every sphere of life are two-fold: resistance by workers, civil society and the state—what Polanyi called the 'double movement' involving marketisation and push-back[13]—and the internal logic of capital itself.

The latest developments in work-related technology, in the form of online or mobile 'gig' platforms, provide an opportunity to get around this lacuna by creating a new form of control: control via the rating and tracking systems of the 'app' rather than control via a human supervisor. But even this has its limits, as this form of control is not a perfect substitute for human supervision, and even if it was it runs up against resistance arising

12 Chapter 6.

13 K. Polanyi, *The Great Transformation: The Political and Economic Origins of Our Time* (Boston: Beacon Press, 1944).

from that contradiction: between having very low labour costs and having a product with the quality that the market will accept. Hence many platform firms fail to make a profit, and some go bust.

That conflict between lowering labour costs and maintaining product quality and workforce stability is not unique to the platform economy, of course. Throughout the economy, workers resist reductions in pay and conditions and, where conditions facilitate it, often act collectively to improve them. Institutional changes driven by financialisation and neo-liberal frameworks have reduced opportunities for collective mobilisation and hence reduced union density, though the actions of individual unions also influence the extent of decline or revival of unionism.

The past and future development of the system is based on, and creates, great inequalities. The most obvious inequalities are of class, as our mode of production is based on class divisions, but there are other important inequalities as well. Prominent among them are gender inequalities.[14] While these have origins in the gendered household division of labour, the evolution of the economic system has reinforced some and created new ones, with gaps in pay between men and women doing similar jobs or between male-dominated and female-dominated occupations that otherwise generate similar economic value. Various devices (including 'merit'-based selection and sex-based harassment) are used to exclude women from positions of power. In recent decades some factors have reduced gender gaps—particularly more progressive *values* that in turn are reflected in less regulatory tolerance of unequal treatment—but other factors have worked in the opposite direction: reduced external regulation, through neo-liberalism, and changing norms about what sort of *behaviour* is acceptable. 'Race' and ethnicity have been used to segregate vulnerable people into the lowest-paid jobs in an economy and to often render them liable to exploitation through payment of low wages or provision of conditions below regulated minimums.

If we cannot predict with accuracy what changes will flow from developments in technology, we can predict, with some uncertainty as to the details, what will happen if nothing changes—most obviously, with the state of the planet. Absent changes in direction, global warming will bring about catastrophic changes to the environment.[15] Anticipating

14 Chapter 8.

15 Chapter 9.

this, research and development focuses on ameliorative technologies with the effect of changing the relative prices and returns on particular investments—for example, new coal-fuelled energy is no longer economic compared to renewable energy. Some types of work will become more difficult, some redundant, some newly attractive. It is unlikely, however, that these changes will be sufficient to prevent catastrophic change unless and until the costs of externalities are effectively priced into production decisions, and other state interventions are likely to be essential.

Potential futures

It would seem there are several potential futures that we could face.

Neo-democracy

One potential future is a more egalitarian one: a new 'social democratic' or 'democratic socialist' future, characterised by a resurgence of labour, reduced inequality and more extensive and new forms of regulation offsetting the failures of neo-liberal approaches. Those new forms of regulation might include some of the more recent, innovative approaches referred to in Chapter 10. Resistance happens, and choices are made. We have already seen how employees want voice at work and they want power to exercise some control over their working lives. Employees learn to cope with or resist insecurity in their jobs and in their pay through unorganised or organised means. Unions have sought to reorganise themselves, devoting more resources to the workplace and sometimes to the formal and informal training of delegates, and greater internal democracy, with varying degrees of enthusiasm and success.[16]

We may see new ways of doing things and of thinking about things: a new vision and new approaches to policy. Unions, other social movements representing women, the underprivileged, community groups and the environment, and intellectuals could be drawn together into a major conversation aimed at developing, articulating and implementing a new vision. In Australia, for example, the almost forgotten Accord between unions and the government of the 1980s was many things, some of which are now irrelevant, but most importantly it was an *alternative vision* of

16 David Peetz and Janis Bailey, 'Dancing Alone: The Australian Union Movement over Three Decades'. *Journal of Industrial Relations* 54, no. 4 (2012): 524–41.

the economy, a challenge to the liberal market orthodoxy of government departments of the day. These days, the prominence given to Thomas Piketty's *Capital in the 21st Century*[17] is not so much a reflection of a great new revelation as it is a reflection of the way the book 'suits the mood of the times'.[18]

Exactly what that more egalitarian, neo-democratic world would look like is hard to say, but later in this chapter I provide some ideas. From the historical examples we have seen so far it would be more like Norway than New Zealand, more like Scandinavia than the Soviet Union. That is, in order to be sustainable it would have both a high level of democracy and a high level of state involvement in the economy, avoiding both the discredited market extremism of 1980s New Zealand and the discredited totalitarian centralism of the former Eastern Bloc countries.

Neo-neoliberalism

A second future may appear to be an even more market-based system than exists at present, characterised by further state retreats from markets and greater embeddedness of market ideals into each aspect of human activity, as ostensibly advocated by many political parties, lobbyists and think-tanks—a new ('neo') neo-liberalism. The hegemony of neo-liberalism seems incompatible with survival of the planet in its present form. However, there is no doubt that neo-liberalism has been resilient in the face of challenges. When the global financial crisis pushed millions out of work globally, the rationale for market liberal policies was demolished. The opaqueness of complex multilayered financial instruments, and the perverse incentives created by reward systems in the finance sector, both results of financialisation, directly created the crisis. Governments and central banks in Europe, the USA and Australia were forced to rescue financial institutions from their own folly. As economist John Quiggin pointed out, the credibility of the economic theories underpinning these policies was destroyed.[19]

17 Robert H. Wade, 'The Piketty Phenomenon and the Future of Inequality'. *Real-World Economics Review* 69 (2014): 2–17.
18 John Quiggin, 'How Thomas Piketty Found a Mass Audience, and What It Means for Public Policy'. *Inside Story*, 30 May 2014.
19 John Quiggin, *Zombie Economics* (New Jersey: Princeton University Press, 2010).

Yet the ideas persisted. Remarkably, within two years Europe was plunged into a new crisis—a crisis of austerity politics—as enthusiasts for market liberal ideas successfully persuaded policy-makers that governments, not banks, were to blame and that workers, not the beneficiaries, needed to endure years of austerity to pay for the fiscal mess that others had created. But does it follow that neo-liberalism will maintain its hegemony in public policy circles? We must wonder whether 'free' markets are themselves just a passing phase, as markets become replaced by monopoly capital. The tendency for capital to seek concentration of markets has been noted by writers since Marx[20] and can be seen in the increasing concentration within industries over the past quarter century.[21] The emergence of digital technology has enabled the concentration of retailing in the hands of Amazon whose owner was, at the time of writing, the richest man in the world,[22] despite substantial losses for Amazon in early years.[23] Amazon is, in many ways, *replacing* the market, as a single website becomes the mechanism by which an increasing number of consumers conduct most of their shopping.[24] The localised interplay between supply and demand becomes replaced by the decisions of Amazon administrators to give or decline prominence in online listings to particular suppliers, on the basis of whatever criteria Amazon determines at the time.[25]

Similarly, it is hard to explain the actions of Uber's investors in continuing to finance a firm that has made billions of dollars in losses, if we see it as simply a firm engaged in a marketplace for rideshare services.[26] Those

20 Karl Marx and Fredrich Engels, *The Communist Manifesto*. Collected Works (Moscow: Progress publishers, 1848; repr., 1977); Raewyn Connell and Terry Irving, *Class Structure in Australian History: Poverty and Progress* (Melbourne: Longman Cheshire, 1992); Michael Gilding, 'Superwealth in Australia: Entrepreneurs, Accumulation and the Capitalist Class'. *Journal of Sociology* 35, no. 2 (1999): 169–71; G. William Domhoff, *Who Rules America? Politics and Social Change* (New York: McGraw-Hill, 2006); Georgina Murray, *Capitalist Networks and Social Power in Australia and New Zealand* (Aldershot: Ashgate, 2006).

21 See Chapter 6.

22 Rebecca Marston, 'Amazon Raises Wages Amid Criticism'. *BBC News*, 2 October 2018, www.bbc.com/news/business-45717768.

23 George Packer, 'Cheap Words'. *New Yorker*, 17 February 2014, www.newyorker.com/magazine/2014/02/17/cheap-words; Alison Griswold and Jason Karaian, 'It Took Amazon 14 Years to Make as Much in Net Profit as It Did Last Quarter'. *Quartz*, 1 February 2018, qz.com/1196256/it-took-amazon-amzn-14-years-to-make-as-much-net-profit-as-it-did-in-the-fourth-quarter-of-2017/.

24 Stacy Mitchell, 'Amazon Doesn't Just Want to Dominate the Market—It Wants to Become the Market'. *The Nation*, 15 February 2018.

25 Ibid.; Julia Angwin and Surya Mattu, 'Amazon Says It Puts Customers First. But Its Pricing Algorithm Doesn't'. *ProPublica*, 20 September 2016, www.propublica.org/article/amazon-says-it-puts-customers-first-but-its-pricing-algorithm-doesnt.

26 Yves Smith, 'Uber Is Headed for a Crash'. Intelligencer, *New York Magazine*, 4 December 2018, nymag.com/intelligencer/2018/12/will-uber-survive-the-next-decade.html.

loss-making investments would be warranted, however, if Uber were to ultimately become a monopoly platform for transport services, replacing taxis and short-haul bus services, and integrated into previously existing train or subway services with which it enters into joint ventures that provide a quarantined revenue stream to Uber.[27] That is, the future of Uber is that of monopoly capital, not of a competing market participant. A free market–driven future seems a mirage, not a genuine option.

Indeed, the idea of a market liberal ideal has never been truly realised and likely never will be.[28] The closest any nation-state has come to it was probably the USA in the late twentieth century, under Reagan, Bush and Bush Jnr, but even then there were many market imperfections and instances of intervention and authoritarian behaviour by the state. And it led, of course, to the very illiberal Trump regime. Indeed, the success of the 2016 Trump campaign and, in the same year, of the Brexit campaign, both point to popular rejection of neo-liberal claims to prosperity and the political consequences of working-class reaction to their failure. This is not to say that neo-liberalism ever held popular sway—opinion polls have long held several tenets of neo-liberalism to be unpopular[29]—but now that unpopularity has demonstrable political consequences. Yet the reaction to market neo-liberalism has not led to a resurgence of social democracy. Indeed, social democratic parties in many countries have been in decline over the past two decades, perhaps because their embrace of some aspects of market neo-liberalism has prevented them from offering an adequate critique and allowed them to be at least partly blamed for the problems that have followed.

Instead, the political beneficiaries in many countries of the failure of neo-liberalism have been the extreme right. Brexit was championed by the xenophobic UK Independence Party and gave the latter a legitimacy it never previously enjoyed. Trump's election has seen some far-right figures move into his circle of advisers (at least on a visiting basis) and the re-energising of far-right groups. Far-right parties in national elections in

27 Sara Salinas, 'Uber and Lyft Are Racing to Own Every Mode of Transportation—They're Getting Close'. *MSNBC Tech*, 9 June 2018.

28 Quiggin, *Zombie Economics*.

29 See Chapter 1.

Europe have achieved votes not seen since World War II.[30] Totalitarian tendencies can be seen in governments in countries such as India, the Philippines, Turkey, Egypt, Brazil, Russia, Hungary, Poland and even Japan.[31] The future portends no neo-neoliberal hegemony.

Neo-totalitarianism

The third potential scenario, then, is of a more totalitarian future, in which inequality is increased, ruling elites are strengthened and suppression of dissent is intensified. It is a spectre of which American sociologist William Robinson warns us.[32] There is no doubt that developments in technology would enhance the potential for state surveillance in such a society. The social futures that we were warned about in *Nineteen Eighty-Four* and *The Handmaid's Tale* are feasible manifestations of this scenario. Inside the workplace, the more immediate future depicted in *The Circle* may be the sugar coating we need to enable the system to reproduce itself; or it just might be a transitory phase to the longer-term misery of *Nineteen Eighty-Four* and *The Handmaid's Tale.*[33] This third scenario seems much more likely than a market ascendancy, because of the very apparent failures of market liberalism and the already evident political manifestations of that failure.

The Trump years were characterised by extensive repudiations of market policies, alongside redistribution to the rich and entrenchment of the power of those already with power. The policies were enthusiastically endorsed by almost all congressional members and most members and supporters of the previously free-market Republican Party. While at the time of writing the prospects for Trump being re-elected seemed less than even, the remarkable thing was that, despite everything that he did in his first two years in office, his approval level through this period bounced

30 BBC News, 'Europe and Nationalism: A Country-by-Country Guide'. *BBC News*, 10 September 2018, www.bbc.com/news/world-europe-36130006; Karoline Postel-Vinay, 'How Neo-Nationalism Went Global'. *The Conversation*, 14 March 2017, theconversation.com/how-neo-nationalism-went-global-74095; Bernard E. Harcourt, 'How Trump Fuels the Fascist Right'. *New York Review of Books*, 29 November 2018, www.nybooks.com/daily/2018/11/29/how-trump-fuels-the-fascist-right/.

31 Postel-Vinay, 'How Neo-Nationalism Went Global'.

32 William I. Robinson, 'Global Capitalism: Crisis of Humanity and the Specter of 21st Century Fascism'. *The World Financial Review*, 27 May 2014, www.worldfinancialreview.com/global-capitalism-crisis-humanity-specter-21st-century-fascism/.

33 See Chapter 3 of this book.

around about two-fifths of voters.[34] While this was one of the poorest approval ratings for first-term modern presidents, none others had behaved in ways that remotely resembled Trump.

I must confess that I was personally surprised by what happened in the Trump years in the USA: not by the behaviour of Trump himself, which could be predicted by his behaviour before being elected, but by the lack of resistance to his approach from within the Republican Party once he became President (and indeed, once he became the official campaign nominee). Seeming adherents to free-market beliefs enthusiastically endorsed or occasionally quietly acquiesced to his regime. On the surface, Trump's mainstream Republican supporters appear to be demonstrating what Orwell in *Nineteen Eighty-Four* called *doublethink*—the power to simultaneously hold two contradictory views. It is slightly more complicated than that, as the rationalising of support for Trump appears to mean that the contradiction is resolved, but in a way that we might not, as rational beings, have expected.

Leon Festinger and colleagues came up with a term to describe the process a decade after *Nineteen Eighty-Four* was published: cognitive dissonance. This was first observed in the 1950s, when researchers infiltrated a group of doomsday cultists. The researchers were curious to know how the cultists would react when the world did not end on the anointed doomsday. But instead of rethinking their beliefs as they waited on that hilltop, the cultists rationalised the non-end of the world in ways that were consistent with their cult's beliefs (God has saved the world because we did those things He wanted us to do). If anything, their adherence to the cult's belief system was strengthened.[35] The conflict between their belief system and reality was resolved by reinterpreting reality. It is the sort of process we see Mae go through in *The Circle*, whereby her initial objections to invasions of privacy by the corporation are overwhelmed by her support for the objectives of the corporation, in which she has a job that she enjoys immensely. The contradiction between her concern for privacy and her support for the organisation that provides her job was eventually resolved in favour of the latter.

34 Nate Silver, 'How Popular Is Donald Trump?'. *Five Thirty Eight*, 14 February 2019, fivethirtyeight.com/trump-approval-ratings/.

35 Leon Festinger, *A Theory of Cognitive Dissonance* (Stanford, CA: Stanford University Press, 1957).

In being surprised by the persistence of support for Trump in the face of his actual behaviour, I had failed to appreciate the strength of cognitive dissonance. To many Republican identifiers, Trump represented conflicts between several of their beliefs. This was resolved by either recasting some of those beliefs, with less important values subordinated to priority values, or reinterpreting what had happened. Thus 'pussy-grabbing' was mere locker-room talk, free-market ideals became the disparaged techniques of 'elites' from the Washington 'swamp', and Trump's regular lies (averaging 15 per day in 2018)[36] were accepted as truths. Any principles regarding the importance of free markets, gender equity,[37] democracy, ethics or honesty were subordinated to values relating in one way or another to the importance of power and entitlements for those with whom Republican voters identified. If a new conflict arose—some new revelation that commentators thought finally signalled the end for Trump—his supporters would almost instinctively dismiss it, not unlike the process of *crimestop* described by Orwell that prevented heretical thoughts from being held. While much has been made of Trump's alleged appeal to white working-class males, this group was arithmetically less important in his total support than the 'traditional' Republican voters whom Trump mostly retained: the average income of 2016 Trump voters was higher than that of Clinton voters.[38] For those who recast their subordinate values and perceptions of reality along these lines, a stream of falsehoods creates an alternative reality[39]—a postmodern, parallel universe—that seems to bear no relation to actual reality. Unfortunately, this parallel universe has little room for a sustainable planet earth in its future.

The fragility of democracy

Some time after Margaret Atwood wrote *The Handmaid's Tale*, she said she did it as a warning of what might happen, not as a prediction of what would happen. Yet in women's marches in the USA, some groups of women have adopted the garments and mannerisms (head bowed,

---

36 Glenn Kessler, 'A Year of Unprecedented Deception: Trump Averaged 15 False Claims a Day in 2015'. *Washington Post*, 30 December 2018. See also Bella DePaulo, 'I Study Liars. I've Never Seen One Like President Trump'. *Washington Post*, 9 December 2017.

37 Jonathan Martin, 'Some in G.O.P. Who Deserted Donald Trump over Lewd Tape Are Returning'. *New York Times*, 12 October 2016.

38 Nicholas Carnes and Noam Lupu, 'It's Time to Bust the Myth: Most Trump Voters Were Not Working Class'. *Washington Post*, 5 June 2017.

39 Denise Clifton, 'A Chilling Theory on Trump's Nonstop Lies'. *Mother Jones*, 3 August 2017.

disengaged) of the handmaids as a protest against the sorts of policies they see the Trump administration pursuing regarding women. The making of the TV series, 30 years after the book was written, was probably accidental in its timing but was seized upon as very prescient by opponents of the administration. That book's depiction of the advances of women in the 1960s and 1970s as being fragile while women remained excluded from positions of power remains relevant, especially as women's share of elected national representatives in the US Republican Party or the Liberal Party of Australia has barely improved in decades.[40]

We like to think of democratic principles as being part of the logic of humanity, and democratic governance as the manifestation of higher civilisation. No democratic country, we are sometimes told, has ever gone to war with another democratic country—though that claim relies entirely on very restrictive definitions of both democracy and war.[41] But it is not just in the USA that political behaviour makes us question whether democratic ideals are supreme. Governments described by various observers as 'extreme right' or 'fascistic' were *elected* (not installed by military juntas) in the late 2010s in countries such as Brazil, Hungary, Poland and the Philippines. Although large-scale migrations have been blamed by some for a shift 'to the right' in Europe—and such migrations are something we will see more of in the future, due to climate change—this hardly explains developments in Poland or Hungary, where there were comparatively few migrants and very few Moslems at the time of writing,[42] let alone the Philippines or Brazil.[43]

40 RMIT ABC Fact Check, 'Fact Check: Is the Level of Liberal Women in Parliament Lower Now Than It Was in 1996?'. *ABC News*, 6 September 2018, www.abc.net.au/news/2018-06-06/fact-check-liberal-women-in-parliament/9796976. The number of Republican women elected to the US House of Representatives was 13 in both 1988 and 2018: en.wikipedia.org/wiki/Women_in_the_United_States_House_of_Representatives.

41 James Lee Ray, 'Wars between Democracies: Rare or Nonexistent?'. *International Interactions* 18, no. 3 (1993): 251–76.

42 Anne Applebaum, 'A Warning from Europe: The Worst Is yet to Come'. *The Atlantic*, October 2018, www.theatlantic.com/magazine/archive/2018/10/poland-polarization/568324/. In 2016, 0.4 per cent of the Hungarian population, and less than 0.1 per cent of the Polish population, was Moslem (compared to 4.9 per cent across Europe). Pew Research Center, 'Europe's Growing Muslim Population' (Pew-Templeton Global Religious Futures project, Pew Research Center, 29 November 2017), www.pewforum.org/wp-content/uploads/sites/7/2017/11/FULL-REPORT-FOR-WEB-POSTING.pdf.

43 Travis Waldron, 'Brazil Is About to Show the World How a Modern Democracy Collapses'. *Huffington Post*, 1 January 2019, www.huffingtonpost.com/entry/brazil-jair-bolsonaro-democracy-threat_us_5c2a30c5e4b08aaf7a929cbb.

A common element in all far-right successes, however, is the ability to blame 'the other' for ills, most of which ultimately arise from the perverse operation of capitalism. The 'other' might be migrants, but they might also be Jews, blacks, Moslems, poor people, or some other existing or imaginary group that constitutes a minority in the country concerned. Fear can be not only beneficial for some politicians but has also been a profitable business model for some media.[44] An 'in' group that is persuaded to see itself under siege (say, because of a declining share of the population) may seek to protect the status quo in any way possible, reverting to 'traditional' behaviour or norms, and feel more negatively toward the 'other'.[45] Thus Lukes referred to 'identity-related' or 'recognitional' domination, where the dominant group 'in control of the means of interpretation and communication, project their own experience and culture as the norm, rendering invisible the perspective of those they dominate, while simultaneously stereotyping them and making them out as "other"'.[46] Yale philosopher Jason Staney explains how 'fascist politics is about identifying enemies, appealing to the in-group (usually the majority group), and smashing truth and replacing it with power'.[47]

Parts of the 'other' are reimagined to become an elite that *really* controls things—hence conspiracy theories abound on the right.[48] This acts to obscure the role of the ruling class. Even people at the core of the ruling class (like Trump himself) become defined as outside the 'elite' and excoriate the redefined elite for their corruption of society. The real or alleged existence of corruption in a previous regime is usually a key part of a fascist strategy, and used to justify radical measures and the weakening or destruction of institutions that protected democracy. Earlier incidents of corruption or violence make it easier to justify widespread violence by the new state. So an authoritarian future may be one in which

44 Mayer, 'Fox News White House'.

45 Olar Khazan, 'People Voted for Trump Because They Were Anxious, Not Poor'. *The Atlantic*, 23 April 2018, www.theatlantic.com/science/archive/2018/04/existential-anxiety-not-poverty-motivates-trump-support/558674/.

46 Steven Lukes, *Power: A Radical View*, 2nd ed. (London: Palgrave, 2005), 120.

47 Interviewed in Sean Illing, 'How Fascism Works'. *Vox*, 19 September 2018, www.vox.com/2018/9/19/17847110/how-fascism-works-donald-trump-jason-stanley.

48 For example, Stephan Lewandowsky, Klaus Oberauer, and Gilles E. Gignac, 'Motivated Rejection of Science: NASA Faked the Moon Landing—Therefore (Climate) Science Is a Hoax: An Anatomy of the Motivated Rejection of Science'. *Psychological Science* 24, no. 5 (2013): 622–33; Stephan Lewandowsky, John Cook, Klaus Oberauer, Scott Brophy, Elisabeth A. Lloyd, and Michael Marriott. 'Recurrent fury: Conspiratorial discourse in the blogosphere triggered by research on the role of conspiracist ideation in climate denial'. *Journal of Social and Political Psychology* 3, no. 1 (2015): 142–78.

domination is achieved initially through seemingly market or democratic means. Democratic rhetoric may then be used to justify antidemocratic intrusions into dissenting groups (as was said in *The Circle*: 'if you aren't transparent, what are you hiding?'),[49] just as the rhetoric of fighting corruption may be used now by those who are themselves corrupt. As dissenting voices—inside the corporation or through the body politic—are increasingly delegitimised and excluded, the capacity for immiseration of those at the bottom increases.

In modern far-right movements, misogyny is a core element, as women, particularly 'feminists', are part of the 'other'. Antifeminist trolling, usually far better organised than observers believe,[50] is a persistent feature of right-wing online activity. But in most scenarios, a violent attack on half the population, challenging the loyalties of all men in heterosexual relationships, would be unsustainable. Hence other 'others'—nonwhites of varying types—must be identified to recruit women, albeit always in minority, to the crusade, so that disrespect towards women can be dismissed as 'locker room talk' and overcome by cognitive dissonance. A counter-scenario is the one posited in *The Handmaid's Tale*, in which women are targeted for subjugation but in which, critically, only a subset—feminists, abortionists and the like—are victimised as the 'other', the elite that secretly controlled things and had to be violently suppressed (including through executions). Although this depiction was more ambitious than most modern fascist movements, elements of this scenario (the subjugation of women) were played out in the period after the Iranian revolution of the 1970s.[51] It evokes substantial resistance;[52] whether that is enough to emulate the fictional fall of Gilead is unknown.

In *Nineteen Eighty-Four* and, to a lesser extent *The Handmaid's Tale*, state power is maintained by a combination of state violence and sophisticated, coordinated systems of surveillance and ideological reproduction that together constitute hegemonic control. By contrast, Trump's America showed a distinct lack of coordination or sophistication. Nor would any future quasi-fascist state be dependent on high coordination or

49 Dave Eggers, *The Circle* (New York: Vintage, 2013), 241.

50 Ginger Gorman, 'Internet Trolls Are Not Who I Thought — They're Even Scarier'. *ABC News*, 1 February 2019, www.abc.net.au/news/2019-02-02/internet-trolls-arent-who-i-thought-ginger-gorman-troll-hunting/10767690.

51 Homa Hoodfar, 'Iranian Women Risk Arrest: Daughters of the Revolution'. *The Conversation*, 6 March 2018, theconversation.com/iranian-women-risk-arrest-daughters-of-the-revolution-92880.

52 Ibid.

sophistication. It would instead rely on the weaknesses of human character that allow oppressive regimes to be built and prosper in the first place. We see this most clearly in *The Circle*'s depiction of cognitive processes that were foreshadowed over half a century earlier in *Nineteen Eighty-Four*'s concept of doublethink. And unlike in *Nineteen Eighty-Four* and *The Handmaid's Tale*, the people in charge of *The Circle* are not, by and large, malevolent or sinister megalomaniacs; they are just mostly people who think they are doing the right thing and progressing ever forwards, but without any dissenting checks or balances against them. One is reminded again, as per Hannah Arendt half a century ago, of the banality of evil.[53]

While the surveillance regimes in Orwell's Oceania are what commentators most commonly allude to, rightly, when warning of state infringements of civil liberties, and the violence of the Ministry of Love is what disturbs us most after seeing a movie or play of Orwell's work, it is Orwell's depictions of the fallibilities of human psychology in the face of a consensus that brooks no dissent that should sound the loudest warnings as we contemplate the future. In the context of force plus hegemony that Gramsci talks of,[54] our focus should be on what happens to both, but ultimately hegemony is the more powerful tool.

If the state in the future may not be the coordinated, sophisticated monolith of *Nineteen Eighty-Four* or *The Handmaid's Tale* (albeit with access to very advanced technology that could enable widespread surveillance), the same need not be true of future corporations—or at least some of them. 'Tech giants' increasingly dominate the corporate world and *The Circle* paints a grim view of the way coordination, technology and culturism combine in that corporation of the near future. It is a world in which employees are both happy and complicit in their own subjugation, in which dissent is performance-managed out of the organisation, much as depicted for the real world by Diane Van den Broek and Hugh Willmott over two decades ago.[55]

53 Hannah Arendt, *Eichmann in Jerusalem: A Report on the Banality of Evil* (New York: Viking, 1963).

54 Antonio Gramsci, *Selection from the Prison Notebooks of Antonio Gramsci* (New York: Lawrence and Wishart, 1971).

55 Diane Van den Broek, 'Human Resource Management, Workforce Control and Union Avoidance: An Australian Case Study'. *Journal of Industrial Relations* 39, no. 3 (1997): 332–48; Hugh Willmott, 'Strength Is Ignorance; Slavery Is Freedom: Managing Culture in Modern Organizations'. *The Journal of Management Studies* 30, no. 4 (1993): 515–52.

If policy-makers do not overcome the divisive forces of modern capitalism, one cannot rule out a violent revolt—but on the basis of what we have seen so far, it seems more likely to be a revolt of the far-right than the far-left. The violent demonstrations of the 2010s decade were mostly demonstrations of the right, not the left.[56] That is why I have given scant attention here to a theoretically fourth alternative future: that of a revolution-driven socialist world. It seems the least probable of any of the outcomes discussed here. While large-scale demonstrations or mobilisations might become part of some neo-democratic political movement and transition, large-scale violence would favour the opposite side.

In the end, it is probably one of two worlds that the *Sliding Doors* of our current choices will eventually open up to: a more egalitarian, neo-democratic one; or an eventually neo-totalitarian one in which the rich prosper at the expense of the rest of the population—possibly (but not with certainty) able to insulate themselves, and only themselves, from the worst effects of catastrophic climate change, transferring the most serious risk in history to the rest of the populace. The space I have devoted here to the neo-totalitarian possibility should not be seen as indicating it is inevitable. It is certainly possible to develop more equal, democratic societies than we presently have. The huge differences in the levels of inequality and other social pathologies between the Scandinavian countries and the Anglophone ones, epitomised by the USA, illustrate the wide range of possibilities that exist—and these are not the only possibilities. What they show is that nothing is inevitable, be it in technology or social organisation. If social and political outcomes were inevitable, every country now would have the same system of government and the same social order, but in practice they differ widely.

56 An exception might be France, but the situation of the yellow vests is complex, and 'the *gilets jaunes* seem more likely to become the French face of Trumpism … than of a more tolerant future'. Adam Gopnik, 'The Yellow Vests and Why There Are So Many Street Protests in France'. *New Yorker*, 6 December 2018, www.newyorker.com/news/daily-comment/the-yellow-vests-and-why-there-are-so-many-street-protests-in-france.

An agenda for a liveable future

What, then, are the characteristics of the alternative to authoritarianism, of more equal, ethical and democratic societies in which a feasible and liveable world of work could exist? To be precise, what are the policy choices that need to be made? In Chapter 10, I have already mentioned three innovative angles that can and need to be taken to policy issues in the face of the changing world of work. Here, I discuss some more.

An ethical economy and polity

The institutions that promote democracy need defending, and *faux democratic* rationales for undermining citizen protections need to be resisted. Ethical considerations should be built into the design of society, of technology (no easy feat) and of the processes of decision-making—something that has already been canvassed here regarding several areas.[57] Is it really *ethical* that a particular process or outcome is in place? This is not the same as giving 'equal time' or 'equal space' to good and evil, in much the same way as many media currently provide 'false balance' by giving a platform to those who deny the scientific reality of climate change.[58] Nor is it the same as 'cooperating' with the powerful after a long period in which they have failed to cooperate with the weak—for example, by 'stacking' ostensibly independent institutions with their own acolytes. Game theory tells us that continuing to cooperate, when the other side does not cooperate, merely reinforces the strength of the other side, and that the only feasible way to avoid 'the suckers' play' is to abandon such cooperation (until the other side credibly agrees to cooperate).[59]

Still, there is an important difference between not providing additional platforms for those who hold power, and suppressing those without power. Often, however, the distinction is lost. It is too easy for progressive governments to slide into repression, perhaps genuinely seeing or, at a minimum, widely portraying the other side as the 'elite', and using that

57 See Chapter 9 and 'Technology and ethics' near the end of Chapter 4.

58 Peter Ellerton, 'The Problem of False Balance When Reporting on Science'. *The Conversation*, 16 July 2014, theconversation.com/the-problem-of-false-balance-when-reporting-on-science-29077.

59 Bernard Keane, 'What Game Theory Says About Labor's Woes'. *Crikey*, 15 August 2011, www.crikey.com.au/2011/08/15/what-game-theory-says-about-labors-woes/.

to rationalise its own excesses. Avoiding 'false balance' does not prevent that from happening. What is required are institutional arrangements that actively prevent slides into authoritarianism from occurring.

These include methods of genuinely separating powers, of giving elected parliaments supremacy over Executives (presidents, prime ministers, and ministers of state),[60] of ensuring continued democratic input into decisions, of limiting donations to election campaigns, of tight auditing and guaranteeing those in positions of power do not financially benefit from any decisions they make, and of placing irrevocable limits on the terms of people in positions of power in an Executive—terms that should be quite short. One- or two-year terms for any Executive would meet these requirements, but would leave much power in the hands of the bureaucratic experts reporting to the Executive. Tim Dunlop's radical solution—sortition (randomly selecting citizens to serve on a rotating Executive for short terms)—needs consideration.[61] Short of that, however, parliamentary systems that have genuinely open elections and have vigorous constraints on the potential for representatives to lose their idealism and be 'bought' by well-resourced interests, as per the intent of the above ideas, are essential. Restrictions on the number of terms served should apply to members of parliament, though terms themselves (i.e. the periods between elections) also need to be fairly short—contrary to the frequently expressed wishes of politicians and bureaucrats themselves, who see long terms and sparse elections as necessary to ensure 'serious' policy can be made, to be swamped or otherwise forgotten at the next election.[62] Neo-liberal and progressive politicians both pine for longer terms to enable their reform vision to be implemented, each ignoring the capacity of the other side to do so and the diminution of democracy that follows.

60 A large study showed that presidential regimes are associated with less favourable economic outcomes, including worse inequality, than parliamentary regimes—likely reflecting the different ways parliamentary and presidential systems shape how competing interests are reflected in institutions. Richard McManus and Gulcin Ozkan, 'Who Does Better for the Economy? Presidents versus Parliamentary Democracies'. *Public Choice* 176, no. 6 (2018): 361–87.

61 Tim Dunlop, *The Future of Everything: Big Audacious Ideas for a Better World* (Sydney: New South Books, 2018).

62 Michelle Grattan, 'Shorten and Turnbull to Talk on Four-Year Terms'. *The Conversation*, 23 July 2017, theconversation.com/shorten-and-turnbull-to-talk-on-four-year-terms-81454.

Technology for the public good

Often the people who are in the best position to regulate specific technologies are the people directly affected. So consultation rights on the introduction of technology at work are important, as is establishing, reinstating or strengthening employees' ability to genuinely negotiate. This would force employers to consider the social implications of their actions. But it would not kill progress. Most employees are cluey enough to know that it is not a good idea to make their own organisation uncompetitive. In German manufacturing, where employees have an institutionalised say in the introduction of technological change through works councils, it appears that 'exposure' to robots is associated with an increased probability that an employee will keep their job.[63] And the better are opportunities for retraining and redeployment, including through public agencies, the greater will be employee acceptance of new technology.

In addition, protections for employees, and for citizens, against surveillance need strength and codification. While in general there are advantages to the state being neutral on the choice of technology for productivity advances, the state has a major role in ensuring that technologies do not have adverse consequences for people. Government innovation policy can have a large impact, especially in smaller economies.[64] We should not pretend that the state has no role in enabling productivity-enhancing technology: you might still be communicating through a phone tethered to a wall with copper wire if it were not for state-funded advances in technology.[65]

While we need to control technological futures, some commonly discussed policies may do more harm than good. This especially applies to generic solutions that assign to technology, such as the 'robot tax' some talk about, which might be used to fund adjustment packages or

63 Wolfgang Dauth et al., 'The Rise of Robots in the German Labour Market'. *Vox*, 19 September 2017.

64 Roy Green and Göran Roos, *Australia's Manufacturing Future* (Canberra: Discussion paper prepared for the Prime Minister's Manufacturing Taskforce, 2012).

65 Mariana Mazzucato, 'Taxpayers Helped Apple, but Apple Won't Help Them'. *Harvard Business Review*, 8 March 2013, hbr.org/2013/03/taxpayers-helped-apple-but-app; Rutger Bregman, 'Look at the Phone in Your Hand—You Can Thank the State for That'. *Guardian*, 12 July 2017, www.theguardian.com/commentisfree/2017/jul/12/phone-state-private-sector-products-investment-innovation.

other policies aimed at ameliorating the effects of technological change.[66] A robot tax would simply increase the labour intensity of production at the margins and lower productivity growth. It would not fundamentally affect who benefited from or who controlled technology. It is possibly the worst proposed response.

That does not mean funds need not be raised. But value attributed to robots is no more valid a source of state revenue than value from other sources. It is indeed very important to put resources, and lots of them, into reskilling and retraining workers. There will be large numbers of workers who will be made redundant from existing industries, and experience tells us they will find it hard to get a new job—this is especially the case for older workers, who often face discrimination in seeking reemployment. Since much of technical education and training in Australia has been essentially privatised, with sometimes disastrous consequences, effectively regearing for reskilling this would actually require quite a lot of effort from government there. Australia in particular has not done it properly in the past, and recommendations in the 1990s to develop or implement even a code of practice on labour adjustment were not seriously pursued.[67]

There is a strong geographic dimension to this. Whole regions will be affected by the loss of jobs while the new jobs will often be elsewhere. Substantial resources need to go to these regions to stop people there from being those who pay for others' rising living standards. This will be a huge task for regions that are not part of major urban centres. It adds a regional aspect to any state innovation policy.

Rethinking revenue

If general revenue does not provide enough resources, then there are other options—better than a robot tax—that, instead of penalising new technology, could be used to redistribute income. Some have been canvassed in contemporary political debate, such as (in Australia) ending

66 Malcolm James, 'Could Bill Gates' Plan to Tax Robots Really Lead to a Brighter Future for All?'. *The Conversation*, 10 March 2017, theconversation.com/could-bill-gates-plan-to-tax-robots-really-lead-to-a-brighter-future-for-all-73395.

67 John Buchanan et al., *Facing Retrenchments: Strategies and Alternatives for Enterprises* (Canberra: Department of Education, Employment and Training, 1992). In the context of Accord VII some work in this regard was commenced by the Office of Labour Market Adjustment and the Department of Industrial Relations, but it was set aside during political controversy surrounding unrelated legislation on unfair dismissals.

'negative gearing',[68] removing the discount for capital gains tax[69] or even amending marginal tax rates.[70] In almost all countries, the top marginal tax rates (i.e. the tax paid on additional income by the highest income earners) were higher in earlier decades than they are now.[71] Low marginal tax rates for top executives not only widen inequality in their own right, they also increase the returns to rent-seekers who cut pay and conditions. Other ideas receive less discussion, such as inheritance taxes. These currently operate in 16 OECD countries[72] and once existed throughout Australia until Queensland Premier Joh Bjelke-Petersen abolished them; he was quickly followed by the other states, fearful of people moving to Queensland to die, and, inexplicably, by the Commonwealth. Yet one estimate is that, over the quarter century to 2050, $30 trillion will be passed on as inheritances in the USA. Small wonder that advisers to wealth managers, if not governments, recognise that 'the scale of [this] transfer … raises the stakes significantly'.[73]

Other options include reviving taxation of net wealth (inheritance taxes are a subset of this), which in the early 1990s was being taxed in a dozen OECD countries, but now only in three.[74] Wealth is not presently taxed in Australia (despite positive opinion-poll results, when it has been tested)[75] or the USA (where it is currently popular and political candidates have started to support it).[76] Taxing *net total* wealth is more efficient and equitable, and potentially raises much more revenue, than taxing *gross*

68 Enabling owners of rental properties to obtain deductions against tax on other income for interest costs on borrowings associated with the rental properties.

69 Allowing part of a capital gain in buying then selling a property to be ignored for taxation purposes.

70 Louis Jacobson, 'Explaining Alexandria Ocasio-Cortez's 70 Percent Marginal Tax Rate Idea'. *Politifact*, 8 January 2019, www.politifact.com/truth-o-meter/article/2019/jan/08/explaining-alexandria-ocasio-cortezs-70-percent-ta/.

71 For example, Paul Krugman, 'The Twinkie Manifesto'. *New York Times*, 19 November 2012, www.nytimes.com/2012/11/19/opinion/krugman-the-twinkie-manifesto.html.

72 Organisation for Economic Co-operation and Development, 'Revenue Statistics: Comparative tables', *OECD Tax Statistics* (database) (Paris: OECD, 2019), doi.org/10.1787/data-00262-en.

73 Alex Pigliucci, Kendra Thompson, and Mark Halverson, *The 'Greater' Wealth Transfer: Capitalizing on the Intergenerational Shift in Wealth*. Wealth and Asset Management Services, Point of View (Arlington, VA: Accenture, 2015), 1.

74 Martin Sandbu, 'The Curious Case of the Missing Wealth Taxes'. *Financial Times*, 6 February 2019, www.businesstelegraph.co.uk/the-curious-case-of-the-missing-wealth-taxes/.

75 In 1984 a wealth tax had been more popular in Australian opinion polling than the capital gains tax that subsequently was introduced. *Bulletin*, 4 December 1984, 25.

76 Matthew Yglesias, 'Taxing the Rich Is Extremely Popular'. *Vox*, 4 February 2019, www.vox.com/2019/2/4/18210370/warren-wealth-tax-poll.

land wealth, which persists in many countries.[77] While there are issues of evasion of total wealth taxes, natural experimental data suggest ways to minimise this.[78] Another option, if enough countries can cooperate, is a 'Tobin tax' on financial transactions, which would raise potentially significant revenue and/or reduce volatility in financial markets.[79]

There are certainly valid arguments for a more generously redistributive tax-transfer system. Thomas Piketty is likely correct in arguing that the great increase in inequality from the late twentieth century, in particular through the increased share going to the very wealthy at the expense of the rest of society, originated with the reduction in top marginal tax rates.[80] Globally, there is widespread agreement (except by those who benefit from the status quo) of the need to take concerted collective action to seriously attack enrichment of the wealthy through tax havens.[81] Credible threats, let alone actions, in this area have a genuine impact on revenue.[82] The 'Overton window'—the range of feasible policy options evident at a particular time—has been shifting back towards such policies for some time, with recent evidence suggesting wide support for such measures.[83]

Expenditure for the common wealth

The money that could be raised by such mechanisms is more than would be needed for labour retraining, but more is needed for other reasons. Branko Milanovic rightly argues for widespread, accessible quality

77 In Australia, these exist as local government 'rates'. Sandbu, 'Curious Case'; Martin Sandbu, 'The Wonderful World of Net Wealth Taxes (Where They Still Exist)'. *Financial Times*, 8 February 2019, www.ft.com/content/c8437204-2adb-11e9-a5ab-ff8ef2b976c7?sharetype=blocked.

78 Juliana Londoño-Vélez and Javier Avila, *Can Wealth Taxation Work in Developing Countries? Quasi-Experimental Evidence from Colombia*. Job Market Paper (Berkeley, CA: UC, 2018), www.google.com/url?q=https%3A%2F%2Fwww.dropbox.com%2Fs%2Fl8vdob4g2z9riti%2FWealthTaxation_LondonoVelez_JMP.pdf%3Fraw%3D1&sa=D&sntz=1&usg=AFQjCNHL46BAhxGyH76yyo_w3vRoagcJ-A.

79 James Tobin, 'A Proposal for International Monetary Reform'. *Eastern Economic Journal* 4, no. 3–4 (1978): 153–59. This is referred to in some circles as the 'Robin Hood' tax.

80 Thomas Piketty, *Capital in the Twenty-First Century* (Cambridge, MA: Harvard University Press, 2014).

81 Facundo Alvaredo et al., *World Inequality Report 2018* (World Inequality Lab/WID.world, 2018); Thomas Piketty, 'Panama Papers: Act Now. Don't Wait for Another Crisis'. *Guardian*, 10 April 2016; David Mistead, 'The Double-Edged Sword of Corporate Tax Avoidance'. *Globe and Mail*, 8 April 2016, www.theglobeandmail.com/globe-investor/investment-ideas/panama-papers-scandal-highlights-corporate-tax-avoidance/article29576260/.

82 Londoño-Vélez and Avila, *Can Wealth Taxation Work*.

83 Yglesias, 'Taxing the Rich'.

education, as it makes high-skilled labour more plentiful and reduces income gaps between skilled and unskilled labour. He contrasts it to the current opposite trend of ever-stronger private education.[84]

Many argue for a universal basic income (UBI),[85] which would provide a living income to everyone in society, regardless of whether or not they were working or even looking for work. There is a lot to be said for this policy, and some jurisdictions have experimented with various limited versions of it. Official evaluation of the Finnish UBI experiment indicates that it does not have adverse effects on employment or employment incentives, but it does improve health and wellbeing outcomes.[86] However, to be effective as a basic income, it could be very expensive.[87] If set at a level that was high enough to provide a good level of income, it would require a level of taxes that was, on average, above what most taxpayers (or at least, most politicians) are presently willing to accept, and if set at a level that was 'affordable' it would likely be either too low to provide a decent income or simply substitute for existing welfare programs. The bigger problem, though, is that in itself this does not deal with the inequality problem or the structural adjustment problem that are at the heart of ensuring the benefits of new technology do not lead to net job destruction. A UBI alone would not stop the remarkable growth in incomes at the very top of society that led to Citigroup economists claiming that the spending behaviour of the rich 'overwhelms that of the "average" consumer',[88] nor the underinvestment in structural adjustment, which between them would stop an adequate level of new job-creation from occurring. In other words, an adequate response to the employment and distributional problems arising from future technologies requires means of redistributing income and wealth away from the richest, which requires consideration of the taxation side of the ledger. A UBI may

84 Branko Milanovic, 'Inequality in the Age of Globalization'. Paper presented at ECFIN's Annual Research Conference, Fostering Inclusive Growth: Inequality and Fairness in Integrated Markets, Lecture in Honor of Anthony A. Atkinson, Brussels, 20 November 2017; Branko Milanovic, *Global Inequality: A New Approach for the Age of Globalization* (Cambridge, MA: Harvard University Press, 2016).

85 Philippe Van Parijs and Yannick Vanderborght, *Basic Income: A Radical Proposal for a Free Society and a Sane Economy* (Cambridge, MA: Harvard University Press, 2017).

86 Olli Kangas et al., *The Basic Income Experiment 2017–2018 in Finland. Preliminary Results.* Reports and Memorandums of the Ministry of Social Affairs and Health 2019:9 (Helsinki: Ministry of Social Affairs and Health, 8 February 2019), urn.fi/URN:ISBN:978-952-00-4035-2.

87 Gerhard Bosch, 'Can a Universal Basic Income Resolve Future Income Security Challenges?' Paper presented at Regulating Decent Work conference, Geneva, 2017.

88 Ajay Kapur et al., 'The Plutonomy Symposium—Rising Tides Lifting Yachts'. *The Global Investigator (Equity Research Global: Equity Strategy)*, 29 September 2006, 7–19.

well be a good idea, but not because of the robots. As it would not, in itself, solve the problem of workers and low-income earners having too little power, it cannot be seen as the overarching solution to problems of inequality. If designed in certain ways, though, it could redress poverty and the financial and physical ill health brought about by underemployment, precarious employment, unemployment and administratively forced employment.

At the same time, useless or counterproductive expenditures must be stopped. The International Monetary Fund (a major neo-liberal institution) estimated energy subsidies at an enormous 6.5 per cent of global GDP in 2015.[89] That said, the bulk of these subsidies come not from financial transfers, or from tax concessions (though both these are significant) but from failing to properly charge for the environmental damage (air pollution and global warming, but also congestion and accidents) that is caused by the activities.[90] In places like Australia, these subsidies represent several times expenditure on matters like early childhood education and care.[91] As the IMF points out, this 'crowd[s] out … potentially productive public spending (for example, on health, education, and infrastructure)' creating 'a drag on economic growth' and 'premature deaths' while 'most of the benefits from energy subsidies are typically captured by rich households'.[92]

Organisational misbehaviour

Alongside rethinking the regulatory arrangements for technology, we should seriously reconsider the legal privileges afforded the owners and beneficiaries of capital through use of the corporate veil. In particular, crimes committed by corporations typically lead only to fines, despite high rates of recidivism among corporate criminals.[93] Unless engaged in fraud,[94] hardly any CEOs or directors ever go to jail or face other personal punishment for misdeeds conducted under their direct or implied

89 David Coady et al., *How Large Are Global Energy Subsidies?* IMF Working Paper WP/15/105 (Washington, DC: International Monetary Fund, 2015).

90 Ibid.

91 Frances Flanagan, 'Climate Change and the New Work Order'. *Inside Story*, 28 February 2019, insidestory.org.au/climate-change-and-the-new-work-order/.

92 Coady et al., *Energy Subsidies*, 4.

93 Joel Bakan, *The Corporation: The Pathological Pursuit of Profit and Power* (London: Constable & Robertson, 2004).

94 An exception, in a small number of jurisdictions, is where directors can be held personally responsible for egregious corporate breaches of occupational health and safety laws.

instruction, in part because of reluctance by corporate regulators,[95] while whistleblowers are harassed into submission.[96] This in turn skews financial incentives, as the disincentives to breaking the law are minimised while the incentives in place favour self-aggrandisement by CEOs and directors.[97] Lawbreaking enables 'accumulation by dispossession'[98] and this in turn increases pressure on other corporate executives to compete by cutting labour conditions faster and further and to set aside any concerns about sustainability. Australian sociologist Andrew Hopkins has suggested that we 'hold top executives and even directors personally and criminally liable when companies fail to take proper account of the interests of consumers, customers, and employees'.[99] Although made in the context of widespread misbehaviour by local banks in the period *after* the global financial crisis, this proposal has broader applicability. Rethinking punishments for corporate misbehaviour is part of a broader project of rethinking the privileges that are given to the corporation.[100] This also frequently requires rethinking the institutional arrangements for regulating corporate behaviour. Boosting the powers of ineffectual institutions may not make any difference if their ineffectiveness is due to industry capture; better (as with some labour compliance institutions) to start again.[101]

State inhibitions on market concentration have faltered since the great antitrust legislation of the USA in the early twentieth century, and these must be revived if citizen power is to have any chance or if worker-cooperatives (as an alternative to capitalist work organisation) are to have any prospects. When Frank Pasquale said, 'Imagine, say, the merger of

95 Jesse Eisinger, *The Chickenshit Club: Why the Justice Department Fails to Prosecute Executives* (New York: Simon & Schuster, 2017); Bernard Keane, 'The Need for a Strong Financial System Justifies ASIC's "Softly Softly" Approach'. *Crikey*, 31 May 2018, www.crikey.com.au/2018/05/31/need-for-strong-financial-system-asics-justification-for-softly-softly/.

96 For example, Adele Ferguson, 'ATO Whistleblower Faces Six Life Sentences, Roughly the Same as Ivan Milat'. *Sydney Morning Herald*, 27 February 2019, www.smh.com.au/business/small-business/ato-whistleblower-faces-six-life-sentences-roughly-the-same-as-ivan-milat-20190226-p510d2.html.

97 David Peetz, 'An Institutional Analysis of the Growth of Executive Remuneration'. *Journal of Industrial Relations* 57, no. 5 (2015): 707–25.

98 David Harvey, 'The "New" Imperialism: Accumulation by Dispossession', *Socialist Register* 40 (2004): 63–87; David Harvey, *The New Imperialism* (Oxford: Oxford University Press, 2003).

99 Andrew Hopkins, 'What Banking Regulators Can Learn from Deepwater Horizon and Other Industrial Catastrophes'. *The Conversation*, 31 January 2019, theconversation.com/what-banking-regulators-can-learn-from-deepwater-horizon-and-other-industrial-catastrophes-108989.

100 Bakan, *Corporation*.

101 Vogel uses the concept of 'deregulatory capture' to describe the success of the finance industry in achieving deregulation. Steven K. Vogel, 'Rethinking Stigler's Theory of Regulation: Regulatory Capture or Deregulatory Capture?'. *Pro-Market* 2018, promarket.org/rethinking-stiglers-theory-regulation-regulatory-capture-deregulatory-capture/.

Microsoft, Apple, Google, and Amazon into one huge company (MAGA), ready to convert the last remnants of the sharing economy into a "taking economy." Such a firm could exercise enormous power: with unprecedented access to consumers, it would be a must-have marketplace, and could use this powerful position to drive very hard bargains with companies',[102] he was inadvertently talking about the world envisaged in *The Circle*. But he was also alluding to the huge advantages monopoly capital *already* possesses in the country that produced Trumpism and celebrated its slogans. There can be a symbiotic relationship between concentrating political and economic power. Powerful governments grant concessions to large corporations that increase the latter's power and they, in turn, provide donations and political support to entrench the position of their allies in government, or even jobs for them after they leave government.[103] In the end, even a seemingly democratically elected government may do nothing to constrain monopoly power, regardless of whether part of it wishes to. This was very much the world of *The Circle*. The potential for gaining profit through the exercise of monopoly power should not be underestimated. The mass of value obtained from all activities is more important to a corporation than the rate at which it is extracted from one worker.[104]

We also need to develop responses to the great freedoms that have been given to financial capital over the past three-plus decades in most industrialised countries. They have clearly helped shift the balance of power in the economy, and the global financial crisis demonstrated that they have not produced net benefits for society. It may seem slightly removed to be talking about regulating the financial sector in response to issues about the future of work; but the key issues about the future of work more concern inequality and power than simply displacement by technology (the latter being a function of inequality and power). Addressing the role of finance is central to addressing inequalities of power. Clearly, more ambitious changes are needed than the piecemeal

102 Frank Pasquale, 'Will Amazon Take over the World?'. *Boston Review*, 20 July 2017, bostonreview.net/class-inequality/frank-pasquale-will-amazon-take-over-world.

103 In Australia, a good source for tracking such events is www.michaelwest.com.au. See also Allan Holmes et al., *Did Billionaires Pay Off Republicans for Passing the Trump Tax Bill?* (Washington DC: Centre for Public Integrity, 7 February 2019), publicintegrity.org/business/taxes/trumps-tax-cuts/did-billionaires-pay-off-republicans-for-passing-the-trump-tax-bill/; Cameron Murray and Paul Frijters, *Game of Mates: How Favours Bleed the Nation* (Publicious, 2017).

104 Karl Marx, *Capital, Volume 1* (London: The Electric Book Company, 1887; repr., 1998), Chapter XI.

reforms that have been considered to date. For example, financial markets themselves were extremely pleased with the relatively small impact on profits likely to arise from the recommendations of a Royal Commission into misconduct in the sector in Australia, despite numerous revelations of extraordinary corporate misbehaviour.[105]

Laws for the workplace

In the workplace, it is easy to get distracted by technological determinism or by talk of the rise of the 'gig economy' or the disappearance of work. But work will continue, people will be employed (to the extent that education and resources are deployed to cope with restructuring) and the employment relationship will persist. So, too, if we do not address it, will the power imbalance in workplaces between labour and capital and the consequences that has for work.[106] The danger technology poses to workers through increased algorithmic management and 'not there' employment is arguably greater than the danger of technological job loss.[107] Much of that must be addressed by broader social and economic policies, as mentioned, but some relates to the specific workplace factors that influence workers' power.

There are changes in several countries needed to the legal and institutional framework for bargaining that affect workers' ability to gain from higher productivity. In Australia, such changes are probably needed more than in most other countries, given the extent of imbalance in the framework in the 2010s; these include enabling multiemployer bargaining, reforming procedures for terminating agreements and industrial action, and indeed reforming the concept of the right to take collective action.[108] Australia clearly needs a new approach to the enforcement of minimum standards, as discussed in Chapter 10. In all countries, core capital—be it in the

105 *Crikey* reported that, in early trading after the release of the Commission's report, the value of NAB shares rose 3.5 per cent, while 'Commonwealth Bank shares rose 4% … and ANZ's 5%. Westpac rose nearly 6%, AMP surged 8% and IOOF 10%.' Glenn Dyer and Bernard Keane, 'Investors Give Banks a Tick in Wake of Royal Commission'. *Crikey*, 5 February 2019.

106 Referred to by Paul Thompson as not the 'bullshit jobs' but 'the bullshit in the jobs (the insecure contracts, the excessive work demands)'. Paul Thompson, 'If There Are So Many "Bullshit Jobs", Should Labour Fight for the Future of Work?'. *Labourlist*, 22 February 2019, labourlist.org/2019/02/if-there-are-so-many-bullshit-jobs-should-labour-fight-for-the-future-of-work/.

107 Brishen Rogers, *Beyond Automation: The Law & Political Economy of Workplace Technological Change* (SSRN, 4 February 2019), ssrn.com/abstract=3327608 or dx.doi.org/10.2139/ssrn.3327608.

108 Tess Hardy, Jim Stanford, and Andrew Stewart, eds, *The Wages Crisis in Australia: What It Is and What to Do About It* (Adelaide: University of Adelaide Press, 2018).

form of franchisors, large brand names or head contractors—needs to be held accountable for underpayment of labour or other law-breaking within the chain. Neither employment law nor competition law should obstruct labour from bargaining with entities other than the direct employer, since 'not there' employment is often used not just to reduce pay and conditions but as a ruse to prevent adequate bargaining. Indeed, competition law should aim to promote the wellbeing of society, and not be a barrier that prevents civil society, including unions, from seeking to improve that wellbeing through putting pressure on the market.

Better regulation of the framework of work is also important for redressing gender imbalances. The more freedom that capital and individual managers have to allocate risk and rewards as they see fit, the more that women, migrants, people of colour and other groups are disadvantaged. Regulation, if designed well, and proximity to it can especially benefit those groups. The gains for many women, for example, in antidiscrimination law over the past three decades (and gains arising from more progressive attitudes towards women's roles) have been largely offset by greater regulation distance through neo-liberalism and weakened collective power, as well as by the greater leniency of permitted *behaviours* in some countries through the rise of neo-totalitarian forces.[109]

Self-organisation

The above changes may alter the degree of inequality and the imbalance of power, but in the end unions and other civil-society organisations must, as discussed in Chapter 7, create within themselves strong organisational capacity. More than anything else, the events that followed the global financial crisis (or Great Recession) of 2008 demonstrated the failure of civil society—in particular, unions, women's groups and other bodies representing workers, children, the environment and the poor—to develop and articulate an alternative policy vision to challenge the failed market-liberal paradigm. This failure raises doubt about the plausibility of the first alternative future mentioned above—a more egalitarian one that matches the very first *Sliding Doors* scenario laid out in Chapter 1.

109 David Peetz and Georgina Murray, 'The Persistence of Gender Gaps'. In *Women, Labor Segmentation and Regulation: Varieties of Gender Gaps*, ed. David Peetz and Georgina Murray (New York: Palgrave Macmillan, 2017), 235–55.

Without a growth of organisational capacity in civil society, including trade unions and nongovernment organisations, workers will lack the power to defend their working conditions or to make fissuring unprofitable, and dissenting voices will lack the power to force change in norms, regulation and the distribution of income and wealth. Dissent is delegitimised in *The Circle*, and when Mae faces critical choices something serious is missing: the collective power of workers to act on informed choices. Yet even in large, nonunionised high-tech firms, workers have shown they will act collectively if sufficiently provoked.[110] Dissent is disorganised and violently suppressed in *Nineteen Eighty-Four*, while in *The Handmaid's Tale* it is violently suppressed but organised and covert. In the very long run, in that last-mentioned book, the malevolent state is overthrown. Unless dissent is organised, however, power ultimately reproduces itself, regardless of the contradictions it creates.

A new citizenship

The issues canvassed in this book are not matters that can be put off. Technological change is going to continue relentlessly. Researchers, in universities and private corporations such as Elon Musk's Neuralink, are working on technology that will enable digital hardware to be implanted within the human body, linking the brain wirelessly with computer networks of the world. It is not a question of *if* this can be done, it is *when*.[111] Already there is talk of a shift to a new form of capitalism—'cognitive capitalism'—based on knowledge as the basic source of value.[112] This would take that process much further. The implications for inequality of opportunity, productivity, income and power could be enormous. Nearly two centuries ago, Percy Shelley wrote of how 'the rich have become richer, and the poor have become poorer'.[113] It is a thought repeated many times—even in a line in a Leonard Cohen song[114]—but one that would barely describe the outcome in the absence of change. If we do not reform

110 Shirin Ghaffary and Eric Johnson, 'After 20,000 Workers Walked out, Google Said It Got the Message. The Workers Disagree'. *Recode*, 21 November 2018, www.recode.net/2018/11/21/18105719/google-walkout-real-change-organizers-protest-discrimination-kara-swisher-recode-decode-podcast.
111 David Peetz and Georgina Murray, 'I, Cyborg: The Life and Work of Digital Humans'. *Griffith Review* 64 (online content) (2019). Watch out for a book on this topic.
112 Yann Moulier Boutang. *Cognitive Capitalism* (Translated by Ed Emery, Cambridge: Polity, 2011).
113 Percy Bysshe Shelley, 'A Defence of Poetry'. In Charles W. Eliot, *English Essays: Sidney to Macaulay*, Vol. XXVII. The Harvard Classics. New York: P.F. Collier & Son, 1909–14; repr. Bartleby.com, 2001, www.bartleby.com/br/02701.html.
114 You can find the idea repeated in Leonard Cohen and Sharon Robinson, *Everybody Knows*, Sony/ATV Music Publishing LLC, 1988.

society's rules now in anticipation of the future, the consequences for the great majority of working people could be devastating, notwithstanding the potentially fantastic improvements that could feasibly be made to many other aspects of people's lives.

With that in mind, our concerns should not be focused on the potential evil that technology might bring and the jobs it might destroy or fundamentally change in the future. Our concern should rather be about what uses can be made of technology in the absence of changes to the distribution of wealth and power, and what needs to be done to ensure that the benefits are not restricted to a few, potentially making the lives of many people worse than they presently are, but are instead accessible to all.

Organisations think of 'organisational citizenship' as depicting 'good' behaviour by employees towards the organisation—doing things not in their job description that make life easier for their fellow workers, their managers or their customers, and that in the end help boost profits. But citizens also have rights, not just responsibilities. We need to think and talk about treating people as *citizens at work*, people with a right to respect, rest, job security, income security and a voice. It means people have a right to decent work. And it can be done, if we make the right choices. As leading Canadian jurist Harry Arthurs said, it is not a question of going back to twentieth-century labour law, as the problems for workers stem from wider forces that 'also adversely affect all citizens in their non-working lives as consumers, borrowers, tenants, and recipients of social goods'.[115] The project is one of restoring the primacy of democratic values and processes over markets and capital. It can be done, but time is not on our side.

115 Harry Arthurs, 'Rethinking Citizenship at Work: Where Do We Go from Here?' Paper presented at New Frontiers for Citizenship at Work conference, Montreal, 2014.

Bibliography

This list excludes newspaper and equivalent articles cited in the text.

Ackroyd, Stephen and Paul Thompson. *Organizational Misbehaviour*. London: Sage, 1999.

ACTRAV Bureau for Workers' Activities. *Just Transition towards Environmentally Sustainable Economies and Societies for All*. Geneva: International Labour Organization, ILO ACTRAV Policy Brief, 2018.

Addo, Michael K. 'Symposium: Human Rights Perspectives of Corporate Groups'. *Connecticut Law Review* 37 (2005): 667–89.

Albarrán, Daniel Gallardo. *A Composite Perspective on British Living Standards during the Industrial Revolution*. Groningen, NL: Groningen Growth and Development Centre, University of Groningen, 2016.

Alcorso, Caroline. *The Effects of Enterprise Bargaining on Employees from NESB*. Report to DIR for 1995 Enterprise Bargaining Report. Canberra: Department of Industrial Relations, 1996.

Alcorso, Caroline and Graham Harrison. *Blue Collar and Beyond: The Experiences of Non-English Speaking Background Women in the Australian Labour Force*. Canberra: Commonwealth State Council on Non-English Speaking Background Women's Issues, Office of Women's Affairs/AGPS, 1993.

Alinsky, Saul D. *Reveille for Radicals*. Chicago: University of Chicago Press, 1946.

——. *Rules for Radicals*. New York: Random House, 1971.

Alkhatib, Ali, Michael S. Bernstein, and Margaret Levi. 'Examining Crowd Work and Gig Work through the Historical Lens of Piecework'. In *CHI'17—Proceedings of the 2017 CHI Conference on Human Factors in Computing Systems*, 4599–616. Denver, CO: Association for Computing Machinery, 2017. doi.org/10.1145/3025453.3025974

Allan, Cameron, Michael O'Donnell, and David Peetz. 'More Tasks, Less Secure, Working Harder: Three Dimensions of Labour Utilisation'. *Journal of Industrial Relations* 41, no. 4 (December 1999): 519–35. doi.org/10.1177/002218569904100403

Allen, Mike. 'How Tech Fuels Authoritarians'. Axios, www.axios.com/big-tech-surveillance-authoritarianism-china-artificial-intelligence-2b91dedb-93a0-460c-a236-4a3bb7cf9c99.html

Alvaredo, Facundo, Lucas Chancel, Thomas Piketty, Emmanuel Saez, and Gabriel Zucman. *World Inequality Report 2018*. World Inequality Lab/WID.world, 2018.

Amadeo, Kimberley. 'Medical Bankruptcy and the Economy'. The Balance (financial advisers), www.thebalance.com/medical-bankruptcy-statistics-4154729

Amnesty International. *28 Years Later, Women in Bhopal Still Waiting for Justice*. New York, 2012.

Anderson, Kevin B. 'Marx's Intertwining of Race and Class during the Civil War in the U.S.'. *Journal of Classical Sociology* 17, no. 1 (2017): 24–36. doi.org/10.1177/1468795X17691387

Angle, Harold L. and James L. Perry. 'Dual Commitment and Labor–Management Relationship Climates'. *Academy of Management Journal* 29, no. 1 (March 1986): 31–50.

Angwin, Julia and Surya Mattu. 'Amazon Says It Puts Customers First. But Its Pricing Algorithm Doesn't'. *ProPublica*, 20 September 2016.

Anner, Mark. 'Corporate Social Responsibility and Freedom of Association Rights: The Precarious Quest for Legitimacy and Control in Global Supply Chains'. *Politics and Society* 40, no. 4 (2012): 609–44. doi.org/10.1177/0032329212460983

Appelbaum, Eileen, Jody Hoffer Gittell, and Carrie Leana. 'High-Performance Work Practices and Sustainable Economic Growth'. Memo to Obama Administration, Brandeis University, 2011.

Applebaum, Anne. 'A Warning from Europe: The Worst Is yet to Come'. *The Atlantic*, October 2018.

Archer, R. 'Organising: An International Perspective'. In *Unions 2001*, edited by Evatt Foundation. Sydney, 1995.

Arendt, Hannah. *Eichmann in Jerusalem: A Report on the Banality of Evil*. New York: Viking, 1963.

Argy, Fred. 'Beware of Economic Fundamentalism (or What Makes a Good Policy Adviser?)'. *Australian Review of Public Affairs Digest* (31 March 2003), www.australianreview.net/digest/2003/03/argy.html

Arndt, Derek S., Molly O. Baringer, and Michael R. Johnson. 'State of the Climate in 2009'. *Bulletin of the American Meteorological Society* 91, no. 7 (2010): S1–S224. doi.org/10.1175/BAMS-91-7-StateoftheClimate

Arnold, A.J. *'Ex Luce Lucellum'? Innovation, Class Interests and Economic Returns in the Nineteenth Century Match Trade*. Exeter: Paper no. 04/06, University of Exeter, 2004.

Arnold, Thomas and Matthais Scheutz. 'The "Big Red Button" Is Too Late: An Alternative Model for the Ethical Evaluation of AI Systems'. *Ethics and Information Technology* 20, no. 1 (2018): 59–69. doi.org/10.1007/s10676-018-9447-7

Arntz, Melanie, Terry Gregory, and Ulrich Zierahn. *The Risk of Automation for Jobs in OECD Countries: A Comparative Analysis*. OECD Social, Employment and Migration Working Paper No. 189. Paris: Organisation for Economic Co-operation and Development, 2016.

Arthurs, Harry. 'Rethinking Citizenship at Work: Where Do We Go from Here?'. In *New Frontiers for Citizenship at Work*. Montréal, 2014.

Asimov, Isaac. *I, Robot*. New York: Gnome Press, 1950.

Asset Owners Disclosure Project. *Active Ownership*. Sydney: AODP, 2017.

——. *AODP Global Climate 500 Asset Owners Index 2017*. Sydney: AODP, 2017.

Association of Professional Engineers, Scientists and Managers Australia. *Women in the Professions Survey Report 2007*. Melbourne: APESMA, 2007.

Atkinson, Anthony B. and Andrew Leigh. 'The Distribution of Top Incomes in Australia'. *Economic Record* 83, no. 262 (2007): 247–61. doi.org/10.1111/j.1475-4932.2007.00412.x

Atkinson, John. *Flexibility, Uncertainty and Manpower Management*. IMS Report No. 89. Brighton, UK: Institute for Manpower Studies, 1985.

——. 'Manpower Strategies for Flexible Organisations'. *Personnel Management* (August 1984): 28–31.

Atwood, Margaret. *Curious Pursuits*. London: Hachette Digital, Little Brown Book Group, 2009.

——. *The Handmaid's Tale*. London: Vintage, 1986.

Australian Bureau of Statistics. 'Characteristics of Employment'. Canberra: AGPS, 6333.0.

——. 'Employee Earnings, Benefits and Trade Union Membership, Australia'. Canberra, 6310.0.

——. 'Employment Arrangements and Superannuation'. Canberra, 6361.0.

——. 'Labour Account Australia, Quarterly Experimental Estimates, September 2017'. Canberra, 6150.0.55.003.

——. 'Labour Force, Australia'. Canberra, 6202.0.

——. 'Recorded Crime—Offenders, Australia, 2014–15'. Canberra, 4519.0.

——. 'Recorded Crime—Victims, Australia, 2014'. Canberra, 4510.0.

——. 'Trade Union Members'. Canberra: AGPS, 6325.0.

——. 'Working Time Arrangements, Australia, November 2012'. Canberra, 6342.0.

Australian Council of Trade Unions (ACTU). *Unions@Work*. Melbourne: ACTU, 1998.

Australian Government. 'Unfair Contracts and Sham Contracts'. Department of Innovation, Industry and Science, www.business.gov.au/people/contractors/independent-contractors/unfair-contracts-and-sham-contracts

Autor, David, David Dorn, Lawrence F. Katz, Christina Patterson, and John Van Reenen. 'Concentrating on the Fall of the Labor Share'. *American Economic Review* 107, no. 5 (2017): 180–85. doi.org/10.1257/aer.p20171102

Babcock, Linda and Sara Laschever. *Women Don't Ask: Negotiation and the Gender Divide*. Princeton, NJ: Princeton University Press, 2003.

Bachrach, Peter and Morton S. Baratz. 'Two Faces of Power'. *American Political Science Review* 56, no. 4947–952 (1962): 947–52.

Bachrach, Peter and Morton S. Baratz. *Power and Poverty: Theory and Practice*. New York: Oxford University Press, 1970.

Bailey, Janis and David Peetz. 'Dancing Alone: The Australian Union Movement over Three Decades'. *Journal of Industrial Relations* 54, no. 4 (2012): 525–41. doi.org/10.1177/0022185612449133

Bailey, Janis, Robin Price, Lin Esders, and Paula McDonald. 'Daggy Shirts, Daggy Slogans? Marketing Unions to Young People'. *Journal of Industrial Relations* 52, no. 1 (2010): 43–60. doi.org/10.1177/0022185609353984

Baird, Marian, Rae Cooper, Elizabeth Hill, Elspeth Probyn, and Ariadne Vromen. *Women and the Future of Work*. Sydney: Australian Women's Working Futures project, University of Sydney Business School, 2018.

Bakan, Joel. *The Corporation: The Pathological Pursuit of Profit and Power*. London: Constable & Robertson, 2004.

Ball, Jeffrey. 'Who Will Pay for Climate Change?' *New Republic*, 3 November 2015.

Banarra Consulting. *2010 Labour Practices in Sustainability Reporting—A Review*. Sydney: Report for the Construction, Forestry, Mining and Energy Union, Mining and Energy Division, 2010.

Bandura, Albert. 'Exercise of Personal and Collective Efficacy in Changing Societies'. In *Self-Efficacy in Changing Societies*, edited by Albert Bandura, 1–45. Cambridge: Cambridge University Press, 1995. doi.org/10.1017/CBO9780511527692.003

——. *Self-Efficacy: The Exercise of Control*. New York: W.H. Freeman & Company, 1997.

Barker, James R. 'Tightening the Iron Cage: Concertive Control in Self-Managing Teams'. *Administrative Science Quarterly* 38, no. 3 (September 1993): 408–37. doi.org/10.2307/2393374

Barnes, Adrian. 'Do They Have to Buy from Burma? A Pre-Emption Analysis of Local Anti-Sweatshop Procurement Laws'. *Columbia Law Review* 107 (2007): 426–56.

Barnes, Katherine and Peter Spearritt, eds. *Drivers of Change for the Australian Labour Market to 2030*. Canberra: Academy of the Social Sciences in Australia, 2014.

Barrett, Rowena and Al Rainnie. 'What's So Special About Small Firms?'. *Work, Employment & Society* 16, no. 3 (2002): 415. doi.org/10.1177/095001702762217416

Barron, Lisa A. 'Ask and You Shall Receive? Gender Differences in Negotiators' Beliefs and Requests for a Higher Salary'. *Human Relations* 56, no. 6 (June 2003): 635–62. doi.org/10.1177/00187267030566001

Barton, Ruth and Peter Fairbrother. 'The Local Is Now Global: Building a Union Coalition in the International Transport and Logistics Sector'. *Relations Industrielles* 64, no. 4 (2009): 685–703. doi.org/10.7202/038879ar

Beamon, Benita. 'Measuring Supply Chain Performance'. *International Journal of Operations and Production Management* 19 (1999): 275–92. doi.org/10.1108/01443579910249714

Beaumont, Phil and Ian Rennie. 'Organisational Culture and Non-Union Status of Small Businesses'. *Industrial Relations Journal* 17, no. 3 (1986): 214–24. doi.org/10.1111/j.1468-2338.1986.tb00539.x

Beck, Ulrich. *Risk Society: Towards a New Modernity*. London: Sage, 1992.

Beckwith, Karen. 'Numbers and Newness: The Descriptive and Substantive Representation of Women'. *Canadian Journal of Political Science* 44, no. 2 (2007): 27–49. doi.org/10.1017/S0008423907070059

Beckwith, Karen and Kimberly Cowell-Meyers. 'Sheer Numbers: Critical Representation Thresholds and Women's Political Representation'. *Perspectives on Politics* 5, no. 3 (2007): 553–65. doi.org/10.1017/S153759270707154X

Bendix, Reinhard. *Max Weber: An Intellectual Portrait.* New York: Anchor Books, 1962.

Berg, Andrew G. and Jonathan D. Ostry. 'Equality and Efficiency: Is There a Trade-Off between the Two or Do They Go Hand in Hand?'. *Finance and Development* 48, no. 3 (September 2011): 12–15.

Berg, Janine. *Income Security in the on-Demand Economy: Findings and Policy Lessons from a Survey of Crowdworkers*. Geneva: Inclusive Labour Markets, Labour Relations and Working Conditions Branch, International Labour Office, 2016.

Berg, Laurie and Bassina Farbenblum. *Wage Theft in Australia: Findings of the National Temporary Migrant Work Survey*. Sydney: Migrant Worker Justice Initiative, 2017.

Berlinski, Claire. *There Is No Alternative: Why Margaret Thatcher Matters.* New York: Basic Books, 2008.

Bertone, Santina. *Enterprise Bargaining and Employees from a Non-English Speaking Background.* Report to DIR for 1994 Enterprise Bargaining Report. Canberra: Department of Industrial Relations, 1995.

Bertone, Santina and Gerry Griffin. *Immigrant Workers and Their Unions.* Canberra: AGPS, 1992.

Best (Kelsey), Catherine. 'Meet the Matchstick Women—the Hidden Victims of the Industrial Revolution'. *The Conversation*, 8 March 2018.

Bhorat, Haroon, Ravi Kanbur, and Natasha Mayet. 'Estimating the Causal Effect of Enforcement on Minimum Wage Compliance: The Case of South Africa'. *Review of Development Economics* 16, no. 4 (2012): 608–23. doi.org/10.1111/rode.12007

Bieler, Andreas. 'Small Nordic Countries and Globalization: Analysing Norwegian Exceptionalism'. *Competition & Change* 16, no. 3 (2012): 224–42. doi.org/10.1179/1024529412Z.00000000015

Bittman, Michael. 'Sunday Working and Family Time'. *Labour and Industry* 16, no. 1 (2005): 59–81. doi.org/10.1080/10301763.2005.10722031

Bittman, Michael, Judith E. Brown, and Judy Wajcman. 'The Mobile Phone, Perpetual Contact and Time Pressure'. *Work Employment and Society* 23, no. 4 (2009): 673–91. doi.org/10.1177/0950017009344910

Black, Sandra E. and Lisa M. Lynch. 'How to Compete: The Impact of Workplace Practices and Information Technology on Productivity'. *The Review of Economics and Statistics* 83, no. 3 (2001): 434–45. doi.org/10.1162/003465 30152480081

Blackburn, William R. *The Sustainability Handbook: The Complete Management Guide to Achieving Social, Economic and Environmental Responsibility*. Washington DC: Earthscan, 2007.

Blanchflower, David G. 'Changes over Time in Union Relative Wage Effects in Great Britain and the United States'. In *The History and Practice of Economics: Essays in Honor of Bernard Corry and Maurice Preston*, edited by Sami Daniel, Philip Arestis, and John Grahl. Edward Elgar, 1999.

Blau, Francine D., Peter Brummund, and Albert Yung-Hsu Liu. *Trends in Occupational Segregation by Gender 1970–2009: Adjusting for the Impact of Changes in the Occupational Coding System*. IZA Discussion Paper No. 6490. Bonn: Forschungsinstitut zur Zukunft der Arbeit, 2012.

Bloom, Peter and Carl Rhodes. *CEO Society: The Corporate Takeover of Everyday Life*. London: Zed, 2018.

Blowfield, Michael and Jedrzej George Frynas. 'Setting New Agendas: Critical Perspectives on Corporate Social Responsibility in the Developing World'. *International Affairs* 81, no. 3 (2005): 499–513. doi.org/10.1111/j.1468-2346.2005.00465.x

Boden, Margaret, Joanna Bryson, Darwin Caldwell, Kerstin Dautenhahn, Lilian Edwards, Sarah Kember, et al. 'Principles of Robotics: Regulating Robots in the Real World'. *Connection Science* 29, no. 2 (2017): 124–29. doi.org/10.1080/09540091.2016.1271400

Bogg, Alan and Tonia Novitz. 'Links between Individual Employment Law and Collective Labour Law: Their Implications for Migrant Workers'. In *Migrants at Work: Immigration and Vulnerability in Labour Law*, edited by Cathryn Costello and Mark Freedland. Oxford: Oxford Scholarship Online, 2014. doi.org/10.1093/acprof:oso/9780198714101.003.0019

Bolton, Sharon C. and Carol Boyd. 'Trolley Dolly or Skilled Emotion Manager? Moving on from Hochschild's Managed Heart'. *Work, Employment & Society* 17, no. 2 (2003): 289–308. doi.org/10.1177/0950017003017002004

Boreham, Paul, Richard Hall, and William Harley. 'Two Paths to Prosperity? Work Organisation and Industrial Relations'. *Work, Employment and Society* 10 (1996): 449–68.

Bosch, Gerhard. 'Can a Universal Basic Income Resolve Future Income Security Challenges?'. In *Regulating Decent Work*. Geneva: International Labour Organization, 2017.

Bourne, Ryan. 'Tony Blair Is Right—Globalisation Is a Fact Not a Choice'. CATO Institute, www.cato.org/publications/commentary/tony-blair-right-globalisation-fact-not-choice

Bowden, Bradley. 'Three Charts On: The Changing Face of Australian Union Members'. *The Conversation*, 4 July 2017.

Boxall, Peter and Peter Haynes. 'Unions and Non-Union Bargaining Agents under the Employment Contracts Act 1991: An Assessment after 12 Months'. *New Zealand Journal of Industrial Relations* 17, no. 2 (August 1992). doi.org/10.26686/nzjir.v17i2.3325

Braverman, Harry. *Labour and Monopoly Capital: The Degradation of Work in the Twentieth Century*. New York & London: Monthly Review Press, 1974.

Bray, Mark and Craig R. Littler. 'The Labour Process and Industrial Relations: Review of the Literature'. *Labour & Industry* 1, no. 3 (1988): 551–87. doi.org/10.1080/10301763.1988.10669058

Britton, Lauren M. and Bryan Semaan. 'Manifesting the Cyborg Via Techno-Body Modification: From Human–Computer Interaction to Integration'. In *CHI 2017—Proceedings of the 2017 ACM SIGCHI Conference on Human Factors in Computing Systems*, 2499–510. Denver: Association for Computing Machinery, 2017. doi.org/10.1145/3022198.3024939

Brochet, Francois, Maria Loumioti, and George Serafeim. *Short-Termism, Investor Clientele, and Firm Risk*. Harvard Business School Accounting & Management Unit Working Paper No. 12-072. Cambridge, MA: Harvard Business School, 2012.

Bronfenbrenner, Kate, Sheldon Friedman, Richard W. Hurd, and Rudolph A. Oswald, eds. *Organising to Win*. Ithaca NY: ILR Press, 1998.

Brooks, Chris and Kim Moody. 'Labor's New Sources of Leverage'. Labor Notes, www.labornotes.org/MoodyInterview

Brosnan, Peter. 'Labour Markets and Social Deprivation'. *Labour and Industry* 7, no. 2 (1996): 3–34. doi.org/10.1080/10301763.1996.10669159

Brosnan, Peter, David Rea, and Moira Wilson. 'Labour Market Segmentation and the State: The New Zealand Experience'. *Cambridge Journal of Economics* 19, no. 5 (1995): 667–96.

Brown, William, Simon Deakin, Maria Hudson, Cliff Pratten, and Paul Ryan. *The Individualisation of Employment Contracts in Britain*. Employment Relations Research Series No. 4. London: Department of Trade and Industry, 1998.

Brownmiller, Susan. A. *Against Our Will: Men, Women, and Rape*. New York: Simon & Schuster, 1975.

Brundtland, Gro Harlem. *Our Common Future: The World Commission on Environment and Development*. Oxford: Oxford University Press, 1987.

Bryson, Alex and Rafael Gomez. *Why Have Workers Stopped Joining Unions?* London: Centre for Economic Performance, London School of Economics and Political Science, 2003.

Buchanan, John and Ron Callus. 'Efficiency and Equity at Work: The Need for Labour Market Regulation in Australia'. *Journal of Industrial Relations* 35, no. 4 (December 1993): 515–37. doi.org/10.1177/002218569303500401

Buchanan, John, D. Campbell, Ron Callus, and Malcolm Rimmer. *Facing Retrenchments: Strategies and Alternatives for Enterprises*. Canberra: Department of Education, Employment and Training/AGPS, 1992.

Burawoy, Michael. 'Between the Labour Process and the State: Changing Face of Factory Regimes under Capitalism'. *American Sociological Review* 48 (October 1983): 587–605. doi.org/10.2307/2094921

——. *Manufacturing Consent*. Chicago: University of Chicago Press, 1979.

Burchell, Jon. 'Just What Should Business Be Responsible For? Understanding the Concept of CSR'. In *The Corporate Social Responsibility Reader*, edited by Jon Burchell. Oxford: Routledge, 2008.

Burgmann, Meredith and Verity Burgmann. *Green Bans*. Sydney: UNSW Press, 1998.

Burkus, David. 'Everyone Likes Flex Time, but We Punish Women Who Use It'. *Harvard Business Review*, 20 February 2017.

Busck, Ole, Herman Knudsen, and Jens Lind. 'Who Is in Control? The Effect of Employee Participation on the Quality of the Work Environment'. In *European Congress of International Industrial Relations Association*. Copenhagen: IIRA, 2010.

Business Council of Australia. *Enterprise-Based Bargaining Units: A Better Way of Working*. Part 1. Melbourne: BCA, 1989.

——. 'The Report That Will Change the Way We Work'. *Business Council Bulletin* 59 (1989): 38–39.

Bussard, Robert L. 'The "Dangerous Class" of Marx and Engels: The Rise of the Idea of the Lumpenproletariat'. *History of European Ideas* 8, no. 6 (2012): 675–92. doi.org/10.1016/0191-6599(87)90164-1

Buultjens, Jeremy. 'Labour Market Deregulation: Does Small Business Care?'. *International Journal of Employment Studies* 2, no. 1 (1994): 132–57.

Cahill, Damien. *The End of Laissez Faire? On the Durability of Embedded Neoliberalism*. Cheltenham: Edward Elgar, 2014.

Cairncross, Grant and Jeremy Buultjens. 'Enterprise Bargaining under the Workplace Relations Act 1996 in Construction and Hospitality Small Businesses: A Comparative Study'. *Journal of Industrial Relations* 48, no. 4 (2006): 475–88. doi.org/10.1177/0022185606066140

Callaghan, George and Paul Thompson. 'Edwards Revisited: Technical Control and Call Centres'. *Economic and Industrial Democracy* 22 (2001): 13–37. doi.org/10.1177/0143831X01221002

Callus, Ron, Jim Kitay, and Paul Sutcliffe. 'Industrial Relations at Small Business Workplaces'. *Small Business Review* 7 (1992): 106–45.

Callus, Ron and Martha Knox. *The Industrial Relations of Migrant Employment*. Canberra: Bureau of Immigration and Population Research/AGPS, 1993.

Callus, Ron, Alison Morehead, Mark Cully, and John Buchanan. *Industrial Relations at Work: The Australian Workplace Industrial Relations Survey*. Canberra: AGPS, 1991.

Campbell, Iain. 'Extended Working Hours in Australia'. *Labour and Industry* 13, no. 1 (August 2002): 91–110. doi.org/10.1080/10301763.2002.10669258

Campbell, Iain, Martina Boese, and Joo-Cheong Tham. 'Inhospitable Workplaces? International Students and Paid Work in Food Services'. *Australian Journal of Social Issues* 51, no. 3 (2016): 279–98. doi.org/10.1002/j.1839-4655.2016.tb01232.x

Campbell, Iain and John Burgess. 'Patchy Progress? Two Decades of Research on Precariousness and Precarious Work in Australia'. *Labour & Industry* 28, no. 1 (2018): 48–67. doi.org/10.1080/10301763.2018.1427424

Cardador, M. Teresa and Brianna Caza. 'The Subtle Stressors Making Women Want to Leave Engineering'. *Harvard Business Review*, 23 November 2018.

Carney, Terry. 'The New Digital Future for Welfare: Debts without Legal Proofs or Moral Authority?'. *UNSW Law Journal Forum* 41, no. 1 (2018).

Carroll, William. 'The Corporate Elite and the Transformation of Finance Capital: A View from Canada'. *Sociological Review* 56, no. s1 (2008): 44–63. doi.org/10.1111/j.1467-954X.2008.00761.x

——. *The Making of a Transnational Capitalist Class*. London: Zed Books, 2010.

Carter, Bob and Rae Cooper. 'The Organizing Model and the Management of Change: A Comparative Study of Unions in Australia and Britain'. *Relations Industrielles* 57, no. 4 (Fall 2002): 712–42. doi.org/10.7202/006907ar

Cascio, Wayne F. 'Downsizing: What Do We Know? What Have We Learned?'. *Academy of Management Executive* 7, no. 1 (1993): 95–104.

Cassells, Rebecca, Yogi Vidyattama, Riyana Miranti, and Justine McNamara. 'The Impact of a Sustained Gender Wage Gap on the Australian Economy'. In *Report to the Office for Women, Department of Families, Community Services, Housing and Indigenous Affairs*. Canberra: NATSEM, University of Canberra, 2009.

Catalyst. 'The Bottom Line: Connecting Corporate Performance and Gender Diversity'. Catalyst, www.catalystwomen.org

Chamorro-Premuzic, Tomas. 'Why Do So Many Incompetent Men Become Leaders?'. *Harvard Business Review blog* (22 August 2013).

Chapman, Ben. 'Gig Economy Ruling: Couriers Carrying Blood for NHS Win Right to Collective Bargaining'. *Independent*, 1 March 2018.

Charlesworth, Sara and Iain Campbell. 'Right to Request Regulation: Two New Australian Models'. *Australian Journal of Labour Law* 21, no. 2 (2008): 1–14.

Charlesworth, Sara and Fiona Macdonald. 'Employment Regulation and Worker-Carers: Reproducing Gender Inequality in the Domestic and Market Spheres?'. In *Women, Labor Segmentation and Regulation: Varieties of Gender Gaps*, edited by David Peetz and Georgina Murray, 79–96. New York: Palgrave Macmillan, 2017. doi.org/10.1057/978-1-137-55495-6_5

Chartered Institute of Personnel and Development. *To Gig or Not to Gig? Stories from the Modern Economy*. London: CIPD, 2017.

Chen, Daniel L. and Jasmin Sethi. *Insiders and Outsiders: Does Forbidding Sexual Harassment Exacerbate Gender Inequality?* John M. Olin Centre for Law Economics and Business. Cambridge, MA: Harvard Law School, 2011.

Childs, Sarah and Mona Lena Krook. 'Should Feminists Give up on Critical Mass? A Contingent Yes'. *Gender and Politics* 2, no. 4 (2006): 522–30. doi.org/10.1017/S1743923X06251146

Chuanli, Wang and Dong Gang. 'Social Responsibilities of Transnational Corporations'. *Frontiers of Law in China* 2, no. 3 (2007): 378–402. doi.org/10.1007/s11463-007-0018-9

Ciulla, Joanne B. 'Ethics and Leadership Effectiveness'. In *The Nature of Leadership*, edited by John. Antonakis, Anna T. Cianciolo and Robert J. Sternberg. Thousand Oaks, CA: Sage, 2004.

Clark, J. 'Full Flexibility and Self-Supervision in an Automated Factory'. In *Human Resource Management and Technical Change*, edited by J. Clark. London: Sage, 1993.

Clean Clothes Campaign. 'Comparison: The Accord on Fire and Building Safety in Bangladesh and the Gap/Walmart Scheme'. www.cleanclothes.org/resources/background/

Clibborn, Stephen. 'Why Undocumented Immigrant Workers Should Have Workplace Rights'. *Economic and Labour Relations Review* 28, no. 3 (2015): 465–73. doi.org/10.1177/1035304615598072

Clifton, Denise. 'A Chilling Theory on Trump's Nonstop Lies'. *Mother Jones*, 3 August 2017.

Climate Central. 'New Analysis Shows Global Exposure to Sea Level Rise'. Climate Central, www.climatecentral.org/news/new-analysis-global-exposure-to-sea-level-rise-flooding-18066

Coady, David, Ian Parry, Louis Sears, and Baoping Shang. *How Large Are Global Energy Subsidies?* IMF Working Paper WP/15/105. Washington, DC: International Monetary Fund, 2015.

Coase, Ronald. 'The Nature of the Firm'. *Economica* 4 (1937): 386–405. doi.org/10.1111/j.1468-0335.1937.tb00002.x

——. 'New Institutional Economics'. *American Economic Review* 88, no. 2 (1998): 72–74.

Cohen, Aaron. 'Dual Commitment to the Organization and the Union: A Multi-Dimensional Approach'. *Relations Industrielles* 60, no. 3 (2005): 432–54. doi.org/10.7202/012154ar

Coles, Amanda. 'Unintended Consequences: Examining the Impact of Tax Credit Programmes on Work in the Canadian Independent Film and Television Production Sector'. *Canadian Journal of Communication* 31, no. 3 (2010): 519–40.

Collier, Ruth Berins and J. David Collier. *Shaping the Political Arena: Critical Junctures, the Labor Movement and Regional Dynamics in Latin America.* Princeton NJ: Princeton University Press, 1991.

Collins, Jock. *Migrant Hands in a Distant Land: Australia's Post-War Immigration.* Sydney: Pluto, 1988.

Collinsville Connect Telecentre. *Collinsville Memoirs* (CD). Collinsville, Qld: Collinsville Connect Telecentre, 2002.

Commonwealth Bureau of Census and Statistics. *Labour Report.* Melbourne, various years.

Conlon, Edward J. and Daniel G. Gallagher. 'Commitment to Employer and Union: Effects of Membership Status'. *Academy of Management Journal* 30, no. 1 (March 1987): 151.

Connell, Raewyn. *Ruling Class, Ruling Culture.* Cambridge: Cambridge University Press, 1977. doi.org/10.1017/CBO9781139085076

——. 'Understanding Neoliberalism'. In *Neoliberalism and Everyday Life*, edited by Susan Braedley and Meg Luxton, 22–36. Montreal, QC, and Kingston, ON: McGill-Queen's University Press, 2010.

Connell, Raewyn and Nour Dados. 'Where in the World Does Neoliberalism Come From? The Market Agenda in Southern Perspective'. *Theory and Society: Renewal and Critique in Social Theory.* 43, no. 2 (2014): 117–38. doi.org/10.1007/s11186-014-9212-9

Connell, Raewyn and Terry Irving. *Class Structure in Australian History: Poverty and Progress*. Melbourne: Longman Cheshire, 1992.

Contu, Alessia and Hugh Willmott. 'The Docudrama: A Situated Learning Experience'. In *Innovations in Teaching Business and Management*, edited by Christine Hockings and Ian Moore, 95–109. Birmingham: SEDA Publications, Staff Educational and Development Association, 2001.

Cook, John, Dana Nuccitelli, Sarah A. Green, Mark Richardson, Bärbel Winkler, Rob Painting, Robert Way, Peter Jacobs, and Andrew Skuce. 'Quantifying the Consensus on Anthropogenic Global Warming in the Scientific Literature'. *Environmental Research Letters* 8, no. 2 (2013). doi.org/10.1088/1748-9326/8/2/024024

Cooper, Andrew J., Luke D. Smillie, and Philip J. Corr. 'A Confirmatory Factor Analysis of the Mini-IPIP Five-Factor Model Personality Scale'. *Personality and Individual Differences* 48, no. 5 (2010): 688–91. doi.org/10.1016/j.paid.2010.01.004

Cooper, Rae. 'The Gender Gap in Union Leadership in Australia: A Qualitative Study'. *Journal of Industrial Relations* 54, no. 2 (2012): 131–46. doi.org/10.1177/0022185612437836

Cotton, Elizabeth and Rebecca Gumbrell-McCormick. 'Global Unions as Imperfect Multilateral Organizations: An International Relations Perspective'. *Economic and Industrial Democracy* 33, no. 4 (2012): 707–28. doi.org/10.1177/0143831X12436616

Cowan, Dallas M., Pamela J. Dopart, Tyler Ferracini, Jennifer Sahmel, Kimberly Merryman, Shannon H. Gaffney, and Dennis J. Paustenbach. 'A Cross-Sectoral Analysis of Reported Corporate Environmental and Sustainability Practices'. *Regulatory Toxicology and Pharmacology* 58, no. 3 (2010): 524–38. doi.org/10.1016/j.yrtph.2010.09.004

Cowan, Ruth Schwartz. *A Social History of American Technology*. Oxford: Oxford University Press, 1997.

Cowgill, Matt. *A Shrinking Slice of the Pie*. Melbourne: Australian Council of Trade Unions, 2013.

Craig, Lyn and Judith E. Brown. 'Weekend Work and Leisure Time with Family and Friends: Who Misses Out?'. *Journal of Marriage and Family* 76, no. 4 (2014): 710–27. doi.org/10.1111/jomf.12127

Cregan, Christina. 'Book Review: Understanding Work and Employment: Industrial Relations'. *Journal of Industrial Relations* 46, no. 1 (March 2004): 137–40. doi.org/10.1111/0022185604046001013

Crenshaw, Kimberlé Williams. 'Demarginalizing the Intersection of Race and Sex: A Black Feminist Critique of Antidiscrimination Doctrine, Feminist Theory and Antiracist Politics'. *University of Chicago Legal Forum* 1989, no. 1 (1989): 139–67.

Cressey, Peter and John MacInnes. 'Voting for Ford: Industrial Democracy and the Control of Labour'. *Capital and Class* 11 (1980): 5–33. doi.org/10.1177/030981688001100101

Crouch, Colin. *Capitalist Diversity and Change: Recombinant Governance and Institutional Entrepreneurs*. Oxford: Oxford University Press, 2005. doi.org/10.1093/acprof:oso/9780199286652.001.0001

Cuevas, Joshua A. 'A New Reality? The Far Right's Use of Cyberharassment against Academics'. American Association of University Professors, 2018.

Curtain, Richard and John Mathews. 'Two Models of Award Restructuring in Australia'. *Labour and Industry* 3, no. 1 (1990): 58–75. doi.org/10.1080/10301763.1990.11673898

Dahl, Robert A. 'The Concept of Power'. *Behavioral Science* 2 (July 1957): 201–15. doi.org/10.1002/bs.3830020303

——. *Who Governs? Democracy and Power in an American City*. Yale Studies in Political Science 4. New Haven: Yale University Press, 1961.

Dahlerup, Drude. 'The Story of the Theory of Critical Mass'. *Gender and Politics* 2, no. 4 (2006): 511–22. doi.org/10.1017/S1743923X0624114X

Dannin, Ellen. *Working Free: The Origins and Impact of New Zealand's Employment Contracts Act*. Auckland: Auckland University Press, 1997.

Data Team. 'Corporate Concentration'. *Economist*, 24 May 2016.

Dauth, Wolfgang, Sebastian Findeisen, Jens Südekum, and Nicole Woessner. 'The Rise of Robots in the German Labour Market'. *Vox*, 19 September 2017.

De Stefano, Valerio. *The Rise of the 'Just-in-Time Workforce': On-Demand Work, Crowdwork and Labour Protection in the 'Gig-Economy'*. Conditions of Work and Employment Series No. 71. Geneva: International Labour Office, 2016.

Deakin, Simon. *The Comparative Evolution of the Employment Relationship*. Centre for Business Research, Working Paper No. 317. Cambridge, UK: University of Cambridge, 2005.

Deal, Terence E. and Allan A. Kennedy. *Corporate Cultures—the Rites and Rituals of Corporate Life*. Massachusetts: Addison-Wesley, 1982.

Deeg, Richard and Iain Hardie. 'What Is Patient Capital and Who Supplies It?'. *Socio-Economic Review* 14, no. 4 (2016): 627–45. doi.org/10.1093/ser/mww025

Delaney, Annie. 'A Comparison of Australian and Indian Women Garment and Footwear Homeworkers'. In *Women, Labor Segmentation and Regulation: Varieties of Gender Gaps*, edited by David Peetz and Georgina Murray, 193–210. New York: Palgrave Macmillan, 2017. doi.org/10.1057/978-1-137-55495-6_11

Department of Employment and Industrial Relations. *Industrial Democracy and Employee Participation: A Policy Discussion Paper*. Canberra: Working Environment Branch, DEIR, and AGPS, 1986.

Department of Industrial Relations. *Enterprise Bargaining in Australia: 1994 Annual Report*. Canberra: AGPS, 1995.

——. *Enterprise Bargaining in Australia: 1995 Annual Report*. Canberra: AGPS, 1996.

Department of Jobs and Small Business. '2018 Employment Projections'. Employment Projections, Department of Jobs and Small Business, lmip.gov.au/default.aspx?LMIP/EmploymentProjections

Desilver, Drew. 'For Most U.S. Workers, Real Wages Have Barely Budged in Decades'. Fact Tank, Pew Research Center, www.pewresearch.org/fact-tank/2018/08/07/for-most-us-workers-real-wages-have-barely-budged-for-decades/

Diesendorf, M. 'Climate Change and the Economy'. Chapter 6. In *Readings in Political Economy: Economics as a Social Science*, edited by George Arygous & Frank Stilwell, 15–18. Melbourne: Pluto Press, 2010.

Dingwall, Doug. 'Centrelink Accused of Intimidating Clients with AFP Letters'. *Australian Financial Review*, 4 August 2017.

Diviney, Emer and Serena Lillywhite. *Ethical Threads: Corporate Social Responsibility in the Australian Garment Industry*. Melbourne: Brotherhood of St Laurence, 2007.

Dobush, Grace. 'Lyft Claims That NYC's New Driver Minimum Wage Makes It Even Harder to Compete with Uber'. *Fortune*, 31 January 2019.

Dockterman, Eliana. 'What Is #Gamergate and Why Are Women Being Threatened About Video Games?'. *Time*, 16 October 2014.

Domenech, Teresa. 'Explainer: What Is a Circular Economy?'. *The Conversation*, 25 July 2014.

Domhoff, G. William. *Who Rules America? Politics and Social Change*. New York: McGraw-Hill, 2006.

Dorman, Peter. 'Financialization and the Incredible Shrinking Time Horizon'. Econospeak, econospeak.blogspot.com.au/2013/05/financialization-and-incredible.html

Dower, Michael. 'The Fourth Wave: The Challenge of Leisure'. *The Architect's Journal* (20 January 1965): 123–90.

Drum, Kevin. 'S&P Admits in Court That Its Ratings Are Ridiculous and No One Should Ever Take Them Seriously'. *Mother Jones*, 8 July 2013.

Dudley, Michael. 'Helping Professionals and Border Force Secrecy: Effective Asylum-seeker Healthcare Requires Independence from Callous Policies'. *Australasian Psychiatry* (2016). doi.org/10.1177/1039856215623354

Dudley, Michael and Fran Gale. 'Psychiatrists as a Moral Community? Psychiatry under the Nazis and Its Contemporary Relevance'. *Australian and New Zealand Journal of Psychiatry* 36 (2002): 585–94. doi.org/10.1046/j.1440-1614.2002.01072.x

Dufour-Poirier, Mélanie and Mélanie Laroche. 'Revitalising Young Workers' Union Participation: A Comparative Analysis of Two Organisations in Quebec (Canada)'. *Industrial Relations Journal* 45, no. 5–6 (2015): 418–33. doi.org/10.1111/irj.12118

Dundon, Tony. 'The Fracturing of Work and Employment Relations'. *Labour and Industry* 29, no. 1 (2019): 6–18. doi.org/10.1080/10301763.2018.1537047

Dundon, Tony, Irena Grugulis, and Adrian Wilkinson. 'Looking out of the Black Hole: Non-Union Relations in an SME'. *Employee Relations* 21 (1999): 251–66. doi.org/10.1108/01425459910273099

Dundon, Tony and Derek Rollison. *Employment Relations in Non-Union Firms*. London: Routledge, 2004. doi.org/10.4324/9780203694558

Dunlop, Tim. *The Future of Everything: Big Audacious Ideas for a Better World.* Sydney: New South Books, 2018.

Dunne, John P., Ronald J. Stouffer, and Jasmin G. John. 'Reductions in Labour Capacity from Heat Stress under Climate Warming'. *Nature Climate Change* 3 (2013): 563–6. doi.org/10.1038/nclimate1827

Durie, John. 'David Jones CEO Mark McInnes Resigns after Sexual Harassment Complaint'. *Australian*, 18 June 2010.

Dyer, Glenn and Bernard Keane. 'Investors Give Banks a Tick in Wake of Royal Commission'. *Crikey*, 5 February 2019.

Edelman, Benjamin. 'Uber Can't Be Fixed — It's Time for Regulators to Shut It Down'. *Harvard Business Review* 21 June 2017. hbr.org/2017/06/uber-cant-be-fixed-its-time-for-regulators-to-shut-it-down

Edis, Tristan. '100% Renewables Is Feasible: Aemo'. *The Australian (Climate Spectator)*, 29 April 2013.

Edwards, Paul K. and Hugh Scullion. *The Social Organisation of Industrial Conflict*. Oxford: Basil Blackwell, 1985.

Edwards, Richard C. *Contested Terrain*. London: Heinemann, 1979.

Eggers, Dave. *The Circle*. New York: Vintage, 2013.

Eidelson, Josh, Hassan Kanu, and Mark Bergen. 'Google Urged the U.S. to Limit Protection for Activist Workers'. *Bloomberg*, 24 January 2019.

Eisinger, Jesse. *The Chickenshit Club: Why the Justice Department Fails to Prosecute Executives*. New York: Simon & Schuster, 2017.

Elbaum, Bernard and Frank Wilkinson. 'Industrial Relations and Uneven Development: A Comparative Study of the American and British Steel Industries'. *Cambridge Journal of Economics* 3, no. 3 (1979): 275–303.

Elger, Tony. 'Task Flexibility and Intensification of Labour in UK Manufacturing in the 1980s'. In *Farewell to Flexibility*, edited by Anna Pollert. Oxford: Basil Blackwell, 1991.

Ellem, Bradon. *Hard Ground: Unions in the Pilbara*. Port Hedland: Pilbara Mineworkers Union, 2004.

——. 'New Unionism in the Old Economy: Community and Collectivism in the Pilbara's Mining Towns'. *Journal of Industrial Relations* 45, no. 4 (Dec 2003 2003): 423–41.

Ellerton, Peter. 'The Problem of False Balance When Reporting on Science'. *The Conversation*, 16 July 2014.

Ellis, Luci and Kathryn Smith. *The Global Upward Trend in the Profit Share*. BIS Working Paper No. 231. Basel: Bank for International Settlements, 2007.

Elson, Charles M. and Craig K. Ferrere. 'Executive Superstars, Peer Groups and Overcompensation: Cause, Effect and Solution'. *Journal of Corporate Law* 38 (2013): 487–537.

EMD Workforce Development. *Migrants and Workplace Bargaining: Australian Case Studies*. Industrial Relations Research Series No. 11, Workplace Bargaining Research Project. Canberra: Department of Industrial Relations, AGPS, 1994.

Emerson, Richard M. 'Power-Dependence Relations'. *American Sociological Review* 27 (1962). doi.org/10.2307/2089716

Ensmenger, Nathan. *The Computer Boys Take Over: Computers, Programmers, and the Politics of Technical Expertise*. Cambridge, MA: MIT Press, 2010. doi.org/10.7551/mitpress/9780262050937.001.0001

Epstein, Marc J. *Making Sustainability Work: Best Practices in Managing and Measuring Corporate Social, Environmental and Economic Impacts*. Sheffield: Greenleaf, 2008. doi.org/10.1177/030630700302900101

Epstein, Marc J. and Marie-Josée Roy. 'Improving Sustainability Performance: Specifying, Implementing and Measuring Key Principles'. *Journal of General Management* 29, no. 1 (2003): 15–31.

Equal Opportunity for Women in the Workplace Agency. *2010 Australian Census of Women in Leadership*. Sydney: EOWA, 2010.

——. *Gender Income Distribution of Top Earners in ASX200 Companies: 2006 EOWA Census of Women in Leadership*. Sydney: EOWA, 2008.

Erickson, Christopher L., Catherine L. Fisk, Ruth Milkman, Daniel J.B. Mitchell, and Kent Wong. 'Justice for Janitors in Los Angeles: Lessons from Three Rounds of Negotiations'. *British Journal of Industrial Relations* 40, no. 3 (September 2002): 543–67.

Esty, Daniel C. and Andrew Winstone. *Green to Gold: How Smart Companies Use Environmental Strategy to Innovate, Create Value and Build Competitive Advantage*. New Haven: Yale University Press, 2006.

European Trade Union Congress. *ETUC Declaration on the Paris Agreement on Climate Change*. Brussels: ETUC, 2016.

Evans, Jon. 'What If Google Unionized?'. *Techcrunch*, 4 November 2018.

Eveline, Joan and Michael Booth. 'Gender and Sexuality in Discourses of Managerial Control: The Case of Women Miners'. *Gender, Work and Organisation* 9, no. 5 (November 2002): 556–78. doi.org/10.1111/1468-0432.00175

Fair Work Commission. '4 Yearly Review of Modern Awards—Penalty Rates'. FWCFB 1001, 2017.

Fairfax, Lisa M. 'The Impact of Stakeholder Rhetoric on Corporate Norms'. *University of Iowa Journal of Corporation Law* 31 (2006): 675–8.

Fairfax, Richard E. (Deputy Assistant Secretary). 'Employer Safety Incentive and Disincentive Policies and Practices'. Occupational Safety and Health Administration, Memorandum for Regional Administrators, Whistleblower Program Administrators. Washington DC: US Department of Labor, 2012.

Farrell, Diana and Fiona Greig. *The Online Platform Economy: Has Growth Peaked?* New York: JPMorgan Chase Institute 2016.

Felton, Ryan. 'Uber Is Doomed'. *Jalopnik*, 24 February 2017.

Feng, Wang. *The End of 'Growth with Equity'? Economic Growth and Income Inequality in East Asia.* Asia Pacific Issues, 101. Honolulu, East-West Center, 2011.

Ferguson, Adele and Klaus Toft. '7-Eleven: The Price of Convenience'. *Four Corners*, Australian Broadcasting Corporation, www.abc.net.au/4corners/stories/2015/08/30/4301164.htm

Ferguson, Adele, Klaus Toft, and Mario Christodoulou. 'Money for Nothing'. *Four Corners*, Australian Broadcasting Corporation, www.abc.net.au/4corners/stories/2016/03/07/4417757.htm

Ferri, Richard E. *The Power of Passive Investing*. Hoboken, NJ: Wiley, 2010.

Festinger, Leon. *A Theory of Cognitive Dissonance*. Stanford, CA: Stanford University Press, 1957.

Findlay, Patricia and Alan McKinlay. 'Union Organising in "Big Blue's" Backyard'. *Industrial Relations Journal* 34, no. 1 (March 2003): 52–66. doi.org/10.1111/1468-2338.00258

Fitzpatrick, Alex. 'Udemy Thinks It's Cracked the Future of Online Education'. *Time*, 12 February 2016.

Fitzroy, Felix R. and John R. Cable. 'Co-operation and Productivity: Some Evidence from West German Experience'. *Journal of Economic Analysis and Workers Management* 14, no. 2 (1980): 163–80.

Flanagan, Frances. 'Climate Change and the New Work Order'. *Inside Story*, 28 February 2019.

Ford, Michelle and Michael Gillan. 'The OECD Guidelines as a Supranational Mechanism of Labor Conflict Resolution'. In *Conflict and its Resolution in the Changing World of Work: A Conference and Special Issue Honoring David B. Lipsky*: DigitalCommons@ILR, 2017.

Forsyth, Anthony. *Victorian Inquiry into the Labour Hire Industry and Insecure Work: Final Report.* Melbourne: Industrial Relations Victoria, Department of Economic Development, Jobs, Transport & Resources, 2016.

Fortuna, W. Harry. 'The Gig Economy Is a Disaster for Workers. Hollywood's Unions Can Help Them Learn to Fight Back'. Quartz, qz.com/1052310/hollywood-unions-offer-the-perfect-model-for-the-beaten-down-workers-of-todays-gig-economy/

Foucault, Michel. *Power/Knowledge: Selected Interviews and Other Writings 1972–77.* Brighton: Harvester, 1980.

Fourastié, J. *Les 40,000 Heures.* Paris: Editions Gonthier, 1965.

Fox, Justin. 'Your Uber Driver Probably Has Another Job'. *Bloomberg*, 20 February 2016.

Frankel, Jeffrey A. 'Globalization of the Economy'. In *Governance in a Globalizing World*, edited by Joseph S. Nye and John D. Donahue, 45–71. Washington DC: Brookings Institution Press, 2000.

Franzway, Suzanne. 'The Changing Sexual Politics of Gender Regulation by Unions'. In *Women, Labor Segmentation and Regulation: Varieties of Gender Gaps*, edited by David Peetz and Georgina Murray, 61–78. New York: Palgrave Macmillan, 2017. doi.org/10.1057/978-1-137-55495-6_4

Franzway, Suzanne, C. Zufferey, and D. Chung. 'Domestic Violence and Women's Employment'. Paper presented at the Our Work, Our Lives National Conference on Women and Industrial Relations, Adelaide, 21 September 2007.

Frase, Peter. 'Delusions of the Tech Bro Intelligentsia'. Jacobin, www.jacobinmag.com/2013/10/delusions-of-the-tech-bro-intelligentsia/

Frazer, Lorelle, Scott Weaven, and Anthony Grace. *Franchising Australia 2014.* Brisbane: Griffith University, 2014.

Freelancers Union and Elance-oDesk. *Freelancing in America: A National Survey of the New Workforce* (New York: Freelancers Union, 2013).

Freeman, Richard B. 'It's Financialization!'. *International Labour Review* 149, no. 2 (2010): 163–83. doi.org/10.1111/j.1564-913X.2010.00082.x

Freeman, Richard B. 'What Do Unions Do ? The 2004 M-Brane Stringtwister Edition'. *Journal of Labor Research* 26, no. 4 (Fall 2005): 642–68. doi.org/10.1007/s12122-005-1003-7

Freeman, Richard B., Peter Boxall, and Peter Haynes, eds. *What Workers Say: Employee Voice in the Anglo-American World.* Ithaca NY: ILR Press, 2007.

Freeman, Richard B. and James L. Medoff. *What Do Unions Do?* New York: Basic Books, 1984.

Freeman, Richard B. and Joel Rogers. *What Workers Want*. Ithaca: ILR Press, 1999.

Frenkel, Stephen J. 'Industrial Sociology and Workplace Relations in Advanced Capitalist Societies'. *International Journal of Comparative Sociology* 27, no. 1–2 (1986): 69–86. doi.org/10.1177/002071528602700105

Frenkel, Stephen J. and David Peetz. 'Enterprise Bargaining: The BCA's Report on Industrial Relations Reform'. *Journal of Industrial Relations* 32, no. 1 (March 1990): 69–99.

Frey, Carl Benedikt and Michael A. Osborne. *The Future of Employment: How Susceptible Are Jobs to Computerisation?* Oxford: Department of Engineering Science, University of Oxford, 2013.

Friedman, Andrew L. *Industry and Labour*. London: Macmillan, 1977.

Friedman, Milton. 'The Social Responsibility of Business Is to Increase Its Profits'. *New York Times Magazine*, 13 September 1970.

Frynas, Jedrzej, Scott Pegg, and J. George Frynas, eds. *Transnational Corporations and Human Rights*. New York: Palgrave Macmillan, 2003. doi.org/10.1057/9781403937520

Fukami, Cynthia V. and Erik W. Larson. 'Commitment to Company and Union: Parallel Models'. *Journal of Applied Psychology* 69, no. 3 (August 1984): 367–71.

Gall, Gregor. 'Is Uber Ruling the Beginning of the End for Bogus Self-Employment?'. *The Conversation*, 5 November 2016.

Gallagher, D.G. 'The Relationship between Organizational and Union Commitment among Federal Government Employees'. *Academy of Management Proceedings* (1984): 319–23.

Gallagher, Daniel G. and Paul F. Clark. 'Research on Union Commitment: Implications for Labor'. *Labor Studies Journal* 14, no. 3 (Spring 1989): 52–71.

Garcia-Bernardo, Javier, Jan Fichtner, Frank W. Takes, and Eelke M. Heemskerk. 'Uncovering Offshore Financial Centers: Conduits and Sinks in the Global Corporate Ownership Network'. *Scientific Reports* 7 (2017). doi.org/10.1038/s41598-017-06322-9

Gardner, Margaret and Gillian Palmer. *Employment Relations: Industrial Relations and Human Resource Management*. Melbourne: Macmillan, 1992. doi.org/10.1007/978-1-349-15133-2

General Accounting Office. *Employee Stock Ownership Plans: Little Evidence of Effects on Corporate Performance.* Washington DC: GAO, 1987.

Gerschwin, Lisa-Ann. *Stung! On Jellyfish Blooms and the Future of the Ocean.* Chicago: University of Chicago Press, 2013.

GESIS. 'European Values Study Data File'. GESIS-Leibniz Institute for Social Sciences (prev. Gesellschaft Sozialwissenschaftlicher Infrastruktureinrich tungen), tinyurl.com/y3fvtjoo

Gibbs, David N. 'Is There Room for the Real World in the Postmodernist Universe?'. In *Beyond the Area Studies Wars: Toward a New International Studies*, edited by Neil L. Waters, 11–28. Hanover: Middlebury College Press, 2000.

Gilding, Michael. 'Superwealth in Australia: Entrepreneurs, Accumulation and the Capitalist Class'. *Journal of Sociology* 35, no. 2 (1999): 169–71. doi.org /10.1177/144078339903500203

Gindling, Tim H. and Katherine Terrell. 'Minimum Wages, Globalization, and Poverty in Honduras'. *World Development* 38, no. 6 (2010): 908–18. doi.org/ 10.1016/j.worlddev.2010.02.013

GlobeScan/BBC World Service. 'Wide Dissatisfaction with Capitalism—Twenty Years after Fall of Berlin Wall'. London: BBC, 2009.

Gomez, Carolina. 'The Relationship between Acculturation, Individualism/ Collectivism and Job Attribute Preferences for Hispanic MBAs'. *Journal of Management Studies* 40, no. 5 (July 2003): 1089–105. doi.org/10.1111/1467-6486.00372

Goodrich, Carter L. *The Frontier of Control: A Study in British Workshop Politics.* London: G. Bell and Sons, 1920.

Gopnik, Adam. 'The Yellow Vests and Why There Are So Many Street Protests in France'. *New Yorker*, 6 December 2018.

Gorman, Ginger. 'Internet Trolls Are Not Who I Thought—They're Even Scarier'. *ABC News*, 1 February 2019.

Gramsci, Antonio. *La Construzione Del Partito Comunista 1923–1926.* Turin: Einaudi, 1971.

——. *Selections from the Prison Notebooks.* London: Lawrence and Wishart, 1971.

Grattan, Michelle. 'Shorten and Turnbull to Talk on Four-Year Terms'. *The Conversation*, 23 July 2017.

Green, Francis. 'Recent Trends in British Trade Union Density: How Much of a Compositional Effect?'. *British Journal of Industrial Relations* 30, no. 3 (January 1992): 445–58. doi.org/10.1111/j.1467-8543.1992.tb00784.x

——. 'Why Has Work Effort Become More Intense?'. *Industrial Relations: A Journal of Economy and Society* 43, no. 4 (2004): 709–41. doi.org/10.1111/j.0019-8676.2004.00359.x

Green, Roy and Göran Roos. *Australia's Manufacturing Future.* Canberra: Discussion paper prepared for the Prime Minister's Manufacturing Taskforce, 2012.

Grey, S. 'Does Size Matter? Critical Mass in New Zealand's Women MPs'. *Parliamentary Affairs* 55, no. 1 (2002): 19–29. doi.org/10.1093/parlij/55.1.19

Griffith University. *Annual Report 2014.* Brisbane: Griffith University, 2014.

Griffith Work Time Project. *Working Time Transformations and Effects.* Brisbane: Queensland Department of Industrial Relations, 2003.

Grimes, Paul F.M. 'The Determinants of Trade Union Membership: Evidence from Two Australian Surveys'. Research School of Social Sciences, The Australian National University, 1994.

Grimshaw, Damian and Jill Rubery. *Undervaluing Women's Work. Manchester: Equal Opportunities Commission.* EOC Working Paper Series. Manchester: Equal Opportunities Commission and European Work and Employment Research Centre, University of Manchester 2007.

Grimsrud, Bjørne and Torunn Kvinge. 'Productivity Puzzles—Should Employee Participation Be an Issue?'. *Nordic Journal of Political Economy* 32, no. 2 (2006): 139–67.

Gruen, David, Brian Gray, and Glenn Stevens. 'Australia'. In *East Asia in Crisis: From Being a Miracle to Needing One?*, edited by Ross H. McLeod and Ross Garnaut, 207–23. London and New York: Routledge, 1998.

Gupta, Sarita, Stephen Lerner, and Joseph A. McCartin. 'It's Not the "Future of Work," It's the Future of Workers That's in Doubt'. *American Prospect*, 31 August 2018.

Hajkowicz, Stefan, Andrew Reeson, Lachlan Rudd, Alexandra Bratanova, Leonie Hodgers, Claire Mason, and Naomi Boughen. *Tomorrow's Digitally Enabled Workforce: Megatrends and Scenarios for Jobs and Employment in Australia over the Coming Twenty Years.* Brisbane: CSIRO, 2016.

Hall, Peter A. and David W. Soskice. *Varieties of Capitalism: The Institutional Foundations of Comparative Advantage*. Oxford: Oxford University Press, 2001. doi.org/10.1093/0199247757.001.0001

Hara, Kotara, Abi Adams, Kristy Milland, Saiph Savage, Chris Callison-Burch, and Jeffrey P. Bigham. 'A Data-Driven Analysis of Workers' Earnings on Amazon Mechanical Turk', paper presented to CHI 2018 conference, Montreal, 21–26 April 2018, arxiv.org/pdf/1712.05796.pdf

Harcourt, Bernard E. 'How Trump Fuels the Fascist Right'. *New York Review of Books*, 29 November 2018.

Harcourt, Mark, Gregor Gall, Margaret Wilson, and Nisha Novell. 'How a Default Union Membership Could Help Reduce Income Inequality'. *The Conversation*, 21 January 2019.

Hardy, Tess, Jim Stanford, and Andrew Stewart, eds. *The Wages Crisis in Australia: What It Is and What to Do About It*. Adelaide: University of Adelaide Press, 2018.

Harley, Bill, Belinda C. Allen, and Leisa D. Sargent. 'High Performance Work Systems and Employee Experience of Work in the Service Sector'. *British Journal of Industrial Relations* 45, no. 3 (2007): 607–33. doi.org/10.1111/j.1467-8543.2007.00630.x

Harpur, Paul. 'Clothing Manufacturing Supply Chains, Contractual Layers and Hold Harmless Clauses: How OHS Duties Can Be Imposed over Retailers'. *Australian Journal of Labor Law* 21, no. 3 (2008): 316–39.

——. 'Labour Rights as Human Rights: Workers' Safety at Work in Australian-Based Supply Chains'. Queensland University of Technology, 2009.

——. 'Regulating Multi-National Corporations through State-Based Laws: Problems with Enforcing Human Rights under the Alien Tort Statute'. *Australian International Law Journal* 13 (2006): 233–46.

Harrison, Ann. *Globalization and Poverty*. NBER Working Paper 12347. Cambridge, MA: National Bureau of Economic Research, 2006.

Harvard Business School. 'How a Short-Term Strategy Can Backfire'. Strategy + Business, Harvard Business School, www.strategy-business.com/article/re00191?pg=all

Harvey, David. 'The "New" Imperialism: Accumulation by Dispossession', *Socialist Register* 40 (2004): 63–87.

——. *The New Imperialism*. Oxford: Oxford University Press, 2003.

Hayhoe, Katharine and Robert E. Kopp. 'What Surprises Lurk within the Climate System?'. *Environmental Research Letters* 11, no. 12 (2016). doi.org/10.1088/1748-9326/11/12/120202

Healy, Geraldine and Gill Kirton. 'Women, Power and Trade Union Government in the UK'. *British Journal of Industrial Relations* 38, no. 3 (2000): 343–60. doi.org/10.1111/1467-8543.00168

Healy, Joshua, Andreas Pekarek, and Daniel Nicholson. 'Gig Economy Businesses Like Uber and Airtasker Need to Evolve to Survive'. *The Conversation*, 4 July 2017.

Hearn, Jeff. 'The Organization(s) of Violence: Men, Gender Relations, Organizations and Violences'. *Human Relations* 47, no. 6 (1994): 731–54. doi.org/10.1177/001872679404700608

Heiler, Kathryn and Richard Rickersgill. 'Shiftwork and Rostering Arrangements in the Australian Mining Industry: An Overview of Key Trends'. *Australian Bulletin of Labour* 27 (2001): 20–42.

Helgeson, Jeffrey. 'American Labor and Working-Class History, 1900–1945'. In *Oxford Research Encyclopedia of American History*. Oxford: Oxford University Press,2016. oxfordre.com/americanhistory/view/10.1093/acrefore/9780199329175.001.0001/acrefore-9780199329175-e-330

Henderson, Troy, Tom Swann, and Jim Stanford. *Under the Employer's Eye: Electronic Monitoring and Surveillance in Australian Workplaces*. Canberra: Centre for Future Work, Australia Institute, 2018.

Herweijer, Celine, N. Patmore, and R. Muir-Wood. 'Catastrophe Risk Models as a New Tool to Investigate the Financial Risks Associated with Climate Change Impacts and Cost-Benefits of Adaptation'. *IOP Conference Series: Earth and Environmental Science* 6 (2009).

Hicks, Marie. *Programmed Inequality: How Britain Discarded Women Technologists and Lost Its Edge in Computing*. Cambridge, MA: MIT Press, 2017.

Hill, Kyle. 'The Overwhelming Odds of Climate Change'. *Scientific American: Blogs* (20 May 2013).

Hill, Steven. 'Good Riddance, Gig Economy: Uber, Ayn Rand and the Awesome Collapse of Silicon Valley's Dream of Destroying Your Job'. *Salon*, www.salon.com/2016/03/27/good_riddance_gig_economy_uber_ayn_rand_and_the_awesome_collapse_of_silicon_valleys_dream_of_destroying_your_job/

Ho, Christina and Caroline Alcorso. 'Migrants and Employment: Challenging the Success Story'. *Journal of Sociology* 40, no. 3 (2004): 237–59. doi.org/10.1177/1440783304045721

Hochschild, Arlie Russell. *The Managed Heart: The Commercialization of Human Feeling* Los Angeles: University of California Press, 1983, repr. 2003.

Holgate, Jane. 'The Sydney Alliance: A Broad-Based Community Organising Potential for Trade Union Transformation?'. *Economic and Industrial Democracy* 39, no. 3 (December 2015).

Holman, Mary A. 'A National Time-Budget for the Year 2000'. *Sociology and Social Research* 46, no. 1 (1961).

Holmes, Allan, Peter Cary, Joe Yerardi, and Chris Zubak-Skees. *Did Billionaires Pay Off Republicans for Passing the Trump Tax Bill?* Washington DC: Centre for Public Integrity, 2019. publicintegrity.org/business/taxes/trumps-tax-cuts/did-billionaires-pay-off-republicans-for-passing-the-trump-tax-bill/

Hood, Christopher. 'A Public Management for All Seasons'. *Public Administration Review* 69, no. 1 (1991): 3–19. doi.org/10.1111/j.1467-9299.1991.tb00779.x

Hoodfar, Homa. 'Iranian Women Risk Arrest: Daughters of the Revolution'. *The Conversation*, 6 March 2018.

Hope, Chris and Kevin Schaefer. 'Economic Impacts of Carbon Dioxide and Methane Released from Thawing Permafrost'. *Nature Climate Change* 6, no. 56–59 (2016).

Hopkins, Andrew. 'What Banking Regulators Can Learn from Deepwater Horizon and Other Industrial Catastrophes'. *The Conversation*, 31 January 2019.

Hopkins, Andrew and Sarah Maslen. *Risky Rewards: How Company Bonuses Affect Safety*. Farnham, UK: Ashgate, 2015.

Horne, Donald. *The Lucky Country: Australia in the Sixties*. Ringwood, Vic.: Penguin, 1964.

Houlihan, Maeve. 'Managing to Manage? Stories from the Call Centre Floor'. *Journal of European Industrial Training* 25, no. 2 (2001): 208–20. doi.org/10.1108/03090590110395816

House of Representatives Standing Committee on Employment and Workplace Relations. *Making It Fair: Pay Equity and Associated Issues Related to Increasing Female Participation in the Workforce*. Canberra: House of Representatives, 2009.

Huff, Darrell. *How to Lie with Statistics*. New York: W.W. Norton & Company, 1954.

Hull, Daryl and Vivienne Read. *Simply the Best: Workplaces in Australia*. Working Paper 88. Sydney: ACIRRT, University of Sydney, 2003.

Human Rights Watch. '"Whoever Raises Their Head Suffers the Most": Workers' Rights in Bangladesh's Garment Factories'. Human Rights Watch, www.hrw.org/report/2015/04/22/whoever-raises-their-head-suffers-most/workers-rights-bangladeshs-garment

Hung, Kai Hsin. 'Tech@Work: Top 6 Disruptive Technologies You Should Know'. ITCILO, International Labour Office.

Hunter, Floyd. *Community Power Structure: A Study of Decision Makers*. Chapel Hill: University of North Carolina Press, 1953.

Hyman, Richard. *Industrial Relations: A Marxist Introduction*. London: Macmillan, 1975. doi.org/10.1007/978-1-349-15623-8

——. *The Political Economy of Industrial Relations*. London: Macmillan, 1989. doi.org/10.1007/978-1-349-19665-4

IBIS World. *Black Coal Mining in Australia*. IBIS World Industry Report B0601. Melbourne: IBIS World, 2016.

——. 'Competitive Landscape'. Australia Industry Reports: Black Coal Mining. Los Angeles: IBIS World, 2015.

IFO Institute for Economic Research. 'Database for Institutional Comparisons in Europe'. University of Munich, www.cesifo-group.de/portal/page/portal/59C1D39D15DD5231E0440003BA988603+%22I+would+consider+equality+more+important%22&cd=1&hl=en&ct=clnk&client=safari

Income Data Services. *Flexible Working*. Study 407. London: IDS, 1988.

Intergovernmental Panel on Climate Change. 'Summary for Policymakers'. In: *Global Warming of 1.5°C*. An IPCC Special Report on the impacts of global warming of 1.5°C above pre-industrial levels and related global greenhouse gas emission pathways, in the context of strengthening the global response to the threat of climate change, sustainable development, and efforts to eradicate poverty, edited by V. Masson-Delmotte et al. Geneva: World Meteorological Organization, 2018.

International Labour Office. *A Challenging Future for the Employment Relationship: Time for Affirmation of Alternatives?* Future of Work Centenary Initiative: Issue Note Series No. 3. Geneva: ILO, 2017.

——. *Economic Security for a Better World.* Geneva: Socio-Economic Security Programme, ILO, 2004.

——. *Future of Work. Inception Report for the Global Commission on Work.* Geneva: ILO, 2017.

——. *Global Wage Report 2016/17.* Geneva: ILO, 2016.

International Labour Organization. 'Employment by Sex and Economic Activity (Thousands)'. ILOSTAT, ILO, www.ilo.org/ilostat/faces/oracle/webcenter/portalapp/pagehierarchy/Page27.jspx

——. 'Gender Gap in Participation Rates Is Not Expected to Improve over the Coming 15 Years'. ILO, www.ilo.org/global/topics/future-of-work/trends/WCMS_545630/lang--en/index.htm

——. 'Migration Is Likely to Intensify in the Future as Decent Work Deficits Remain Widespread'. ILO.

——. *Statistics of Trade Union Membership.* Geneva: ILO Bureau of Statistics, 2006.

Isaac, Joe. *Small Business and Industrial Relations: Some Policy Implications.* Industrial Relations Research Series No. 8. Canberra: Department of Industrial Relations, 1993.

——. 'Why Are Australian Wages Lagging and What Can Be Done About It?'. *Australian Economic Review* 51, no. 2 (2018): 175–90. doi.org/10.1111/1467-8462.12270

Isaac, Joe, Steve Kates, David Peetz, Chris Fisher, Rob Macklin, and Mark Short. *A Survey of Small Business and Industrial Relations.* Industrial Relations Research Series No. 7, Department of Industrial Relations. Canberra, 1993.

Itkowitz, Colby, Dino Grandoni, and Jeff Stein. 'AFL-CIO Criticizes Green New Deal, Calling It "Not Achievable or Realistic"'. *Washington Post,* 12 March 2019.

Iverson, Roderick D. and Sarosh C. Kuruvilla. *Does Dual Commitment Underline Company and Union Commitment? An Application of Second Order Confirmatory Analysis.* Working Paper 67. Melbourne: Centre for Industrial Relations and Labour Studies, University of Melbourne, 1992.

Jackson, Andrew and Grant Schellenberg. *Unions, Collective Bargaining and Labour Market Outcomes for Canadian Working Women: Past Gains and Future Challenges.* Research Report 11, Canadian Labour Congress, 1999.

Jacobs, Jerry A. and Kathleen Gerson. 'Overworked Individuals or Overworked Families?'. *Work and Occupations* 28, no. 1 (2001): 40–63. doi.org/10.1177/0730888401028001004

Jacobson, Louis. 'Explaining Alexandria Ocasio-Cortez's 70 Percent Marginal Tax Rate Idea'. *Politifact*, 8 January 2019.

James, Malcolm. 'Could Bill Gates' Plan to Tax Robots Really Lead to a Brighter Future for All?'. *The Conversation*, 10 March 2017.

Jarley, Paul. 'Unions as Social Capital: Renewal through a Return to the Logic of Mutual Aid?'. *Labor Studies Journal* 29, no. 4 (Winter 2005): 1–26. doi.org/10.1353/lab.2005.0011

Jaynes, Stephen. 'The Control of Workplace Culture: A Critical Perspective'. In *Current Research in Industrial Relations*, edited by Tom Bramble, Bill Harley, Richard Hall and Gillian Whitehouse, 182–89. Brisbane: Association of Industrial Relations Academics of Australia and New Zealand, 1997.

Johnston, Hannah and Chris Land-Kazlauskas. *Organizing on-Demand: Representation, Voice, and Collective Bargaining in the Gig Economy*. Conditions of Work and Employment Series No. 94 Geneva: Inclusive Labour Markets, Labour Relations and Working Conditions Branch, International Labour Office, 2018.

Johnstone, Richard and Therese Wilson. 'Take Me to Your Employer: The Organizational Reach of Occupational Health and Safety Regulation'. *Australian Journal of Labour Law* 19 (2006): 3–26.

Jones, Derek C. and Jan Svejnar. 'The Economic Performance of Participatory and Self-Managed Firms: A Historical Perspective and a Review'. In *Participatory and Self-Managed Firms*, edited by Derek C. Jones and Jan Svejnar, 3–16. Lexington, MA: DC Heath & Co, 1982.

Jones, Peter, Daphne Comfort, and David Hillier. 'What's in Store? Retail Marketing and Corporate Social Responsibility'. *Marketing Intelligence & Planning* 25, no. 1 (2007): 17–30. doi.org/10.1108/02634500710722371

Kahn, Herman and Anthony J. Wiener. *The Year 2000: A Framework for Speculation on the Next Thirty-Three Years*. New York: Macmillan, 1967.

Kahneman, Daniel. 'The Surety of Fools (Don't Blink! The Hazards of Confidence)'. *New York Times*, 19 October 2011, MM30.

——. *Thinking, Fast and Slow*. New York: Farrar, Straus and Giroux, 2011.

Kaine, Sarah, Emmanuel Josserand, and Martijn Boersma. 'How to Stop Businesses Stealing from Their Employees'. *The Conversation*, 8 September 2017.

Kaine, Sarah, Danielle Logue, and Emmanuel Josserand. 'The "Uberisation" of Work Is Driving People to Co-operatives'. *The Conversation*, 28 September 2016.

Kangas, Olli, Signe Jauhiainen, Miska Simanainen, and Minna Ylikännö. *The Basic Income Experiment 2017–2018 in Finland. Preliminary Results*. Reports and Memorandums of the Ministry of Social Affairs and Health 2019:9. Helsinki: Ministry of Social Affairs and Health, 2019.

Kanter, Rosabeth Moss. 'Leadership and the Psychology of Turnarounds'. *Harvard Business Review* (June 2003).

——. *Men and Women of the Corporation*. New York: Basic Books, 1977.

——. 'Some Effects of Proportions on Group Life: Skewed Sex Ratios and Responses to Token Women'. *American Journal of Sociology* 82, no. 5 (March 1977). doi.org/10.1086/226425

Kaplan, M. *Leisure: Theory and Policy*. New York: Wiley, 1975.

Kapur, Ajay, Niall Macleod, and Narendra Singh. 'Plutonomy: Buying Luxury, Explaining Global Imbalances'. In *Citigroup Equity Strategy Industry Note*. Citigroup Capital Markets, 2005.

——. 'Revisiting Plutonomy: The Rich Getting Richer'. In *Citigroup Equity Strategy Industry Note*. Citigroup Capital Markets, 2006.

Kapur, Ajay, Niall MacLeod, Narendra Singh, Hao Hong, and Audrey Seybert. 'The Plutonomy Symposium—Rising Tides Lifting Yachts'. *The Global Investigator (Equity Research Global: Equity Strategy)*, 29 September 2006, 7–19.

Karabarbounis, Loukas and Brent Neiman. 'The Global Decline of the Labor Share'. *Quarterly Journal of Economics* 129, no. 1 (2013): 61–103. doi.org/10.1093/qje/qjt032

Katz, Lawrence F. and Alan B. Krueger. *The Rise and Nature of Alternative Work Arrangements in the United States, 1995–2015*. NBER Working Paper No. 22667. Washington DC: National Bureau of Economic Research, 2016.

Keane, Bernard. 'The Looming Crisis for Women in Oz Tech'. *Crikey*, 16 March 2016.

——. 'The Need for a Strong Financial System Justifies ASIC's "Softly Softly" Approach'. *Crikey*, 31 May 2018.

——. 'Rape Fears and Harassment, but Bright Spots for Women in Tech, Too'. *Crikey*, 18 March 2016.

——. 'What Game Theory Says About Labor's Woes'. *Crikey*, 15 August 2011.

——. 'What's Driving Women out of Tech Industries?'. *Crikey*, 17 March 2016.

Keenoy, Tom and Di Kelly. *The Employment Relationship in Australia*, 2nd ed. Sydney: Harcourt, 1998.

Kelly, Caroline and Sara Breinlinger. 'Identity and Injustice: Exploring Women's Participation in Collective Action'. *Journal of Community & Applied Social Psychology* 5 (1995): 41–57. doi.org/10.1002/casp.2450050104

Kelly, John. E. 'British Trade Unionism 1979–89: Change, Continuity and Contradictions'. *Work, Employment and Society* special issue (1990): 29–60. doi.org/10.1177/0950017090004005003

——. *Rethinking Industrial Relations: Mobilization, Collectivism, and Long Waves*. Routledge Studies in Employment Relations. London, New York: Routledge, 1998.

Kelly, Paul. *The End of Certainty: The Story of the 1980s*. Sydney: Allen & Unwin, 1992.

Kernaghan, Charles, Jonathann Giammarco, Barbara Briggs, Alexandra Hallock, and Thomas Donoso. *Making Barbie, Thomas & Friends, and Other Toys for Wal-Mart: The Xin Yi Factory in China*. National Labor Committee (USA), 2007.

Keynes, John Maynard. 'Economic Possibilities for Our Grandchildren'. In *Essays in Persuasion*. London: Palgrave Macmillan, 1930, repr. 2010. doi.org/10.1007/978-1-349-59072-8_25

——. *The General Theory of Employment, Interest, and Money*. London: Macmillan, 1936.

Khazan, Olar. 'People Voted for Trump Because They Were Anxious, Not Poor'. *The Atlantic*, 23 April 2018.

Kiatpongsan, S. and M.I. Norton. 'How Much (More) Should CEOs Make? A Universal Desire for More Equal Pay'. *Perspectives on Psychological Science* 9, no. 6 (2014): 587–93. doi.org/10.1177/1745691614549773

Kilhoffer, Zachary, Karolien Lenaerts, and Miroslav Beblavý. *The Platform Economy and Industrial Relations: Applying the Old Framework to the New Reality*. CEPS Report No. 2017/12. Brussels, Centre for European Policy Studies, 2017.

Killaly, Jim. 'Fair Game: Is Australian Vulnerable or Getting Its Fair Share?'. *Journal of Australian Taxation* 19, no. 3 (2017): 1–194.

Kirchhoff, Jörg W. and Jan C. Karlsson. 'Expansion of Output: Organizational Misbehaviour in Public Enterprises'. *Economic and Industrial Democracy* 34, no. 1 (2013): 107–22. doi.org/10.1177/0143831X12439113

Kitay, Jim. 'The Labour Process: Still Stuck? Still a Perspective? Still Useful?'. *Electronic Journal of Radical Organisation Theory* 3, no. 1 (1997): 1–10.

Kitching, John. *Exploring the UK Freelance Workforce in 2015*. London: Association of Independent Professionals and the Self-Employed, 2016.

Klein, Naomi. *No Logo: Taking Aim at the Brand Bullies*. New York: Picador, 2000.

——. *The Shock Doctrine: The Rise of Disaster Capitalism*. Toronto: Knopf, 2007.

Klikauer, Thomas. 'What Is Managerialism?'. *Critical Sociology* 41, no. 7–8 (2015). doi.org/10.1177/0896920513501351

Knights, David and Darren McCabe. 'Ain't Misbehavin'?'. *Sociology* 34, no. 3 (2000): 421–36.

Knights, David and Hugh Willmott. *Management Lives: Power and Identity in Work Organizations*. London: Sage, 1999.

Kochan, Thomas A, Katerina Bezrukova, Robin Ely, Susan Jackson, Aparna Joshi, Karen Jehn, Jonathan Leonard, David Levine, and David Thomas. 'The Effects of Diversity on Business Performance: Report of the Diversity Research Network'. *Human Resource Management* 42, no. 1 (2003): 3–21. doi.org/10.1002/hrm.10061

Kochan, Thomas A. 'Video: All Innovations Are Local'. In *Shaping the Future of Work*. Cambridge, MA: MIT and EdX, 2017.

Kochan, Thomas, Duanyi Yang, Erin L. Kelly, and Will Kimball. 'Who Wants to Join a Union? A Growing Number of Americans'. *The Conversation*, 31 August 2018.

Kossen, Chris and Cec Pedersen. 'Older Workers in Australia: The Myths, the Realities and the Battle over Workforce "Flexibility"'. *Journal of Management & Organization* 14 (2008): 73–84.

Kotchen, Matthew J., Zachary M. Turk, and Anthony A. Leiserowitz. 'Public Willingness to Pay for a US Carbon Tax and Preferences for Spending the Revenue'. *Environmental Research Letters* 12, no. 9 (2017). doi.org/10.1088/1748-9326/aa822a

Kotter, John P. and James L. Heskett. *Corporate Culture and Performance.* New York: Free Press, 1992.

Krugman, Paul. 'The Twinkie Manifesto'. *New York Times*, 19 November 2012.

Kruse, Douglas. *Employee Ownership and Employee Attitudes: Two Case Studies.* Pennsylvania: Norwood Editions, 1984.

Kruszelnicki, Karl. 'Road Trip to Future Travel'. *Great Moments in Science*, Australian Broadcasting Corporation, 29 May 2018. www.abc.net.au/radionational/programs/greatmomentsinscience/lessons-from-first-road-trip/9795122

Kun, Michael S. and Kevin D. Sullivan. 'California Supreme Court Adopts "ABC Test" for Independent Contractors'. Wage and Hour Defense Blog, Epstein Becker Green, www.wagehourblog.com/

Lambert, Phil. 'The Future of Work and Skills'. *Professional Educator* 17, no. 2/3 (2017): 15–17.

Lammers, Joris, Diederik A. Stapel, and Adam D. Galinsky. 'Power Increases Hypocrisy: Moralizing in Reasoning, Immorality in Behavior'. *Psychological Science* 21, no. 5 (2010): 737–44. doi.org/10.1177/0956797610368810

Laper, Glenn W. 'Lombard Odier Launches Climate Bond Fund with AIM'. Nordsip (Nordic Sustainable Investment Platform), nordsip.com/2017/03/06/lombard-odier-launches-climate-bond-fund-with-aim/

Laß, Inga and Mark Wooden. 'The Structure of the Wage Gap for Temporary Workers: Evidence from Australian Panel Data'. *British Journal of Industrial Relations* (2019). doi.org/10.1111/bjir.12458

Learning and Skills Council. *Skills in England 2007 Volume 2: Research Report.* Coventry: LSC, 2007.

Lebowitz, Todd. 'California's Top Court Creates New Test for Independent Contractor vs. Employee, Re-Interprets 102-Year Old Definition'. Who is my employee?, Baker Hostetler LLP, whoismyemployee.com/

Lee, Jenny and Charles Fahey. 'A Boom for Whom? Some Developments in the Australian Labour Market, 1870–1891'. *Labour History—A Journal of Labour and Social History* 50 (May 1986): 1–27.

Legge, Karen. *Human Resource Management: Rhetorics and Realities.* Management, Work & Organisations Series. Basingstoke, England: Macmillan Business, 1995. doi.org/10.1007/978-1-349-24156-9

Leigh, Andrew and Adam Triggs. 'A Few Big Firms'. *The Monthly*, 17 May 2017.

Lepanjuuri, Katriina, Robert Wishart, and Peter Cornick. *The Characteristics of Those in the Gig Economy*. London: Department for Business, Energy & Industrial Strategy, 2018.

Lever-Tracy, Constance and Michael Quinlan. *A Divided Working Class*. New York: RKP, 1988.

Lévesque, Christian and Gregor Murray. 'Local Versus Global: Activating Local Union Power in the Global Economy'. *Labor Studies Journal* 27, no. 3 (Fall 2002): 39–65. doi.org/10.1177/0160449X0202700304

——. 'Understanding Union Power: Resources and Capabilities for Renewing Union Capacity'. *Transfer—European Review of Labour and Research* 16, no. 3 (2010): 333–50. doi.org/10.1177/1024258910373867

Lewandowsky, Stephan, John Cook, Klaus Oberauer, Scott Brophy, Elisabeth A. Lloyd, and Michael Marriott. 'Recurrent fury: Conspiratorial discourse in the blogosphere triggered by research on the role of conspiracist ideation in climate denial.' *Journal of Social and Political Psychology* 3, no. 1 (2015): 142–78.

Lewandowsky, Stephan, Klaus Oberauer, and Gilles E. Gignac. 'Motivated Rejection of Science: NASA Faked the Moon Landing—Therefore (Climate) Science Is a Hoax: An Anatomy of the Motivated Rejection of Science'. *Psychological Science* 24, no. 5 (May 2013): 622–33. doi.org/10.1177/0956797612457686

Lewis, Dianne. 'Five Years on—the Organizational Culture Saga Revisited'. *Leadership & Organization Development Journal* 23, no. 5 (2002): 280–87. doi.org/10.1108/01437730210435992

Li, YaoTai. 'Constituting Coethnic Exploitation: The Economic and Cultural Meanings of Cash in Hand Jobs for Ethnic Chinese Migrants in Australia'. *Critical Sociology* 43, no. 6 (2017): 919–32.

Lippel, Katherine, Ellen MacEachen, Ron Saunders, Natalia Werhun, Kosny Agnieszka, Liz Mansfield, Christine Carrasco, and Diana Pugliese. 'Legal Protections Governing the Occupational Safety and Health and Workers' Compensation of Temporary Employment Agency Workers in Canada: Reflections on Regulatory Effectiveness'. *Policy and Practice in Health and Safety* 9, no. 2 (2011): 69–90. doi.org/10.1080/14774003.2011.11667762

Liu, Jia, Tian-Ming Fu, Zengguang Cheng, Guosong Hong, Tao Zhou, Lihua Jin, et al. 'Syringe-Injectable Electronics'. *Nature Nanotechnology* 10 (June 2015): 629–36. doi.org/10.1038/nnano.2015.115

Londoño-Vélez, Juliana and Javier Avila. *Can Wealth Taxation Work in Developing Countries? Quasi-Experimental Evidence from Colombia*. Job Market Paper. Berkeley, CA: UC, 2018. eml.berkeley.edu//~saez/course/londono-wealth 2018.pdf

Lubin, David A. and Daniel C. Esty. 'The Big Idea: The Sustainability Imperative'. *Harvard Business Review*, May 2010, 42–50.

Lukes, Steven. *Power: A Radical View*. London: Macmillan, 1974. doi.org/10.1007/978-1-349-02248-9

——. *Power: A Radical View*, 2nd ed. London: Palgrave, 2005. doi.org/10.1007/978-0-230-80257-5

Lutz, William. *Doublespeak*. 1st ed. New York: Harper & Row, 1989.

Lysy, Frank J. 'Why Wages Have Stagnated While GDP Has Grown: The Proximate Factors'. An Economic Sense, aneconomicsense.org/2015/02/13/why-wages-have-stagnated-while-gdp-has-grown-the-proximate-factors/

Maatz, Lisa M. 'The Awful Truth Behind the Gender Pay Gap'. *ForbesWoman*, 7 April 2014.

Mabey, Christopher and Graeme Salaman. *Strategic Human Resource Management*. Oxford: Blackwell, 1995.

Magenau, John M., James E. Martin, and Melanie M. Peterson. 'Dual and Unilateral Commitment among Stewards and Rank-and-File Union Members'. *Academy of Management Journal* 31 (1988): 359–76.

Mallory, Greg. *Uncharted Waters: Social Responsibility in Australian Trade Unions*. Brisbane: Boolarong Press, 2005.

Malmendier, Ulrike and Geoffrey Tate. 'Superstar CEOs'. *Quarterly Journal of Economics* 24 (2009): 1593–638. doi.org/10.1162/qjec.2009.124.4.1593

Mandel, Ernest. *Late Capitalism*. London: New Left Books, 1972.

Mann, Michael. *The Hockey Stick and the Climate Wars: Dispatches from the Front Lines*. New York: Columbia University Press, 2012. doi.org/10.7312/mann15254

Marchington, Mick. 'Shop-Floor Control and Industrial Relations'. In *The Control of Work*, edited by John Purcell and Robin Smith. London: Macmillan, 1979. doi.org/10.1007/978-1-349-03356-0_6

Markey, Ray, Joseph McIvor, and Chris F. Wright. *Climate Change and the Australian Workplace: Final Report for the Australian Department of Industry on State of Knowledge on Climate Change, Work and Employment.* Sydney: Macquarie University, 2014.

Marx, Karl. *Capital, Volume 1.* London: The Electric Book Company, 1887, repr. 1998.

——. *Capital, Volume 2.* London: The Electric Book Company, 1885, repr. 1998.

——. *The Eighteenth Brumaire of Louis Bonaparte.* London: The Electric Book Company, 1852, repr. 1998.

Marx, Karl and Fredrich Engels. *The Communist Manifesto.* Collected Works. Moscow: Progress publishers, 1848, repr. 1977.

Masterman-Smith, Helen. 'Green Collaring a Capital Crisis?'. *Labour and Industry* 20, no. 3 (April 2010): 317–30. doi.org/10.1080/10301763.2010.10669406

May, Robyn, David Peetz, and Glenda Strachan. 'The Casual Academic Workforce and Labour Market Segmentation in Australia'. *Labour and Industry* 23, no. 3 (2013): 258–75. doi.org/10.1080/10301763.2013.839085

Mayer, Jane. 'The Making of the Fox News White House'. *New Yorker*, 11 March 2019.

Mayne, Stephen, 'McInnes is back, but is Lew's blokey board ready for backlash?'. *Crikey*, 25 March 2011, www.crikey.com.au/2011/03/25/mcinnes-is-back-but-is-lew%e2%80%99s-blokey-board-ready-for-the-backlash/

Mazzucato, Mariana. 'Taxpayers Helped Apple, but Apple Won't Help Them'. *Harvard Business Review*, 8 March 2013.

McElwee, Sean and Amy Traub. 'Don't Believe the Wal-Mart Hype: Here's Proof It Still Isn't Paying Its Workers Enough'. *Salon*, 19 September 2015.

McMahon, Anne M. 'Does Workplace Diversity Matter? A Survey of Empirical Studies on Diversity and Firm Performance, 2000–09'. *Journal of Diversity Management* 5, no. 2 (2010): 37–48.

McManus, Richard and Gulcin Ozkan. 'Who Does Better for the Economy? Presidents Versus Parliamentary Democracies'. *Public Choice* 176, no. 6 (May 2018): 361–87. doi.org/10.1007/s11127-018-0552-2

McPherson, Mevyl. 'Workforce Diversity: Evidence of Positive Outcomes and How to Achieve Them. A Review of the Literature'. In *Labour, Employment and Work.* Wellington: Victoria University of Wellington, 2008.

Mealor, Tony. *ICI Australia: The Botany Experience*. Sydney: School of Industrial Relations and Organisational Behaviour, University of New South Wales, 1992.

Meek, V. Lynn. 'Organisational Culture: Origins and Weaknesses'. *Organisational Studies* 9, no. 4 (1988): 453–73. doi.org/10.1177/017084068800900401

Menegus, Bryan. 'Google Agreed to Pay Execs Accused of Sexual Harassment $135 Million'. *Gizmodo*, 11 March 2019.

Mercer, Jeffrey. 'Corporate Social Responsibility and Its Importance to Consumers'. The Claremont Graduate University, 2003.

Milanovic, Branko. *Global Income Inequality by the Numbers: In History and Now*. Policy Research Working Paper 6259. Washington DC: Development Research Group, World Bank, 2012.

——. *Global Inequality: A New Approach for the Age of Globalization*. Cambridge, MA: Harvard University Press, 2016. doi.org/10.4159/9780674969797

——. 'Inequality in the Age of Globalization'. In *ECFIN's Annual Research Conference, Fostering Inclusive Growth: Inequality and Fairness in Integrated Markets*. Lecture in Honor of Anthony A. Atkinson. Brussels: European Commission, 2017.

Milgram, Stanley. *Obedience to Authority*. New York: Harper & Row, 1974.

Miliband, Ralph. *The State in Capitalist Society*. New York: Basic, 1969.

Militantcentrist. 'Union-Busting & You: Wal-Mart's Handy Guide to Preventing Union Organization'. *Daily Kos*, 25 September 2012. www.dailykos.com/stories/2012/9/25/1136113/-Union-Busting-You-Wal-Mart-s-Handy-Guideto-Preventing-Union-Organization

Mills, C. Wright. *The Power Elite*. New York: Oxford University Press, 1956.

Ming-Xiao, Wang, Zhang Tao, Xie Miao-Rong, Zhang Bin, and Jia Ming-Qiu. 'Analysis of National Coal-Mining Accident Data in China, 2001–2008'. *Public Health Reports* 126, no. 2 (2011): 270–75. doi.org/10.1177/003335491112600218

Minter, Kate. 'Negotiating Labour Standards in the Gig Economy: Airtasker and Unions New South Wales'. *Economic and Labour Relations Review* 28, no. 3 (2017): 438–54. doi.org/10.1177/1035304617724305

Mintzberg, Henry. 'Strategy Formulation as a Historical Process'. *International Studies of Management & Organization* 7, no. 2 (Summer 1977): 28–40. doi.org/10.1080/00208825.1977.11656225

Mitchell, Richard and Joel Fetter. 'Human Resource Management and Individualisation in Australian Law'. *Journal of Industrial Relations* 45, no. 3 (September 2003): 292–325. doi.org/10.1111/1472-9296.00085

Mitchell, Stacy. 'Amazon Doesn't Just Want to Dominate the Market—It Wants to Become the Market'. *The Nation*, 15 February 2018.

Mokyr, Joel. 'Long-Term Economic Growth and the History of Technology'. In *Handbook of Economic Growth,* edited by Philippe Aghion and Steven N. Durlauf, 1113–80, 2005.

Morck, Randall. *Behavioral Finance in Corporate Governance—Independent Directors and Non-Executive Chairs.* Discussion Paper No. 2037. Cambridge, MA: Harvard Institute of Economic Research, 2004.

Morehead, Alison, Mairi Steele, Michael J. Alexander, Kerry Stephen, and Linton Duffin. *Changes at Work: The 1995 Australian Workplace Industrial Relations Survey.* South Melbourne: Longman, 1997.

Morgan, Gareth. *Images of Organisation.* London: Sage, 1986.

Moulier Boutang, Yann. *Cognitive Capitalism.* (Translated by Ed Emery.) Cambridge: Polity, 2011.

Muir, Kathie. *Worth Fighting For: Inside the Your Rights at Work Campaign.* Sydney: UNSW Press, 2008.

Muir, Kathie and David Peetz. 'Not Dead Yet: The Australian Union Movement and the Defeat of a Government'. *Social Movement Studies* 9, no. 2 (April 2010): 215–28. doi.org/10.1080/14742831003603380

Munoz, Eduardo. 'Walmart Warns Workers Not to Use App Helping Them Understand Company's Labor Rules'. RT, www.rt.com/usa/367062-walmart-worker-app-workit/

Murphy, Jason. 'Climate Change Could Make the World "Uninsurable"'. *Crikey*, 14 March 2019.

Murray, Cameron and Paul Frijters. *Game of Mates: How Favours Bleed the Nation.* Publicious, 2017.

Murray, Georgina. *Capitalist Networks and Social Power in Australia and New Zealand.* Aldershot: Ashgate, 2006.

Murray, Georgina and David Peetz. 'Financial Markets, Climate Change, and Paradoxes of Coordination and Intervention'. *Perspectives on Global Development and Technology* 15, no. 5 (2016): 455–79. doi.org/10.1163/15691497-12341402

——. 'Ideology Down under and the Shifting Sands of Individualism'. In *Labour and Employment in a Globalising World: Autonomy, Collectives and Political Dilemmas*, edited by Christian Azais. Brussels: PEI Peter Lang, 2010.

——. 'Plutonomy and the One Per Cent'. In *Challenging the Orthodoxy: Reflections on Frank Stilwell's Contribution to Political Economy*, edited by Susan Schroeder and Lynne Chester, 129–48. Sydney: Springer, 2013.

——. 'Restructuring of Corporate Ownership in Australia through the Global Financial Crisis,'. *Journal of Australian Political Economy* 71 (Winter 2013): 76–105.

——. *Women of the Coal Rushes*. Sydney: UNSW Press, 2010.

Murray, Georgina, David Peetz, and Olav Muurlink. 'Structuring Gender Relations among Coal Mine Workers'. In *Women at Work: Labor Segmentation and Regulation*, edited by D. Peetz and G. Murray, 119–36. New York: Palgrave Macmillan, 2017. doi.org/10.1057/978-1-137-55495-6_7

——. *Women and Work in Australian Mining*. Brisbane: Centre for Work, Organisation and Wellbeing, Griffith University, 2012.

Murray, Georgina and John Scott. *Financial Elites and Transnational Business: Who Rules the World? Edward Elgar, Cheltenham*. Cheltenham: Edward Elgar, 2012. doi.org/10.4337/9780857935526

Myers, Joe. 'Swearing on Social Media Really Could Cost You Your Job'. World Economic Forum, 2017.

New York Times Editorial, The. *Climate Refugees: How Global Change Is Displacing Millions*. New York: New York Times, 2017.

Nguyen, Olivia and Trinh Nguyen. 'Exclusive: Exploitation of Vietnamese Students Rampant among Melbourne Businesses'. SBS Vietnamese (Special Broadcasting Service), 20 April 2017. sbs.com.au/yourlanguage/vietnamese/en/explainer/exclusive-exploitation-vietnamese-students-rampant-among-melbourne-businesses

Niederle, Muriel and Lise Vesterlund. *Do Women Shy Away from Competition? Do Men Compete Too Much?* NBER Working Paper No. 11474. Cambridge, MA: National Bureau of Economic Research, 2005.

Nienhüser, Werner. 'Employees Want Democracy in the Workplace'. *Magazin Mitbestimmung*, Hans-Böckler-Stiftung, www.boeckler.de/66359.htm

——. 'Resource Dependence Theory—How Well Does It Explain Behavior of Organizations?'. *Management Revue* 19, no. 1–2 (2008): 9–32. doi.org/10.5771/0935-9915-2008-1-2-9

Noon, Mike. 'Pointless Diversity Training: Unconscious Bias, New Racism and Agency'. *Work, Employment and Society* 32, no. 1 (2018): 198–209. doi.org/10.1177/0950017017719841

Noon, Mike and Paul Blyton. *The Realities of Work: Experiencing Work and Employment in Contemporary Society*. Basingstoke: Palgrave Macmillan, 2002. doi.org/10.1007/978-1-4039-1445-3

Norges Bank Investment Management. *NBIM Quarterly Performance Report; First Quarter 2008*. Oslo: Norges Bank, 2008.

Nossar, Igor, Richard Johnstone, Anna Macklin, and Michael Rawling. 'Protective Legal Regulation for Home-Based Workers in Australian Textile, Clothing and Footwear Supply Chains'. *Journal of Industrial Relations* 57, no. 4 (2015): 585–603. doi.org/10.1177/0022185615582236

Nossar, Igor, Richard Johnstone, and Michael Quinlan. 'Regulating Supply Chains to Address the Occupational Health and Safety Problems Associated with Precarious Employment: The Case of Home-Based Clothing Workers in Australia'. *Australian Journal of Labour Law* 17 (2004): 137–64.

Novak, Matt. 'Bullshit Article About Bullshit Automation Promises Bullshit Life of Leisure'. *Gizmodo*, 16 October 2017.

O'Donnell, Michael. 'Empowerment or Enslavement? Lean Production, Immigrant Women and Service Work in Public Hospitals'. *Labour and Industry* 6, no. 3 (October 1995): 73–94. doi.org/10.1080/10301763.1995.10669145

O'Neill, Cathy. *Weapons of Math Destruction: How Big Data Increases Inequality and Threatens Democracy*. New York: Crown Publishing Group, 2016.

Ogbonna, Emmanuel. 'Organisation Culture and Human Resource Management: Dilemmas and Contradictions'. In *Reassessing Human Resource Management*, edited by P. Blyton and P. Turnbull, 74–96. London: Sage, 1992.

Oreskes, Naomi and Erik Conway. *Merchants of Doubt: How a Handful of Scientists Obscured the Truth on Issues From Tobacco Smoke to Global Warming*. London: Bloomsbury, 2010.

Organisation for Economic Co-operation and Development. *Chapter 1. Knowledge Economies: Trends and Features*. OECD Science, Technology and Industry Scoreboard 2015. Paris: OECD, 2015.

——. *Employment Outlook*. Paris: OECD, 2017.

——. *Employment Outlook*. Paris: OECD, 2009.

——. *Making Globalisation Work: Better Lives for All*. Key Issues Paper, Meeting of the OECD Council at Ministerial Level. Paris: OECD, 2017.

——. *The OECD Jobs Study: Facts, Analysis, Strategy*. Paris: OECD, 1994.

——. 'OECD Productivity Database'. Paris: OECD, 2006. Now accessible via www.oecd.org/std/productivity-stats/

Orwell, George. *Nineteen Eighty-Four: A Novel*. Harmondsworth: Penguin, 1949, repr. 1976.

Osberg, Lars and Timothy Smeeding. '"Fair" Inequality? Attitudes toward Pay Differentials: The United States in Comparative Perspective'. *American Sociological Review* 71, no. 3 (2006): 450–73. doi.org/10.1177/000312240607100305

Oxenbridge, Sarah. 'The Individualisation of Employment Relations in New Zealand: Trends and Outcomes'. In *Employment Relations: Individualisation and Union Exclusion—an International Study*, edited by Stephen Deery and Richard Mitchell, 227–50. Sydney: Federation Press, 1999.

Oxfam Australia. *The Hidden Billions: How Tax Havens Impact Lives at Home and Abroad*. Oxfam, 2016.

Palley, Thomas I. 'Financialization: What It Is and Why It Matters'. Working Paper No. 525. Annandale-on-Hudson, NY: Levy Economics Institute, 2007.

Palmer, Charis and Sunanda Creagh. 'Climate Change Linked to Declines in Labour Productivity'. *The Conversation*, 25 February 2013.

Parijs, Philippe Van and Yannick Vanderborght. *Basic Income: A Radical Proposal for a Free Society and a Sane Economy*. Cambridge, MA: Harvard University Press, 2017. doi.org/10.4159/9780674978072

Parker, Jane and Julie Douglas. 'Can Women's Structures Help New Zealand and UK Trade Unions' Revival?'. *Journal of Industrial Relations* 52, no. 4 (2010): 439–58. doi.org/10.1177/0022185610375508

Pasquale, Frank. 'Will Amazon Take over the World?'. *Boston Review*, 20 July 2017.

Peetz, David. 'Aim for Gains, Not Profits'. *The Australian* Higher Education Supplement, 6 September 2006, 30.

——. 'Are Collective Identity and Action Being Squashed by Individualism?'. In *Work and Identity: Contemporary Perspectives on Workplace Diversity*, edited by Shalene Werth and Charlotte Brownlow. New York: Palgrave, 2018. doi.org/10.1007/978-3-319-73936-6_11

——. 'Are Individualistic Attitudes Killing Collectivism?'. *Transfer—European Review of Labour and Research* 16, no. 3 (2010): 383–98. doi.org/10.1177/1024258910373869

——. *Brave New Workplace: How Individual Contracts Are Changing Our Jobs*. Sydney: Allen & Unwin, 2006.

——. 'The Choices We Make—a "Sliding Doors" Moment'. *Griffith Review* 45 (July 2014): 44–75.

——. 'Co-operative Values, Institutions and Free Riding in Australia: Can It Learn from Canada?'. *Relations Industrielles/Industrial Relations* 60, no. 4 (2005): 709–36.

——. 'Collateral Damage: Women and the Workchoices Battlefield'. *Hecate* 33, no. 1 (May 2007): 61–80.

——. 'Debt in Paradise: On the Ground with Wage Theft'. *Griffith Review* 61 (July 2018): 185–91.

——. 'Decollectivist Strategies in Oceania'. *Relations Industrielles* 57, no. 2 (Spring 2002): 252–81. doi.org/10.7202/006780ar

——. 'Does Industrial Relations Policy Affect Productivity?'. *Australian Bulletin of Labour* 38, no. 4 (2012): 268–92.

——. 'Hollow Shells: The Alleged Link between Individual Contracting and Productivity'. *Journal of Australian Political Economy* 56 (2005): 32–55.

——. *The Impact of the Penalty Rates Decision on Australian and Victorian Workers in Retail and Hospitality Industries*. Melbourne: Department of Economic Development, Jobs Transport and Resources Commissioned Research Report, 2017.

——. 'Industrial Action, the Right to Strike, Ballots and the Fair Work Act in International Context'. *Australian Journal of Labour Law* 29 (2016): 133–53.

——. 'Industrial Conflict with Awards, Choices and Fairness'. In *Rediscovering Collective Bargaining: Australia's Fair Work Act in International Perspective*, edited by Anthony Forsyth and Breen Creighton, 159–81. New York: Routledge, 2012.

——. 'An Institutional Analysis of the Growth of Executive Remuneration'. *Journal of Industrial Relations* 57, no. 5 (November 2015): 707–25. doi.org/10.1177/0022185615590903

——. 'The Labour Share, Power and Financialisation'. *Journal of Australian Political Economy* 81 (2018): 33–51.

——. *The Operation of the Queensland Workers' Compensation Scheme*. Report of the Second Five Yearly Review of the Scheme. Brisbane: Parliament of Queensland, 2018.

——. 'Protection and the Labour Movement'. *Journal of Australian Political Economy* 12/13 (June 1982): 62–73.

——. 'Regulation Distance, Labour Segmentation & Gender Gaps'. *Cambridge Journal of Economics* 39, no. 2 (November 2015): 345–62. doi.org/10.1093/cje/beu054

——. *The Relationship between Collective Representation and National Pension Fund Outcomes*. Melbourne: Industry Super, 2019.

——. 'Sympathy for the Devil? Attitudes to Australian Unions'. *Australian Journal of Political Science* 37, no. 1 (March 2002): 57–80. doi.org/10.1080/13603100220119029

——. 'Trend Analysis of Union Membership'. *Australian Journal of Labour Economics* 8, no. 1 (2005): 1–24.

——. *Unions in a Contrary World: The Future of the Australian Trade Union Movement*. Cambridge: Cambridge University Press, 1998. doi.org/10.1017/CBO9781139106818

——. 'Why Establish Non-Representative Organisations? Rethinking the Role, Form and Target of Think Tanks'. In *Think-Tanks: Key Spaces in the Global Structure of Power*, edited by Alejandra Salas-Porras and Georgina Murray. New York: Palgrave Macmillan, 2017.

——. 'Workplace Cooperation, Conflict, Influence and Union Membership'. In *Contemporary Research on Unions: Theory, Membership, Organisation and Non-Standard Employment*, edited by G. Griffin. Monograph No. 8, 309–46. Melbourne: National Key Centre in Industrial Relations, 1996.

Peetz, David and Michael Alexander. 'A Synthesis of Research on Training of Union Delegates'. *Industrial Relations Journal* 44, no. 4 (2013): 425–42. doi.org/10.1111/irj.12023

Peetz, David, Cameron Allan, and Michael O'Donnell. 'Are Australians Really Unhappier with Their Bosses Because They're Working Harder? Perspiration and Persuasion in Modern Work'. Rethinking Institutions for Work and Employment, Selected Papers from the XXXVIII Annual Canadian Industrial Relations Association Conference, Quebec, 26–28 May 2001.

Peetz, David and Janis Bailey. 'Dancing Alone: The Australian Union Movement over Three Decades'. *Journal of Industrial Relations* 54, no. 4 (2012): 524–41. doi.org/10.1177/0022185612449133

——. 'Neoliberal Evolution and Union Responses in Australia'. In *International Handbook on Labour Unions: Responses to Neo-Liberalism*, edited by G. Gall, A. Wilkinson, and R. Hurd, 62–81. Cheltenham: Edward Elgar, 2011. doi.org/10.4337/9780857938053.00009

Peetz, David, Scott Bruynius, and Georgina Murray. 'Choice and the Impact of Changes to Sunday Premiums in the Australian Retail and Hospitality Industries'. *Journal of Industrial Relations* (2019). doi.org/10.1177/0022185618814578

Peetz, David and Ann Frost. 'Employee Voice in the Anglo-American World: What Does It Mean for Unions?'. In *What Workers Say: Employee Voice in the Anglo-American World*, edited by Richard B. Freeman, Peter Boxall, and Peter Haynes. Ithaca NY: ILR Press, 2007.

Peetz, David, Chris Houghton, and Barbara Pocock. 'Organisers' Roles Transformed? Australian Union Organizers and Changing Union Strategy'. *Journal of Industrial Relations* 49, no. 2 (2005): 151–66. doi.org/10.1177/0022185607074907

Peetz, David, Stephane Le Queux, and Ann Frost. 'The Global Financial Crisis and Employment Relations'. In *The Future of Employment Relations: New Paradigms, New Approaches*, edited by Adrian Wilkinson and Keith Townsend, 193–214. Basingstoke: Palgrave Macmillan, 2011. doi.org/10.1057/9780230349421_11

Peetz, David and Georgina Murray. 'Class, Attitudes and Climate Change'. In *Public Opinion, Campaign Politics and Media Audiences: New Perspectives on Australian Politics*, edited by Bridget Griffen-Foley and Sean R. Scalmer. Melbourne: Melbourne University Press, 2017.

——. 'Conflicts within Transnational Finance Capital and the Motivations of Climate-Interested Investors'. In *Globalization and Transnational Capitalism in Asia and Oceania*, edited by Jeb Sprague, 163–79: Routledge, 2015.

——. 'The Financialisation of Global Corporate Ownership'. In *Financial Elites and Transnational Business: Who Rules the World?*, edited by Georgina Murray and John Scott. Cheltenham: Edward Elgar, 2012. doi.org/10.4337/9780857935526.00007

——. 'Financialization of Corporate Ownership and Implications for the Potential for Climate Action'. In *Institutional Investors' Power to Change Corporate Behavior: International Perspectives, Critical Studies on Corporate Responsibility, Governance and Sustainability*, edited by Suzanne Young and Stephen Gates, 99–125. Bingley, UK: Emerald, 2013. doi.org/10.1108/S2043-9059(2013)0000005013

——. *Global Wellbeing and Climate-Interested Investors' Motives*. Working Paper. Brisbane: Centre for Work, Organisation and Wellbeing, Griffith University, 2013.

——. 'The Government Is Swimming against the Tide on Westpac's Adani Decision'. *The Conversation*, 3 May 2017.

——. 'I, Cyborg: The Life and Work of Digital Humans'. *Griffith Review* 64 (May 2019). griffithreview.com/articles/i-cyborg-digital-humans/

——. 'The Persistence of Gender Gaps'. In *Women, Labor Segmentation and Regulation: Varieties of Gender Gaps*, edited by David Peetz and Georgina Murray, 235–55. New York: Palgrave Macmillan, 2017. doi.org/10.1057/978-1-137-55495-6

——. 'The "Powerful Women Paradox": Why Women at the Top Still Miss Out'. In *Macht Und Employment Relations. Festschrift Für Werner Nienhüser*, edited by H. Hossfeld and R. Ortlieb, 181–86. Mering, Bayern: Rainer Hampp Verlag, 2013.

——. *Women, Labor Segmentation and Regulation: Varieties of Gender Gaps*. New York: Palgrave Macmillan, 2017. doi.org/10.1057/978-1-137-55495-6

——. 'Women's Employment, Segregation and Skills in the Future of Work'. *Labour and Industry* 29, no. 1 (2019): 132–48. doi.org/10.1080/10301763.2019.1565294

——. '"You Get Really Old, Really Quick": Involuntary Long Hours in the Mining Industry'. *Journal of Industrial Relations* 53, no. 1 (2011): 13–29. doi.org/10.1177/0022185610390294

Peetz, David, Georgina Murray, Ian Lowe, and Christopher Wright. *Corporations, Their Associations, and Climate Action*. Canberra: Association of Industrial Relations Academics of Australia and New Zealand/SSRN, 2017.

Peetz, David, Georgina Murray, and Olav Muurlink. *Work and Hours Amongst Mining and Energy Workers*. Brisbane: Centre for Work, Organisation and Wellbeing, Griffith University, 2012.

Peetz, David, Georgina Murray, Olav Muurlink, and Maggie May. 'The Meaning and Making of Union Delegate Networks'. *Economic and Labour Relations Review* 26, no. 4 (December 2015): 596–613. doi.org/10.1177/1035304615614717

Peetz, David, Georgina Murray, and Werner Nienhüser. 'The New Structuring of Corporate Ownership'. *Globalizations* 10, no. 5 (2013): 711–30. doi.org/10.1080/14747731.2013.828965

Peetz, David, Georgina Murray, and Mahan Poorhosseinzadeh. 'Why Do Women at the Top of Organizations Do Worse?'. In *Women, Labor Segmentation and Regulation: Varieties of Gender Gaps*, edited by David Peetz and Georgina Murray. New York: Palgrave Macmillan, 2017. doi.org/10.1057/978-1-137-55495-6

Peetz, David, Olav Muurlink, Keith Townsend, Cameron Allan, and Andrea Fox. 'Quality and Quantity in Work–Home Conflict: Nature and Direction of Effects of Work on Employees' Personal Relationships and Partners'. *Australian Bulletin of Labour* 37, no. 2 (2011): 138–63.

Peetz, David and Barbara Pocock. 'An Analysis of Workplace Representatives, Union Power and Democracy in Australia'. *British Journal of Industrial Relations* 47, no. 4 (December 2009): 623–52. doi.org/10.1111/j.1467-8543.2009.00736.x

——. 'Community Activists, Coalitions and Unionism'. In *Trade Unions in the Community: Values, Issues, Shared Interests and Alliances*, edited by D. Buttigieg, S. Cockfield, R. Cooney, M. Jerrard and A. Rainnie. Adelaide: Heidelberg Press, 2007.

——. 'Organising and Delegates: An Overview'. Association of Industrial Relations Academics of Australia and New Zealand conference, Sydney, February 2005.

Peetz, David and Alison Preston. 'Individual Contracting, Collective Bargaining and Wages in Australia'. *Industrial Relations Journal* 40, no. 5 (September 2009): 444–61. doi.org/10.1111/j.1468-2338.2009.00537.x

Peetz, David, Robin Price, and Janis Bailey. 'Ageing Australian Unions and the "Youth Problem"'. In *Young People and Trade Unions: A Global View*, edited by Lefteris Kretsos and Andrew Hodder. Palgrave Macmillan, 2015.

Peetz, David, David Quinn, Leah Edwards, and Peter Riedel. 'Workplace Bargaining in New Zealand: Radical Change at Work'. In *Workplace Bargaining in the International Context*, edited by David Peetz, Alison Preston and Jim Docherty. Workplace Bargaining Research Project. Canberra: Department of Industrial Relations and Australian Government Publishing Service, 1993.

Peetz, David and Trish Todd. *Globalisation and Employment Relations in Malaysia.* Bangkok: International Labour Office, 2000.

Peetz, David, Keith Townsend, Robert Russell, Chris Houghton, Andrea Fox, and Cameron Allan. 'Race against Time: Extended Hours in Australia'. *Australian Bulletin of Labour* 29, no. 2 (June 2003): 126–42.

Peetz, David, Carol Webb, and Meredith Jones. 'Activism Amongst Workplace Union Delegates'. *International Journal of Employment Studies* 10, no. 2 (October 2002): 83–108.

Peetz, David and Serena Yu. *Explaining Recent Trends in Collective Bargaining.* Research Report 4/2017. Melbourne: Fair Work Commission, 2017.

Pennington, Randy G. 'Change Performance to Change the Culture'. *Industrial and Commercial Training* 35, no. 6 (2003): 251–55.

Perez, Thomas. 'Video: A Message from Former US Secretary of Labor Thomas Perez to the Next Generation Workforce'. In *Shaping the Future of Work.* Cambridge, MA: MIT and EdX, 2017.

Peters, Thomas J. and Robert H. Waterman. *In Search of Excellence.* New York: Harper & Row, 1982.

Pew Research Center. 'Europe's Growing Muslim Population'. Pew–Templeton Global Religious Futures project, Pew Research Center, www.pewforum.org/wp-content/uploads/sites/7/2017/11/FULL-REPORT-FOR-WEB-POSTING.pdf

Pfeffer, Jeffrey. *Power in Organizations.* Pitman, 1981.

Pfeffer, Jeffrey and Gerald R. Salancik. *The External Control of Organizations. A Resource Dependence Perspective.* New York: Harper & Row, 1978.

Phelan, Julie E., and Laurie A. Rudman. 'Prejudice toward Female Leaders: Backlash Effects and Women's Impression Management Dilemma'. *Social and Personality Psychology Compass* 4, no. 10 (2010): 807–20. doi.org/10.1111/j.1751-9004.2010.00306.x

Pheysey, Diana C. *Organisational Cultures: Types and Transformations.* London: Routledge, 1993.

Philips, Christopher B. 'The Case for Indexing'. Vanguard Research. Valley Forge, PA: The Vanguard Group, 2011.

Phillips, Ken. *Independence and the Death of Employment.* Ballan, Vic.: Connor Court Publishing, 2008.

Pigliucci, Alex, Kendra Thompson, and Mark Halverson. *The "Greater" Wealth Transfer: Capitalizing on the Intergenerational Shift in Wealth.* Wealth and Asset Management Services, Point of View. Arlington, VA: Accenture, 2015.

Piguet, Etienne, Antoine Pécoud, and Paul de Guchteneire. 'Migration and Climate Change: An Overview'. *Refugee Survey Quarterly* 33, no. 3 (2011): 1–23. doi.org/10.1093/rsq/hdr006

Piketty, Thomas. *Capital in the Twenty-First Century*. Cambridge, MA: Harvard University Press, 2014. doi.org/10.4159/9780674369542

——. 'Panama Papers: Act Now. Don't Wait for Another Crisis'. *Guardian*, 10 April 2016.

Pocock, Barbara. 'Gender and Activism in Australian Unions'. *Journal of Industrial Relations* 37, no. 3 (September 1995): 377–400. doi.org/10.1177/002218569503700303

——. 'Institutional Sclerosis: Prospects for Trade Union Transformation'. *Labour & Industry* 9, no. 1 (1998): 17–33. doi.org/10.1080/10301763.1998.10669184

——. *The Labour Market Ate My Babies.* Sydney: Federation Press, 2006.

——. 'Women Count: Women in South Australian Trade Unions'. Adelaide: Centre for Labour Studies, University of Adelaide, 1992.

——. *The Work–Life Collision.* Sydney: Federation Press, 2003.

——. 'Work/Care Regimes: Institutions, Culture and Behaviour and the Australian Case'. *Gender, Work & Organization* 12, no. 1 (2005): 32–49. doi.org/10.1111/j.1468-0432.2005.00261.x

Pocock, Barbara and Natalie Skinner. *The Australian Work and Life Index (AWALI).* Adelaide: Centre for Work + Life, University of South Australia, 2009.

Pocock, Barbara, Sara Charlesworth, and Janine Chapman. 'Work–Family and Work–Life Pressures in Australia: Advancing Gender Equality in "Good Times"?'. *International Journal of Sociology and Social Policy* 33, no. 9/10 (2013): 594–612. doi.org/10.1108/IJSSP-11-2012-0100

Pocock, Barbara, Rosslyn Prosser, and Ken Bridge. *'Only a Casual…': How Casual Work Affects Employees, Households and Communities in Australia.* Adelaide: Labour Studies, School of Social Sciences, University of Adelaide, 2004.

Pokarier, Christopher James. 'Politics of Foreign Direct Investment in Australia 1960–96'. The Australian National University, 2000.

Polanyi K. *The Great Transformation: The Political and Economic Origins of Our Time.* Boston: Beacon Press, 1944.

Pollert, Anna, ed. *Farewell to Flexibility.* Oxford: Basil Blackwell, 1991.

——. 'The Flexible Firm: Fixation or Fact?'. *Work, Employment and Society* 2, no. 3 (1988): 281–316. doi.org/10.1177/0950017088002003002

Pontusson, Jonas. 'Unionization, Inequality and Redistribution'. *British Journal of Industrial Relations* 51, no. 4 (2013): 797–825.

Postel-Vinay, Karoline. 'How Neo-Nationalism Went Global'. *The Conversation,* 14 March 2017.

Poulantzas, Nicos. *State, Power, and Socialism.* Translated by Patrick Camiller. London: Verso, 1980.

Poulantzas, Nicos and Ralph Miliband. 'The Problem of the Capitalist State'. In *Ideology in Social Science: Readings in Critical Social Theory,* edited by R. Blackburn, 238–62. New York: Pantheon Books.

Powell, James. 'The State of Climate Science: A Thorough Review of the Scientific Literature on Global Warming'. Science Progress, Center for American Progress, scienceprogress.org/2012/11/27479/

Power, Margaret. 'Woman's Work Is Never Done—by Men: A Socio-Economic Model of Sex Typing in Occupations'. *Journal of Industrial Relations* 17, no. 3 (September 1975). doi.org/10.1177/002218567501700301

Pressman, Jeffrey L. and Aaron Wildavsky. *Implementation: How Great Expectations in Washington Are Dashed in Oakland; or Why It's Amazing That Federal Programs Work at All, This Being a Saga of the Economic Development Administration as Told by Two Sympathetic Observers Who Seek to Build Morals on a Foundation of Ruined Hopes.* Berkeley: University of California Press, 1973.

Preston, Alison C. 'Female Earnings in Australia: An Analysis of 1991 Census Data'. *Australian Bulletin of Labour* 26, no. 1 (2000): 38–58.

Price, Robin. 'Controlling Routine Front Line Service Workers: An Australian Retail Supermarket Case'. *Work, Employment and Society* 30, no. 6 (2016): 915–31. doi.org/10.1177/0950017015601778

Pruett, Duncan. *Looking for a Quick Fix: How Weak Social Auditing Is Keeping Workers in Sweatshops*. Amsterdam: Clean Clothes Campaign, 2005.

Purcell, John. 'Mapping Management Styles in Employee Relations'. *Journal of Management Studies* (1987): 205–23. doi.org/10.1111/j.1467-6486.1987.tb00462.x

Pusey, Michael. *Economic Rationalism in Canberra: A Nation-Building State Changes Its Mind.* Cambridge, UK: Cambridge University Press, 2003.

Pusey, Michael and Nick Turnbull. 'Have Australians Embraced Economic Reform?'. In *Australian Social Attitudes: The First Report*, edited by Shaun Wilson et al., 161–81. Sydney: UNSW Press, 2005.

Quiggin, John. 'Globalisation, Neoliberalism and Inequality in Australia'. *Economic and Labour Relations Review* 10, no. 2 (1999): 240–59. doi.org/10.1177/103530469901000206

——. 'How Thomas Piketty Found a Mass Audience, and What It Means for Public Policy'. *Inside Story* (30 May 2014).

——. 'In Praise of Credentialism'. *Inside Story*, 27 February 2017.

——. 'Social Democracy and Market Reform in Australia and New Zealand'. *Oxford Review of Economic Policy* 14, no. 1 (1998): 76–95. doi.org/10.1093/oxrep/14.1.76

——. *Zombie Economics*. New Jersey: Princeton University Press, 2010.

Quinlan, Michael. *The Effects of Non-Standard Forms of Employment on Worker Health and Safety*. Conditions of Work and Employment Series No. 67. Geneva: International Labour Office, Inclusive Labour Markets, Labour Relations and Working Conditions Branch, 2015.

Quinlan, Michael, Philip Bohle, and Felicity Lamm. *Managing Occupational Health and Safety: A Multidisciplinary Approach*. Palgrave Macmillan, 2010.

Rafferty, Mike and Serena Yu. *Shifting Risk: Work and Working Life in Australia.* A report for the Australian Council of Trade Unions. Sydney: Workplace Research Centre, University of Sydney, 2010.

Rahwan, Iyad. 'Society-in-the-Loop: Programming the Algorithmic Social Contract'. *Ethics and Information Technology* 20, no. 1 (2018): 5–14. doi.org/10.1007/s10676-017-9430-8

Ram, Monder and Paul K. Edwards. 'Praising Caesar Not Burying Him: What We Know About Employment Relations in Small Firms'. *Work, Employment and Society* 17, no. 4 (2003): 719–30. doi.org/10.1177/0950017003174006

Rasmussen, E. and J. Deeks. 'Contested Outcomes: Assessing the Impacts of the Employment Contracts Act'. *California Western International Law Journal* 28 (1997): 275–96.

Ray, James Lee. 'Wars between Democracies: Rare or Nonexistent?'. *International Interactions* 18, no. 3 (1993): 251–76. doi.org/10.1080/03050629308434807

Rebhun, Uzi. 'A Double Disadvantage? Immigration, Gender, and Employment Status in Israel.'. *European Journal of Population* 24, no. 1 (2008): 8–113. doi.org/10.1007/s10680-007-9137-3

Reeder, Ern. 'The Fast Food Industry'. In *Technology and the Labour Process*, edited by Evan Willis. Sydney: Allen & Unwin, 1988.

Rees, Gareth and Sarah Fielder. 'The Services Economy, Subcontracting and the New Employment Relations: Contract Catering and Cleaning'. *Work, Employment and Society* 6, no. 3 (September 1992): 73–94. doi.org/10.1177/095001709263003

Reeve, Belinda H., Dorothy H. Broom, Lyndall Strazdins, and Megan Shipley. 'Regulation, Managerial Discretion and Family-Friendliness in Australia's Changing Industrial Relations Environment'. *Journal of Industrial Relations* 54, no. 1 (2012): 57–74. doi.org/10.1177/0022185611432385

Regalado, Antonio. 'With Neuralink, Elon Musk Promises Human-to-Human Telepathy. Don't Believe It'. *MIT Technology Review*, 22 April 2017.

Reinecke, Juliane and Jimmy Donaghey. 'After Rana Plaza: Building Coalitional Power for Labour Rights between Unions and (Consumption-Based) Social Movement Organisations'. *Organization* 22, no. 5 (2015): 720–40. doi.org/10.1177/1350508415585028

Ressia, Sue. 'Starting from Scratch: Skilled Dual Career Migrant Couples and Their Search for Employment in South East Queensland'. *International Journal of Employment Studies* 18, no. 1 (2010): 63–88.

Rhodes, Carl. '"Command and Control" Banks Have Got Ethics and Culture All Wrong'. *The Conversation*, 18 March 2016.

Riaño, Yvonne and Nadia Baghdadi. 'Understanding the Labour Market Participation of Skilled Immigrant Women in Switzerland: The Interplay of Class, Ethnicity, and Gender'. *International Migration and Integration* 8, no. 2 (2007): 163–83. doi.org/10.1007/s12134-007-0012-1

Richard, Michael Graham. 'This Striking Chart Shows Why Solar Power Will Take over the World'. *Treehugger*, www.treehugger.com/renewable-energy/striking-chart-showing-solar-power-will-take-over-world.html

Richard, Orlando C. 'Racial Diversity, Business Strategy, and Firm Performance: A Resource-Based View'. *Academy of Management Journal* 43, no. 2 (2000): 164–77.

Rimmer, Malcolm. 'Work Place Unionism'. In *Australian Unions: An Industrial Relations Perspective*, edited by William Ford and David Plowman, 122–44. Melbourne: Macmillan, 1989. doi.org/10.1007/978-1-349-11088-9_6

Rimmer, Russell and Sheila Rimmer. *More Brilliant Careers*. Canberra: AGPS, 1994.

Robinson, William I. 'Global Capitalism: Crisis of Humanity and the Specter of 21st Century Fascism'. *The World Financial Review*, 2014. doi.org/10.1017/CBO9781107590250

Robinson, William I. and Jerry Harris. 'Towards a Global Ruling Class? Globalisation and the Transnational Capitalist Class'. *Science and Society* 64, no. 1 (2000): 11.

Rockefeller Foundation and Global Strategy Group. *CEOs & Gender: A Media Analysis*. New York: Rockefeller Foundation, 2016.

——. *Women in Leadership: Why It Matters*. New York: Rockefeller Foundation, 2016.

Rogers, Brishen. *Beyond Automation: The Law & Political Economy of Workplace Technological Change*. SSRN, 2019.

Rosenzweig, Philip. 'The Halo Effect and the Challenge of Management Inquiry: A Dialog between Phil Rosenzweig and Paul Olk'. *Journal of Management Inquiry* 19 (2010): 48–54. doi.org/10.1177/1056492609347567

Rosti, Luisa, Chikara Yamaguchi, and Carolina Castagnetti. 'Educational Performance as Signalling Device: Evidence from Italy'. *Economics Bulletin* 9, no. 4 (2005): 1–7.

Roy, Donald. 'Quota Restriction and Goldbricking in a Machine Shop'. *American Journal of Sociology* 57, no. 5 (1952): 427–42. doi.org/10.1086/221011

Royal Commission into Misconduct in the Banking, Superannuation and Financial Services Industry. *Final Report*. Canberra: Australian Government, 2019.

Rubin, Larry. 'Unions Are All in for People's Climate March, April 29'. *People's World*, 10 April 2017.

Rynderman, John and Catherine Flynn. '"We Didn't Bring the Treasure of Pharaoh": Skilled Migrants' Experiences of Employment Seeking and Settling in Australia'. *International Social Work* 59, no. 2 (2016): 266–83. doi.org/10.1177/0020872813519659

Salas-Porras, Alejandra and Georgina Murray, eds. *Think Tanks and Global Politics: Key Spaces in the Structure of Power*. Singapore: Palgrave Macmillan, 2017. doi.org/10.1057/978-1-137-56756-7

Salvati, Michele. 'A Long Cycle in Industrial Relations'. *Labour* 3, no. 1 (1989): 42–72. doi.org/10.1111/j.1467-9914.1989.tb00148.x

Sapinski, Jean Philippe. 'Climate Capitalism and the Global Corporate Elite Network'. *Environmental Sociology* 1, no. 4 (2015): 268–79. doi.org/10.1080/23251042.2015.1111490

Sassoon, Anne Showstack, ed. *Approaches to Gramsci*. London: Writers and Readers Publishing Cooperative Society, 1982.

Saul, John Ralston. *The Collapse of Globalism: And the Reinvention of the World*. London: Atlantic, 2005.

Savage, Mike. 'Individuality and Class: The Rise and Fall of the Gentlemanly Social Contract in Britain'. In *Social Contracts under Stress: The Middle Classes of America, Europe, and Japan at the Turn of the Century*, edited by Olivier Zunz, Leonard James Schoppa and Nobuhiro Hiwatari, 47–65. New York: Russell Sage, 2002.

Schein, Edgar H. 'Culture: The Missing Concept in Organization Studies'. *Administrative Science Quarterly* 41, no. 2 (June 1996): 229–40. doi.org/10.2307/2393715

——. *Organisational Culture and Leadership*. San Francisco: Jossey-Bass, 1986.

Schein, Edgar H., I. Schneier, and C.H. Barker. *Coercive Persuasion: A Socio-Psychological Analysis of the 'Brainwashing' of American Civilian Prisoners by the Chinese Communists*. New York: Norton, 1961.

Schnabel, Claus. 'Union Membership and Density: Some (Not So) Stylized Facts and Challenges'. *European Journal of Industrial Relations* 19, no. 3 (2013): 255–72. doi.org/10.1177/0959680113493373

Scholz, Trebor and Nathan Schneider. *Ours to Hack and to Own: The Rise of Platform Cooperativism, a New Vision for the Future of Work and a Fairer Internet*. New York: OR Books, 2017. doi.org/10.2307/j.ctv62hfq7

Schulze-Cleven, Tobias and Jennifer R. Olson. 'Worlds of Higher Education Transformed: Toward Varieties of Academic Capitalism'. *Higher Education* 73 (2017): 813–31. doi.org/10.1007/s10734-017-0123-3

Seccombe, Mike. 'The Truth About Wage Stagnation'. *Saturday Paper*, 12 May 2018.

Sheehy, Benedict. 'Corporations and Social Costs: The Wal-Mart Case Study'. *University of Pittsburgh Journal of Law and Commerce* 24 (2004): 1–39.

Shenker-Osorio, Anat. *Don't Buy It: The Trouble with Talking Nonsense About the Economy*. New York: Public Affairs, 2012.

Short, John Rennie. 'Globalization and Its Discontents: Why There's a Backlash and How It Needs to Change'. *Conversation*, 29 November 2016.

Silver, Beverly J. *Forces of Labor: Workers' Movements and Globalization since 1870*. Cambridge, UK: Cambridge University Press, 2003. doi.org/10.1017/CBO9780511615702

Singleton, Gwynneth. 'Corporatism or Labourism? The Australian Labour Movement in Accord'. *Journal of Commonwealth and Comparative Politics* 28, no. 2 (1990): 162–82. doi.org/10.1080/14662049008447586

Sisson, Keith and Paul Marginson. *'Soft Regulation'—Travesty of the Real Thing or New Dimension?* ESRC 'One Europe or Several' Programme, Working Paper 32/01. Brighton: University of Sussex, Sussex European Institute, 2001.

Skinner, Natalie and Janine Chapman. 'Work–Life Balance and Family Friendly Policies'. *Evidence Base* 2013, no. 4 (2013): 1–17. doi.org/10.4225/50/558217B4DE473

Skinner, Natalie, Claire Hutchinson, and Barbara Pocock. *The Big Squeeze: Australian Work and Life Index 2012*. Adelaide: Centre for Work + Life, University of South Australia, 2012.

Skinner, Natalie and Barbara Pocock. 'Flexibility and Work–Life Interference in Australia'. *Journal of Industrial Relations* 53, no. 1 (2011): 65–82. doi.org/10.1177/0022185610390297

——. *The Persistent Challenge: Living, Working and Caring in Australia in 2014*. The Australian Work and Life Index 2014. Adelaide: Centre for Work + Life, University of South Australia, 2014.

——. *Work, Life & Workplace Culture: The Australian Work and Life Index 2008*. Adelaide: Centre for Work + Life, University of South Australia, 2008.

Smedley, Audrey. 'The History of the Idea of Race. And Why It Matters'. In *Race, Human Variation and Disease: Consensus and Frontiers*. Warrenton, VA: American Anthropological Association, 2007.

Smith, Aaron. *Gig Work, Online Selling and Home Sharing*. Pew Research Center, 2016.

Smith, Yves. 'Uber Is Headed for a Crash'. Intelligencer, *New York Magazine*, nymag.com/intelligencer/2018/12/will-uber-survive-the-next-decade.html

Snape, Ed and Andy W. Chan. 'Commitment to Company and Union: Evidence from Hong Kong'. *Industrial Relations* 39, no. 3 (July 2000): 445–59. doi.org/10.1111/0019-8676.00175

Sobyra, Robert. 'Australian Jobs Aren't Becoming Less Secure'. *The Conversation*, 17 July 2018.

Soons, Oscar C. 'Inequality and Financialization'. Senior Honors Projects. Paper 492, University of Rhode Island, digitalcommons.uri.edu/srhonorsprog/492?utm_source=digitalcommons.uri.edu%2Fsrhonorsprog%2F492&utm_medium=PDF&utm_campaign=PDFCoverPages

Stanford, Jim. 'The Declining Labour Share in Australia: Definition, Measurement, and International Comparisons'. *Journal of Australian Political Economy* 81 (2018): 11–32.

Statista. 'Female Labor Participation Rate in China from 2007 to 2017'. Statista, www.statista.com/statistics/252721/female-labor-force-participation-rate-in-china/

Steketee, Mike. 'Government by Algorithm'. *Inside Story*, 5 April 2018.

Stewart, Andrew, Anthony Forsyth, Mark Irving, Richard Johnstone, and Shae McCrystal. *Creighton & Stewart's Labour Law*, 5th ed. Sydney: Federation Press, 2016.

Stewart, Andrew and Rosemary Owen. *Experience or Exploitation? The Nature, Prevalence and Regulation of Unpaid Work Experience, Internships and Trial Periods in Australia*. Report for the Fair Work Ombudsman. Adelaide: University of Adelaide, 2013.

Stewart, Andrew, Jim Stanford, and Tess Hardy, eds. *The Wages Crisis in Australia: What It Is and What to Do About It*. Adelaide: University of Adelaide Press, 2018. doi.org/10.20851/wages-crisis

Stewart, John. *Evolution's Arrow: The Direction of Evolution and the Future of Humanity*. Canberra: Chapman Press, 2000.

Stiglitz, Joseph E. 'A Rigged Economy'. *Scientific American*, 1 November 2018. doi.org/10.1038/scientificamerican1118-56

Stilwell, Frank. *Political Economy: The Contest of Economic Ideas*. South Melbourne: Oxford University Press, 2002.

Stilwell, Frank and Kirrily Jordan. *Who Gets What? Analysing Economic Inequality in Australia*. Cambridge University Press, 2007. doi.org/10.1017/CBO9780511481314

Stoller, Matt. 'S&P—"Our Ratings in the Mortgage-Backed Securities Area Were Not Venal"'. *Naked Capitalism*, 12 August 2011.

Storer, D. and K. Hargreaves. 'Migrant Women in Industry'. In *Social Policy and Problems of the Workforce, Vol. 1,* edited by S. Staats, 39–104. Melbourne: Social Welfare Unit, Australian Council of Trade Unions, 1976.

Storm, Servaas. *Labor Laws and Manufacturing Performance in India: How Priors Trump Evidence and Progress Gets Stalled.* Working Paper No. 90. New York: Institute for New Economic Thinking, January 2019.

Strachan, Glenda and John Burgess. 'Employment Restructuring, Enterprise Bargaining and Employment Conditions for Women Workers'. Paper presented at the Current Research in Industrial Relations conference, Brisbane, AIRAANZ, 1997.

Strachan, Glenda, Carolyn Troup, David Peetz, Gillian Whitehouse, Kaye Broadbent, and Janis Bailey. *Work and Careers in Australian Universities: Report on Employee Survey*. Brisbane: Centre for Work, Organisation and Wellbeing, Griffith University, 2012.

Stratmann, Thomas. 'The Market for Congressional Votes: Is Timing of Contributions Everything?'. *Journal of Law and Economics* 41, no. 1 (April 1998): 85–114.

Strauss, George. 'Workers' Participation in Management'. In *Employment Relations: The Psychology of Influence and Control at Work*, edited by Jean F. Hartley and Geoffrey M. Stevenson, 291–311. Cambridge, MA: Blackwell, 1992.

Streeck, Wolfgang. 'The Uncertainties of Management and the Management of Uncertainty'. *Work, Employment and Society* 1, no. 2 (1987): 281–308. doi.org/10.1177/0950017087001003002

Strobl, Eric and Frank Walsh. 'Minimum Wages and Compliance: The Case of Trinidad and Tobago'. *Economic Development and Cultural Change* 51, no. 2 (2003): 427–50. doi.org/10.1086/346051

Stromback, Thorsten. *The Earnings of Migrants in Australia*. Conference Paper No. 46. Canberra: Bureau of Labour Market Research, 1984.

Sturdy, Andrew, Christopher Wright, and Nick Wylie. *Management as Consultancy: Neo-Bureaucracy and the Consultant Manager*. Cambridge, UK: Cambridge University Press, 2015. doi.org/10.1017/CBO9781139108065

Summers, Anne. 'The Education of David Morrison'. *Anne Summers Reports* 11 (2015): 22–34.

Suta, Cornelia, Luca Barbieri, and Mike May-Gillings. 'Future Employment and Automation'. *Quaderni Fondazione G. Brodolini: Studi e Ricerche* 61 (2018): 17–43.

Syed, Jawad and Peter A. Murray. 'Combating the English Language Deficit: The Labour Market Experiences of Migrant Women in Australia'. *Human Resource Management Journal* 19, no. 4 (2009): 413–32. doi.org/10.1111/j.1748-8583.2009.00106.x

Take, Ingo. 'The Hanseatic League as an Early Example of Cross-Border Governance?'. *Journal of European Integration History* 23, no. 1 (2017): 71–96. doi.org/10.5771/0947-9511-2017-1-71

Taksa, Lucy. 'The Cultural Diffusion of Scientific Management: The United States and New South Wales'. *Journal of Industrial Relations* 37, no. 3 (1995): 427–61. doi.org/10.1177/002218569503700305

Tattersall, Amanda. *Power in Coalition: Strategies for Strong Unions and Social Change*. Ithaca, NY: Cornell University Press, 2010.

Taylor, Frederick Winslow. *The Principles of Scientific Management*. New York: Harper & Brothers, 1911.

Teicher, Julian, Amanda Pyman, Peter Holland, and Brian Cooper. 'Employee Voice in Australia'. In *What Workers Say: Employee Voice in the Anglo-American World*, edited by Richard B. Freeman, Peter Boxall and Peter Haynes. Ithaca NY: ILR Press, 2007.

Tenbrunsel, Ann and Jordan Thomas. *The Street, the Bull and the Crisis: A Survey of the US & UK Financial Services Industry*. New York: University of Notre Dame and Labaton Sucharow LLP, 2015.

Terrell, Josh, Andrew Kofink, Justin Middleton, Clarissa Rainear, Emerson Murphy-Hill, Chris Parnin, and Jon Stallings. 'Gender Bias in Open Source: Pull Request Acceptance of Women Versus Men'. *Peer Journal of Computer Science* 3, no. 1 (May 2017), doi.org/10.7287/peerj.preprints.1733v2

Terry, Deborah J. and Nerina L. Jimmieson. 'Work Control and Employee Well-Being: A Decade Review'. In *International Review of Industrial and Organizational Psychology*, edited by Cary L. Cooper and Ivan T. Robertson. Chichester: John Wiley & Sons, 1999.

Thapa, Prem J. 'On the Risk of Unemployment: A Comparative Assessment of the Labour Market Success of Migrants in Australia'. *Australian Journal of Labour Economics* 7, no. 2 (2004): 199–229.

Tharenou, Phyllis. 'The Work of Feminists Is Not Yet Done: The Gender Pay Gap—a Stubborn Anachronism'. *Sex Roles* 68, no. 3–4 (February 2013): 198–206. doi.org/10.1007/s11199-012-0221-8

The Economist. 'Why Bitcoin Uses So Much Energy'. *Economist*, 9 July 2018.

Thompson, Paul. 'The Capitalist Labour Process: Concepts and Connections'. *Capital and Class* 100 (Spring 2010). doi.org/10.1177/0309816809353475

——. 'If There Are So Many "Bullshit Jobs", Should Labour Fight for the Future of Work?'. *Labourlist*, 22 February 2019.

——. *The Nature of Work: An Introduction to Debates on the Labour Process*. Hampshire: Macmillan, 1989. doi.org/10.1007/978-1-349-20028-3

Thorpe, Mindy. 'Outworkers'. In *Pay Equity in Queensland*, edited by David Peetz and Rosemary Hunter, 99–114. Brisbane: Centre for Research on Employment and Work and Socio Legal Research Centre, Report to Department of Employment Training and Industrial Relations, Queensland Government Submission, Pay Equity Inquiry, Queensland Industrial Relations Commission, No. B1568 of 2000, 2000.

Tobin, James. 'A Proposal for International Monetary Reform'. *Eastern Economic Journal* 4, no. 3–4 (1978): 153–59.

Tolliday, Steven and Jonathan Zeitlin, eds. *Between Fordism and Flexibility: The Automobile Industry and Its Workers*. New York: Berg, 1992.

Toner, Phillip. 'Long Run Shifts in the Industry and Workforce Structure of the Australian Construction Industry: Implications for a Sustainable Labour Supply'. In *Reworking Work: AIRAANZ 2005*, 503–9. Sydney: Association of Industrial Relations Academics of Australia and New Zealand, 2005.

Töngür, Ünal and Adem Yavuz Elveren. 'Deunionization and Pay Inequality in OECD Countries: A Panel Granger Causality Approach'. *Economic Modelling 38* (2014): 417–25.

Tourish, Dennis, David Collinson, and James R. Barker. 'Manufacturing Conformity: Leadership through Coercive Persuasion in Business Organisations'. *M@n@gement* 12, no. 5 (2009): 360–83.

Townsend, Keith and Sue Hutchinson. 'Line Managers in Industrial Relations: Where Are We Now and Where to Next?'. *Journal of Industrial Relations* 59, no. 2 (2017): 139–52. doi.org/10.1177/0022185616671163

Trades Union Congress. *Investment Chains: Addressing Corporate and Investor Short-Termism*. London: TUC, 2006.

Triandis, Hatty C. and Theodore M. Singelis. 'Training to Recognize Individual Differences in Collectivism and Individualism within Culture'. *International Journal of Intercultural Relations* 22, no. 1 (February 1998): 35–47. doi.org/10.1016/S0147-1767(97)00034-5

Tridico, Pasquale. 'The Determinants of Income Inequality in OECD Countries'. *Cambridge Journal of Economics* 42, no. 4 (2018):1009–42.

Underhill, Elsa. 'Changing Work and OHS: The Challenge of Labour Hire Employment'. Paper presented at the New Economies: New Industrial Relations conference, Noosa, February 2004.

Unions NSW. *Innovation or Exploitation: Busting the Airtasker Myth*. Sydney: Unions NSW, 2016.

United Nations. 'Human Development Report 2004: Statistics'. New York: United Nations Development Programme, 2004.

United Nations Conference on Trade and Development. *Trade and Development Report; Capital Accumulation, Growth and Structural Change*. UNCTAD/TDR/2003. New York and Geneva: United Nations, 2003.

United Nations Principles for Responsible Investment. 'FAQs'. UNPRI, www.unpri.org/about-pri/faqs/

Vaile, Mark. 'The Practical Benefits of Globalisation and the New Economy'. Trade Minister's Luncheon, Business Club Australia, Darling Harbour, Sydney, trademinister.gov.au/speeches/2000/000922_globalisation.html

Valkenburg, Ben. 'Individualization, Participation and Solidarity'. *European Journal of Industrial Relations* 1, no. 1 (1995): 129–44.

Vamplew, Peter, Richard Dazeley, Cameron Foale, Sally Firmin, and Jane Mummery. 'Human-Aligned Artificial Intelligence Is a Multiobjective Problem'. *Ethics and Information Technology* 20, no. 1 (2018): 27–40. doi.org/10.1007/s10676-017-9440-6

Van Barneveld, Kristin. 'Under the Covers: Negotiating Australian Workplace Agreements: Two Cases'. Paper presented at the Current Research in Industrial Relations conference, Adelaide, 4–6 February 1999.

Van den Broek, Diane. 'Human Resource Management, Workforce Control and Union Avoidance: An Australian Case Study'. *Journal of Industrial Relations* 39, no. 3 (September 1997): 332–48. doi.org/10.1177/002218569703900302

Van Fossen, Anthony, B. 'Money Laundering, Global Financial Instability, and Tax Havens in the Pacific Islands'. *The Contemporary Pacific* 15, no. 2 (2003): 237–75. doi.org/10.1353/cp.2003.0058

Van Reenen, John. 'Research: The Rise of Superstar Firms Has Been Better for Investors Than for Employees'. *Harvard Business Review*, 11 May 2017.

van Wanrooy, Brigid, Sally Wright, John Buchanan, Susanna Baldwin, and Shaun Wilson. *Australia at Work: In a Changing World.* Sydney: Workplace Research Centre, University of Sydney, 2009.

Vandenbergh, Michael P. 'The New Wal-Mart Effect: The Role of Private Contracting in Global Governance'. *UCLA Law Review* 54 (2007): 913–70.

Vardi, Moshe Y. 'Cars Are Regulated for Safety—Why Not Information Technology?'. *The Conversation*, 22 March 2019.

Veal, Anthony James. 'The Leisure Society I: Myths and Misconceptions, 1960–1979'. *World Leisure Journal* 53, no. 3 (2011): 206–27. doi.org/10.1080/04419057.2011.606826

Veblen, Thorstein. *The Theory of the Leisure Class: An Economic Study of Institutions.* London: George Allen & Unwin, 1925, repr. 1970.

Velayutham, Selvaraj. 'Precarious Experiences of Indians in Australia on 457 Temporary Work Visas'. *Economic and Labour Relations Review* 24, no. 3 (2013): 340–61. doi.org/10.1177/1035304613495268

Verick, Sher. 'Female Labor Force Participation in Developing Countries'. *IZA World of Labor* 87 (January 2014): 1–10. doi.org/10.15185/izawol.87

Vicario, Michela Del, Alessandro Bessib, Fabiana Zolloa, Fabio Petronic, Antonio Scalaa, Guido Caldarellia, H. Eugene Stanleye, and Walter Quattrociocchia. 'The Spreading of Misinformation Online'. *Proceedings of the National Academy of Sciences* 113, no. 3 (2016): 554–9.

vida. 'Betriebsrat Für Fahrradzustelldienst Foodora'. vida (Austrian transport and service union), www.vida.at/cms/S03/S03_0.a/1342577497037/home/artikel/betriebsrat-fuer-fahrradzustelldienst-foodora

Visser, Jelle. 'Data Base on Institutional Characteristics of Trade Unions, Wage Setting, State Intervention and Social Pacts, 1960–2011 (ICTWSS), Version 4.0'. Amsterdam: Amsterdam Institute for Advanced Labour Studies AIAS, University of Amsterdam, 2013.

——. 'Trends in Trade Union Membership'. In *Employment Outlook*, 97–134. Paris: Organisation for Economic Co-operation and Development, 1991.

Von Bergen, C.W., B. Soper, and J.A. Parnell. 'Workforce Diversity and Organisational Performance'. *Equal Opportunities International* 24, no. 3/4 (2005): 1–16. doi.org/10.1108/02610150510788033

Wade, Robert H. 'The Piketty Phenomenon and the Future of Inequality'. *Real-World Economics Review*, 69 (2014): 2–17.

Wade, Robert H. and Silla Sigurgeirsdottir. 'Iceland's Rise, Fall, Stabilisation and Beyond'. *Cambridge Journal of Economics* 36 (2012): 127–44. doi.org/10.1093/cje/ber038

Wajcman, Judy. 'Life in the Fast Lane? Towards a Sociology of Technology and Time'. *British Journal of Sociology* 59, no. 1 (2008): 59–77. doi.org/10.1111/j.1468-4446.2007.00182.x

Wal-Mart Stores Inc. 'A Manager's Toolbox to Remaining Union Free'. Unpublished company document, 1997.

Walby, Sylvia, Jude Towers, and Brian Francis. 'Mainstreaming Domestic and Gender-Based Violence into Sociology and the Criminology of Violence'. *Sociological Review* 62, no. S2 (2014): 187–214. doi.org/10.1111/1467-954X.12198

Walley, Linda, Margaret Steinberg, and David Warner. *The Mature Age Labour Force*. Workforce Strategy Unit, Employment Taskforce, Monograph series No. 2. Brisbane: Department of Employment, Training and Industrial Relations, 1999.

Wallimann, Isidor, Nicholas Tatsis, and George V. Zito. 'On Max Weber's Definition of Power'. *Australian and New Zealand Journal of Sociology* 13, no. 3 (December 1977): 231–35. doi.org/10.1177/144078337701300308

Walsh, Frank and Eric Strobl. 'Recent Trends in Trade Union Membership in Ireland'. *Economic and Social Review* 40, no. 1 (Spring 2009): 117–38.

Walton, Richard E. 'From Control to Commitment in the Workplace'. *Harvard Business Review* 85, no. 2 (March 1985): 77–84.

Waring, Peter. 'The Paradox of Prerogative in Participative Organisations: The Manipulation of Corporate Culture?'. In *Current Research in Industrial Relations, Proceedings of the 12th AIRAANZ Conference*, edited by R. Harbridge et al., 423–30. Wellington: Association of Industrial Relations Academics of Australia and New Zealand, 1998.

Weber, Max. *The Protestant Ethic and the Spirit of Capitalism*. Routledge, repr. 2013.

Weigand, Robert A. 'Organizational Diversity, Profits and Returns in U.S. Firms'. *Problems and Perspectives in Management* 5, no. 3 (2007): 69–83.

Weil, David. 'Creating a Strategic Enforcement Approach to Address Wage Theft: One Academic's Journey in Organizational Change'. *Journal of Industrial Relations* 60, no. 3 (2018): 437–60. doi.org/10.1177/0022185618765551

——. *The Fissured Workplace: Why Work Became So Bad for So Many and What Can Be Done to Improve It*. Cambridge: Harvard University Press, 2014. doi.org/10.4159/9780674726123

Werth, Shalene. 'Stigma, Stress and Emotional Labour: Experiences of Women with Chronic Illness at Work'. In *Proceedings of 25th AIRAANZ Conference*. Auckland, 2011.

Werth, Shalene, David Peetz, and Kaye Broadbent. 'Issues of Power and Disclosure for Women with Chronic Illness in Their Places of Work'. In *Work and Identity: Contemporary Perspectives on Workplace Diversity*, edited by Shalene Werth and Charlotte Brownlow. New York: Palgrave, 2018.

West, Michael. 'Multinationals' Brazen Tax Avoidance'. *Saturday Paper*, 13–19 May 2017.

Western, Bruce, and Jake Rosenfeld. 'Unions, Norms, and the Rise in U.S. Wage Inequality'. *American Sociological Review* 76, no. 4 (August 2011): 513–37.

White, Alex. *Social Media for Unions*. Melbourne: Aleithia Media and Communications, 2010.

Whitehouse, Gillian. 'A Cross-National Comparison of Gender Gaps'. In *Women, Labor Segmentation and Regulation: Varieties of Gender Gaps*, edited by David Peetz and Georgina Murray. New York and London: Palgrave Macmillan, 2017. doi.org/10.1057/978-1-137-55495-6_6

——. 'Recent Trends in Pay Equity: Beyond the Aggregate Statistics'. Paper presented at the Research on Work, Employment and Industrial Relations conference 2000, *Proceedings of 14th AIRAANZ conference*, Newcastle, February 2000.

——. 'Unequal Pay: A Comparative Study of Australia, Canada, Sweden and the U.K'. *Labour & Industry* 3, no. 2–3 (1990): 354–71. doi.org/10.1080/10301763.1990.10669092

Whyte, Jemima, Jonathan Shapiro, Sarah Thompson, and Joyce Moullakis. 'Inside ANZ's Toxic Culture: The High-Octane World of Dealing Rooms'. *Australian Financial Review*, 15 January 2016.

Wik, Martin, Brett F. Thornton, David Bastviken, Jo Uhlbäck, and Patrick M. Crill. 'Biased Sampling of Methane Release from Northern Lakes: A Problem for Extrapolation'. *Geophysical Research Letters* 43, no. 3 (2016): 1256–62. doi.org/10.1002/2015GL066501

Wilkinson, Adrian and Tony Dundon. 'Employment Relations in Smaller Firms'. In *Handbook of Employment Relations, Law and Practice,* 4th ed., edited by B. Towers, 288–307. London: Kogan Page, 2003.

Wilkinson, Adrian, Mick Marchington, John Goodman, and Peter Ackers. 'Total Quality Management and Employee Involvement'. *Human Resource Management Journal* 2, no. 4 (1992): 1–20. doi.org/10.1111/j.1748-8583.1992.tb00263.x

Williamson, Oliver E. *Institutions of Capitalism.* New York: Free Press, 1985.

——. *Markets and Hierarchies: Analysis and Antitrust Implications.* New York: Free Press, 1975.

Willmott, Hugh. 'Strength Is Ignorance; Slavery Is Freedom: Managing Culture in Modern Organizations'. *The Journal of Management Studies* 30, no. 4 (July 1993): 515–52. doi.org/10.1111/j.1467-6486.1993.tb00315.x

Wilson, Shaun, Gabrielle Meagher, and Trevor Breusch. 'Where to for the Welfare State'. In *Australian Social Attitudes: The First Report,* edited by Shaun Wilson et al., 101–21. Sydney: UNSW Press, 2005.

Wood, A.J., M. Graham, V. Lehdonvirta, and I. Hjorth. 'Good Gig, Bad Gig: Autonomy and Algorithmic Control in the Global Gig Economy'. *Work, Employment and Society* 33, no. 1 (2018): 56–75.

Wooden, Mark. 'Factcheck: Has the Level of Casual Employment in Australia Stayed Steady for the Past 18 Years?'. *The Conversation*, 23 March 2016.

——. 'The Impact of Redundancy on Subsequent Labour Market Experience'. *Journal of Industrial Relations* 30, no. 1 (1988): 3–31. doi.org/10.1177/002218568803000101

Woods, Stephen A. and Sarah E. Hampson. 'Measuring the Big Five with Single Items Using a Bipolar Response Scale'. *European Journal of Personality* 19 (2005): 373–90. doi.org/10.1002/per.542

Workplace Gender Equality Agency. *Gender Pay Gap Statistics*. Sydney: WGEA, 2013.

World Bank. 'Merchandise Trade (% of GDP)'. Databank, World Bank, data.worldbank.org/indicator/TG.VAL.TOTL.GD.ZS

Woyzbun, Kirsten, Susan Beitz, and Katherine Barnes. 'Industry Transformation'. In *Drivers of Change for the Australian Labour Market to 2030*, edited by Katherine Barnes and Peter Spearritt, 17–34. Canberra: Academy of the Social Sciences in Australia, 2014.

Wright, Christopher. *The Management of Labour: A History of Australian Employers*. Australian Studies in Labour Relations 4. Melbourne: Oxford University Press, 1995.

Wright, Christopher and John Lund. 'Best Practice Taylorism: "Yankee Speed-up" in Australian Grocery Distribution'. *Journal of Industrial Relations* 38, no. 2 (June 1996): 196–212. doi.org/10.1177/002218569603800202

Wright, Erik Olin. *Understanding Class*. London: Verso, 2015.

Yan, Jack. 'Corporate Responsibility and the Brands of Tomorrow'. *Brand Management* 10, no. 4/5 (2003): 290–302. doi.org/10.1057/palgrave.bm.2540125

Yap, A., A. Wazlawek, B. Lucas, A. Cuddy, and D. Carney. 'The Ergonomics of Dishonesty: The Effect of Incidental Posture on Stealing, Cheating, and Traffic Violations'. *Psychological Science* 24, no. 11 (2013): 2281–89. doi.org/10.1177/0956797613492425

Zimbardo, Philip. 'Stanford Prison Experiment: A Simulation Study of the Psychology of Imprisonment' (2015), www.prisonexp.org

Zoll, Rainer. 'Failing to Modernize?'. *European Journal of Industrial Relations* 1, no. 1 (1995): 119–28.